"In an Inescapable Network of Mutuality"

"In an Inescapable Network of Mutuality"

Martin Luther King, Jr. and the Globalization of an Ethical Ideal

Edited by

LEWIS V. BALDWIN and PAUL R. DEKAR

Foreword by

VICKI L. CRAWFORD

 CASCADE *Books* · Eugene, Oregon

"IN AN INESCAPABLE NETWORK OF MUTUALITY"
Martin Luther King, Jr. and the Globalization of an Ethical Ideal

Cascade Books
An Imprint of Wipf and Stock Publishers
199 W. 8th Ave., Suite 3
Eugene, OR 97401

www.wipfandstock.com

ISBN 13: 978-1-61097-434-9

Cataloguing-in-Publication Data

"In an inescapable network of mutuality" : Martin Luther King, Jr. and the globalization of an ethical ideal / edited by Lewis V. Baldwin and Paul R. Dekar ; foreword by Vicki L. Crawford.

xxxii + 376 p. ; 23 cm. Includes bibliographical references and index.

ISBN 13: 978-1-61097-434-9

1. King, Martin Luther, Jr., 1929–1968. 2. Globalization—Moral and ethical aspects. I. Crawofrd, Vicki L. II. Baldwin, Lewis V., 1949–. III. Dekar, Paul R. IV. Title.

BJ1275 .I5 2013

Manufactured in the U.S.A.

In gratitude to the Martin Luther King, Jr. Collections
at Morehouse College, Boston University, and the King Center in Atlanta
for preserving the legacy of a world citizen

Contents

Contributors

Lewis V. Baldwin is Professor of Religious Studies at Vanderbilt University in Nashville, Tennessee. He has written scores of articles and several books on various aspects of African American religion and culture, and has lectured and taught courses on Martin Luther King, Jr. for some thirty years. He has received numerous honors and awards for his scholarship on King and the civil rights movement. Among his publications are *There Is a Balm in Gilead: The Cultural Roots of Martin Luther King, Jr.* (1991); *To Make the Wounded Whole: The Cultural Legacy of Martin Luther King, Jr.* (1992); *Toward the Beloved Community: Martin Luther King, Jr. and South Africa* (1995); *The Voice of Conscience: The Church in the Mind of Martin Luther King, Jr.* (2010); and *Never to Leave Us Alone: The Prayer Life of Martin Luther King, Jr.* (2010).

Peter Cousins holds degrees from Merton College, Oxford University, and the Department of Peace Studies at Bradford University in the United Kingdom. He has served as an international accompanier-human rights observer with the U.S. Fellowship of Reconciliation in San José de Apartadó and Bogotá, Colombia. He has also worked in support of asylum seekers and the homeless across Great Britain, and currently practices as a community mediator in the south of England.

Vicki L. Crawford is Director of the Morehouse College Martin Luther King, Jr. Collection and a scholar of the civil rights movement, focusing on the role of women. She is the editor of the groundbreaking volume of essays, *Women in the Civil Rights Movement: Trailblazers and Torchbearers* (1990), which was one of the first publications to address the underrepresented role of women in the African American freedom struggle. Her book chapters and essays have appeared in *The American Woman 2000; Black Women in America: An Historical Encyclopedia* (1994); *Sisters in the Struggle: Women in the Civil Rights and Black Power Movements* (2001); and *The Journal of African American History.*

Crystal A. DeGregory teaches History at Tennessee State University in Nashville, Tennessee. Her research explores the interrelationship between black struggles for freedom, justice, and equality, with a special focus on the activist qualities of historically black colleges and universities (HBCU). Her work has appeared in several publications, among which are *The Tennessee State University Journal; Encyclopedia of African American Popular Culture; Tennessee Historical Quarterly; African American National Biography;* and *Freedom Facts and Firsts: 400 Years of the African American Civil Rights Experience* (2009), edited by Linda T. Wynn and Jessie Carney Smith.

Paul R. Dekar is Professor Emeritus of Evangelism and Mission, Memphis Theological Seminary, Memphis, Tennessee. He has received numerous grants and awards, and has lectured in parts of the United States, Canada, and Australia. Among his publications are *Crossing Barriers in World Mission* (1983); *For the Healing of Nations* (1993); *Creating the Beloved Community: A History of the Fellowship of Reconciliation* (2005); *Community of the Transfiguration: Journey of a New Monastic Community* (2008); *Building a Culture of Peace: Baptist Peace Fellowship of North America* (2009); and *Thomas Merton: Twentieth-Century Wisdom for Twenty-First Century Living* (2011).

Noel Leo Erskine is Professor of Theology and Ethics at Candler School of Theology and the Graduate School of Arts and Sciences at Emory University in Atlanta, Georgia. He has authored and edited some eleven books, among which are *King Among the Theologians* (1994); *From Garvey to Marley: Rastafari Theology* (2005); and *Black Theology and Pedagogy* (2008).

Everett Gendler is an ordained Conservative Rabbi with an extensive history of involvement in progressive causes, such as Jewish nonviolence, the egalitarian Jewish Havurah movement, and Jewish environmentalism. In the 1950s and 1960s he served as rabbi to a number of congregations in Mexico (1957–59), Brazil (1961), and Cuba (1968–69), and worked with Martin Luther King, Jr. on various occasions between August 1962 and

March 1968. Since 1995, the year of his retirement, he has been involved with a Nonviolence Training Project for the Tibetan exile community in Dharamsala, India. His articles and ideas have appeared in *Tikkun* and in such volumes as *Protest: Pacifism and Politics* (1968); *A Conflict of Loyalties: The Case of Selective Conscientious Objection* (1968); *The Challenge of Shalom: The Jewish Tradition of Peace and Justice* (1994); *The Greening of Faith: God, the Environment, and the Good Life* (1997); *Torah of the Earth* (2000); and *Jewish Mysticism and the Spiritual Life: Classical Texts, Contemporary Reflections* (2010).

Mary Gendler is a retired clinical psychologist. She and her husband, Rabbi Everett Gendler, were involved with Martin Luther King, Jr. and civil rights activities in the American South in the 1960s. During the 1960s and 1970s, she and Rabbi Gendler participated in several alternative residential communities, including Ivan Illich's Centro Intercultural de Documentación in Cuernavaca, Mexico (1968–69), and the interracial and interreligious living center Packard Manse in Stoughton, Massachusetts (1969–71). She worked as a clinical psychologist from 1973 to 1995. Since 1995, she, along with her husband, has been involved in community education work among Tibetan exiles on Strategic Nonviolent Struggle in Dharamsala, India.

Mary Elizabeth King is Professor of Peace and Conflict Studies at the University of Peace, an affiliate of the United Nations, and a Scholar-in-Residence with the American University's School of International Service in Washington, DC. She is also Distinguished Fellow of the Rothermere American Institute at the University of Oxford in Britain. Her *Freedom Song: A Personal Story of the 1960s Civil Rights Movement* (1987), which highlights her experiences working for four years with the Student Nonviolent Coordinating Committee (SNCC) and at times with Martin Luther King, Jr., won a Robert F. Kennedy Memorial Book Award. She has received numerous other honors and awards, including a James M. Lawson Award for Nonviolent Achievement, the 2003 Jamnalal Bajaj International Award in Mumbai, India, and the 2009 El-Hibri Peace Education Prize. Her books include *Mahatma Gandhi and Martin Luther King, Jr.: The Power of Nonviolent Action* (2002; originally 1999); *A Quiet Revolution: The First Palestinian Intifada and Nonviolent Resistance* (2007); and *The New York Times on Emerging Democracies in Eastern Europe* (2009).

Roy Money is a biostatistician in the Psychiatry Department at Yale University in New Haven, Connecticut. He was a founding member of the Southern Student Organizing Committee in 1964 and has remained involved in social justice struggles. He has written numerous book reviews for *Turning Wheel*, the journal of the Buddhist Peace Fellowship, and some of his research focuses on areas of congruence between Martin Luther King, Jr.'s idea of the "beloved community" and the central Buddhist concept of "dependent origination," "interdependent arising," or "interbeing."

Thomas A. Mulhall is an independent researcher trained in International Peace Studies at the Irish School of Ecumenics, Trinity College Dublin. He has done extensive research on the life and thought of Martin Luther King, Jr., and is the author of a number of forthcoming articles on the subject. He is currently completing the first book on King and the World Council of Churches (WCC).

Francisco Rodés teaches Latin American Church History at the Ecumenical Seminary in Matanzas, Cuba, and is also pastor emeritus of the First Baptist Church in that city, where he served for thirty-seven years. He is director of the Kairos Community Center, a ministry of First Baptist in Matanzas. His other involvements include first president of the Fraternity of Cuban Baptist Churches, national coordinator of the Evangelical Prison Chaplaincy of Cuba, membership in the Baptist World Alliance Peace Commission, and founder of the Coordination of Baptist Students and Workers of Cuba, a kind of Baptist Peace Fellowship.

John J. Thatamanil is an Associate Professor of Theology and World Religions at Union Theological Seminary in New York, New York. He has taught widely in the areas of comparative theology, theologies of religious pluralism, Hindu-Christian dialogue, Buddhist-Christian dialogue, and Eastern Orthodox theology and spirituality, and is the author of *The Immanent Divine: God, Creation, and the Human Predicament—An East-West Conversation* (2006). His forthcoming book is tentatively titled, *Religious Diversity after "Religion": Rethinking Theologies of Religious Pluralism.*

Linda T. Wynn teaches in the Department of History and Political Science at Fisk University in Nashville, Tennessee, and is also the Assistant Director for State Programs with the Tennessee Historical Commission. In addition to coediting *Profiles of African Americans in Tennessee* (1996) with Bobby L. Lovett, and *Freedom Facts and Firsts: 400 Years of the African American Civil Rights Experience* (2009) with Jessie Carney Smith, she is a major contributor to *The Tennessee Encyclopedia of Culture and History*. Her chapters on the African American civil and human rights struggle have appeared in *The History of African Americans in Tennessee: Trials and Triumphs* (2002); *Tennessee Women: Their Lives and Times* (2009); and the latest edition of *The African American Almanac*.

Acknowledgments

THE IDEA FOR THIS book blossomed out of our participation in activities surrounding the fortieth anniversary of the assassination of Martin Luther King, Jr. At that time, in April 2008, we participated in a number of activities at the Civil Rights Museum in Memphis, Tennessee, and presented papers at Memphis State University. Inspired by what we saw, heard, shared, and experienced, we also discussed the possibility of collaborating on a book on the global King. This book is the product of our collaboration and of our continuing encounter with King as an intellectual and spiritual source.

The effort and goodwill of a number of very special individuals made this volume possible. Warmest thanks are extended to Cynthia Lewis and Elaine Hall, who work in the library and archives at the Martin Luther King, Jr. Center for Nonviolent Social Change, Inc. in Atlanta, Georgia. The King documents they provided were especially important to the completion of some of the chapters of this work.

We thank Vicki L. Crawford, the Director of the Morehouse College Martin Luther King, Jr. Collection, for her support and encouragement. Despite her own crowded schedule, she graciously accepted our invitation to write the foreword to this book. Because we share her devotion to the preservation and advancement of the King legacy, we agreed to donate all proceeds from this book to the Morehouse King Collection.

Christian Amondson and others at Wipf and Stock Publishers deserve a special word of gratitude for their patience and support. Despite our inability to meet deadlines, which is typically the case with collaborative efforts of this nature, the people at Wipf and Stock never put pressure on us. Their understanding and willingness to bear with us helped make this a truly pleasurable experience.

The contributors to this volume, who come from many backgrounds and parts of this nation and the world, deserve special praise and thanks for their willingness to offer interpretations of King in a global context, for the time they devoted to research and to writing excellent chapters, and for agreeing to make this book and the proceeds that derive from it a gift to the Martin Luther King, Jr. Collection at Morehouse College. The contributors worked patiently and graciously with us, always responding promptly and positively to our requests for revisions and improvements. All of these contributors are deeply interested in King and in the enduring struggle for global justice, democratic freedoms, and human rights, and they provide rich, incisive, and provocative essays. We are certain that readers will learn from all of them.

Foreword

Vicki L. Crawford

THE SCHOLARSHIP ON MARTIN Luther King, Jr. has expanded significantly over the past decade, enriching our understanding of the confluence of factors that shaped his life. Several excellent biographies of King along with numerous specialized studies in such fields as theology, sociology, religion, history, and political science have deepened our understanding of King's intellectual and spiritual roots while tracing the trajectory that resulted in his ascendancy as a world leader. King scholars have benefited immensely from the rich corpus of writings left by King himself. These sources include the Papers of Martin Luther King, Jr. at Stanford University, the extensive manuscript collections at Boston University, and the more recently acquired Morehouse College Martin Luther King, Jr. Collection. These repositories contain a wealth of King's sermons, speeches, correspondence and other writings that embody King's remarkable standing in the nation and the world.

Studies of King and the African-American freedom struggle have advanced through three phases. The first phase emphasized King's rise to national leadership, beginning with the Montgomery Bus Boycott in 1955–56, continuing through the major civil rights campaigns in Birmingham, Selma, Albany, and St. Augustine, and ending with King's assassination in Memphis, Tennessee, in April 1968. Later studies critiqued this "Montgomery to Memphis" periodization and shifted emphasis away from King to the importance of local community leaders who organized and sustained movements throughout the South. Writing during the decades of the 1980s and early 1990s, scholars in this phase illuminated the roles of lesser-known activists, such as Ella Baker, Bayard Rustin, and James Lawson, many of whom were close to King and a vital part of his interlocking network of support. More recently, scholarship on King and the movement encompasses a fuller, more nuanced view. While recognizing King's significance, these studies also focus on the interplay between national and local leaders and highlight aspects of movement history that have received far less emphasis. For example, new studies of King focus on the years following the 1963 March on Washington as they examine King's incisive critique of American domestic and foreign policies, specifically focusing on his stance against the war in Vietnam and advocacy for world peace. Along these lines, current scholarship on King emphasizes his role as a global figure, or as one whose influence extended beyond the United States to other democratic freedom struggles throughout the world. While some scholars have argued that King became increasingly more radical in the years following 1964, as he spoke out against the ravages of war, rich archival documentation depicts a man who was deeply concerned with the world, particularly Africa, Asia, Latin America and the Caribbean, very early in his life.

This current volume of essays, coedited by eminent King scholar Lewis V. Baldwin, along with Paul R. Dekar, significantly advances this historiographic turn toward King's international prominence as it presents an engaging collection of essays that explicate and expound on King's communitarian ideals in the advancement of human rights. The insightful essays in this volume frame King's thought and action in the context of globalization, a concept in today's parlance that addresses the profound political and economic transformations in national economies that result from developments in media, information technology, and transportation and communication systems. Through the process of globalization, the gap between wealthy and poor countries has widened to the extent that large sectors of the world's population face widespread poverty and enormous levels of social and economic inequalities.

The emergence of globalization began in the twentieth century, during King's lifetime. In his final book, *Where Do We Go From Here: Chaos or Community?* (1967), King acknowledged the rapidly developing scientific and technological advances that deepened chasms of difference. He warned that "when machines and computers, profit motives and property rights are considered more important than people, the giant triplets of racism, materialism, and militarism are incapable of being conquered." King understood with great clarity and depth how worldwide systems create and exploit differences. From this understanding, he developed the concept of the "world house," or the "worldwide neighborhood," where all of humanity would be valued and interconnected through the practice of peace, nonviolence, and love. As King articulated it, the full realization of the world house would require a global nonviolent strategy of resistance to eradicate the triple evils of racism, poverty, and militarism, as well as other forms of oppression.

Perhaps one of King's most notable contributions to the struggle for civil and human rights was his ability to connect the African American freedom struggle to the anticolonial and anti-imperialist struggles of the twentieth century. The contributors to *"In an Inescapable Network of Mutuality"* have done a superb job of presenting this global King and reminding us that he was a "citizen of the world." Through a close reading and examination of King's speeches and writings, the authors in this volume trace King's understanding of these interconnections, as early as his formative years, continuing through his extensive education, travel, and activism. Reflecting a rich tapestry of multidisciplinary perspectives, this volume's contributors are diverse themselves, representing a range of backgrounds that provides a unique interpretive lens for "reading Martin Luther King, Jr. in context and beyond context," to quote Lewis V. Baldwin in the book's introduction. Baldwin, Dekar, and the other contributors portray King as not only an important historical figure, but also as a compelling and present-day voice who calls us to action.

Collectively, these groundbreaking essays document King's critical engagement with a wide and diverse network of people, ideas, and movements that helped shape his ethical, spiritual, and global understandings. Several chapters trace and include discussions of King's journey to nonviolent civil resistance, owing considerable credit to human rights and peace activists such as Bayard Rustin and Glenn Smiley. As several essays clarify, King was nurtured through long-standing networks of support that included African-American leaders and others who held deep knowledge and experience with nonviolence. African-American community contact with the ideas of Mohandas K. Gandhi and nonviolence predated the freedom struggle of the 1950s, as leaders such as Benjamin E. Mays, Howard Thurman, and Mordecai Johnson traveled to India in the 1920s where they met and studied the Indian leader. Also, King inspired and, in turn, received moral support from the Fellowship of Reconciliation (FOR), as Dekar notes, extending his global outreach. Moreover, King was directly connected to the leadership of the World Council of Churches, where he influenced the Council's antiracism and antiwar positions.

It is worth noting that Baldwin and Dekar have also included essays that do not shy away from critiques of King's leadership. In "Beyond Patriarchy: The Meaning of Martin Luther King, Jr. for the Women of the World," written by Linda T. Wynn, a frank discussion points out the disjunctions between King's clearly formulated concept of the "beloved community" and his conventional views on women. Here we encounter a King whose ideals sometimes exceeded his own personal limitations. While King was an outspoken critic of racism, materialism, and militarism, his critique of structural forms of oppression failed to include patriarchy, a formidable oppression that restricts the freedom of a vast and disproportionate share of the world's women. But Wynn contends that despite this omission, King's ethic of global human rights is still instructive in today's struggle for women's equality.

The final section of *"In an Inescapable Network of Mutuality"* offers important contemporary explorations of King's meaning for nation-building and the expansion of democratic freedoms throughout the world. In varying contexts, including the Caribbean, Latin America, and the Middle East, the authors deftly analyze King's legacy and ponder its possibilities for world peace and social justice amidst escalating violence, irresolvable differences, and continuing turmoil. Taken together, these essays extend the conversation around King's global vision as they provide thought-provoking and inspiring new streams of inquiry into the application of King's principles in our time. As a whole, this volume makes a significant contribution to King scholarship, extending its analysis beyond the conventional as it calls our attention to the relevance of King's global ideas in a twenty-first-century world.

General Introduction

Martin Luther King, Jr. in a Global Context

Lewis V. Baldwin and Paul R. Dekar

"THE DREAMER" IS THE title by which Martin Luther King, Jr. is still known, admired, and respected around the world. Indeed, his contributions in many different spheres—religion, theology, philosophy, culture, ethics, politics, and social activism—are increasingly assuming global relevance and significance. Perhaps more than ever before, people worldwide appeal to King as the quintessential *idealist, spiritual leader, human rights advocate,* and *social change agent,* thus establishing King's importance as a historical figure who actually transcends both his past and his immediate geographical context in terms of his meaning, authority, and inspiration for the current and subsequent generations.

The world in which King lived, traveled, and functioned had already become *globalized* on so many levels, scientifically and technologically, and King's image of the world as "a single neighborhood" and emphasis on both "the interrelated structure of all reality" and "the social nature of human existence" shows that he understood this better than even many of the most perceptive thinkers and activists in his time. Also, King's commitment to the actualization of what he variously called "the beloved community," "the world house," "the worldwide neighborhood," "a new kind of man," "a new world," and "a new world order" allows us to study him as both a global figure and a forerunner of much of what is currently identified with globalization theory and practice.

This book goes beyond the conventional findings and claims of the scholarship on King to probe King's international connections and impact. The purpose is not only to retrieve the historical King, but also to foster critical engagement with King in a twenty-first-century world. The essential question, then, is one of contextualization. What happens when King's ideas and methods are contextualized in his own time, place, and generation, and in ours as well? Is King really meaningful and relevant in this contemporary age of globalization? How are we to understand and interpret King's message to and enduring impact on various parts of the world? What is the meaning of King's life and legacy for a multicultural and multi-religious world—a world in which there are different and competing folkways, ideologies, and modes of thinking about life and ultimate reality? This book addresses these basic questions to some extent, while deliberately avoiding the tendency to embellish and sanitize King's ideas and to distort and manipulate his image.

Convinced that a single-authored work on the global King would perhaps be less appealing, informative, provocative, and challenging, we set out to assemble an impressive array of contributors from various parts of the world to produce a piece that is both multi-authored and multidisciplinary in focus. Some of the contributors to this volume are educators and scholars, others are religious leaders, still others are activists, and a few have lived and continue to live and function in all of these worlds. Some might be realistically characterized as "the intellectual-activist type," or what Antonio Gramsci labels "the organic intellectual," for they have, at particular times in their lives, combined ideas and the life of the mind with a commitment to social activism and social change.

In any case, all of the contributors were selected for essentially three reasons. First, because their various cultural backgrounds, social locations, and walks of life, so to speak, make them ideally suited to reflect, in clear and profound ways, on King as a social prophet and activist with global status. Second, they offer a rich variety of perspectives—historical, cultural, religious, ethical, social, and political—which have developed out of their own life involvements, experiences, and struggles in different geographical contexts. Finally, they are especially equipped to explain how King might speak eloquently and authoritatively to a new generation of intellectuals and activists across the globe today.

There are three major parts to this book. Part I, titled "For a World Made New: Exposing the Global Martin Luther King, Jr.," consists of three chapters. Chapter 1, written by the religious historian Lewis V. Baldwin, discusses King in his own global context while also treating him as a forerunner and critic of much of what is defined as globalization theory and practice today, particularly as this relates to the call for global justice, the advancement of democratic freedoms and human rights, and the transnational sharing and/or exchange of the kinds of ideas, values, and material goods that serve the most cherished intellectual, cultural, economic, social, political, and religious interests of the entire human family. Baldwin reminds us that King was indeed a global figure, "a citizen of the world," at heart and in mind, and that any understanding of King that ignores or downplays his global significance and impact is deeply distorted at best. Baldwin further contends that a serious study of King and globalization, which should begin with a consideration of his vision of the "world house," reminds us of how certain ideas and modes of thinking about life, humanity, and the world extend across generations.

This first chapter essentially concerns reading Martin Luther King, Jr. in context and beyond context, and it prepares the ground for the content that unfolds in the subsequent chapters. The chapter actually draws on Baldwin's *Toward the Beloved Community: Martin Luther King, Jr. and South Africa* (1995), which was the first book-length work published on the global King. Readers of this chapter are challenged to understand King as a religious leader, idealist, and activist in his own historical context, and also as a historical figure who is meaningful, authoritative, and inspirational for millions worldwide who remember and are still influenced by his efforts to create a world free of bigotry, intolerance, injustice, and violence. King emerges here as not merely a figure of the past, but of the present and future as well. While King no longer lives, his words, ideas, and activities are of enduring value for a world that must still, as King so often put it, make a choice between "nonviolent coexistence" and "violent coannihilation."

Chapter 2 is coauthored by Baldwin and Paul R. Dekar, professor emeritus of Evangelism and Mission at Memphis Theological Seminary. This chapter highlights King's message to what King labeled the "white world" and the "colored world." Particular attention is devoted to how King described or defined these two worlds, and to the different ways in which he approached them on the levels of both ideas and activism. It is clear that King had both the same and different messages for these two worlds, for he understood essential differences between them even as he struggled for a sense of global oneness. Baldwin and Dekar employ King's image of the world as "a single neighborhood" to show that King's sense of both a "white world" and a "colored world" was realistic and not necessarily inconsistent with his ideal of a global beloved community, and that King ultimately had a vision of world community that included peoples of all colors and creeds. King knew that pushing a particularistic agenda in a global context, rooted in race and color differences, was not only immoral and unethical, but also impractical and unrealistic.

Drawing on Baldwin's published books and articles on King and Africa, and on Dekar's speeches and published and unpublished essays on King and Latin America and the Caribbean, this second chapter builds on the first one, particularly in terms of establishing King as a thinker and activist of global status. It reveals that King's world vision, and his sense of the American Negro's role in the actualization of that vision, grew out of his travels, observations, and study of the vast landscape of humanity. Chapter 2 also explains King's meaning and relevance for white peoples and peoples of color worldwide today, a topic that has been woefully neglected in the extant scholarship on this phenomenal figure. Chapters 1 and 2, when considered jointly, actually frame the general concern of *"In an Inescapable Network of Mutuality": Martin Luther King, Jr. and the Globalization of an Ethical Ideal,* thus opening the way for the more topic-specific concerns treated in the subsequent chapters of this volume.

Chapter 3, the last in Part I, focuses essentially on the meaning of Martin Luther King, Jr. for the women of the world. Written by Linda T. Wynn, who teaches courses on women and civil rights at Fisk University, this chapter convincingly argues that King's androcentric leadership style, rhetoric, dialogues with others, and policy solutions were partriarchal-based and customary to other male civil rights and church leaders of his time. Wynn goes on to maintain that King and other male leaders lacked genuine respect for black women as leaders in the civil rights movement, that they never seriously addressed the need for women's liberation, and that King's own male-dominated, charismatic leadership model was antithetical to his beloved community vision and ideal. But in a stunning and yet perceptive conclusion, Wynn contends that King's ethical discourse, which is centered in the beloved community and which affirms "the interrelatedness of all life" and "the social nature of human existence," can be of some positive value and use to women worldwide, especially as they elucidate and/or address the problem of female exclusion and subordination. Wynn's suggestion that King's ethos still speaks to issues that are pertinent to women everywhere will undoubtedly be questioned and even rejected by the most radical feminists and womanists, but it is well advanced and solidly grounded in a careful reading of King sources, and it will most certainly trigger considerable scholarly discussion and debate. The need for such discussion and debate in the academy, the church, and in world circles cannot be overstated in this age of globalization.

This third chapter is really groundbreaking in that it explores King's meaning and relevance for women in a global context. No scholar, male or female, has seriously taken this approach up to this point. Wynn is not afraid to be critical of King, even as she finds meaning and potential in his world vision. She is convinced that King's message remains instructive for women in the "world house," and especially for women who are still oppressed by what she calls "male-dominated global institutions."

Part II is titled "A Global Quest for Common Ground: Martin Luther King, Jr. and the Power of Interreligious and Intercultural Learning," and it includes chapters 4–8. Chapter 4 examines the ways in which King and the World Council of Churches (WCC) influenced each other in their efforts to end the Vietnam War and global racism. Contributed by Thomas A. Mulhall, an independent researcher trained in International Peace Studies at the Irish School of Ecumenics, Trinity College in Dublin, and the author of a forthcoming work on King and the WCC, this chapter shows that both King and the WCC were aware of "the changing world order" in the 1960s, and that both provide an essential model for how humans as a whole should relate to each other in a world that has become "a global village." Mulhall's chapter is particularly engaging and refreshing at a time when more and more questions are being raised about the ability of the church universal to remain a living, vital organism, and, more specifically, about its capacity to spearhead purposeful Christian witness and praxis in the world in this new century and millennium.

Mulhall's chapter actually breaks new ground, for despite King's occasional comments about the WCC in relation to issues of race and war, no scholar has written at such length on the topic. Mulhall skillfully corrects this pattern of omission in King studies, thus opening yet another window from which we might view and assess the significance of the global Martin Luther King, Jr. Mulhall's probing remarks and rich insights are obviously informed by both his interest in the global King and his background and interest in global peace studies.

Chapter 5 discusses the Fellowship of Reconciliation (FOR) as a critical element in King's adoption, appropriation, and application of Gandhian nonviolence. Authored by Paul R. Dekar, a scholar and FOR activist, it builds on the discussion in chapter 4, providing another angle from which to assess and analyze global Christian influences on King. Having authored a wonderful book highlighting his own views about and experiences with the FOR, titled *Creating the Beloved Community: A Journey with the Fellowship of Reconciliation* (2005), Dekar begins with a powerful discussion of the rise of the FOR in Britain and the United States as embodiments of Christian nonviolence during the second decade of the twentieth century. He moves on to explain the FOR's impact, through figures like Bayard Rustin, Glenn Smiley, and others, on both King and the black freedom movement in the United States in the 1950s and 1960s. This chapter is immensely important for those who wish to better understand how the black freedom movement interacted with, and was influenced by, certain personalities and forces clamoring and struggling for global peace, particularly within the ranks of the FOR.

King's involvements with and indebtedness to the FOR is a largely unknown and unexplored aspect of the historiography of the modern civil rights movement. This fifth chapter helps fill this gap in King scholarship, while also further enlightening us about the deep religious roots of King's nonviolent theory and praxis. Dekar reminds us that King read and applied Gandhi through the prism of Christian influences, a point often overlooked by those who attribute Kingian nonviolence and civil disobedience to foreign and non-Christian sources.

Chapter 6 takes a different slant, focusing primarily on how the black American community, under King's leadership, answered "a poignant invitation" to learn from Mahatma Gandhi and India. Provided by John J. Thatamanil, an Associate Professor of Theology and World Religions at New York's Union Theological Seminary, this chapter speaks more specifically to the black community's "open-hearted reception" to the theory and practice of Gandhian nonviolence. As Thatamanil puts it, King and his people in America responded in positive ways to Gandhi's call for "the hospitality of receiving," and their willingness to embrace Gandhian ideas and methods constituted "a moment of interreligious receptivity." Thatamanil is equally perceptive in underscoring those theological convictions and resources that enabled King to become "a hospitable recipient of Gandhian wisdom." At the same time, Thatamanil readily acknowledges Gandhi's appreciation for the lessons of the black struggle in America, especially as expressed in the Negro spirituals. While his primary focus is on what King inherited from Gandhi, Thatamanil is sensitive to areas of similarity and interchangeability between the Indian people and black Americans, especially in the realm of values. Clearly, this is why the southern Negroes could adopt and adapt Gandhian ideas and methods without doing essential violence to their own Christian faith and worldview.

Generally speaking, Thatamanil is interested in showing how certain kinds of values and traditions transcend religious and cultural differences. His insistence that there was a genuine reciprocity and a vital spiritual kinship that joined the communities and movements of Gandhi and King, particularly at the levels of ideas and methods, is quite convincing, and it suggests possibilities for interreligious and intercultural dialogue and learning today. In other words, Thatamanil offers other examples of how Gandhi, King, and the movements they led might be meaningful or relevant for today's hostile, violent, and fragmented world.

Chapter 7 advances this position to another level, with special attention to Gandhian and Kingian nonviolence as a moral imperative for action in the globalized world. Written by Mary E. King, a professor of Peace and Conflict Studies at the University of Peace, an affiliate of the United Nations, this chapter begins with an interesting and provocative discussion of how Gandhi's ideas, strategies, and tactics from India's struggle for independence were adopted and practically applied by King and others in the struggle against Jim Crow in the southern United States in the 1950s and 1960s. While arguing that King found in Gandhi's thought and social praxis rich resources and opportunities for learning, Mary King is also mindful of the creative and distinctive cast King brought to his own perspective on and practice of nonviolent civil disobedience. Her chapter, like John Thatamanil's, offers rich insights into how the Indian people and blacks in America were positively transformed through their encounters with each other. Both are far more interested in what the two peoples shared than what they did not share.

Mary King is also interested in appeals to Gandhi's and King's authority and inspiration by the generations that have followed them. She notes that the ideas and methods of Gandhi and King have been appropriated and applied by any number of peoples and recent popular movements, including the Poles, East Germans, Czechs and Slovaks, the Burmese, Palestinians, Guatemalans, and the Thais. Mary King goes on to conclude that nonviolent civil disobedience has increased in political significance on virtually every continent since King's murder. According to Mary King, perhaps the greatest testament to the power of the legacy of Gandhi and King is the fact that oppressed peoples today are far more efficient and effective in using creative nonviolent means than oppressors are in developing and employing new methods of repression.

In chapter 8, Roy Money, a biostatistician in the psychiatry department at Yale University, examines King's language of interdependence as repeatedly and consistently expressed in variations of two phrases; namely, "a network of mutuality" and "the interrelatedness of all life." King's use of this language, Money contends, distinguished him from other civil rights leaders in his time. Money goes on to identify the main sources of King's "language of interdependence," while also pointing to other sources that are especially relevant to that language. Money maintains that there is a rich history of similar language in Buddhist literature, as evident in the concepts of "interbeing," "interdependent arising," or "dependent origination," which provide a larger context for understanding this kind of language. Money also suggests that King's "language of interdependence" is essentially restated in the Dalai Lama's call for the development of "universal responsibility."

This eighth chapter speaks perceptively to King's ability to craft language that was not only powerful and persuasive, but also universal, inclusive, and redemptive. King's "language of interdependence," as Money suggests, affords yet another vantage point from which to assess the dimensions of his world vision. Such an approach is at best refreshing, enlightening, and stimulating, for it lays bare a side of King that is too often slighted even by scholars who treat him as a homiletician and rhetorician.

Part III is titled "Linked in a Single Garment of Destiny: Martin Luther King, Jr., Nation-Building, and the Challenges of an Interdependent World," and it consists of chapters 9–14. In chapter 9, Noel Leo Erskine, Professor of Theology and Ethics at Candler School of Theology, asserts that King-led civil rights campaigns in America proved enormously significant for people in the Caribbean as they sought to understand and pursue nation-building. Some of the values of King, writes Erskine, were transported to the Caribbean, especially the emphasis on human dignity, economic empowerment and equality, and the beloved community ideal. At the same time, Erskine dispels any notion that the movements in the Caribbean and the southern United States were identical, declaring that the challenge for Caribbean people in the 1950s and 1960s was not Jim Crow and racial integration but the overthrow of imperialist policies and a lifestyle of dependence fostered by colonialism. According to Erskine, this explains why Marcus M. Garvey, the Jamaican-born Pan-Africanist and advocate for African repatriation, was more influential in some circles than King. Even so, one ultimately has to think in terms of how both figures came together in the consciousness of Caribbean people.

As Erskine observes, King's protest tactics never really registered with great force among most Caribbean people, largely because they failed to see the need for racial integration, and because of the pervasive view that church leaders should not seriously engage matters of a political nature. Thus, one has to speak in terms of King's ambiguous legacy in the Caribbean—ambiguous in the sense that it is subject to more than one interpretation. Although not as extensive as the Haitian leader François Duvalier's book-length tribute to King, Erskine's chapter is in some ways the strongest statement available on King's meaning for the Caribbean.

In chapter 10, Crystal A. DeGregory, who teaches history at Tennessee State University in Nashville, Tennessee, traces the relationship between King-led civil rights campaigns in America and Lynden O. Pindling-led Progressive Liberal Party activities in the Bahamas, declaring that this is part of the "largely unexplored global dimensions of King's life and work." DeGregory reminds us that the Commonwealth of the Bahamas and its transformation from a British colonial outpost to a black independent nation paralleled developments with King and the civil rights movement. According to DeGregory, it was through Pindling that King's influence was most significantly felt in the Bahamas. The relationship between the struggles in the Bahamas and the United States, says DeGregory, was supremely embodied in the personalities, tactics, and aspirations of King and Pindling.

This tenth chapter also breaks new ground in the scholarship on Martin Luther King, Jr., for no scholar has written in such compelling terms about King's meaning for people in the Commonwealth of the Bahamas. As one who has thoroughly researched both the path toward nationhood in the Bahamas and the struggle for civil rights in America, DeGregory is eminently qualified to write with authority about these issues. Needless to say, her chapter adds yet another piece to the puzzle that *was* and *is* the global King.

Chapter 11 was written by Peter Cousins, an Oxford University-trained peace activist who served as an international accompanier and human rights observer with the U.S. Fellowship of Reconciliation in San José de Apartadó and Bogotá, Colombia. Cousins examines the influence of King across Latin America, with a particular focus on citizen-led, nonviolent initiatives in Colombia that draw on and reflect King's thinking. He also discusses the declining significance of nonviolence in national reform movements in parts of Latin America, where even many young Catholic priests have joined or are joining guerilla movements. This chapter, much like Noel Erskine's, points to the ambiguous side of the King legacy, particularly as it relates to Latin America.

Cousins is highly sensitive to what King thought about America's role in the world, and especially in Latin America. Moreover, Cousins suggests that King, in relating to Latin America, sought to embody the best of what he felt the United States could and should be within the global community—namely, a nation that relates to the rest of the world with understanding, compassion, and goodwill, not out of ignorance, arrogance, and military might. Here the global King is viewed and discussed from the perspective of one who is, in his own right, both a scholar and social activist.

King's significance for Latin America is explored in a somewhat different vein by Francisco Rodés, who teaches church history at the Ecumenical Seminary in Matanzas, Cuba, and who serves as pastor of the First Baptist Church there. In chapter 12, Rodés highlights the inspiration and example of Martin Luther King, Jr. for Cubans, especially when it comes to social causes and a sense of social responsibility and commitment. In Rodés's estimation, King also showed Cubans, including himself, how the church might serve as a reservoir of hope and change, thus contributing to the increased interest in Christianity in Cuba after the King assassination. The role of the churches in solidifying the Cuban people around just causes and popular education is, for Rodés, in part a testimony to the power of King's legacy.

Rodés identifies two major developments that reflect King's enduring influence for this generation of Cubans. One is the Martin Luther King, Jr. Memorial Center, "a macro-ecumenical organization of Christian inspiration" that is based among the Cuban people and their churches. The other is Latin American liberation theology, "a popular theology that is critical, liberating, and contextualized." Rodés asserts that King's legacy, through the King Memorial Center, is actually linked to certain streams of this liberation theology.

Chapter 13, authored by Rabbi Everett Gendler, discusses King in relation to the Holy Land and the Middle East crisis, a subject also treated to some extent in Rabbi Marc Schneier's *Shared Dreams: Martin Luther King, Jr. and the Jewish Community* (1999). Gendler, a retired rabbi who marched with King in Albany, Birmingham, and Selma, and who has taught nonviolent ideas and methods in various parts of the world, including the Teaching Training School for the exile school system in Dharamsala, India, discusses the impact King might have had had he visited the Holy Land and given his active support to a peaceful resolution of the seemingly intractable Israeli-Palestinian conflict. According to Rabbi Gendler, King, like Gandhi, never took to the Holy Land his charismatic embodiment of "the efficacy and power of nonviolence." Gendler is much more sensitive than Rabbi Schneier to what he terms "the tragedy of King's absence in the Holy Land." Had King visited and gotten involved in that part of the world, Gendler surmises, he may well have affected its destiny in positive and profound ways in his time.

Rabbi Gendler concludes that if King were alive today, the question of a peaceful end to the Israeli-Palestinian crisis would perhaps receive immediate and careful scrutiny from him. Such a conclusion is difficult to dismiss, especially since King had moved toward a more enlightened and explicit globalism by the time of his death. Rabbi Gendler imagines King coming up with an "economic-religious-spiritual approach" to "the perplexing problem of settlements," which fuels the Israeli-Palestinian conflict, taking into account those who are displaced in the process. Rabbi Gendler goes on to highlight King's belief, expressed in 1967, that the United Nations should get involved to insure Israel's right to exist in a state of security, and the Palestinians' right to a life free of poverty. In the final analysis, Rabbi Gendler is convinced that these and any other approaches recommended and pursued by King would affirm "the basic human needs and dignity of all the contenders."

Chapter 14 is the last one in Part III. Contributed by Mary Gendler, a retired clinical psychologist, who has also taught nonviolence at the Teachers Training Institute in Dharamsala, India, this chapter treats the meaning of King for Tibetans who struggle under Chinese occupation. Recalling the experiences she and her husband, Rabbi Everett Gendler, have had with Tibetan exiles in India, Mary Gendler reports that many Tibetans see parallels between King's struggle in America and their own, and that they have evidenced a willingness to relate the issues King faced to their own personal struggles. Mary Gendler also insists that King's vision of a just and peaceful world is echoed in recent times by the Dalai Lama and the Tibetan people, who are also clamoring for and in search of freedom, justice, and human dignity through nonviolence. Thus, Martin Luther King, Jr. and the Tibetan Plateau are not "an unlikely pairing."

Mary Gendler's chapter, like others in this volume, gives readers a sense of King's continuing global impact. This, too, is an example of how we might move beyond the historical King, or the King who actually lived, spoke, and struggled, to interpret King beyond context. For Mary Gendler, and for other contributors to this volume, reflecting on King's ideas and struggles in different times and places does not necessarily present an insurmountable historical problem. Hence, these contributors constantly move between historical analysis and contemporary issues in their treatments of King.

For so many people, thinking of King in global terms amounts to a venture into the horizon of the unfamiliar. By orienting the focus to the global King, this book transcends the King who is routinely identified with the United States and its race problem, and it reveals that King played and continues to play a far more significant role in furthering world peace and community than is usually known or imagined. This volume also exposes readers to some of the best current thinking concerning the global King and his legacy. It reconstructs hitherto neglected aspects of King's life and enduring global impact, and is therefore a distinctive and original contribution to the field of King studies.

There is a new surge of interest in King as a global figure, a trend initially sparked by Lewis V. Baldwin's *Toward the Beloved Community: Martin Luther King, Jr. and South Africa* (1995), and reinforced by the appearance of Hak Joon Lee's *The Great World House: Martin Luther King, Jr. and Global Ethics* (2011) and Lewis V. Baldwin's edited collection of King documents, titled *"In a Single Garment of Destiny": A Vision of Global Justice* (2012). *"In an Inescapable Network of Mutuality": Martin Luther King, Jr. and the Globalization of an Ethical Ideal* is a timely and useful collection that has the potential to crystallize this important trend. If this happens, our greatest hopes and expectations will be realized.

PART ONE

For a World Made New

Exposing the Global Martin Luther King, Jr.

1

Living in the "World House"

Martin Luther King, Jr. and Globalization as Theory and Praxis

Lewis V. Baldwin

However deeply American Negroes are caught in the struggle to be at last at home in our homeland of the United States, we cannot ignore the larger world house in which we are also dwellers.

MARTIN LUTHER KING, JR.[1]

THE CURRENT FERMENT IN the scholarship on Martin Luther King, Jr. is leading to a new appreciation of his relevance and significance in this modern era of globalization.[2] While any discussion of King in relation to

---

1. Martin Luther King, Jr., *Where Do We Go from Here: Chaos or Community?* (Boston: Beacon, 1968) 167.

2. Because globalization is a new and largely untested concept in King studies, this is one angle from which scholars might break new ground in the scholarship on King. Important contributions toward this effort are made in Lewis V. Baldwin, *Toward the*

contemporary perspectives on globalization is fraught with risk, given that he is a figure from the past, it is not excessive to contend that the civil rights leader was both a precursor to and a critic of much of what is defined as globalization theory and praxis today. Moreover, King continues to have a profound impact on the world—religiously, socially, politically, and otherwise—and his insights, values, and activities still inform many facets of world cultures. Thus, it is not odd or peculiar to speak of the global Martin Luther King, Jr., and to consider how his ideal of the "world house," or his communitarian ideal, might take on new hues and pertinence[3] for those who wish and struggle for a more legitimate globalization in today's astoundingly altered and vastly different world.

TOWARD A NEW WORLD ORDER: THE CHALLENGE OF GLOBAL CITIZENSHIP

In his last two books, King was clearly speaking to the challenge of global citizenship, and of living and surviving in what he regarded as an increasingly globalized world. In his *Trumpet of Conscience* (1967), he defined his own quest for justice, peace, and human equality in global terms, declaring that "I speak as a citizen of the world."[4] In his *Where Do We Go from Here: Chaos or Community?* (1967), King variously described peoples across the earth as part of a "world house," a "worldwide neighborhood," a "single neighborhood," or a "human family," which stood in dire need of healthier ways of being globally connected and integrated. He wrote:

Beloved Community: Martin Luther King, Jr. and South Africa (Cleveland: Pilgrim, 1995) 1–185; Lewis V. Baldwin, "Martin Luther King, Jr. as a National and International Symbol of Community," *The A.M.E. Zion Quarterly Review* 101 (1989) 2–4; Lawrence E. Carter et al., *Global Ethical Options in the Tradition of Gandhi, King, and Ikeda* (New York: Weatherhill, 2001) 21–133; and Hak Joon Lee, *The Great World House: Martin Luther King, Jr. and Global Ethics* (Cleveland: Pilgrim, 2011) 15–200.

3. For some of the earliest attempts to uncover the global King and the universal implications of his communitarian ideal, see Lewis V. Baldwin, *To Make the Wounded Whole: The Cultural Legacy of Martin Luther King, Jr.* (Minneapolis: Fortress, 1992) 245–313; Baldwin, *Toward the Beloved Community*, 1–185; and Lewis V. Baldwin, *The Voice of Conscience: The Church in the Mind of Martin Luther King, Jr.* (New York: Oxford University Press, 2010) 181–216.

4. Martin Luther King, Jr., *The Trumpet of Conscience* (New York: Harper & Row, 1967) 31.

This is the great new problem of mankind. We have inherited a
large house, a great "world house" in which we have to live together—black and white, Easterner and Westerner, Gentile and
Jew, Catholic and Protestant, Moslem and Hindu—a family un-
duly separated in ideas, culture, and interest, who, because we can
never again live apart, must learn somehow to live with each other
in peace.[5]

Clearly, the concept of the *global* was not foreign to King. He envisioned a totally integrated world, undiminished and undeterred by human
differences, and committed to the ethical norms of love, justice, equal opportunity, peace, and community.[6] This was consistent with King's personal
idealism, which affirmed the dignity and worth of all human personality
and the communitarian and/or social nature of human existence.[7] I submit
that King's "world house" vision is still meaningful, and especially so in a
context in which globalization theorists and activists are calling for global
justice, the advancement of democratic freedoms and human rights, and
the transnational sharing and/or exchange of the kinds of ideas, values,
and material goods that serve the most cherished intellectual, cultural, economic, social, political, and religious interests of the entire human family.[8]
Indeed, any serious study of King and globalization should remind us of
how certain modes of thinking about life, humanity, and the world might
extend across generations and geographical and cultural boundaries.

The world is now interconnected in ways that King could only have
imagined in his time. Even so, associating King with globalization, in a
historic sense, is not oxymoronic. The term and concept of globalization

---

5. King, *Where Do We Go from Here?*, 167; James M. Washington, ed., *A Testament of Hope: The Essential Writings and Speeches of Martin Luther King, Jr.* (New York: Harper-Collins, 1991) 209; and Martin Luther King, Jr., "Moral and Religious Imperatives for Brotherhood," unpublished version of a speech delivered at Congregation B'nai Jeshu-run, New York, New York (February 9, 1963), The Library and Archives of The Martin Luther King, Jr. Center for Nonviolent Social Change, Inc., Atlanta, Georgia, 2.

6. Baldwin, *Toward the Beloved Community*, 2–3.

7. See Rufus Burrow, Jr., *God and Human Dignity: The Personalism, Theology, and Ethics of Martin Luther King, Jr.* (Notre Dame: University of Notre Dame Press, 2006) 157–61.

8. This point is supported by a careful reading of Lee, *Great World House*, 15. Focus-ing extensively on King's global ministry and cosmopolitanism, Lee argues that King's ethical insights and experiences and his political praxis are rich resources for fashioning a constructive global ethics. Lee goes on to explain how "Kingian global ethics" engages both "ethical deliberations" and "public practice."

would have been familiar to King in the 1960s. In fact, the term *globalization* was first widely used by economists and other social scientists in the 1960s,[9] when King and his activities at home and abroad dominated much of global consciousness. Since the 1980s, the term has achieved widespread use in the mainstream social media, and it is now "one of the most fashionable buzzwords" in contemporary academic and political debate and discourse.[10] Driven primarily by powerful international corporations that benefit enormously from the movement of capital, goods, and technology across borders, globalization is commonly described as "a process by which regional economies, societies, and cultures have become integrated through a global network of communication, transportation, and trade." The term is most often used "to refer to economic globalization," or "the integration of national economies into the international economy through trade, foreign direct investment, capital flows, migration, and the spread of technology." Globalization "can also refer to the transnational circulation of ideas, languages, or popular culture through acculturation."[11] Amazingly, one finds in globalization theory and praxis today echoes of some of what King had in mind when he spoke of the "world house," the "worldwide neighborhood," or the "new world order" as "the great new problem of mankind."[12]

9. See "Globalization," *Wikipedia, the Free Encyclopedia*, 1–2. Online: http://en.wikipedia.org/wiki/Globalization.

10. Ibid.; and "Globalization," *Stanford Encyclopedia of Philosophy*, 1–2. Online: http://plato.stanford.edu/entries/globalization/.

11. "Globalization," 1; Joseph E. Stiglitz, *Globalization and Its Discontents* (New York: Norton, 2002) 9–10; Thad Williamson et al., *Making a Place for Community: Local Democracy in a Global Era* (New York: Routledge, 2002) 28; and Kent E. Richter et al., *Understanding Religion in a Global Society* (Thomson Wadsworth, 2005) 10.

12. King, *Where Do We Go from Here?*, 167–91; and Martin Luther King, Jr., "Desireability of Being Maladjusted," unpublished version of a sermon (January 13, 1958), King Center Library and Archives, 1. King also used terms like "new world," "new order," "new age," and "new humanity" in expressing his vision of a globally connected and integrated world. See Clayborne Carson et al., eds., *The Papers of Martin Luther King, Jr.*, vol. 3, *Birth of a New Age, December 1955–December 1956* (Berkeley: University of California Press, 1997) 342, 462, and 478; Clayborne Carson et al., eds., *The Papers of Martin Luther King, Jr.*, vol. 4, *Symbol of the Movement, January 1957–December 1958* (Berkeley: University of California Press, 2000) 82–83; Clayborne Carson et al., eds., *The Papers of Martin Luther King, Jr.*, vol. 5, *Threshold of a New Decade, January 1959–December 1960* (Berkeley: University of California Press, 2005) 355, 425, and 576; Clayborne Carson et al., eds., *The Papers of Martin Luther King, Jr.*, vol. 6, *Advocate of the Social Gospel, September 1948–March 1963* (Berkeley: University of California Press, 2007) 182–83; Martin Luther King, Jr., "Doubts and Certainties Link: Transcript of an Interview," London, England (Winter 1968), King Center Library and Archives, 5; and Baldwin, *To Make the Wounded Whole*, 286.

King prefigured contemporary globalization theorists and activists in highlighting the need for a fresh core of globally shared values. In other words, how should we approach the question of global justice? How should we address the many enduring threats to democratic freedoms and human rights worldwide? What is our responsibility in the face of the globalization of racism? How concerned should we be about poverty, economic injustice, and the poor? What should be our response to the redefinition of the role of women and other marginalized groups in this global age? How should we deal with the problem of war and human destruction? What should we do about the degradation and destruction of the environment? What does globalization mean in terms of religion and its changing contexts? In the context of globalization, should we be uncritical supporters of the status quo or advocates for diversity and the celebration of human differences?[13]

Unlike most economists and other social scientists today, King approached these questions as a philosopher and theologian, giving far more priority to the moral and/or ethical than to economic and political considerations. And perhaps more importantly, King called for "a revolution of values to accompany the scientific and freedom revolutions engulfing the earth" in his time. Here he had in mind the shift from "a thing-oriented" society and world to "a person-oriented" society and world, the expression of loyalties that are "ecumenical" rather than "sectional" in scope, and the movement beyond the idea that "self-preservation is the first law of life" to the principle that "other-preservation is the first law of life."[14] King was really talking about a radical reconstruction of global society with an accent on the highest human values—values that would draw on the very best qualities of people from every part of the globe. Currently, globalization is widely considered a real threat to "traditional values," especially in rural areas, but this is not consistent with King's idea of "a revolution of values."[15]

The concerns that separate King and globalization theory and praxis today are glaringly evident in the case of global justice issues. King's oft-repeated declaration that "injustice anywhere is a threat to justice everywhere," and that the prophet of God is never an outsider where injustice

13. Stiglitz, *Globalization and Its Discontents*, 218–19.

14. King, *Where Do We Go from Here?*, 180, 186, and 190.

15. Critics of globalization lament its threat to human values, and especially traditional values. See Stiglitz, *Globalization and Its Discontents*, 247; and King, *Where Do We Go from Here?*, 186.

exists,[16] mirrored both his commitment to global justice and his awareness of the ever-growing global nature of his daily life and activities. In
other words, King did not separate injustice in Birmingham and Selma
from injustice in Johannesburg, Hanoi, and Moscow, and he considered
his nonviolent dissent and activism in America a part of his larger struggle
for global justice, which involved, among other things, fund-raising, the
call for economic and diplomatic sanctions against South Africa, and the
signing of appeals, petitions, and declarations aimed at the more humane
treatment of Jews in Russia and rice farmers in Vietnam. King was unequivocally a global justice advocate and activist whose perspective was
enriched by both his world travels and his encounter with different peoples
and cultures.[17]

Some supporters of globalization in our times raise the banner of global justice as "the equitable treatment" of individuals, groups, and nations,[18]
and claim to pursue it as a higher humanitarian principle, but too many
of them, in contrast to King, seem more concerned about controlling the
expansion of world markets and preserving their status as power elites than
about altruistic love and the unselfish and legitimate exercise of power.[19]
The problem is further complicated by the lack of a globally acceptable and
functional criterion for determining what justice really means, and how
it can best be administered across geographical and cultural boundaries.[20]

The same might be said regarding the advocacy and promotion of
democratic freedoms and human rights. Undoubtedly, these concerns surface in the language and on the mission agenda of both King and many who
currently manage globalization. King maintained that much of the human
inequality and social injustice throughout the world resulted from either
the unwarranted abridgement or the total lack of democratic freedoms,
which always require radical structural changes in societies. Convinced that
his own quest for participatory democracy for black and white Americans
meant little in a larger world bereft of basic democratic freedoms, King

16. Martin Luther King, Jr., *Why We Can't Wait* (New York: New American Library,
1964) 77.

17. This claim is substantiated in Baldwin, *Toward the Beloved Community*, 10–63.

18. See Thomas Pogge, *World Poverty and Human Rights* (Cambridge: Polity, 2002)
31.

19. If antiglobalizationists are to be taken seriously, this is most certainly the case. See
"Anti-globalization Movement," *Wikipedia, the Free Encyclopedia*, 1–2. Online: http://
en.wikipedia.org/wiki/Anti-globalization_movement.

20. This is profoundly discussed in Pogge, *World Poverty and Human Rights*, 33.

delighted in the forward march of what he called "a world-wide freedom revolution." Indeed, he viewed the struggle for democracy in America as "a significant part of a world development,"[21] in which people everywhere were revolting against systems of tyranny and oligarchy and clamoring for political and constitutional power.

But King also held that the United States, which paraded as the leader of the free world, could not assume a leadership role in this global revolution as long as her own democracy remained "flawed both economically and socially," and if she persisted in giving materialism, power, and supremacy over other nations primacy over the spiritual and moral dimensions of life.[22] In an increasingly globalized world, King also addressed the danger inherent in America's Manichean division of the world into *us* and *them*, noting how such an outlook could only lead to her diminished global role. His hope was that his own country would play a more positive and creative role in the flowering of more genuine patterns of global democracy. As far as King was concerned, the American Negro, "by taking to the streets and there giving practical lessons of democracy's defaults and shortcomings," through nonviolent direct action, was keeping alive this hope, directing it toward a global messianic objective.[23] King's thoughts on these matters are still relevant, and they stand as a challenge to those globalizationists who believe unquestionably that the United States should have the vanguard role in the spread of democratic freedoms.

Theoretically, globalization affirms the need for a healthy leveling of democracy in the direction of greater rights and privileges for human beings everywhere. The idea is that democracy should be what Anja Weiss calls "a global institution"[24]—that people who are "significantly and legitimately affected" by governmental or political decisions should have "a roughly equal opportunity" to influence those decisions "directly or through elected

---

21. King, *Where Do We Go from Here?*, 169; and Martin Luther King, Jr., "Statement to the Press at the Beginning of the Youth Leadership Conference," Raleigh, North Carolina (April 15, 1960), King Center Library and Archives, 1.

22. Washington, *Testament of Hope*, 314; King, "Doubts and Certainties Link," 5; and Baldwin, *To Make the Wounded Whole*, 286.

23. Martin Luther King, Jr., *Where Do We Go from Here?*, unpublished draft (1967), King Center Library and Archives, 9–10; and Lewis V. Baldwin, *There Is a Balm in Gilead: The Cultural Roots of Martin Luther King, Jr.* (Minneapolis: Fortress, 1991) 242–43.

24. Anja Weiss, "The Racism of Globalization," in *The Globalization of Racism*, ed. Donaldo Macedo and Panayota Gounari (Boulder, CO: Paradigm, 2006) 128.

delegates or representatives."[25] These ideas evidently square with King's. But on a practical level, globalization too often serves the interests of the so-called developed countries themselves, thereby undermining community democracy, or the empowerment of local communities, and also the sovereignty of the nation-state. Joseph E. Stiglitz elaborates the point in his book *Globalization and Its Discontents*, in which he writes that

> Globalization, as it has been advocated, often seems to replace the old dictatorships of national elites with new dictatorships of international finance. Countries are effectively told that if they don't follow certain conditions, the capital markets or the IMF will refuse to lend them money. They are basically forced to give up parts of their sovereignty, to let capricious capital markets, including the speculators whose only concerns are short-term rather than the long-term growth of the country and the improvement of living standards, "discipline" them, telling them what they should and should not do.[26]

In her critique of globalization, Amy Chua highlights the problematic phrase "market democracy," questioning the view that the combination of electoral freedom and laissez-faire economics is transforming individuals into "civic-minded citizens and consumers" and the world into "a community of modernized, peace-loving nations." Chua concludes that the world's "market-dominant minorities"—the power elite in the United States, the Chinese in Southeast Asia, the Croatians in the former Yugoslavia, whites in southern Africa and Latin America, Indians in East Africa, the Lebanese in West Africa, and Jews in post-Communist Russia—are benefiting from economic power and wealth disproportionately to their numbers, and are actually undermining democracy and contributing to cycles of ethnic tension and global violence that are potentially catastrophic for humans everywhere.[27] Obviously, this is antithetical to what King envisioned when he spoke of the advancement of the kind of democratic freedoms that insure genuine human community, peace, and global stability.

Some globalizationists are fundamentally in agreement with King in refusing to separate democratic freedoms and/or civil liberties from human

25. Pogge, *World Poverty and Human Rights*, 184.

26. See Stiglitz, *Globalization and Its Discontents*, 247; and Williamson et al., *Making a Place for Community*, 25–99, 267–68, 270, 292, 295–97, and 310–22.

27. Amy Chua, *World on Fire: How Exporting Free Market Democracy Breeds Ethnic Hatred and Global Instability* (New York: Doubleday, 2003).

rights. The language of the global King actually takes us beyond democracy and civil rights in America to the more general question of human rights in the international arena. King believed that human rights should be universalized in principle and practice. In his very last speech, "I See the Promised Land," delivered in Memphis on the night before his assassination, he spoke of "the human rights revolution" pervading the world, noting that its aim was to free the destitute, weak, and victimized from hurt, want, and neglect.[28] King's understanding of human rights was rooted in the principle of *imago Dei*, or the idea that human worth is related to and ultimately grounded in God.[29]

The theoreticians of globalization in this modern era are not likely to use the language that King employed, but globalization is advancing the idea of universal human rights by putting to the forefront a concept that King consistently espoused; namely, that "all people share a common human-ness and should be afforded equally respect, fairness, and justice."[30] Globalization embraces the idea of "human rights fulfillment" and also a keen sense of the need for international alliances to prevent human rights abuses.[31] As Richard Horton puts it in his book *Health Wars on the Global Front Lines of Modern Medicine*, "Human rights are increasingly recognized as global norms, regardless of national laws."[32] Moreover, globalization seeks to dispel the notion that nations can choose either to agree or disagree about these matters, with each committing itself to human rights standards appropriate to its history, culture, population size, geopolitical context, and stage of development. The problem actually surfaces in the absence of a single, global standard of human rights that all peoples and countries are willing to embrace unequivocally. Even so, the hope is that the nations of the world can, despite their differences, at least share in a common culture of decency and respect for human rights. King supremely embodied and acted on this hope, and this is why his name has become associated with a globalized rights culture.

28. Washington, *Testament of Hope*, 280.

29. King, "Moral and Religious Imperatives for Brotherhood," 1.

30. Richter et al., *Understanding Religion in a Global Society*, 192–93.

31. Pogge, *World Poverty and Human Rights*, 188.

32. Richard Horton, *Health Wars on the Global Front Lines of Modern Medicine* (New York: New York Review of Books, 2003) 472.

ON THE INTERRELATED STRUCTURE OF REALITY:
OVERCOMING BARRIERS

Martin Luther King, Jr.'s ethic of global human rights grew out of a deep sensitivity to the interplay of oppressions based on race, class, gender, and religion. King did not separate one form of oppression from the others, and this, too, speaks to the profundity of his global vision. He was really ahead of his time in perceiving the challenges posed by the globalization of racism. Convinced that racism existed as an international phenomenon,[33] King became the world's conscience and voice as he sought to forge new paths toward an authentically multiracial and multiethnic world. Indeed, he was a pioneer in addressing the urgent necessity for a kind of global organizing in the assault on racial and ethnic antagonisms and divisions. Speaking of the artificial barriers that separate people along the lines of race, King, in his "South Africa Benefit Speech" given in New York in December 1965, declared that "the whole human race will benefit when it ends the abomination that has diminished the stature of man for too long."[34]

Some interpreters of globalization theory and praxis are calling our attention to "new forms of racism" that are being manifested globally, in the form of ethnic cleansing, culture wars, terrorism, Zionism, anti-immigration, and intensified xenophobia. These issues have been addressed in recent years in the United Nations (U.N.) conferences on world racism, meetings that have not been heavily supported by the United States and other major powers and their allies.[35] Obviously, we do not live in a post-racial world, and we are not restricted to the white-black binary that framed so much of the racial discourse in King's age. So in a real sense, the question looms larger and with more complexity: how do we deal with the new global color line issues of the twenty-first century?[36]

By benefiting some nations and cultures more than others, particularly from an economic standpoint, globalization is creating a climate for

33. King, *Where Do We Go from Here?*, 173.

34. Martin Luther King, Jr., "South Africa Benefit Speech," unpublished version, delivered at Hunter College, New York, New York (December 10, 1965) 5–6; and Baldwin, *Toward the Beloved Community*, 50.

35. Lynn Huntley, "Combating Racism in a Global Era," *New Crisis* 108 (2001) 24–26; Bill Nichols, "Powell Will Not Attend U.N. Conference on Racism," *USA Today*, August 27, 2001, 13A; "U.S. Will Boycott Racism Meeting," *The Tennessean*, April 19, 2009, 4A; and Baldwin, *Voice of Conscience*, 239.

36. Macedo and Gounari, *Globalization of Racism*, 6–238.

racial and ethnic tensions and conflict. In fact, globalization today is actu-ally associated with structural racism, and globalization theorists and activ-ists are thus ill-prepared to come up with workable strategies to dismantle the ideology and structures that undergird racial polarization and racist practices.[37] At a time when right-wing extremists around the world are fan-ning the flames of bigotry and intolerance, globalization could benefit from an urgent retelling of King's continuing significance for a new generation and its concerns relative to race. As suggested previously, King envisioned a new global spirit that knows no racial, ethnic, or tribal boundaries, and he consistently pointed to the inspiring possibilities for human reconciliation and community. His lifelong fidelity to a global "beloved community" still stands as a prophetic indictment against those globalizationists who simply refuse to truly commit themselves to the banishment of racism from the face of the earth.[38]

The concerns of King and contemporary globalization also never re-ally intersect when it comes to the problems of poverty, economic injustice, and class differences. King felt that these problems had to be solved as a precondition for living creatively and productively in the "world house." He lamented the fact that "two-thirds of the peoples of the world" were "under-nourished, ill-housed, shabbily clad," and had "never seen a physician or a dentist." He wondered why hunger, privation, and disease could exist in any land given the abundance of human and material resources, and also the knowledge of vitamins, nutrition, the chemistry of food, and the environ-ment, "to provide all mankind with the basic necessities of life," despite "the enormous acceleration in the rate of growth of the world's population."[39]

Convinced that space and resources should never be limited to certain peoples and nations, King called for more enlightened global economic policies, with a particular emphasis on the need for "an all-out world war against poverty."[40] Evidently, King was thinking of something far more in-novative and/or creative than U.N.-sponsored world food summits and programs, world health assemblies to monitor infectious diseases, and rais-ing the standards of living generally for people, especially in the case of developing countries—concepts associated with globalization today.[41] In a

37. Ibid., 10–33.

38. See ibid., 6–238.

39. King, *Where Do We Go from Here?*, 176–77.

40. Ibid., 178.

41. Pogge, *World Poverty and Human Rights*, 10; and Horton, *Health Wars*, 129.

more general sense, King opted for the kind of global coalition-building and activism that would lead to the complete dismantling of the structures that breed poverty, economic injustice, and glaring class distinctions worldwide.

The moral responsibility for this "world-wide war against poverty," King thought, rested with the wealthy, developed nations—the United States, Britain, Russia, Canada, Australia, and those of Western Europe—many of which had solidified their wealth and power by exploiting the countries of the so-called Third World. For King, the global struggle against poverty and economic injustice necessarily involved revolting against the "subversive influence" of imperialism, colonialism, and neocolonialism, to which the technology and wealth of the great powers, and especially the Western world, had for too long been devoted.[42] King urged the rich nations to provide capital and technical assistance to poor nations, not "as a surreptitious means to control" them, but with the goal of developing the underdeveloped, schooling the unschooled, and feeding the unfed.[43]

The economic currents driving globalization in these times seem unreceptive to the type of new global economic strategies that King felt would best benefit poor persons and nations. In fact, economic globalization is identified with the very structures that King so vehemently critiqued—namely, corporate capitalism. The large multinational corporations, with their unregulated power exercised in financial markets and through trade agreements, are clearly more interested in maximizing profit than in honoring work safety standards, fair hiring and compensation guidelines, and environmental conservation standards.[44] To be sure, economic globalization has resulted in a higher quality of life for millions throughout the world, and it has benefited countries that have taken advantage of it by seeking debt relief, new markets for their exports, and foreign investment; but it is also contributing to what Thomas Pogge calls "the appalling trajectory of world poverty and global inequality."[45]

42. King, *Where Do We Go from Here?*, 57 and 178–79; Martin Luther King, Jr., "Statement Regarding the Legitimacy of the Struggle in Montgomery, Alabama," unpublished version (May 4, 1956), King Center Library and Archives, 1; and Baldwin, *Toward the Beloved Community*, 247.

43. King, *Where Do We Go from Here?*, 178–79; and Baldwin, *To Make the Wounded Whole*, 266–67.

44. See "Anti-globalization Movement," 1.

45. Stiglitz, *Globalization and Its Discontents*, 4 and 248; and Pogge, *World Poverty and Human Rights*, 19.

The greatest beneficiaries of economic globalization are not poor individuals and nations, but transnational corporations and global lenders such as the World Trade Organization (WTO), the Free Trade Area of the Americas (FTAA), the World Bank, and the International Monetary Fund (IMF). This can only breed enduring problems in a world in which virtually every economy is linked to international financial and commodity markets, and in which the world economy is teetering on the edge of the abyss.[46] Furthermore, because economic globalization encourages decision-making based on ideology and politics rather than moral and/or ethical imperatives, it is fundamentally antithetical to King's vision of the "beloved community" or "world house," which embraces economic egalitarianism as an ethical ideal.[47]

But what is missing in the values and ethos of both the global King and economic globalization are penetrating critiques of the subordination and marginalization of women. The essential dignity and worth of women is emphatically proclaimed in the rhetoric of both King and the managers of globalization. At times, King insisted that "women must be respected as human beings and not treated as mere means," and he delighted in the thought that "one of the great contributions that Christianity has made to the world is that of lifting the status of womanhood from that of an insignificant child-bearer to a position of dignity and honor and respect."[48] King also collaborated with female activists such as Dorothy I. Height and the former first lady Eleanor Roosevelt in appeals calling for worldwide protests against the apartheid regime in South Africa; but, interestingly enough, King did not make the liberation of women a critical part of his global human rights agenda, even when he turned his attention to the South African problem, the crisis in the Middle East, the evils of colonialism in Africa and Asia, and the grinding poverty in Latin America and the Caribbean.[49]

46. See Pogge, *World Poverty and Human Rights*, 19–20; Stiglitz, *Globalization and Its Discontents*, 4–5, 10, and 247–49; and "Anti-globalization Movement," 1. One of the most interesting critiques of economic globalization is Stan G. Duncan, *The Greatest Story Oversold: Understanding Economic Globalization* (Maryknoll, NY: Orbis, 2011).

47. King, *Where Do We Go from Here?*, 176–81; and Baldwin, *To Make the Wounded Whole*, 254–55 and 263–68.

48. Carson et al., *Papers*, 6:212; and Baldwin, *Voice of Conscience*, 203.

49. At the time of Mrs. Roosevelt's death in November 1962, King declared that she "will remain a symbol of world citizenship." See Martin Luther King, Jr., "Epitaph for a First Lady: Eleanor Roosevelt," unpublished statement (November 24, 1962) 1; Eleanor Roosevelt, Bishop James A. Pike, and Martin Luther King, Jr. to the Friends and Supporters of the American Committee on Africa, unpublished version of a letter (July 1957),

It is better to say that King's efforts benefited women in some ways and harmed them in others. Women's liberation was inspired by his nonviolent crusade for equality, even as he did little to encourage female leadership in the global struggles for liberation.[50] Furthermore, while it is true that King himself was sexist, his communitarian ideal, as expressed through the metaphors of the "world house" and the "beloved community," was not,[51] for one finds here the idea of a mutually dependent, even symbiotic, liberation for both the oppressed and the oppressors, irrespective of gender difference. The point is that the freedom of all oppressed people from injustice and exploitation also requires the liberation of their oppressors from fear, greed, and ignorance. This kind of global liberation ethic stands as an important and unique component of King's thought and praxis.

Globalization as we know it in contemporary times is redefining the roles and changing the status of women in ways that King never witnessed, but not always in a liberating fashion, especially in developing nations. Through its new and advanced information, communication, and transportation technologies, globalization is increasing our awareness concerning women's issues and the status of women worldwide. Women's rights are now widely accepted as part of a larger crusade for global human rights and social justice, and have become a pressing issue for transnational advocacy networks and intergovernmental organizations such as the U.N. The results of such trends are formal agreements and programs targeting women's issues, and new standards and/or guidelines for the treatment of women.[52] Moreover, economic globalization is resulting in new opportunities and resources for women, particularly from the standpoint of health

---

King Center Library and Archives, 1–2; "Declaration of Conscience: An Appeal to South Africa," drafted by the American Committee on Africa (December 10, 1962), King Center Library and Archives, 1; and Baldwin, *Toward the Beloved Community*, 15–19.

50. John J. Ansbro, *Martin Luther King, Jr.: The Making of a Mind* (Maryknoll, NY: Orbis, 1982) xv; and Lewis V. Baldwin and Amiri YaSin Al-Hadid, *Between Cross and Crescent: Christian and Muslim Perspectives on Malcolm and Martin* (Gainesville: University Press of Florida, 2002) 181–99.

51. Baldwin and Al-Hadid, *Between Cross and Crescent*, 403 n. 43.

52. These insights are based on a careful reading of Richter et al., *Understanding Religion in a Global Society*, 376–77; Candace C. Archer, "Women and Globalization," in *Women and Politics around the World: A Comparative History and Survey*, ed. Joyce Gelb and Marian L. Palley (Santa Barbara, CA: ABC-CLIO, 2009) 1:17–23; and "How Does Globalization Affect Women?," *The Globalization Website*, 1. Online: http://www.sociology.emory.edu/globalization/issues02.html.

and child-care concerns.[53] King envisioned and spoke to such possibilities in his own time, particularly as he thought in terms of a "revolution" of human values and priorities.

But globalization has not yet liberated women from patriarchal domination and the division of labor, and from the larger problems of poverty and economic inequality. Men are in control of the instruments of production and of formal economic policymaking on a global scale. In an insightful study titled, "Globalization and Women," Elaine Coburn has reported that women comprise "less than six percent of the governors of the World Bank, less than three percent of the IMF board of governors," and, until recently, "less than eight percent of the trade experts consulted by the World Trade Organization in its Dispute Resolutions Body."[54] Also, women are still disproportionately represented among the low-wage workers of the world, and they are not receiving an equal share of the benefits of cooperative production.[55] Female representation in global politics is equally dismal. Coburn tells us that "less than fifteen percent of legislators worldwide are women" and that "women are less likely than men to hold ministerial positions in economics-related areas like finance, trade, industry and agriculture."[56] In such a climate, ethical dialogue with both King and globalization can yield insights as the human family moves from *what is* to *what ought to be* in the sphere of gender equality and inclusiveness.

The same might be said of religion and the ways in which it is being redefined in today's global society. One finds in both King and globalization a sense of the growing interconnectedness of religious life and how it is altering the activities of persons and communities on a planetary-wide stage.[57] King lamented the fact that he lived in a rapidly changing world in which ignorance and misunderstanding too often greeted religious differences, or in which there was too little respect for the rich and abounding diversity of the world's faith traditions. As a man of the church, King envisioned that institution's future encounter with globalization, and in his

---

53. "Women and Globalization: A Study of 180 Countries, 1975–2000," *International Organization* 60 (2006) 293–333.

54. Elaine Coburn, "Globalization and Women," in *Gendered Intersections: A Collection of Readings for Women's and Gender Studies*, ed. Leslie Biggs and Pamela Downe (Black Point, NS: Fernwood, 2005) 3–4.

55. "How Does Globalization Affect Women?," 1.

56. Coburn, "Globalization and Women," 3.

57. Richter et al., *Understanding Religion in a Global Society*, 384.

estimation this entailed, among other things, developing a healthy respect and appreciation for Hinduism, Buddhism, Judaism, Islam, and other great world religions.[58] King's "world house" or "beloved community" ideal actually amounted to a sort of overarching *telos* that embraces all of the major religions as valid pointers to the Supreme Being.

King concluded that the love ethic is "that force which all the great religions have seen as the supreme unifying principle of life,"[59] and that these religions combined are sources of universal and timeless ethical values that are vital to the struggle for a global "beloved community." Interestingly enough, this was part of King's creative interpretation of the kingdom of God motif; namely, that there is a universal path to the kingdom that intersects with people of all faith claims. "God has intended through all religions to keep intact the brotherhood of man," said King in a letter to schoolchildren in 1961.[60] Although he worked from his own Christian base, the pan-religious character of both his civil rights and global human rights campaigns was unmistakable. Clearly, King's openness to the ideas of Mohandas K. Gandhi, and his association and collaborative efforts for peace with the Buddhist monk Thich Nhat Hanh, the Muslim spokesman Muhammad Ali, and the Jewish rabbis Abraham J. Heschel and Everett Gendler, were symbolic of how certain kinds of values move across different religions and cultures.[61] Undoubtedly, King contributed enormously to interfaith understanding and cooperation in the 1950s and 1960s, and, in so doing, he offered a paradigm for how religion might best intersect with a global justice and human rights agenda.

58. Clayborne Carson et al., eds., *The Papers of Martin Luther King, Jr.*, vol. 1, *Called to Serve, January 1929–June 1948* (Berkeley: University of California Press, 1992) 211 and 281; Carson et al., *Papers*, 4:471–72; Martin Luther King, Jr. to Dr. Harold E. Fey, unpublished letter, King Center Library and Archives, 3; Martin Luther King, Jr. to Mr. M. Bernard Resnikoff (September 17, 1961), unpublished letter, King Center Library and Archives, 1; Baldwin and Al-Hadid, *Between Cross and Crescent*, 115–27; and Baldwin, *Voice of Conscience*, 201–16.

59. King, *Where Do We Go from Here?*, 190–91; and "An Interview with Martin Luther King, Jr.," unpublished version prepared for *Redbook* magazine (November 5, 1964), King Center Library and Archives, 1–2.

60. Martin Luther King, Jr. to Mr. L. F. Palmer, unpublished letter dictated to James R. Wood (February 23, 1961), King Center Library and Archives, 2.

61. Even King scholars have failed to grasp the genuine reciprocity and deep spiritual kinship that joined the cultures and movements of King, Gandhi, Hanh, and Heschel and Gendler. See Baldwin, *Voice of Conscience*, 213.

The forces of globalization today are increasingly breaking down barriers that separate people, and are thereby presenting many new opportunities and challenges for all of the great world religions. King said almost a half-century ago that "we live in a world of geographical oneness" due to our scientific and technological genius, and that "we are challenged now to make it spiritually one," or one in terms of "brotherhood."[62] These words ring with more of a piercing urgency now than they did then. Among the urgent issues confronting the great religions are human rights and social justice and the need to be a collective force for good in a world of plurality and difference, suffering and conflict.

Some supporters of globalization view the different faith communities and traditions as key sources of the kinds of ethical ideas and values that serve the best interests of humankind as a whole, but unfortunately, the various faiths are still being used to feed tendencies toward inequality, injustice, intolerance, and oppression. In more specific terms, religion is too frequently employed to reinforce the global status quo—to discourage genuinely ethical behavior, prophetic critique, and cooperative social activism, and to anchor patriarchal structures that subordinate women, economic and political systems that favor the rich and powerful, and cultural barriers that incite discord, hostility, and even violence. King's vision of a globalized world in which the various religions cease fighting among themselves over truth claims, while spearheading and enriching the quest for greater human rights and freedoms, must still be seriously considered among the broad spectrum of looming possibilities. Perhaps the greater challenge is to overcome the individualistic tendencies that too often afflict religion in global society,[63] to engage in fruitful interreligious dialogue and action, and to become a formidable, unified, and constructive force in bringing the principle of the "beloved community" to vivid life.

There is also the question of how interfaith encounters and dialogue might focus more attention on the issues of war and peace in this modern age of globalization. As a person of faith, first and foremost, and as one mindful of the unholy alliance between religion and war historically, King entertained this question consistently and with a keen sense of urgency. Convinced that violence in any form is intrinsically immoral, he held that surviving in the "world house" hinged on the human capacity to find

---

62. Washington, *Testament of Hope*, 209.

63. Richter et al., *Understanding Religion in a Global Society*, 362.

some "alternative to war and human destruction."[64] King literally agonized over the fact that "the best brains in the highly developed nations of the world are devoted to military technology," or to the proliferation of nuclear weapons and other weapons of mass destruction, and he categorically rejected the rationale for using military force to try to remedy the world's problems.[65] Ever mindful of the catastrophic consequences of war, and especially its toll in human suffering, health threats, death, and environmental destruction, King denounced the "arms race" and enlisted the commitment of the world religions and of humanity in general in what he termed the "peace race."[66] In King's estimation, humanity stood at a crossroads where the choice between nonviolent coexistence and violent coannihilation had never been clearer and more urgent.[67]

King maintained that all war was "obsolete"—that it no longer served a useful purpose, especially considering the stockpiles of weapons of mass destruction and the mounting capacity of humans for global self-destruction.[68] Even the idea of military intervention on humanitarian grounds was morally repulsive to him. Thus, he spoke in terms of the purpose and value of human life and of globalizing the nonviolent ethic. At one point in his *Trumpet of Conscience*, King suggested "that modern man really go all out to study the meaning of nonviolence, its philosophy and its strategy," and at another he asserted that in an increasingly interconnected world, "nonviolence is no longer an option for intellectual analysis, it is an imperative for action."[69] But King's most significant and far-reaching influence came through his involvement with the peace movement and the more global antiwar activities in his time, much of which entailed making speeches, fund-raising, participating in street demonstrations, and signing declarations and appeals against the conflicts in Vietnam and other parts of the so-called Third World.

64. King, *Where Do We Go from Here?*, 181.

65. Ibid.

66. "An Interview with Martin Luther King, Jr.," 1–2; Martin Luther King, Jr., "What Are Your New Year's Resolutions?," unpublished version of a sermon, New York, New York (January 7, 1968), King Center Library and Archives, 3; Martin Luther King, Jr., "An Address at the Fiftieth Anniversary of the Women's International League for Peace and Freedom," unpublished version of a speech, Philadelphia, Pennsylvania (October 15, 1965), King Center Library and Archives, 11; and Baldwin, *Voice of Conscience*, 244.

67. King, *Where Do We Go from Here?*, 191.

68. Ibid., 181 and 183.

69. King, *Trumpet of Conscience*, 64 and 68.

Perhaps it is in relation to the timeless themes of war and peace that King is most meaningful for the globalization process today, and more specifically for globalization thought and praxis. The emergence of a more economically interconnected and interdependent world has not eliminated the prospects and the reality of war. Some social critics argue, and convincingly so, that globalization actually "promotes the conditions for war." As Steven Staples points out, "Ethnic and religious differences mask the underlying economic causes of more than thirty wars raging around the world today." Staples goes on to say that "inequality, competition for dwindling resources, and environmental degradation are factors in the outbreak of armed conflict that is worsened by free trade."[70] According to Staples and Antulio J. Echevarria, globalization promotes war by "exacerbating basic feelings of enmity among different cultures," by promoting "corporate security over human security," by requiring "police and military protection of corporate interests," by giving priority to "military spending over social spending," and by undermining "grassroots peace work."[71] Richard Horton, another critic, goes further, insisting that "globalization has fostered the conditions that will permit acts of biowar," such as anthrax infections, "to flourish."[72] Nothing could be more disturbing at a time when Muslim extremists think in terms of "world jihad," and the rest of humanity speaks of the urgency of "the global war on terror."

Clearly, King remains a refreshing voice in the debate around the ethics of war and peace in this age of globalization. He compels us to rethink and reimagine key questions about how war and peace issues are being framed in the world's religions, in the circles of political and governmental power, and in the larger public discourse worldwide. King also provides a paradigm for addressing and ultimately eliminating war and its threat to the "beloved community," or the "world house." In the face of the immense spiral of violence across the earth, and especially war and terrorism, globalization's recognition of the growing importance of the

70. Steven Staples, "Ten Ways Globalization Promotes Militarism," 1. Online: http://rense.com/general41/prono.htm. P. R. Goldstone, "Does Globalization Bring War or Peace?," 1–2. Online: http://www.alternet.org/world/62848. Antulio J. Echevarria II, "Globalization and the Nature of War," 1–2. Online: http://www.strategicstudiesinstitute.army.mil/pubs/display.cfm?pubID=215.

71. Echevarria, "Globalization and the Nature of War," 1–2; and Staples, "How Globalization Promotes War," 1.

72. Horton, *Health Wars*, 127.

U.N. as a transnational organization actually recalls King, who described the U.N. as "a gesture in the direction of nonviolence on a world scale."[73] One might also claim that in the midst of the tension and uncertainty of the changing times, King's sense of a globalized world in which indigenous peoples enjoy basic human rights and freedoms while assuming diverse roles in the quest for world peace seems an unrealistic scenario, to say nothing of his vision of a "world house" completely free of war. In any case, globalization theorists and activists who currently claim to abhor war and to understand the need for world peace are, in one sense, a tribute to the resiliency of King's spirit; but it is the actual pursuit of peace through moral and practical methods, and especially nonviolent means, that is far more important.

As Joseph E. Stiglitz has noted, globalization has brought many benefits in terms of the increased interdependence among peoples worldwide, more accessibility to markets and technology, opportunities for trade, better health standards, and a greater interest in human rights, democratic freedoms, and social justice. Better and more accessible means of transportation, improved communication through the Internet, satellite, cable, and other sources, and the easier flow of goods, services, capital, and knowledge across borders are all great benefits.[74] Even so, we have not evolved into the kind of global society that King envisioned and expressed in his use of the metaphors of the "beloved community" and the "world house." In a world in which the actions of the United States and other powerful countries are antiglobalist on so many fronts, King still challenges us not only to avoid the perils of isolationism, but also to proclaim the ideal of a truly integrated and interdependent world, a common humanity, and equality before the God who is the parent of us all. King said the following in one of his last books, *Where Do We Go from Here: Chaos or Community?*, as he challenged humans to rethink questions about themselves and about what it really means to be interconnected, interrelated, and interdependent in a global context:

> Every nation is an heir of a vast treasury of ideas and labor to which both the living and the dead of all nations have contributed. Whether we realize it or not, each of us lives eternally "in the red." We are everlasting debtors to known and unknown men

73. King, *Where Do We Go from Here?*, 184.
74. Stiglitz, *Globalization and Its Discontents*, 4–5, 214, and 248.

and women. When we arise in the morning, we go into the bath-
room where we reach for a sponge which is provided for us by
a Pacific Islander. We reach for soap that is created for us by a
European. Then at the table we drink coffee which is provided for
us by a South American, or tea by a Chinese or cocoa by a West
African. Before we leave for our jobs we are already beholden to
more than half of the world.[75]

King's ideas and values, and especially his communitarian ethic, can
be useful in reshaping globalization, or in making it more ethical, equitable, humane, and productive, so that there is no longer a threat to the
freedoms, cultural identities, and values of certain peoples, and that all
peoples and countries can have an equal voice in the policies that impact
their lives daily. King's "beloved community" ideal offers hard insights
and creative ways to approach the rich varieties and complexities of human experience, and it calls into question the idea of globalization as an
effort to impose the power and values of one country over others. By engaging that ideal, the different peoples of the world can become more sensitive to their rich interconnectedness and moral responsibilities toward
each other, and to the stakes and possibilities of international relations.
In short, King's image of the "beloved community" or the "world house"
provides a model for alternative and new kinds of reflection around the
issues of globalization.[76]

King thought in terms of the globalization of an ethical ideal, and he
has a lot to say about the role of ethics in the face of rapid globalization.
This is not likely to be understood by those who assume that associating
King with modern globalization is somehow oxymoronic. It is not simply
a matter of forming images of King purely as a response to the global challenges of today, but of considering his enduring challenge and relevance
for a rapidly changing and increasingly pluralistic world. Clearly, King,
with the foresight, instinct, and discernment of a prophet, had a sense of
the challenges that modern globalization would pose for all humanity.
Thus, it is perfectly logical to place his ideas about community in the context of globalization, especially at a time when some critics are charging
that globalization is actually polarizing humanity and resulting in an even
more unjust world. After all, the ultimate challenge still involves, as King

---

75. King, *Where Do We Go from Here?*, 181; and King, *Trumpet of Conscience*, 69–70.
76. King, *Where Do We Go from Here?*, 167–91.

said a half-century ago, affirming and investing in our common humanity and saving our common "world house."[77]

77. Ibid.

2

Becoming "a Single Neighborhood"
Martin Luther King, Jr. on the "White" and "Colored" Worlds

Lewis V. Baldwin and Paul R. Dekar

Now this is a bit humorous but I am trying to laugh a basic fact into all of us: the world has become a single neighborhood. Through our scientific genius we have made the world a neighborhood; now through our moral and spiritual development we must make of it a brotherhood.

MARTIN LUTHER KING, JR.[1]

MARTIN LUTHER KING, JR. understood and shared W. E. B. DuBois's concern about the centrality of "the color line" in international politics and relations. Both spoke at times about the "white world" and the "colored world,"[2] and about the need to overcome the glaring racial divide that had

1. James M. Washington, ed., *A Testament of Hope: The Essential Writings and Speeches of Martin Luther King, Jr.* (New York: HarperCollins, 1991) 209.

2. W. E. B. DuBois, *The Souls of Black Folk* (1903), in *Three Negro Classics* (New York:

long undermined possibilities for global community and peace. But King, in word and deed, seemed more intentional about translating certain kinds of ethical and spiritual principles, particularly relative to what he termed "the beloved community,"[3] into a global reality. Convinced that the survival of humans hinged on their capacity to "develop a world perspective," King envisioned "a new kind of man,"[4] a humanity that would no longer give materialism, power, and supremacy over other peoples and nations primacy over the moral and spiritual dimensions of life. At the same time, King struggled to eliminate the attitudes and the various artificial human barriers that kept individuals and nations from truly experiencing the beloved community.

Having already discussed King as both a global figure and a forerunner of globalization theory and praxis, the purpose here is to explore more specifically King's challenge to the white and colored worlds. Clearly, King had a rare facility in engaging the most pressing questions and the most critical issues confronting these vastly diverse worlds, particularly as they pertained to the specific roles these worlds might assume in eliminating what he labeled "the giant triplets" or "the evil triumvirate"—namely, racism, poverty, and militarism.[5] The point is to highlight the messages that King conveyed to the white and colored worlds and also his vital potential as a rich source of ideas for these worlds today. The discussion will close with reflections on the continuing liberative potential of King's beloved community ideal for the white and colored worlds.

Avon, 1963) 221; W. E. B. DuBois, *Dusk of Dawn: An Essay toward an Autobiography of a Race Concept* (New York: Schocken, 1968) 134–220; and Martin Luther King, Jr., *Where Do We Go from Here: Chaos or Community?* (Boston: Beacon, 1968) 174 and 176.

3. Martin Luther King, Jr., *Why We Can't Wait* (New York: New American Library, 1963) 45; and Martin Luther King, Jr., *Stride Toward Freedom: The Montgomery Story* (New York: Harper & Row, 1958) 105–7.

4. Martin Luther King, Jr., "Doubts and Certainties Link: Transcript of an Interview," London, England (Winter 1968), The Library and Archives of the Martin Luther King, Jr. Center for Nonviolent Social Change, Inc., Atlanta, Georgia, 5; and Lewis V. Baldwin, *To Make the Wounded Whole: The Cultural Legacy of Martin Luther King, Jr.* (Minneapolis: Fortress, 1992) 286.

5. King, *Where Do We Go from Here?*, 186; and Baldwin, *To Make the Wounded Whole*, 258.

ENDING THE THREAT OF A "RACE WAR": A CHALLENGE TO THE "WHITE WORLD"

Martin Luther King, Jr. understood that the world in which he traveled and functioned was essentially controlled by the un-colored and the un-poor. In his estimation, the un-colored and the un-poor constituted what he variously characterized as "the white Western world," "the house of the West," or yesterday's "enslavers" and "colonial masters." Generally speaking, King had in mind the United States, Britain, Russia, Canada, and the nations of Western Europe. He declared repeatedly that these nations had figured prominently in the rise and development of white supremacist attitudes and structures as a global problem.[6] Responding to a question from an interviewer in London, England, in the winter of 1968, King stated:

> I think we have to honestly admit that the problems in the world today, as they relate to the question of race, must be blamed on the whole doctrine of white supremacy, the whole doctrine of racism, and these doctrines came into being through the white race and the exploitation of the colored peoples of the world.[7]

Noting that "the cup of endurance has run over," King spoke of "a deep determination on the part of peoples of color to be freed from all of the shackles of the past." He went on to assert, in a moment of stern prophecy, that if the "white world" failed to cultivate "the spirit" and "the readjusting qualities" necessary to overcome racism, "then we can end up with a kind of race war."[8] King pointed specifically to the threat posed by institutionalized white supremacy in America, by South Africa's "national policy and practice" of white rule, by Portugal's continuing "practices of slave labor and subjugation in Angola," and by the British-backed Ian Smith government and its racist and exploitative actions against the natives of Rhodesia. For King, these were prime examples of "white men building empires on the sweat and suffering of colored people." While labeling the Union of South Africa "the classic example of organized and institutionalized" white supremacy, King insisted that its existence was "virtually made possible by the economic policies" of the United States and Great Britain, powerful nations that professed "to be moral bastions of our Western world."[9]

6. King, *Where Do We Go from Here?*, 173–91.

7. King, "Doubts and Certainties Link," 1–2.

8. Ibid.

9. King, *Where Do We Go from Here?*, 173–74; "King Accuses USA and Britain of

For King, the tragic effects of global racism required a swift, creative, and persistent response from the white world. Noting that "racial injustice is a constant threat to the peace and to the harmony of the world," as "great a threat to the human race as the atomic bomb,"[10] he urged the United States, Canada, and the nations of Europe to attack the problem within their own boundaries through government action and initiatives, while also employing worldwide economic sanctions against South African apartheid and other white supremacist systems in countries like Rhodesia (Zimbabwe) and Angola.[11] King insisted that such a commitment should not ignore colonialism and neocolonialism, which he viewed as "racism in its most sophisticated form."[12] He detected in colonialism and neocolonialism highly structured and deeply entrenched racism that spread its vicious tentacles across Africa, Asia, the Caribbean, and Latin America.

While highlighting the need for the white world to put its vast resources and manpower to the service of banishing racism from the face of the earth, King did not overlook the more critical role that the global community as a whole could assume in this necessary quest. "Among the moral imperatives of our time," he wrote, "we are challenged to work all over the world with unshakable determination to wipe out the last vestiges of racism."[13] In King's estimation, the United Nations (U.N.) was most important in this regard, particularly in light of its mission as a force for global human rights and peace. While he was never really clear about the specific steps the U.N. could take in attacking racism as an international problem,

---

Bolstering Racial Segregation in South Africa," *Relay News in English*, London, England (8 December 1964) 1–2; and Lewis V. Baldwin, *Toward the Beloved Community: Martin Luther King, Jr. and South Africa* (Cleveland: Pilgrim, 1995) 34–57.

10. Martin Luther King, Jr., "Radio Interview Regarding the Neobel Peace Prize," unpublished transcript, Oslo, Norway (9 December 1964), King Center Library and Archives, 4.

11. Martin Luther King, Jr., *The Trumpet of Conscience* (New York: Harper & Row, 1967) 63; *Four Decades of Concern: Martin Luther King, Jr. and South Africa*, printed by The Martin Luther King, Jr. Center for Nonviolent Social Change, Inc., Atlanta, Georgia (1 August 1986) 23; King, *Where Do We Go from Here?*, 173–74; Martin Luther King, Jr., "On the World Taking a Stand on Rhodesia," unpublished statement, Paris, France (25 October 1965), King Center Library and Archives, 1; and "Introduction to *Southwest Africa: The UN's Stepchild*," in Clayborne Carson et al., eds., *The Papers of Martin Luther King, Jr.*, vol. 5, *Threshold of a New Decade, January 1959–December 1960* (Berkeley: University of California Press, 2005) 298–99.

12. King, *Where Do We Go from Here?*, 175.

13. Ibid., 173.

he did raise the need for that family of nations to pursue creative and constructive ways of employing its potential as an "international conciliator" and as a global forum for diplomatic and economic interaction to promote the idea that there are no superior and inferior races.[14]

King was adamantly opposed to any military option on the part of the U.N. to deal with white supremacist regimes in places like South Africa. Instead, he maintained that such regimes afforded opportunities to exploit "the international potential of nonviolence." In his own thinking, King was not being unrealistic or impractical in suggesting such a path, especially since, as he put it, "Nonviolence has been practiced within national borders in India, the U.S., and in regions of Africa with spectacular success."[15] But King had to face the fact that the white world, which had long profited politically and economically from both the global structures of white supremacy and the lingering, antiquated thinking about race and ethnicity, was ill-prepared to seriously consider, let alone embrace, what he called "a potent nonviolent path" toward the complete eradication of the problem.[16]

But King remained cautiously optimistic, and he was not deterred by any suggestion that the white world was irredeemable when it came to the problems of race and racism. He hoped that his own country would take on the leadership role in an international effort to wipe out racism, especially since she paraded as the model for how genuine democracy might unfold on a global scale. Thus, he called for the kind of "foreign policy" that would be "consistent with our own democratic posture," while insisting that "a strong functional attitude" against "racism at home" would "consequently evolve" into "a strong functional attitude against racism in our foreign policy." For King, it was "unthinkable" that his own country would allow itself, "knowingly or unknowingly," to "be a party" to the continued political and economic domination of peoples of color in other parts of the world.[17]

14. Martin Luther King, Jr., "Statement on Vietnam," unpublished document (5 October 1965), King Center Library and Archives, 1; Martin Luther King, Jr., "The Negro Looks at Africa," unpublished version of essay (8 December 1962), King Center Library and Archives, 3; M. S. Handler, "Negroes Ask Role in Foreign Policy: Leaders to Meet in Capital—White House Interested," *New York Times*, 9 July 1964, L15; and "U.S. Negroes' Goal: To Set Africa Policy," *U.S. News & World Report*, 11 January 1965, 60–61.

15. *Four Decades of Concern*, 21; and Baldwin, *Toward the Beloved Community*, 49.

16. *Four Decades of Concern*, 21; and Baldwin, *Toward the Beloved Community*, 49.

17. Martin Luther King, Jr., "Statement at the American Negro Leadership Conference on Africa," Arden House, Harriman, New York (24 November 1962), King Center Library and Archives, 2.

In King's estimation, the critical role that the white world could play in forging interracial coalitions of conscience against racism was not to be overlooked. He affirmed, with intense feeling, the need for "an international alliance of peoples of all nations against racism," declaring that "the whole human race will benefit when it ends the abomination that has diminished the stature of man for too long."[18] To demonstrate the power of such an interracial coalition of conscience in a global context, King worked with Eleanor Roosevelt and Bishop James A. Pike in sponsoring and promoting, under the auspices of the American Committee on Africa (ACOA), the "Declaration of Conscience," a document proclaiming "December 10, 1957, Human Rights Day, as a Day of Protest against the organized inhumanity of the South African government and its *apartheid* policies."[19] That document solicited the moral support and the signatures of religious leaders, educators, social activists, and heads of state from many parts of the world.[20] The same occurred on December 10, 1962, when King, in connection with both the ACOA and the American Negro Leadership Conference on Africa (ANLCA), became a cosponsor with the South African leader Albert J. Luthuli of a worldwide "Appeal for Action Against Apartheid," which was "in the nature of a follow-up on our 1957 Declaration of Conscience."[21] King had every reason to think that his involvements in such noble ventures might be symbolically and practically important, and indeed a model not only for white people, but for peoples of goodwill worldwide who were open to forming coalitions to fight and ultimately destroy racism.

Religion and education were equally important to King as he considered the contribution that the white world might make to the struggle against racism. Since Christianity was such a pervasive presence in the

18. *Four Decades of Concern*, 22–23; and Baldwin, *Toward the Beloved Community*, 49–50.

19. "Declaration of Conscience: An Appeal to South Africa," drafted by the American Committee on Africa (10 December 1957), King Center Library and Archives, 1; Eleanor Roosevelt, James A. Pike, and Martin Luther King, Jr. to Friends and Supporters of the ACOA (July 1957), The Martin Luther King, Jr. Papers, Special Collections, Mugar Memorial Library, Boston University, 1–2; and Baldwin, *Toward the Beloved Community*, 15–16. Many of the ACOA documents with which King was involved can be found in the ACOA Collection, The Amistad Center, Tulane University, New Orleans, Louisiana.

20. George M. Houser, *No One Can Stop the Rain: Glimpses of Africa's Liberation Struggle* (New York: Pilgrim, 1989) 124; and Baldwin, *Toward the Beloved Community*, 17.

21. "Appeal for Action Against Apartheid," ACOA Campaign (July 1962), King Center Library and Archives, 1–2; and Baldwin, *Toward the Beloved Community*, 36–37.

white world, and especially the white Western world, King, who was first and foremost a Christian pastor, naturally felt that churches should be at the vanguard of such a struggle. "Christianity should be a crusade not against infidels but against injustice,"[22] he thought, as he pondered both the depth of the world's race problem and the white churches' preoccupation with a certain brand of missionary activity. In March 1957, while in Ghana, he predicted that the World Council of Churches (WCC) would "hound every Christian layman everywhere with a nagging conscience" around the issues of race.[23] During a trip to London in the fall of 1964, King proudly noted that Pope Paul VI and the Catholic Church had categorically denounced racism as "morally wrong."[24] As far as King was concerned, these were hopeful signs, but they fell far short of what the world's Christian churches in the West, with their vast resources, were capable of providing.

Also, King was deeply troubled by the actions of the Southern Baptist Convention in the United States and the Dutch Reformed Protestant Church in South Africa, both of which were actually bastions of white supremacy and racial segregation.[25] Convinced that racism in any form scarred and divided the Body of Christ, he appealed to the churches of the United States, Canada, and Eastern and Western Europe to transcend their doctrinal and cultural differences in a joint effort to dismantle the race-caste system wherever it exists.[26] In a larger sense, King thought in terms of a crusade against global racism that would involve not only the Christian

22. Harry Golden, "Only in America: Brave Clergymen," *Chicago Defender*, May 29–June 4, 1965, 8. King believed that white churches, instead of trying desperately to convert the world to Christianity, should devote more time to integrating their own ranks and becoming sites for cross-racial ministries. See Martin Luther King, Jr. and Wyatt Tee Walker to Mr. John Collins and The Student Interracial Ministry Committee, New York, New York (March 29, 1961), King Center Library and Archives, 1–2.

23. "Conversation in Ghana," *Christian Century* 74.15 (April 10, 1957) 446–48.

24. "Race Problem Warning to Britain: 'Keep Vigilant,' Says Dr. King," *Irish News*, London, England, September 24, 1964; and "Martin Luther King to Meet with Pope Paul," press release given by Barbara Suarez to *Associated Press, New York Times, United Press International, Atlanta Constitution* (September 16, 1964), Memphis Theological Seminary Library, 1.

25. W. W. Bottoms, "'I Still Stand by Nonviolence,' Says Luther King," *The Baptist Times*, September 24, 1964, 9; Clayborne Carson et al., eds., *The Papers of Martin Luther King, Jr.*, vol. 6, *Advocate of the Social Gospel, September 1948–March 1963* (Berkeley: University of California Press, 2007) 442; and Lewis V. Baldwin, *The Voice of Conscience: The Church in the Mind of Martin Luther King, Jr.* (New York: Oxford University Press, 2010) 156–59 and 185–87.

26. Baldwin, *Voice of Conscience*, 182–216; and King, *Why We Can't Wait*, 91.

churches but representatives of Hinduism, Buddhism, Judaism, Islam, and the other great world religions as well.[27] This idea of a pan-religious crusade against global racism was unique for King's time, but it was most certainly consistent with King's claim that the "Hindu-Moslem-Christian-Jewish-Buddhist belief about ultimate reality is beautifully summed up in the first epistle of Saint John," which makes love of God and love of neighbor equally essential.[28] King appropriated and practically applied this idea by uniting with representatives of many of the great world religions in promoting antiracism appeals such as the "Declaration of Conscience" and "Appeal for Action Against Apartheid."

Because the white world stood at the center of so much that had occurred in terms of the "scientific and technological revolutions," with its great minds and highly reputable college and university systems, King was always mindful of the possible impact that the right kind of education could have in transforming the minds and/or the thinking of white supremacists. In other words, he felt that in the struggle for a world free of racial injustice, education could possibly do for the *mind* what religion was capable of doing for the *heart*. Of course, he had in mind the kind of education that encourages a "devotion to the search for truth," an "open and analytical mind," and "a refusal to abandon the best lights of reason."[29] King believed that the proper use of functioning and expanding cultures of learning could move white people beyond that maze of myths and stereotypes that they had imposed upon peoples of color worldwide. It could also instill in white people a healthy sense of themselves as individuals who can only find real meaning and authentic existence through relations with other humans, irrespective of differences in pigmentation.[30] In general terms, the purpose of education in the white world for King had to involve, on many levels, creating an atmosphere that fosters understanding, self-worth, an ethic of

27. Baldwin, *Voice of Conscience*, 182–216.

28. King, *Where Do We Go from Here?*, 190–91; and Washington, *Testament of Hope*, 632.

29. King, *Where Do We Go from Here?*, 168; Martin Luther King, Jr., *Strength to Love* (Philadelphia: Fortress, 1981) 147; Martin Luther King, Jr., "Field of Education a Battleground," unpublished version of a speech delivered to the United Federation of Teachers, New York, New York (July 15, 1965), King Center Library and Archives, 1; Martin Luther King, Jr., "An Address at Syracuse University," Syracuse, New York, unpublished version (July 15, 1965) 1; Martin Luther King, Jr., "Revolution in the Classroom," unpublished version of a speech, Georgia Teachers and Education Association, Atlanta, Georgia (July 31, 1967) 1–8; and Baldwin, *Toward the Beloved Community*, 182–83.

30. Baldwin, *Toward the Beloved Community*, 182–83.

mutual acceptance, a genuine respect for human differences, shared power, and a commitment to interpersonal and intergroup living.[31] Knowing that education had been used effectively in instilling and advancing attitudes of white supremacy across the globe, King felt that it might also be employed successfully in a purging of those attitudes.

As one might imagine, King's message to the white world about racism did not exclude anti-Semitism, which had for centuries been pervasive in one form or another in that world. For King, anti-Semitism was as evil and sinful as the white supremacy that haunted peoples of color in various parts of the world. Put another way, he saw racism in all forms as equally problematic, especially from a spiritual and ethical standpoint. Nothing concerned him more "than the continued religious and personal persecution of Jews in the Soviet Union." Thus, he insisted that "the cultural and religious deprivation of some three million Jews" in that part of the world had to be "completely exposed" and the conditions "changed."[32] At the same time, King was equally concerned about those Jews in the United States, Europe, and the State of Israel who too often appeared to be willing partners in sustaining the structures of white supremacy worldwide. Evidently, racism in any form was abhorrent to King, and he was always clamoring for a higher consciousness on the part of the global community regarding this problem. This should be accounted a fundamental aspect of the King legacy.

King's message to the white world about poverty and economic justice was no less compelling and provocative. Indeed, he focused on "the white race" and its "exploitation of the colored peoples of the world"[33] with telling insight, giving some attention to the potential devastating consequences. He was well informed about the involvement of the United States and European nations in the long history of slavery, segregation, colonialism, and neocolonialism, so there was never any question in his mind about the indebtedness of the white world to peoples of color. He was unalterably convinced that all of "the wealthy nations"—the United States, Britain, Russia, Canada, Australia, and those of Western Europe—had "a moral obligation to provide capital and technical assistance" to underdeveloped countries in Africa, Asia, the Caribbean, Latin America, and other parts of the so-called

31. Ibid.

32. Martin Luther King, Jr. to Rabbi Seymour J. Cohen, New York, New York (September 8, 1965), King Center Library and Archives, 1.

33. King, "Doubts and Certainties Link," 1.

Third World. King recommended "a massive, sustained Marshall Plan" for these countries, but he insisted that such aid from the white world should be used "to develop the underdeveloped, school the unschooled, and feed the unfed," and not as a surreptitious design "to control the poor nations."[34] In King's thinking, any foreign policy motivated by a desire for world domination rather than "a compassionate and committed effort" to wipe out "poverty, ignorance, and disease"[35] was doomed to failure.

Bridging "the social and economic gulf between the *haves* and the *have nots* of the world" was central to King's vision of a global beloved community or "a worldwide fellowship."[36] But the real challenge involved educating the white world and bringing it to a true understanding of its role in compensating for the evils of its history, past and present. Few in the white world, particularly among the ruling elites, were prepared to take King's challenge about the white world's moral obligation to the peoples of darker hue seriously, to say nothing of embracing and following through on it. The same might be said about King's warning that a gross neglect of the problems of poverty and illiteracy in the colored world could lead many of its poor nations to embrace Communism or military dictatorships.[37] Hence, it was not at all surprising that King became such a target of ridicule and rejection by whites in nations like the United States and South Africa.[38] After all, his worldview and value systems conflicted in so many ways with theirs, making a meeting of the minds and hearts virtually impossible.

This was also glaringly evident in the white world's failure to respond to King's strong and persistent challenge around the issues of violence or, more specifically, war and human destruction. In King's mind, the white world's history of violence against peoples of color epitomized what he termed "man's inhumanity to man." He pointed to the brutal enslavement of Africans, "the physical extermination of the American Indian," and the forced colonization of peoples in Africa, Asia, the Caribbean, and Latin America, and he spoke plainly of the folly and the self-defeating notion of imitating the violence of white people, their "most brutal" and "most uncivilized value."[39] King was most critical of the United States, "the

---

34. King, *Where Do We Go from Here?*, 178.

35. Ibid., 178–79.

36. Martin Luther King, Jr., "The Octopus of Poverty," *The Mennonite* 80.1 (1965) 4.

37. Carson et al., eds., *Papers*, 5:143.

38. Baldwin, *Toward the Beloved Community*, 18.

39. King, *Where Do We Go from Here?*, 64 and 71–80. Mohandas K. Gandhi shared

greatest purveyor of violence in the world today,"[40] noting particularly her "arrogance of power," which was rapidly pushing "the whole world closer to a nuclear confrontation—a third world war."[41] King lamented the fact that all too many government officials and heads of state "do not follow Gandhi literally," failing to "apply his spirit to domestic and international problems."[42] "It has been my consistent belief and position," King wrote, "that nonviolence is the only true solution to the social problems of the world." "More than ever before," he commented, "the Gandhian method of nonviolent direct action must be applied in international affairs."[43]

The Vietnam War was for King not only a stunning abuse of American military might, but also an indication that the white West had not completely surrendered its drive for world domination. He knew of France's colonization of Vietnam, and he denounced America's involvement in that country as "cruel" and "senseless."[44] David Halberstam's claim that King did "not particularly think of the war in Vietnam as a racial one (although the phrase 'killing little brown children in Vietnam' slips in)"[45] is highly questionable, for King understood clearly that the denial of self-determination to peoples of color had for centuries been a by-product of white supremacist views and policies. King called for the U.N.'s involvement in the Vietnam Conflict, noting that that body "can now realize its potential as an international conciliator which should be supported by the forces of good will in every nation."[46] "The alternative to strengthening the United Nations and thereby disarming the whole world," he argued, "may well be

---

this perspective on the white world, noting on one occasion that "the people of Europe are sure to perish if they continue to be violent." See Thomas Merton, ed., *Gandhi on Nonviolence: A Selection from the Writings of Mahatma Gandhi* (New York: New Directions, 1965) 34.

40. Washington, *Testament of Hope*, 233.

41. King, "Doubts and Certainties Link," 9.

42. Martin Luther King, Jr., "Farewell Statement," New Delhi, India, unpublished version (March 9, 1959), King Center Library and Archives, 1.

43. Martin Luther King, Jr. to Mr. G. Ramachandran, New Delhi, India, dictated to Miss. D. McDonald (December 20, 1961), King Center Library and Archives, 1.

44. Martin Luther King, Jr., "Stop the Bombing," *Pacific: War—Peace—International Cooperation* 2.1 (May/June 1967) 19.

45. David Halberstam, "When 'Civil Rights' and 'Peace' Join Forces," in *Martin Luther King, Jr.: A Profile*, ed. C. Eric Lincoln, rev. ed. (New York: Hill & Wang, 1987) 207; Washington, *Testament of Hope*, 235; and Baldwin, *To Make the Wounded Whole*, 277.

46. Martin Luther King, Jr., "Vietnam: A Statement by Martin Luther King, Jr.," for immediate release (October 5, 1965), King Center Library and Archives, 1.

a civilization plunged into the abyss of annihilation."[47] Strangely enough, King felt that within this international forum, the United States could "lead the way" in a "revolution of values" that could possibly give "the pursuit of peace" precedence over "the pursuit of war."[48]

King determined that the "arms race" necessarily had to be replaced by the "peace race,"[49] but he wondered if the white world had the moral capacity and the will to see and accept this pressing reality. Describing himself as "a voice of reason," King declared that "we must all speak out in a multitude of voices," for "the thunder of our voices will be the only sound stronger than the blast of bombs and the clamor of war hysteria."[50] This message was aimed particularly at white churches and Jewish synagogues and their leadership, which King urged to become a major, positive force in eradicating war and in establishing a culture of peace. He encouraged white churches to reclaim both Jesus' image as "the prince of peace" and "the sacrificial spirit of the early church," thereby enhancing their prophetic witness against all wars.[51] The moral commitment to overcome the evils of war, King contended, had to be deeper and more consistent among Christians and the adherents of the other great world religions as well.[52] As King observed, "peace-loving people" of all faiths and ideologies had to rely less on "military power" and more on their "moral power," while realizing "that peace is not only a goal which we all seek," but also "a means by which we reach that goal."[53] He was audacious and creative when thinking through the possibilities inherent in a global nonviolent strategy.

King ultimately became convinced that white youth were potentially a powerful force in the white world's effort to deal positively and creatively with both the external barriers (i.e., racism, poverty, war) and the internal

47. Martin Luther King, Jr., "Why We are Here," unpublished version of a speech at the SCOPE Orientation (June 15, 1965), King Center Library and Archives, 2.

48. Washington, *Testament of Hope*, 241.

49. Martin Luther King, Jr., "An Address at the Synagogue Council of America," unpublished version (December 5, 1965), King Center Library and Archives, 11; and Baldwin, *Voice of Conscience*, 99.

50. King, "Vietnam," 1; and King, "Stop the Bombing," 19.

51. Baldwin, *Voice of Conscience*, 97–99; and Martin Luther King, Jr., "Peace: God's Man's Business," *Chicago Defender*, January 1–7, 1966, 10.

52. "Transcript of Remarks by Martin Luther King, Jr.," unpublished version prepared for *Redbook* magazine, November 5, 1964, 1–3.

53. "Martin Luther King, Jr. and Goldberg of the UN: War Statements," unpublished version (September 10, 1965), King Center Library and Archives, 1.

barriers (i.e., fear, greed, ignorance, hatred) to world peace and community. Thus, he urged white youth to join in what he labeled a "new order."[54] King seemed quite impressed with the young whites whom he included among "the radicals," or those who had come to see and accept "that only by *structural* change can current evils be eliminated."[55] King had actually marched with some of these young whites in both the civil rights and the peace movements, and he had come to see that many of them were generally more receptive than their elders to joining alliances and working with peoples of color in the interest of much-needed social change. Youngsters imbued with this kind of outlook on life and the world, many of whom were students in colleges and universities in the United States, England, South Africa, and other countries,[56] kept King from giving up completely on the possibility that white people might become a truly positive and effective force for change across the globe.

King traveled throughout the United States, Europe, and other parts of the white world during his thirteen years of public leadership in campaigns for civil and human rights, and based on what he saw, heard, and experienced, he concluded that "the rolling tide of world opinion" was on the side of those who struggled for the full actualization of the beloved community. Reflecting on his European tour in March 1966, King happily reported that "we share in the deepest recesses of our hearts a longing for the oneness of mankind" and for "the dawning of a new day when the manmade barriers of race and nation no longer divide us."[57] King made the point differently and more emphatically in a speech in Stockholm, Sweden, around that same time, asserting that "I still have a dream that one day black and white men, brown and yellow men, Protestant, Catholic, Jew,

---

54. "King Urges Youth Join in New Order," *Athens Messenger* (Athens, Ohio), December 30, 1959, 1 and 16.

55. King, *Trumpet of Conscience*, 39–44.

56. Ibid.; "King Urges Youth Join in New Order," 1 and 16; and Baldwin, *Toward the Beloved Community*, 57–61.

57. Martin Luther King, Jr., "European Tour," unpublished version of a speech (March 1966), King Center Library and Archives, 1. For more of King's reflections on his experiences in Europe, see Martin Luther King, Jr., "East or West—God's Children," unpublished version of a speech, Berlin, Germany (September 13, 1964) 1–16; Martin Luther King, Jr., "Revolution and Redemption," unpublished version of a closing address at the European Baptist Assembly, Amsterdam, Holland (August 16, 1964) 1–11; and Martin Luther King, Jr., "A Lecture," under the auspices of The Federation Protestante de France Mutualite, Paris, France (October 24, 1965), King Center Library and Archives, 1–18.

believer and unbeliever will coexist in a world where [humans] are judged by the content of their character rather than the color of their skins or the nature of their heritage."[58]

Needless to say, King redefined what the policies and practices of the white world toward peoples of color should be. He envisioned a world in which there were no dominant and subordinate nations, or developed and underdeveloped countries; but he knew that the coming of this "new world" required a revolution in the thinking of white people, or an expanded understanding of what it means to live in a racially, culturally, religiously, and ideologically diverse world. And interestingly enough, King saw that revolution taking place in the minds of growing numbers of whites who questioned the values of the "old world" while siding with peoples of color in their struggles for "a new world."[59]

RESISTING THE OLD ORDER: A MESSAGE FOR AND ABOUT THE "COLORED WORLD"

Martin Luther King, Jr.'s deep interest in the plight of peoples of color worldwide extended at least as far back as his undergraduate years at Morehouse College in Atlanta, Georgia, in the mid- and late 1940s.[60] Much of this interest developed in the context of discussions in the classroom about race and world problems.[61] Also, African heads of state, academics, religious leaders, and activists appeared at times on the Morehouse campus, and occasionally there were a few African students, all building on the ideas and insights King gained through close interaction with his professors and peers.[62] When King was catapulted to the ranks of civil rights leadership a decade later, his contacts with peoples of color increased significantly, and

58. Martin Luther King, Jr., "En Granslos Kval Pa Operan: Remarks," unpublished version, Stockholm, Sweden (March 31, 1966), King Center Library and Archives, 3.

59. Carson et al., *Papers*, 6:182–84; and Clayborne Carson and Peter Holloran, eds., *A Knock at Midnight—Inspiration from the Great Sermons of Reverend Martin Luther King, Jr.* (New York: Warner, 1998) 186.

60. Michael Long argues that "King's vision" embraced "international topics even in high school." See Michael G. Long, *Against Us, but for Us: Martin Luther King, Jr. and the State* (Macon, GA: Mercer University Press, 2002) 6 n. 17.

61. Martin Luther King, Jr., *The Autobiography of Martin Luther King, Jr.*, ed. Clayborne Carson (New York: Warner, 1998) 13–16 and 23.

62. Baldwin, *Toward the Beloved Community*, 8–9.

his sense of the colored world grew and became more enlightened through reading and his travels, observations, and experiences at home and abroad.

In May 1956, as the bus boycott gained momentum, King expressed delight that "this movement in Montgomery is a part" of the "overall movement" in which "oppressed people" in "the Third World" are "revolting against the imperialism and colonialism that have too long existed."[63] In his use of terms such as "Third World," "colored world," or "underdeveloped countries," King had in mind primarily the inhabitants of Africa, the Caribbean, Latin America, and Asia. These peoples figured prominently in his definition of "the least of these,"[64] especially when he spoke in global terms. Also included were the millions of people of color scattered throughout North America, Europe, and Australia.

African peoples stood at the very center of King's consciousness of and vision for the world. This was only natural for one who considered himself a descendant of Africans who were tragically enslaved in America. In his speeches and sermons in black churches in Montgomery as early as the late 1950s, King occasionally alluded to "a close relationship between the black struggle in America and the struggle for independence in Africa."[65] By the 1960s, King was reminding his people that they had "a moral as well as a practical responsibility to keep the civil rights movement in America close to our African brothers."[66] His recognition of bonds and obligations between peoples of African ancestry everywhere actually informed and conditioned his response and approach to the problems faced by all peoples of color across the globe.

King's trips to Africa in 1957 and India in 1959 loomed large and heightened his sense of how he might best approach the struggles of peoples of color at the levels of both ideas and activism. At the invitation of Prime Minister Kwame Nkrumah, King attended and witnessed the independence celebrations of Ghana in the spring of 1957, an event that inspired him and

63. Martin Luther King, Jr., "Statement Regarding the Legitimacy of the Struggle in Montgomery, Alabama," unpublished version (May 4, 1956), King Papers, Special Collections, Mugar Memorial Library, Boston University, 1.

64. King, "Revolution and Redemption," 9; and Baldwin, *Voice of Conscience*, 92–93 and 294 n. 211.

65. Coretta Scott King, *My Life with Martin Luther King, Jr.* (New York: Holt, 1993) 142–43.

66. Martin Luther King, Jr. to Theodore E. Brown, New York, New York (April 1, 1963), King Center Library and Archives, 1; and Baldwin, *To Make the Wounded Whole*, 163.

left a lasting impression. Reflecting on the occasion, the civil rights leader spoke of "a close bond between the American Negro and the Negroes of the Gold Coast," and he declared that an "independent Negro nation in Ghana" highlighted the fact "that in our own nation elementary rights of citizenship and equality" are "still unrealized" for "the Southern Negro." King went on to claim that Ghana represented "a victorious sector in the worldwide movement of colonial peoples toward the dawn of freedom."[67] The trip to Ghana was "King's first sojourn on the continent" of his forebears,[68] and it gave him a view of both the beauty and the hardships of Africa that he had not gotten from all the books he had read and the lectures and sermons he had heard. Although the impact of colonialism was evident, as he encountered servants everywhere in Accra, King learned that all of Africa was not "primitive and dirty," a reality that surfaced more prominently in his thinking as he and his wife Coretta traveled through Lagos and Kano in Nigeria. But the images of servants bowing and cringing in Ghana, and of people living under extreme "conditions of filth and squalor" in Nigeria, greatly disturbed King, particularly as he compared this to "the grandeur of England and the Empire."[69]

King left Africa with a renewed sense of mission as it related to both civil rights in America and human rights in Africa. He shared his experiences and observations with friends and supporters in Montgomery and elsewhere in the United States on several occasions. In his first sermon after his return from Africa, titled, "The Birth of a New Nation," delivered at his Dexter Avenue Baptist Church in Montgomery, King drew on the story of the Israelites in Egyptian bondage in framing "his impressions of Ghana's battle against colonialism"; he declared that "this is something of the story of every people struggling for freedom."[70] This was yet another indication of King's refusal to separate the civil rights movement in America from the struggles against colonialism in the colored world, for he had often used

67. Martin Luther King, Jr., "A Statement Regarding the Invitation from Prime Minister Kwame Nkrumah," unpublished (March 1957), King Center Library and Archives, 1; Martin Luther King, Jr. to Kwame Nkrumah, Accra, Ghana (April 17, 1959), King Center Library and Archives, 1; and Baldwin, *To Make the Wounded Whole*, 166–67.

68. "Conversation in Ghana: Editorial Correspondence," *Christian Century* 74.15 (April 10, 1957) 446–47; and Baldwin, *To Make the Wounded Whole*, 167.

69. Scott King, *My Life with Martin Luther King, Jr.*, 143–46.

70. Clayborne Carson et al., eds., *The Papers of Martin Luther King, Jr.*, vol. 4, *Symbol of the Movement, January 1957–December 1958* (Berkeley: University of California Press, 2000) 155–67; and King, *Autobiography of Martin Luther King, Jr.*, 111–16.

that same exodus story and its rich source of language and metaphors to instill a collective memory of American Negroes and their struggle from bondage and segregation toward freedom and self-determination.[71]

Convinced that the struggle for freedom and participatory democracy in the United States could not be won as long as Africans languished under the yoke of colonialism, King soon joined the American Committee on Africa (ACOA), a New York–based organization comprised largely of Christian pacifists, which had formed in 1951 as Americans for South African Resistance (AFSAR). The ACOA was an interracial group with international connections, and through it King supported African anticolonial struggles across the continent, occasionally making financial contributions and signing letters, appeals, petitions, and declarations. King's involvement with the "Declaration of Conscience" (1957) and "Appeal for Action Against Apartheid" (1962), referred to earlier, actually grew out of these connections.[72] His decision to combine his civil rights activities through his Southern Christian Leadership Conference (SCLC) with support for the active agenda of the ACOA spoke volumes about how he perceived his own role in freeing Africa, and ultimately the colored world as a whole, from colonialism and imperialism.

King's trip to India in 1959 impacted his sense of mission on yet another level. While in "the land of Gandhi," he met and discussed nonviolence and the anticolonial struggles of peoples of color with Gandhi's relatives and with Africans studying in India. Recalling the influence of those encounters on his personal growth and on his perspective on the challenges confronting the oppressed, King wrote, "I left India more convinced than ever before that nonviolent resistance is the most potent weapon available to oppressed people in their struggle for freedom."[73] King had come to see more clearly the great success achieved through nonviolence in Montgomery, in India, and in Ghana and other regions of Africa, and he had reason to believe that that method would work even in a place like South Africa.

71. Martin Luther King, Jr., "A Christian Movement in a Revolutionary Age," unpublished version of a speech (Fall 1966), King Center Library and Archives, 1–2; King, "A Lecture," 3–5; Martin Luther King, Jr., "But, If Not . . . ," unpublished version of a sermon (November 5, 1967), King Center Library and Archives, 2; Martin Luther King, Jr., "Why We Must Go to Washington," unpublished version of a speech, SCLC retreat (January 15, 1968) 14; and Baldwin, *Voice of Conscience*, 105.

72. Baldwin, *Toward the Beloved Community*, 14–21.

73. Washington, *Testament of Hope*, 25; and Baldwin, *Toward the Beloved Community*, 12.

Thus, he envisioned a future in which peoples of color would ultimately end colonial domination of their lands via nonviolent action. Also, King himself, as a result of his experiences in India, came to accept nonviolence as not merely a social ethic, or as a tactic for attacking social evil, but as a personal ethic as well, or as a personal way of life.[74] This personal development would have tremendous implications as far as King's future involvements with and influences on liberation movements in the Third World were concerned.

By the early 1960s, King was raising "the need for some type of continued organizational setup to relate the American Negro with Africa and its many problems."[75] He suggested that "one of the means by which" his own country "could demonstrate sincerity of purpose" was "a broader use of Negro Americans in our diplomatic corps that serve the independent and emergent nations"[76] of Africa. In November 1964, King, supported by George M. Houser and other liberal whites in the ACOA, joined Roy Wilkins of the National Association for the Advancement of Colored People (NAACP), Whitney M. Young of the National Urban League, A. Philip Randolph of the Brotherhood of Sleeping Car Porters, James Farmer of the Congress of Racial Equality (CORE), Dorothy I. Height of the National Council of Negro Women (NCNW), and other civil rights leaders in forming the American Negro Leadership Conference on Africa (ANLCA), another organization through which "African issues" were addressed.[77] The ACOA and the ANLCA became equally important for King in terms of both his advocacy for African liberation and his financial and moral support for this cause.

Aside from his work with these groups, King continued to raise money and to meet with college presidents and governmental officials on behalf of African students interested in studying in the United States, a practice he had begun and pursued on a more serious note while serving as pastor of the Dexter Avenue Baptist Church in Montgomery in the late fifties. In King's judgment, all of his activities were an expression of "our deep

74. "Conversation in Ghana," 446–48; *Four Decades of Concern*, 21; and Baldwin, *Toward the Beloved Community*, 10.

75. King to Brown (April 1, 1963) 1–2.

76. Martin Luther King, Jr., "The Negro Looks at Africa," unpublished version of a statement (December 8, 1962), King Center Library and Archives, 3.

77. Houser, *No One Can Stop the Rain*, 266; George M. Houser to Martin Luther King, Jr. (June 5, 1962), King Center Library and Archives, 1; and Baldwin, *Toward the Beloved Community*, 38–39 and 206 n. 57.

sympathy with our African brothers in the struggle for freedom and human dignity" and of "our awareness of the oneness of our struggle," and they "contribute in some little way toward the development of persons to take over leadership responsibilities on that great continent."[78] Moreover, this special concern and support for anticolonial struggles throughout Africa was consistent with, not antithetical to, King's vision of a global beloved community.[79]

That vision included peoples of African descent in the Caribbean and Latin America as well. King knew the histories of these peoples' struggles with slavery and colonialism and the enduring impact on these lands. He actually visited Jamaica and Brazil and referred at times to events as they unfolded throughout the Caribbean and Latin America, frequently stressing the bonds and obligations between their inhabitants and Negroes in America. In London in late 1964, King met with people from parts of the Caribbean, South America, Africa, India, and Pakistan and participated in a "movement to bring together colored people in the London area" to address "a growing color or race problem" there, a problem stemming from "the large number of persons that migrated to England from various points of the British Commonwealth." King also spoke at that time about the evils of apartheid in South Africa and of the need for a collective effort on the part of peoples of color in dismantling that country's apartheid regime. It is important to observe that no issue in the West Indies or Latin America, with the possible exception of poverty in places like Haiti, commanded King's attention as did the campaign against South African apartheid.[80]

78. Martin Luther King, Jr. to Mr. John C. Miyengi (June 1, 1959), King Center Library and Archives, 1; Martin Luther King, Jr., "Recommendations to the Board of the SCLC," The Southern Christian Leadership Conference Meeting, Columbia, South Carolina (September 29–October 1, 1959), King Center Library and Archives, 3; Martin Luther King, Jr. to Amin Msowoya (September 19, 1960), King Papers, Special Collections, Mugar Memorial Library, Boston University, 1; *The Crusader: SCLC, Inc.* (November 1959) 4; Ouma Namwambe to Martin Luther King, Jr. (June 10, 1961), King Center Library and Archives, 1; and Baldwin, *To Make the Wounded Whole*, 179–83.

79. Baldwin, *Toward the Beloved Community*, 187–88 n. 2 and 189–244.

80. Martin Luther King, Jr., "Dreams of Brighter Tomorrows," unpublished version of a speech (March 1965), King Center Library and Archives, 1–2; Martin Luther King, Jr., "Interview Regarding Nobel Peace Prize," unpublished version (November 9, 1964), King Center Library and Archives, 1–2; Baldwin, *To Make the Wounded Whole*, 178; Baldwin, *Toward the Beloved Community*, 45; Paul R. Dekar, "Introduction: The Inspiration of Martin Luther King, Jr. for Nonviolent Justice Seekers in Latin America and the Caribbean," in *Nonviolence for the Third Millennium: The Legacy and the Future*, unpublished manuscript (n.d.), 3–4; and Paul R. Dekar, "Introduction: The Appropriation of King in Violent Contexts," unpublished manuscript (n.d.), 3–4.

In a speech given at the University of the West Indies in Mona, Jamaica, in June 1965, King alluded to the "magnificent drama of independence taking place on the stage of Asian and African history, and in the Caribbean area"—developments that, as he described them, reveal "to us that the old order of colonialism is passing away."[81] This address reflected King's growing attention to global affairs. He expounded once again themes that had long animated him, such as the interrelated structure of reality, the need to eradicate racism in any form, the need for a united witness and struggle against colonialism, and peace. King knew of, appreciated, and celebrated the Jamaican-born leader Marcus M. Garvey's mass crusade to liberate and empower West Indians and other peoples of African ancestry generations earlier, irrespective of his denunciation of Garvey's dream of African repatriation as impractical and unrealistic.[82] Garvey's work with blacks in the United States and abroad, much like King's own civil rights activities with West Indian blacks such as Harry Belafonte, Stokely Carmichael, and Sidney Poitier in this country, underscored the fact that the past and future of West Indians and other peoples of African descent were intertwined.[83]

King's sense of the challenges confronting Latin America owed much to both his communication with activists and his very limited travels in that part of the world. As early as 1959, he exchanged letters and ideas with Deolinda Rodrigues, an advocate for African "freedom and independence" who was studying in Brazil.[84] From June 24 to July 3, 1960, King attended the tenth annual Baptist World Alliance meeting in Rio de Janeiro, Brazil,[85] an experience that must have further enlightened him about the tragic and lingering effects of both slavery and colonialism. Six years later, King, in *Where Do We Go from Here: Chaos or Community?*, one of his last books,

81. Martin Luther King, Jr., "Address at Valedictory Service," University of the West Indies, Mona, Jamaica (June 20, 1965), King Center Library and Archives, 2; and Baldwin, *To Make the Wounded Whole*, 177–78.

82. King, *Why We Can't Wait*, 35; Dekar, "Introduction: The Appropriation of King," 6; and Baldwin, *To Make the Wounded Whole*, 8, 20–26, and 177.

83. Baldwin, *To Make the Wounded Whole*, 177.

84. Deolinda Rodrigues to Martin Luther King, Jr. (December 30, 1959), unpublished version, King Papers, Special Collections, Mugar Memorial Library, Boston University, 1; and Martin Luther King, Jr. to Deolinda Rodrigues (December 21, 1959), King Papers, Special Collections, Mugar Memorial Library, Boston University, 1.

85. Martin Luther King, Jr. to T. Y. Rogers (June 18, 1960), unpublished version, King Center Library and Archives, 1; and Baldwin, *To Make the Wounded Whole*, 171.

condemned poverty in Mexico as well as neocolonial economic exploitation and military adventures by the United States in Latin America as a whole. King used the image of erecting a "world house" and urged building on a foundation that required completing the worldwide freedom revolution, humanizing technology, ending racism, eliminating poverty on an international scale, and finding alternatives to war and human destruction.[86] As far as King was concerned, all of these steps were crucial to the global struggle against racism, poverty, and militarism.

The Cuban Missile Crisis, which occurred in October 1962 and which escalated tensions between the United States and the Soviet Union, heightened King's concern about both the independence of Latin American countries and the threat of nuclear conflict. King seriously studied and denounced the crisis not only because it dwarfed other important issues, but also because it made Cuba essentially a pawn in a power struggle between the world's two superpowers. Although King was generally pleased with President John F. Kennedy's decision to blockade Cuba to prevent the delivery of jet aircraft and military supplies by the Russians, King believed nevertheless that the confrontation proved the necessity for a greater affirmation of world peace. "Every one of us knows full well that we came dreadfully close to the precipice of nuclear war in 1962," King recalled later. He went on to note that "there is a grave danger, however, that our 'success' in handling the Cuban crisis could be misused." "We must not allow the delicate balance that has been established in matters of foreign policy to be destroyed by our arrogance,"[87] King added. With the Cuban crisis successfully resolved, King argued that it was time for the United States to turn its undivided attention to "disarmament" on the world stage and to "improved health and educational programs" at home.[88]

For King, the Middle East crisis stood as perhaps the most enduring reminder of the need for global action around the issues of disarmament, poverty, and illiteracy. Although King never made an issue of race when discussing the Arab-Israeli conflict, he was deeply concerned about the

86. King, *Where Do We Go from Here?*, 167–73 and 178; and Dekar, "Introduction: The Appropriation of King," 4.

87. Dekar, "Introduction: The Inspiration of Martin Luther King, Jr.," 3; Martin Luther King, Jr., "New Year Hopes," *New York Amsterdam News*, January 5, 1963, 9; and Baldwin, *To Make the Wounded Whole*, 270–71.

88. King, "New Year Hopes," 9; and Clayborne Carson et al., *A Guide to Research on Martin Luther King, Jr., and the Modern Black Freedom Struggle*, Occasional Publications in Bibliography 1 (Stanford: Stanford University Libraries, 1989) 68.

welfare and survival of the Palestinians and peoples of color generally in the Arab world. In his mind, being pro-Israel and pro-Palestinian at the same time was perfectly logical. Thus, the disputes between the Arabs and the Israelis over the West Bank and the Golan Heights greatly disturbed him, to say nothing of the violence that too often surfaced from both sides. Convinced that "the Arab world is in a state of imposed poverty and backwardness that must threaten peace and harmony," King called in 1967 for the type of U.N. action that would lead to "Arab development." "After all," he maintained, "the Arab world is that Third World of poverty and illiteracy and disease, and it is time now to have a Marshall Plan for the Middle East."[89] But even at that point, King understood that any global action that favored the Palestinians over the Israelis or the Israelis over the Palestinians carried serious international costs, and so he recommended a bilateral approach that would serve the best interests of both—territorially, politically, economically, and otherwise. In more specific terms, King pushed for a U.N. policy that would embody and advance the related concerns of "security" for Israel and "development" for the Palestinians.[90] Interestingly enough, King's thoughts and actions around these issues occurred during a period when almost three times as many Americans sympathized with the Israelis as sympathized with the Palestinians.

But when it came to world problems, King never determined what was right or wrong by taking a Gallup poll of the majority opinion.[91] Many of the unpopular positions he took involved the struggles of peoples of color in Asia against colonialism and imperialism, and global strategies for their independence, uplift, and empowerment. While King was always troubled by the U.S. bombing of Nagasaki and Hiroshima in Japan during World War II, he delighted in "the decolonization and liberation" of nations in Asia since that time.[92] He found in the struggle of India against British

89. "Resolution on the Middle East: Draft of a Statement Regarding the SCLC's Participation at the National Conference on New Politics," Chicago, Illinois, unpublished document (September 1967), King Center Library and Archives, 1; and "Martin Luther King, Jr. Radio Interview," on *Issues and Answers* with Tom Jerriel, ABC Atlanta Bureau Chief, and John Casserly, ABC Washington correspondent, unpublished document (June 18, 1967), King Center Library and Archives, 13–14.

90. "Resolution on the Middle East," 1; and "Martin Luther King, Jr. Radio Interview," 13–14.

91. Martin Luther King, Jr., "An Address at the Ministers' Leadership Training Program," Miami, Florida (February 19–23, 1968), King Center Library and Archives, 2.

92. King, *Why We Can't Wait*, 21.

colonial domination a model for all people who struggled for freedom and national independence, especially since Mohandas Gandhi led his people "without lifting one gun" and "without uttering one curse word."[93] For King, the fact that Britain no longer ruled "all of India" and "most of China" testified to the power of the human spirit and its thirst for freedom.[94] However, he cautioned the leaders of these decolonized and liberated countries against imitating the behavior and policies of their former colonial masters or enslavers and thereby substituting one form of tyranny for another. His hope was that they would approach the challenges of nation-building and nationhood with more sanity and reasonableness, thus becoming models for nations with similar histories.

King recognized that the "postcolonial period" had become "more difficult and precarious" than the colonial struggles themselves, especially since much still had to be done—in terms of eliminating the vicious race-caste-tribal system, grinding poverty, lack of capital, and war—before countries in Asia could realize the fullness of their potential as members of the family of nations.[95] In King's estimation, the condition of the untouchables in India epitomized the lingering challenge posed by the race-caste-tribal system in certain decolonized countries. He compared their problem to "the race problem in America," but he was quick to point out that "India appears to be integrating its untouchables faster" than America "is integrating its Negro minority." King also noted that in contrast to the American South, government, religious, and educational leaders and institutions in India "have publicly endorsed the integration laws." King went on to credit Gandhi, who fasted until the doors of the Hindu temples in India were open to the untouchables, for breaking the backbone of untouchability. He felt that the Indian leader actually set the standard for how issues of race, caste, and tribalism might be handled within parts of Asia, Africa, and other newly decolonized countries.[96]

Although King knew about poverty in the lands and villages of peoples of color all over the world, he witnessed the problem in magnified form while visiting India in 1959. The nagging problems of unemployment, food shortages, and housing, coupled with the uncontrollable birth rates and the gripping problems of overpopulation, touched the depths of his

---

93. Carson et al., *Papers*, 5:148.

94. Ibid., 4:164.

95. King, *Where Do We Go from Here?*, 179.

96. Carson et al., *Papers*, 5:143 and 154–55; and Washington, *Testament of Hope*, 28.

soul, leading him to urge "America and other nations of the West" to "extend generous economic and technical aid to India immediately."[97] At the same time, King acknowledged that the people of India, like others in Asia and Africa, the Caribbean, and Latin America, were "trying desperately to solve" their own problems, and that they would not accept aid "if strings are attached to it." He referred to "the larger nations" such as India and China and to the "many nations in Asia and Africa and all over South America" that were grappling with the enormity of the problem of "the population explosion," knowing that it represents as much a "threat to mankind as the problem of war."[98] King was always mindful that the decolonized nations had much to lose by relying too much on their former colonizers for solutions, and that such a practice was at the root of emerging trends in neocolonialism, or the economic domination of Third World countries by the West.[99] For King, nothing short of genuine freedom, independence, and empowerment for the colored world would suffice, especially if it was to have any control at all over its destiny.

King's fears about too much meddling in the affairs of Third World countries on the part of former colonizers were realized in the Vietnam War. He lamented the devastating impact that this conflict was having on the whole of Southeast Asia, especially with the U.S. military buildup in Thailand and its interference in Cambodia and Laos. In graphic detail, King noted how the U.S. bombings in South Vietnam had destroyed villages, family ties, land, crops, and even the unified Buddhist Church, "the nation's only non-Communist revolutionary political force."[100] Thus, he urged the United States to end "all bombing in North and South Vietnam," to create an "atmosphere for negotiation" by declaring "a unilateral cease-fire," to cease military buildup and interference in Thailand, Laos, and other countries, to accept the involvement of South Vietnam's National Liberation Front "in any meaningful negotiations" and any future Vietnamese government, and to "remove all foreign troops from Vietnam in accordance with the 1954 Geneva Agreement."[101] King also called for "the recognition of

97. King, *Where Do We Go from Here?*, 177; and Carson et al., *Papers*, 5:143.

98. "Interview with Martin Luther King, Jr.," *The Today Show* with Hugh Downs, unpublished transcript (April 18, 1966), King Center Library and Archives, 4; and Carson et al., *Papers*, 5:143.

99. Carson et al., *Papers*, 5:143; and King, *Where Do We Go from Here?*, 175 and 178.

100. Washington, *Testament of Hope*, 236 and 239; and Baldwin, *Voice of Conscience*, 199.

101. Washington, *Testament of Hope*, 239.

China" and her admittance to the United Nations, declaring that such a move was essential to bringing "about peace in that very turbulent situation" in Southeast Asia.[102]

King's message and efforts were consistent with his belief that the American Negro had a special role to play not only in freeing "our African brothers," but the entire colored world. In an article in September 1964, King, reflecting on the large numbers of people who showed up to hear him speak during a recent tour of Europe, insisted that this confirmed "my belief that the Negro is now in a position to lead the world." "As the Negro goes," he added, "so does the world. We are the conscience of the Western world."[103] Three years later, King, in *Where Do We Go from Here: Chaos or Community?*, asserted that the "hard cold facts" indicated "that the hope of the people of color in the world may well rest with the American Negro and his ability to reform the structure of racist imperialism from within," thereby turning "the technology and wealth of the West to the task of liberating the world from want."[104] This responsibility fell to American Negroes, King held, because they were possibly the most well educated and materially affluent among the world's people of color, and also because of their commitment to nonviolence as demonstrated in the context of the civil rights movement in America. King knew that through their folklore, art, spiritual values, and the movement itself, American Negroes were already having perhaps a greater impact on the world than any other single people in Western society.[105] Therefore, he always interpreted the civil rights movement not only in terms of its significance for peoples of color, but the entire

102. "Interview with Martin Luther King, Jr.," *The Today Show*, 3; and Carson et al., *Papers*, 5:347.

103. Martin Luther King, Jr., "Untitled Column on European Tour," typed version prepared for *New York Amsterdam News*, September 17, 1964, King Center Library and Archives, 2.

104. King, *Where Do We Go from Here?*, 57. In "A Testament of Hope," an essay published posthumously, King noted that "American Negroes" in "decision-making positions" could give "encouragement to the underprivileged and disenfranchised in other lands." He continued: "I don't think it can work the other way around. I don't think the nonwhites in other parts of the world can really be of any concrete help to us, given their own problems of development and self-determination." King also said that "American Negroes can be a bridge between white civilization and the nonwhite nations of the world, because we have roots in both." See Washington, *Testament of Hope*, 318–19.

105. Lewis V. Baldwin et al., *The Legacy of Martin Luther King, Jr.: The Boundaries of Law, Politics, and Religion* (Notre Dame: University of Notre Dame Press, 2002) 21 and 263.

world. The image of "the 'new Negro' as heralding a 'new world order' to replace the 'old order' of colonialism, exploitation, and segregation"[106] was endlessly fascinating for King—and quite reassuring as he struggled and sacrificed his life daily for the realization of this global ideal.

In the same vein, King understood that peoples of color elsewhere in the world were fully capable of leading their own struggles and planning their own destinies, and that the Negro in America also had much to learn from them.[107] Hence, King believed that the Negro's encounter with other peoples of color across the world—with their religions, cultures, and ways of thinking and living—afforded rich and illimitable opportunities for both learning and a fruitful exchange of ideas. He had witnessed this in his own people's encounter with Gandhi and the Indian struggle for independence.[108] What King ultimately hoped for was a world in which peoples of color embraced and shared ideas and strategies for freedom with each other, thereby blazing new paths toward the complete actualization of a global beloved community that includes all humans.

Again, King's choice to convey a special message and set of values to the colored world was not inconsistent with his global beloved community ideal. He understood that the vast complex of experiences among peoples of color generally was unique and quite different from what most of "the white world"[109] had known, thus exposing the need to approach each with a message that best applied to its particular experiential-historical context and place in the global community. But when King thought in terms of the whole world becoming "a neighborhood," he was envisioning a course that would ultimately involve the mingling of the highest human values of peoples from every part of the globe, irrespective of race, the badge of color, or any other artificial human barrier, for that matter.[110] Clearly, this speaks to King as an intriguing blend of the *realist* and the *idealist*—the *realist* who could not logically exclude race and/or color in his analysis of the human condition, and the *idealist* who was in search of a world in which racial and color categories would not be a serious consideration at all.

106. Clayborne Carson et al., eds., *The Papers of Martin Luther King, Jr.,* vol. 3, *Birth of a New Age, December 1955–December 1956* (Berkeley: University of California Press, 1997) 451 and 462.

107. Baldwin, *Toward the Beloved Community,* 54.

108. Baldwin, *Voice of Conscience,* 206–7.

109. King, "Doubts and Certainties Link," 2.

110. Washington, *Testament of Hope,* 209; and Baldwin, *To Make the Wounded Whole,* 286.

THE ENDURING SEARCH FOR THE IDEAL WORLD: A VISION UNREALIZED

Martin Luther King, Jr.'s heart and mind were in harmony with all people who envisioned and struggled for a world in which the idea that the color of a person's skin determines the content of that person's character is categorically and universally rejected.[111] This, he often said, would be "the day not of the white man, not of the black man," but "of man as man." King obviously had in mind a globally responsible ethic that embraces the fact that neither whites nor peoples of color worldwide can be truly liberated until all are free, nor can they reach their fullest potential as human beings without each other.[112] This was the profundity of King's communitarian vision. But the enduring question is, where is the world today in terms of the actualization of that vision? Have we really become that "single neighborhood" that King spoke of in the last years of his life?

There is a sense in which the white world and the colored world still exist, despite the revolutionary changes that have occurred in the half-century since King's death. Stunning advancements in science and technology have not altered this global reality. Although human societies throughout the world have become more pluralistic in terms of their racial and ethnic character, there are still questions about the extent to which they have become authentically integrated. Antiquated thinking about race, color, and ethnicity and personal and institutionalized racism still fragment the cultural, social, and political landscapes on a global scale.[113] The world is indeed what King called "a single neighborhood," but only in a geographical sense. Although the amazing advancements in science and technology have brought humans closer in a physical sense, anti-immigrant fears, racial profiling, ethnic cleansing, staggering economic woes, and global terrorism are sparking new trends in the polarization and tensions that exist between peoples of different races and ethnic backgrounds across the globe. Hence, the essential challenge, as King said, involves creating a world in which our "moral and spiritual development" is commensurate with our "scientific and technological revolutions."[114] This is the key to creating a world that is in the fullest sense "a single neighborhood."

111. Carson et al., *Papers*, 5:499.

112. Baldwin, *Toward the Beloved Community*, 2.

113. Baldwin, *Voice of Conscience*, 238.

114. Washington, *Testament of Hope*, 209; Carson et al., *Papers*, 6:86, 159, and 338; Carson et al., *Papers*, 3:414; and King, *Where Do We Go from Here?*, 168.

A serious reading of King suggests three levels on which we might construct the kind of ethical value system needed to bring into being the ideal world. They involve learning how to sustain diversity in positive and meaningful ways, developing a determination to overcome an obsession with materialism and greed, and nurturing a genuine adherence to the idea that the "forces of spiritual might" are much more powerful "in the universe" than the "forces of military might."[115] A few words on each of these are in order if we are to understand more fully the global King.

King concluded that the growing pluralization of the world demanded a movement away from viewing diversity as a weakness to legitimizing and celebrating it as a source of strength. This was for King not simply a matter of extinguishing the "flame of intolerance,"[116] but of dispelling the myth of superior and inferior races, removing all racial and ethnic barriers to human community, eliminating poverty and hunger, and creating the atmosphere for "mutual acceptance" and "genuine intergroup" and "interpersonal living." In practical terms, this meant seeking "new ways of human beings living together, free from the spiritual deformation of race hatred" and "of war and economic injustice," a vision that, according to King, "does not belong" to peoples of color alone but "is the yearning of mankind."[117] In an ethical vein, this involves envisioning the beloved community as the regulating and the highest human ideal. In a theological context, it is about affirming that "God's love is universal and inclusive of all."[118] In the politico-economic realm, this translates into institutions and structures that meet the material and non-material needs of people on a nondiscriminatory basis.

The possibility of the actualization of such a human ideal in history was never seriously doubted by King, for he witnessed approximations of the beloved community in history, and especially in the contexts of both the civil rights crusade and liberation movements abroad, in which peoples of all nationalities, races, and faiths united in common causes. King knew that there were many in both the white and colored worlds who opposed all forms of bigotry and intolerance and who embraced diversity

115. Carson et al., *Papers*, 5:145; Clayborne Carson et al., eds., *The Papers of Martin Luther King, Jr.*, vol. 2, *Rediscovering Precious Values, July 1951–November 1955* (Berkeley: University of California Press, 1994) 248 and 294; and Carson et al., *Papers*, 3:462.

116. Carson et al., *Papers*, 6:214.

117. Ibid., 5:120 and 191; and King, *Where Do We Go from Here?*, 72–83.

118. Carson et al., *Papers*, 2:325.

wholeheartedly.[119] When thinking of diversity in a global sense, King envisioned moving beyond the old paternalism, which had too long defined relations between the rich and poor nations, to a legitimate partnership in which the ideas and the contributions of all nations to human enlightenment, uplift, and empowerment are viewed and appreciated equally. King insisted that all people, and especially the affluent and powerful, had to understand that the colored peoples of Africa, Asia, and other parts of the globe were "an integral part of the history which is reshaping the world, replacing a dying order with modern democracy."[120] Clearly, much has occurred in the last half-century—the dismantling of the apartheid regime in South Africa, the disappearance of the great wall that once separated East and West Germany, U.N. conferences on racism, and recent pro-democracy movements in Africa and the Middle East—to affirm the timelessness of such concerns as those raised by King.

King lamented the extent to which peoples throughout the world were caught in the grip of materialism and greed. He spoke of "a practical materialism," which "means living as if there [is] nothing else that [has] reality but fame and material objects."[121] He denounced "the false gods of science, money, and pleasure," declaring that "these ends may result in some material satisfaction," but humans ultimately "cannot live by bread alone." King observed that the more humans feed their material hunger, the closer they come to spiritual famine.[122] Noting that "the bourgeoisie—white, black or brown—behaves about the same the world over" in terms of their greed and materialism, King stressed the need for a more charitable spirit that seriously addresses the needs of the poor and neglected. On the global scale, this meant developing "a spirit of international brotherhood, not national selfishness."[123] From a biblical standpoint, the Good Samaritan on the Jericho road was, in King's estimation, a model for how individuals, groups, and nations might overcome the lure of materialism and greed, while taking on a genuine and constructive ethic of giving and sharing.[124]

When it came to the question of the supremacy of the "forces of spiritual might" over the "forces of military might," King could not have been

119. Ibid., 6:195.

120. Ibid., 5:120 and 447.

121. Ibid., 5:413.

122. Ibid., 6:203.

123. Ibid., 5:231.

124. King, *Strength to Love*, 26–35.

more insightful, especially in his own time.[125] He detected that there were many forces reshaping the world, such as politics and religion, but he wanted to live in a world in which spiritual values were held in higher esteem than the military-industrial complex. King argued that war, like racism and the neglect of the poor and marginalized, constituted "a spiritual problem" that required spiritual leadership and a conscious and persistent movement toward "spiritual ends," especially if humans were to live in what he termed "a war-less world." Thus, he urged humans to stop paying "lip service to the spiritual life," and he turned to "the weapons of the spirit" in an effort to achieve global justice and peace.[126]

The culture of nonviolence in our world has diminished over time, and few seem really interested in what King said about the dire consequences of violence. It could be argued that the continuation of war across the vast landscape of humanity reflects not only a deep spiritual malady, but also the essential failure of King's global nonviolent strategy. But King's ideas are very much alive and relevant, and a critical engagement with this phenomenal figure around matters of the *spiritual* and the *ethical* is still vitally necessary in this new and even more dangerous and challenging world.

125. Carson et al., *Papers*, 5:145.

126. Ibid., 4:103; Carson et al., *Papers*, 6:86 and 535; Carson et al., *Papers*, 3:181 and 471; Carson et al., *Papers*, 2:248 and 294.

3

Beyond Patriarchy

*The Meaning of Martin Luther King, Jr.
for the Women of the World*

Linda T. Wynn

Freedom, self-determination and world peace are nothing if not women's issues and they cannot be achieved without the active involvement of women.

CORETTA SCOTT KING[1]

IN NOVEMBER AND DECEMBER 1967, Martin Luther King, Jr. delivered five
lectures for the Canadian Broadcasting Corporation's (CBC) Massey Lectures. These lectures included his Christmas Eve sermon, "A Christmas Sermon on Peace," broadcasted live from Ebenezer Baptist Church in Atlanta,
Georgia. Later, CBC published the lecture series under the title *Conscience*

---

1. *Four Decades of Concern: Martin Luther King, Jr.* (Atlanta: Martin Luther King,
Jr. Center for Nonviolent Social Change, 1986) 31. Also quoted in Lewis V. Baldwin, *To
Make the Wounded Whole: The Cultural Legacy of Martin Luther King, Jr.* (Minneapolis:
Fortress, 1992) 240.

for Change. In 1968, subsequent to Dr. King's assassination, the book was republished as *The Trumpet of Conscience,* for which his widow, Coretta Scott King, wrote the foreword. In *The Trumpet of Conscience* and *Where Do We Go From Here: Chaos or Community?*, Dr. King put forth his vision and mission for human equality in global terms. Speaking as a "citizen of the world,"[2] he articulated his global vision in his 1967 Christmas Eve sermon:

> It really boils down to this: that all life is interrelated. We are all caught in an inescapable network of mutuality, tied into a single garment of destiny. Whatever affects one directly, affects all indirectly. We are made to live together because of the interrelated structure of reality. Did you ever stop to think that you can't leave for your job in the morning without being dependent on most of the world? You get up in the morning and go to the bathroom and reach over for the sponge, and that's handed to you by a Pacific Islander. You reach for a bar of soap, and that's given to you at the hands of a Frenchman. And then you go into the kitchen to drink your coffee for the morning, and that's poured into your cup by a South American. And maybe you want tea: that's poured into your cup by a Chinese. Or maybe you're desirous of having cocoa for breakfast, and that's poured into your cup by a West African. And then you reach over for your toast, and that's given to you at the hands of an English-speaking farmer, not to mention the baker. And before you finish eating breakfast in the morning, you've depended on more than half of the world. This is the way our universe is structured, this is its interrelated quality. We aren't going to have peace on earth until we recognize this basic fact of the interrelated structure of all reality.[3]

While Dr. King did not use the term globalization, he clearly articulated the multidimensional concept and process that has made humanity increasingly interdependent. Throughout *Where Do We Go from Here: Chaos or Community?*, King made reference to those who populate the global community as part of a "world house," a "worldwide neighborhood," or a "human family."[4] With these cognitive thought processes about

2. Martin Luther King, Jr., *The Trumpet of Conscience* (New York: Harper & Row, 1967) 31.

3. James M. Washington, ed., *A Testament of Hope: The Essential Writings and Speeches of Martin Luther King, Jr.* (New York: HarperCollins, 1986) 254.

4. See Martin Luther King, Jr., *Where Do We Go from Here: Chaos or Community?* (Boston: Beacon, 1968) 167–91.

globalization, King presaged his time, as he drew a parallel to global justice, the advancement of democratic freedoms and human rights, and the intercontinental exchange of a particular set of ideas and principles. These ideals were developed during his activism in the movement to gain the civil rights of American blacks and to secure their full citizenship status as guaranteed by the country's legal instrumentalities. Although King's guiding principles were originally aimed at the lack of racial inclusiveness in America, they were also instructive for women in the world house who were oppressed by male-dominated global institutions.

SEXISM AND THE MAKING OF A MOVEMENT: HISTORICAL REFLECTIONS

Between the 1955–1956 Montgomery bus boycott and the 1968 Memphis sanitation workers' strike, Dr. King connected African Americans' dreams of liberty, equality, and justice with global dreams of political and economic equality. Often he referenced the African American movement for civil rights as one manifestation of a global human rights revolution that called for economic rights to work, income, housing, and security. In 1956, King spoke about his dream for a world in which "privilege and property [would be] widely distributed, a world in which men will no longer take the necessities from the masses to give luxuries to the classes," a "world in which men will throw down the sword," thereby coming to the point where they could care for and assist others, especially those who were among the world's underprivileged.[5] Two years later, King called for world disarmament and a global war on poverty. However, the repetitive playing of King's "I Have a Dream" speech has bulldozed his vision of a just society based on "a radical redistribution of economic and political power." It has cleared his "American Dream" sermon and it takes no notice of the King who, as early as the 1950s, called for world disarmament, an end to apartheid in South Africa, a global war on poverty, and "special treatment" to assist African Americans to overcome historic racism. His radicalism, which was there throughout his career and not just in the last year of his life, has been taken out of the historical photograph.[6] As noted historian C. Vann Woodward

5. Clayborne Carson et al., eds., *The Papers of Martin Luther King, Jr.*, vol. 3, *Birth of a New Age, December 1955–December 1956* (Berkley: University of California Press, 1997) 346.

6. Harvard Sitkoff, preface to *King: Pilgrimage to the Mountaintop* (New York: Hill & Wang, 2007).

wrote, "The twilight zone that lies between memory and written history is one of the favorite breeding places of mythology."[7]

In his July 4, 1965, "American Dream" sermon, King stated, "I still have a dream that one day all of God's children will have food and clothing and material well-being for their bodies, culture and education for their minds, and freedom for their spirits."[8] In contrast to popular culture's belief about King in the 1950s, he was never a civil rights leader unconcerned with the national political economy. He, like the civil rights organizations of the 1930s, pursued a twofold agenda of civil rights and economic justice designed to benefit women as well as men. As cited in "Social Policies, Civil Rights, and Poverty," by Charles V. Hamilton and Dona C. Hamilton, "race has always been fused with class in the political struggle to obtain equitable policies" for American blacks.[9]

The March on Washington for Jobs and Freedom pushed to the forefront economic needs and demands that reflected the movement's broadening social base. Many of the women active in the movement spoke of securing civil, political, and economic rights, and they, like King, also considered these ideals as human rights that were mutually reinforcing and communal or international in scope.

Although women were the predominate force as grassroots leaders in community-based organizing for civil rights, King's dialogue, classic models of leadership, and policy solutions were patriarchal-based and customary to many of his contemporary male civil rights leaders and heads of congregations. While dedicated to the African American struggle for civil rights, women involved in the movement wanted respect for their contributions, for their ability to organize their communities, and for issues that were of concern to them. However, for most of King's leadership, the "Negro" in his rhetoric was gendered male, commonly seen as the family breadwinner and as asserting himself in politics as a courageous fighter for freedom. In a May 1964 *Life* magazine preview of his book *Why We Can't Wait*, King said, "The Negro does not want to languish on the welfare rolls

7. C. Vann Woodward, *The Strange Career of Jim Crow*, 3rd. ed. (New York: Oxford University Press, 1974) xvi.

8. Wolfgang Mieder, *"Making a Way Out of No Way": Martin Luther King's Sermonic Proverbial Rhetoric* (New York: Peter Lang, 2010) 398.

9. Charles V. Hamilton and Dona C. Hamilton, "Social Policies, Civil Rights, and Poverty," in *Fighting Poverty: What Works and What Doesn't*, ed. Sheldon H. Danziger and Daniel H. Weinberg (Cambridge: Harvard University Press, 1986) 286–311.

anymore than the next man." Black men deserve a "family wage" sufficient to support their wives and children.[10] But, it must be remembered that married black women had long been vested in the income-earning workforce. Not all black women agreed with King's gender-specific language, and some challenged him. However, it was not until the 1970s that black feminism developed as an independent theory.

King was the most well-known leader of the modern black freedom struggle of the 1950s and 1960s, both nationally and internationally. His willingness to demolish the walls of injustice in order to erect a house constructed on the foundation of justice is virtually unparalleled in America's history. His conviction and faith gave him the wherewithal and fortitude not to accept anything less than full equality for African Americans and the disadvantaged as a whole. King remained true to his convictions and did not yield to the temptation to prosper materially from his fame. Even though King was deeply grounded in his spiritual underpinning, he ultimately advanced a liberal theological point of view not only to crusade against racial discrimination within the black community but also to fight class discrimination. He used his spiritual beliefs to convey the ideals of racial justice and social liberation, and these ideals had universal or global appeal. King's philosophy inspired the women's liberation movement. Notwithstanding, the evidence suggests that he did very little to advance female leadership in the global struggles for liberation.[11] Moreover, the campaigns that King planned and led for the civil rights of his people did not provide a paradigm for the full inclusion of women leaders.

However, while King spoke of or made inferences about a global community, his parlance, while inclusive in intent, used gender-specific language to convey his ideas about a "world house." King not only used gender-specific language but was also viewed as sexist toward women— and especially strong women who actively participated in the movement.[12]

10. Martin Luther King, Jr., "Why We Can't Wait," *Life* 55.2 (1964) 98–99; and Martin Luther King, Jr., *Why We Can't Wait* (New York: New American Library, 1963) 136.

11. John J. Ansbro, *Martin Luther King, Jr.: The Making of a Mind* (Maryknoll, NY: Orbis, 1982) xv; Lewis V. Baldwin and Amiri YaSin Al-Hadid, *Between Cross and Crescent: Christian and Muslim Perspectives on Malcolm and Martin* (Gainesville: University Press of Florida, 2002) 181–99; Michael Eric Dyson, *I May Not Get There with You: The True Martin Luther King, Jr.* (New York: Simon & Schuster, 2000) 127.

12. David J. Garrow, *Bearing the Cross: Martin Luther King, Jr., and the Southern Christian Leadership Conference* (New York: William Morrow, 1986) 375–76 and 617. In addition to Garrow, Taylor Branch also spoke of King's sexual liaisons, as did Michael Friedly and David Galen in their *Martin Luther King, Jr.: The FBI File* (New York: Carroll

He worked with women activists like Eleanor Roosevelt in 1957, on the American Committee on Africa (ACOA), and with Dorothy Irene Height five years later on the American Negro Leadership Conference on Africa (ANLCA) against South African apartheid, a metastasized cancer that was also invasive in the sociopolitical structure of America. Yet, as Lewis V. Baldwin points out in chapter 1, when King turned his attention toward the crisis in the Middle East, the evils of colonialism in Africa and Asia, or the socioeconomic problems in the Caribbean and Latin America, he did not make the liberation of women a critical part of his global human rights agenda.[13] Even though King was chauvinist in his attitude toward women and did not make the liberation of women a critical part of his global human rights agenda, this chapter concludes that the ideas and social praxis of the world's most recognized leader of the 1950s and 1960s civil rights movement still has relevance for women across the globe.

King entered the modern civil rights movement after moving to Montgomery, Alabama, in 1954, shortly after the U.S. Supreme Court's unanimous enunciation in the *Brown vs. Board of Education* decision. He had accepted the Dexter Avenue Baptist Church's call to become its pastor. The Reverend Vernon Johns, an activist in his own right, preceded King at Dexter Avenue, and his activism affected the incoming pastor. *In Stride Toward Freedom*, Dexter's twentieth pastor described Johns as "a brilliant preacher with a creative mind" and "a fearless man, [who] never allowed an injustice to come to his attention without speaking out against it."[14] As Dexter's pastor from 1947 to 1952, Johns advocated for the civil rights of African Americans in the former capital of the Confederacy. He urged his congregation to challenge the traditional status quo, a defiant stance that he himself adopted. In response to discrimination on city buses, Johns once disembarked in protest and demanded a refund. His early activism and challenges to the power structure paved the way for Dexter's congregation

---

& Graf, 1993) 66 and 623–26. Also see Ralph D. Abernathy, *And the Wall Came Tumbling Down: An Autobiography* (New York: Harper & Row, 1989) 434–36 and 470–75; Stephen B. Oates, *Let the Trumpet Sound: The Life of Martin Luther King, Jr.* (New York: Harper & Row, 1982) 265 and 283; Lewis V. Baldwin, *There Is a Balm in Gilead: The Cultural Roots of Martin Luther King, Jr.* (Minneapolis: Fortress, 1991) 155.

13. Also see Baldwin, *To Make the Wounded Whole*, 205–9; and Lewis V. Baldwin, *Toward the Beloved Community: Martin Luther King, Jr. and South Africa* (Cleveland: Pilgrim, 1995) 15–19 and 36–38.

14. Martin Luther King, Jr., *Stride Toward Freedom: The Montgomery Story* (New York: Harper & Row, 1958) 38.

to accept King's social activism and enabled King to become a leader in the Montgomery bus boycott.

Soon after his arrival as pastor, Dr. King presented the congregants of Dexter Avenue Baptist Church with a six-page pastoral letter called "Recommendation to the Dexter Avenue Baptist Church for the Fiscal Year 1954–55."[15] It detailed plans for fund-raising, organizational innovations, and church renovation and expansion, and it ended by asserting his need for a full-time secretary.[16] However, embedded in the middle of the letter, there was mention of the Social and Political Action Committee, which had been created to keep the congregation "intelligently informed about the social, political, and economic situation."[17] This Social and Political Action Committee, in which women participated fully, existed prior to King's becoming Dexter Avenue's pastor.

The Women's Political Council (WPC) was an organization founded in Montgomery in 1946 by Mary Fair Burks, JoAnn Robinson, Irene West, Uretta Adair, and others because the local League of Women Voters refused to integrate or work with them on projects in which they had a common interest. The WPC had issued numerous official complaints to functionaries of the Montgomery City Bus Lines regarding insolent bus drivers and unjust seating arrangements throughout the early 1950s.[18] Robinson's book, *The Montgomery Bus Boycott and the Women Who Started It,* noted that the evolution of activists in Montgomery's infrastructure, for all practical purposes, did not include King and his fellow ministers.[19]

Several months before King's arrival in Montgomery, members of the WPC met with Mayor W. A. Gayle and outlined the changes they sought for Montgomery's bus system. These included no one standing over empty seats; a decree that black individuals not be made to pay at the front of

15. Charles Marsh, *The Beloved Community: How Faith Shapes Social Justice, from the Civil Rights Movement to Today* (New York: Basic Books, 2005) 14.

16. Ibid.

17. Ibid.; and Clayborne Carson, "Martin Luther King, Jr., and the African-American Social Gospel," in *African-American Christianity*, ed. Paul E. Johnson (Berkeley: University of California Press, 1994) 159–77.

18. Mary Fair Burks, "Women in the Montgomery Bus Boycott," in *Women in the Civil Rights Movement: Trailblazers and Torchbearers, 1941–1965,* ed. Vicki L. Crawford et al. (Bloomington: Indiana University Press, 1993) 71–83.

19. *The Montgomery Bus Boycott and the Women Who Started It: The Memoir of Jo Ann Gibson Robinson,* ed. David J. Garrow (Knoxville: University of Tennessee Press, 1987) 19–179.

the bus and enter from the rear; and a policy that would require buses to stop at every corner in black residential areas, as they did in white communities. When the meeting failed to produce any change at all, Jo Ann Robinson, the WPC president, reiterated the council's requests four days after the unanimous *Brown v. Board of Education* decision. In a letter to Mayor Gayle, dated May 21, 1954, she stated that "there has been talk from twenty-five or more local organizations of planning a city-wide boycott of buses."[20] Along with the actions of women in bringing forth the Montgomery bus boycott and the refusal of Rosa Parks to give up her bus seat, it was ultimately the legal action taken on behalf of Claudette Colvin, Mary Louise Smith, Aurelia Browder, and Susie McDonald that ended segregated public transportation in Montgomery. On November 13, 1956, the U.S. Supreme Court upheld the U.S. district court's decision in *Browder v. Gayle*, proclaiming that bus segregation violated the due process and equal protection clause of the Fourteenth Amendment.[21] Later, King did note Parks' refusal to further condone the oppressors' tactics when he stated, "She was anchored to that seat by the accumulated indignities of days gone by and the boundless aspirations of generations yet unborn. She was a victim of both the forces of history and the forces of destiny. She had been tracked down by the *Zeitgeist*—the spirit of the time."[22] After the bus boycott ended, it should also be noted that Ella Baker gave King the idea for establishing an umbrella organization that became the Southern Christian Leadership Conference.[23] While men were noted early on in the scholarship on the movement, the dynamic role women played in the modern struggle for freedom, equality, and justice for American blacks was not seriously considered until much later.

20. Jo Ann Robinson to Mayor W. A. Gayle (May 21, 1954), unpublished version, Alabama State University, Montgomery, Alabama; and Garrow, *Montgomery Bus Boycott*, x.

21. *Browder v. Gayle*, 352 U.S. 903 (1956). Jeanetta Reese was one of the original plaintiffs. However, outside pressure convinced her to withdraw from the case. Fred Gray, one of the attorneys, made the decision not to include Rosa Parks in the case to avoid the perception that he, King, and others "were trying to circumvent and enjoin the criminal prosecution of Mrs. Parks" on other charges. See Fred Gray, *Bus Ride to Justice: Changing the System by the System: The Life and Works of Fred Gray* (Montgomery, AL: Black Belt, 1995) 69.

22. King, *Stride Toward Freedom*, 29.

23. Crawford et al., *Women in the Civil Rights Movement*, 54; and Baldwin and Al-Hadid, *Between Cross and Crescent*, 188.

Since the publication in 1990 of Vicki L. Crawford, Jacqueline Anne Rouse, and Barbara Woods' *Women in the Civil Rights Movement: Trailblazers and Torchbearers, 1941–1965*, historians have explored women's involvement in the civil rights movement. This work was the last volume in *Black Women in United States History*, a sixteen-volume series edited by Darlene Clark Hine. *Women in the Civil Rights Movement: Trailblazers and Torchbearers, 1941–1965* grew out of the realization that women were being left out or at best marginalized in the modern civil rights movement narrative. Marymal Dryden understood that the participation of many women in the movement had not received the same media attention as their male counterparts. She wanted to learn more about the trailblazing "women whose heroic acts initiated specific events" and about those bearing the torch, "who continue to carry on the struggle for reform."[24]

Now there are biographies on movement activists such as Rosa Parks, Septima Clark, Ella Baker, Fannie Lou Hamer, Lillian Smith, and Anne Braden.[25] In addition to these biographies, there are several autobiographies that have facilitated the understanding of the intersection of gender roles in the movement as well as the numerous projects that give discourse on the treatment of women in the civil rights movement. The autobiographies include such women as Anne Moody, Pauli Murray, Constance Baker Motley, Daisy Bates, Patricia Stephens Due and Tananarive Due, Lillian Smith, Dorothy Irene Height, Mamie Till-Mobley, Amelia Boynton Robinson,

---

24. The papers that comprise *Women in the Civil Rights Movement* were originally presented at a conference held at the Martin Luther King, Jr. Center for Nonviolent Social Change on October 12–15, 1988. It was cosponsored by the Division of Continuing Education of Georgia State University. The conference came about because of Marymal Dryden's viewing of the television documentary *Eyes on the Prize* in 1987. See Crawford et al., *Women in the Civil Rights Movement*, xiii and xv.

25. See Anne C. Loveland, *Lillian Smith: A Southerner Confronting the South* (Baton Rouge: Louisiana State University Press, 1986); Kay Mills, *This Little Light of Mine: The Life of Fannie Lou Hamer* (New York: Penguin,1993); Joanne Grant, *Ella Baker: Freedom Bound* (New York: Wiley, 1998); Chana Kai Lee, *For Freedom's Sake: The Life of Fannie Lou Hamer* (Urbana: University of Illinois Press, 1999); Douglas Brinkley, *Rosa Parks: A Life* (New York: Penguin, 2000); Catherine Fosl, *Subversive Southerner: Anne Braden and the Struggle for Radical Justice in the Cold War South* (New York: Palgrave, 2002); Barbara Ransby, *Ella Baker and the Black Freedom Movement: A Radical Democratic Vision* (Chapel Hill: University of North Carolina Press, 2003); and Katherine Mellen Charron, *Freedom's Teacher: The Life of Septima Clark* (Chapel Hill: University of North Carolina Press, 2009).

Myrlie Evers-Williams, Johnnie Rebecca Carr, and Jo Ann Robinson, to name a few.[26]

A review of the scholarship on women in the civil rights movement discloses that many scholars came to the same judgment—namely, that women out-numbered men as participants in the movement. In *The Autobiography of Medgar Evers*, Manning Marable asserts, "Women were the foundation of the movement's success." He argues that the foundation was quantitative, that "women are more likely than males to emerge as critical leaders in most working-class and poor neighborhoods. Women activists are far more prevalent than males in the building of civic capacity."[27] As illustrated by Bernice McNair Barnett in *Invisible Southern Black Women Leaders in the Civil Rights Movement: The Triple Constraints of Gender, Race, and Class*, women started, facilitated, and assisted in sustaining the yearlong Montgomery bus boycott. Following the arrest of Rosa Parks on December 1, 1955, for refusing to relinquish her seat on the Cleveland Street bus driven by James F. Blake, Jo Ann Robinson of the Women's Political Council wrote and mimeographed more than thirty thousand leaflets that called for a one-day bus boycott on December 5.[28] Yet, prior to Parks,

26. A selective listing of autobiographies includes Lillian Smith, *Killers of the Dream* (New York: Norton, 1961); Anne Moody, *Coming of Age in Mississippi* (New York: Dial, 1968); Septima Clark with LeGette Blythe, *Echo in My Soul* (New York: Dutton, 1962); Pauli Murray, *The Autobiography of a Black Activist, Lawyer, Priest, and Poet* (Knoxville: University of Tennessee Press, 1987); Garrow, *The Montgomery Bus Boycott*; Daisy Bates, *The Long Shadow of Little Rock* (Fayetteville: University of Arkansas Press, 1987); Johnnie Rebecca Carr with Randall Williams, *Johnnie: The Life of Johnnie Rebecca Carr, with Her Friends Rosa Parks, E. D. Nixon, Martin Luther King, Jr., and Others in the Montgomery Civil Rights Struggle* (Montgomery, AL: Black Belt, 1996); Constance Baker Motley, *Equal Justice Under the Law: An Autobiography* (New York: Farrar, Straus & Giroux, 1999); Amelia Boynton Robinson, *Bridges Across Jordan* (Washington, DC: Schiller Institute, 1991); Myrlie Evers-Williams, *Watch Me Fly: What I Learned on Becoming the Woman I Was Meant to Be* (Boston: Little, Brown, 1999); Patricia Stephens Due and Tananarive Due, *Freedom in the Family: A Mother-Daughter Memoir of the Fight for Civil Rights* (New York: One World, 2003); Mamie Till-Mosley with Christopher Benson, *Death of Innocence: The Story of the Hate that Changed America* (New York: Random House, 2003); and Dorothy I. Height, *Open Wide the Freedom Gates: A Memoir* (New York: Public Affairs, 2005).

27. Manning Marable, "Introduction: A Servant-Leader of the People—Medgar Wiley Evers (1925–1963)," in *The Autobiography of Medgar Evers: A Hero's Life and Legacy Revealed Through His Writings, Letters, and Speeches*, ed. Myrlie Evers-Williams and Manning Marable (New York: Basic Books, 2005) xviii.

28. Bernice McNair Barnett, "Invisible Southern Black Women Leaders in the Civil Rights Movement: The Triple Constraints of Gender, Race, and Class," *Gender & Society*

numerous other women (including fifteen-year-old Claudette Colvin, who had been manhandled, arrested, and indicted for refusing to give up her seat on the Highland Gardens bus near Dexter Avenue Baptist Church) experienced the wrath of white bus drivers. Even Thurgood Marshall forewarned almost a decade earlier that the invective insults and maltreatment of black women on public transportation was "dynamite."[29] Colvin's arrest galvanized many of the WPC to begin planning for a boycott. The WPC had long concluded that a boycott of Montgomery's bus company would bring down the walls of black segregation. As Robinson stated, a bus boycott would be a way "not just to teach a lesson but to break the system. We knew if the women supported it, the men would go along."[30] After all, the maltreatment of black women on public conveyances had been taking place since the nineteenth century. Black women such as Sojourner Truth and Ida B. Wells, among others, protested against segregated public transportation. Black American resistance to segregated transit began in the wake of Reconstruction and escalated in response to the vicious treatment that blacks, and especially women, faced on Southern streetcars in the late nineteenth century. The segregation of public conveyances continued in the early twentieth century, and black Americans sought redress to these issues that reflected the *Zeitgeist* of the time. At the turn of the century, according to August A. Meier and Elliot Rudwick, boycotts were waged in over twenty-five cities against unequal segregated transit by black communities in the South, and especially between 1900 and 1906.[31]

On public conveyances such as trains and streetcars, black women, both middle-class and working-class, had long made arguments for their right to be seated. As Blair L. M. Kelley asserts, among such voices of advocacy were the antebellum black New Yorker Elizabeth Jennings and

7 (1993) 178.

29. Danielle L. McGuire, *At the Dark End of the Street: Black Women, Rape, and Resistance—A New History of the Civil Rights Movement from Rosa Parks to the Rise of Black Power* (New York: Vintage, 2012) 83.

30. Paula Giddings, *When and Where I Enter: The Impact of Black Women on Race and Sex in America* (New York: William Morrow, 1984) 264. A close reading of Dr. King's *Stride Toward Freedom*, an account of the yearlong boycott, reveals that except for a brief notice of Parks and the WPC, there is very little recognition of the WPC's achievements.

31. August A. Meier and Elliott Rudwick, "The Boycott Movement against Jim Crow Streetcars in the South, 1900–1906," *Journal of American History* 55 (1969) 756–75. It should be noted that Montgomery, Alabama, witnessed one of these early transit boycotts. There was a Montgomery streetcar boycott from 1900 to 1902 to protest segregated public transportation service.

the Virginia clubwoman Maggie Lena Walker, in addition to the numerous unknown black domestics and other common laborers who followed them. Their active involvements made the movement possible. The legal proceedings brought forth by these women and their clarion calls to speak out in opposition to segregated streetcars are reminders that black women were also at the forefront of defending their rights. The women of this period exposed the senselessness of racial segregation. As domestic workers, black women with white children and the white elderly in their care were permitted to sit in the white sections of public conveyances, but, as passengers without white children or the elderly, transportation officials assaulted them for sitting in those same seats. When women challenged the color line head-on, they often faced attacks just as violent and inhumane as those perpetrated against black men. As black women were barred, beaten, and ejected from moving streetcars, physically pulled from their seats in ladies' railcars, or made to stand on the outdoor platforms of moving trains, they exposed the truth about segregation. Segregation was not about separation and protection of "white womanhood," but about violence and stigma. Shaped by this force, women became some of the most effective leaders and protesters in the fight for full citizenship and dignity.[32] From early in the twentieth century, American black women made up a large percentage of the passengers on public transportation and met head-on the uncivil behavior and handling by white drivers, as well as the capricious enforcement of segregation laws. As Paula Giddings points out, "there had always been a tinderbox quality to the ill treatment of black women on public conveyances.[33]

In 1892, activist, educator, and "race woman" Anna Julia Cooper wrote about the "voiceless black women of America," who were confronted by both "a woman question and a race problem" and who were expected to choose between their own needs and the well-being of their race.[34] Despite their marginalization, nineteenth-century black women waged crusades against sexism in their communities. They were critical of black male leadership and spoke candidly about gender tensions within the race. Historian

32. Blair L. M. Kelley, *Right to Ride: Streetcar Boycotts and African American Citizenship in the Era of Plessy v. Ferguson* (Chapel Hill: University of North Carolina Press, 2010) 11.

33. Giddings, *When and Where I Enter*, 262.

34. Charles Lemert and Esme Bhan, eds., *The Voice of Anna Julia Cooper: Including A Voice from the South and Other Important Essays, Papers, and Letters* (Lanham, MD: Rowman & Littlefield, 1998) 112.

Deborah Gray White noted that black women of this era believed that "black female issues and issues of race were identical."[35]

Male leaders of the movement more often than not overlooked even those women in positions of leadership, who were instrumental in aiding their communities in marshaling their moral boldness to defy white supremacy. Often exposed to sexism within the movement, these women understood that the movement, contrary to popular memory, was not one of great speeches given by King, interspersed with images from Montgomery, Little Rock, lunch counter sit-ins, Freedom Rides, Ole Miss, Birmingham, the March on Washington for Jobs and Freedom, Freedom Summer, and Selma. "The tendency in the popular imagination and in much of the [early] scholarship has been to reduce the movement to stirring speeches—given by men—and dramatic demonstrations—led by men," writes Charles M. Payne. Payne adds: "The everyday maintenance of the movement, women's work, overwhelmingly, is effectively devalued, sinking beneath the level of our sight."[36]

The declarations of the modern movement's participants themselves demonstrate the kind of sexism women endured. Additionally, the behavior of the movement's male leadership is also illustrative of the sexism and marginalization of women within the movement. Having said that, it must be taken into account that many of the movement's participants and activists did not converse forthrightly about gender relations in the movement until after the second wave of the women's movement in America drastically changed the discursive discourse and restructured personal and public memory. Most women active in the movement for equality, justice, and freedom did not publicly criticize or comment on gender relations. That assessment was made during the years when gender consciousness came into full focus. With ties to the civil rights movement of the 1950s and 1960s, the new women's movement took on a wider agenda than that of the women's suffrage movement; it fought for equal rights and it looked at gender differently than the preceding wave of activists.

Like Jo Ann Robinson and the WPC, Stokely Carmichael (also known as Kwame Ture), himself no stranger to gender controversy in the movement, stated that "the ones who came out first for the movement were

35. Deborah Gray White, *Too Heavy a Load: Black Women in Defense of Themselves, 1894–1994* (New York: Norton, 1999) 54.

36. Charles M. Payne, *I've Got the Light of Freedom: The Organizing Tradition and the Mississippi Freedom Struggle* (Berkeley: University of California Press, 1995) 276.

women. If you follow the mass meetings, not the stuff on TV, you'd find women out there giving all the direction. As a matter of fact we used to say, 'Once you got the women, the men got to come.'"[37] Ella Baker, national organizer, strategist, visionary with the Southern Christian Leadership Conference (SCLC), and the woman who aided the students conducting the 1960 sit-in movement and in establishing the Student Nonviolent Co-ordinating Committee (SNCC), was most attuned to the movement's demeaning treatment of women. She noted that "the movement of the 1950s and 1960s was carried largely by women. . . . It's true that the number of women who carried the movement is much larger than that of men."[38]

Congressman John Lewis echoes the sentiments of others who gave ordinary women recognition for their eagerness to join in and assist the movement in any way that they could. In *Walking with the Wind*, Lewis credits such women with helping SNCC workers in the Deep South in their organizing efforts:

> One group of people who helped us . . . in these communities were [sic] the local women, the matriarchal heads of so many of these households. Over and over again we found that it was these wom-en—wives and mothers in their forties and fifties, hardworking, humorous, no-nonsense, incredibly resilient women who had car-ried such an unimaginable weight through their own lives and had been through so much unspeakable hell that there was nothing left on this earth for them to be afraid of—who showed *us* the way to mobilize in towns and communities where they lived. No one was

---

37. Lynne Olson, *Freedom's Daughters: The Unsung Heroines of the Civil Rights Move-ment from 1830 to 1970* (New York: Scribner, 2001) 15. Stokely Carmichael's statements about black women at a SNCC retreat in Waveland, Mississippi, caused him to be viewed as a sexist. When called upon to comment on the "position" of women in the organiza-tion, he stated that "the proper position of women in the movement is prone." However, in memoirs published after his death in 1998, he professed that the retort was meant to be funny, made to a group of SNCC friends relaxing on a pier after a long day of debate. See Casey Hayden, "Fields of Blue," in *Deep in Our Hearts: Nine White Women in the Free-dom Movement*, ed. Constance Curry et al. (Athens: University of Georgia Press, 2000) 366. For Stokely Carmichael's account, see Stokely Carmichael and Ekwueme Michael Thelwell, *Ready for Revolution: The Life and Struggles of Stokely Carmichael (Kwame Ture)* (New York: Scribner, 2003). Also see Mary Elizabeth King, *Freedom Song: A Personal Story of the 1960s Civil Rights Movement* (New York: William Morrow, 1987) 451–52.

38. See Vicki L. Crawford's "Beyond the Human Self: Grassroots Activists in the Mis-sissippi Civil Rights Movement," in Crawford et al., *Women in the Civil Rights Movement*, 13–28.

more ready, eager and willing to climb on the Freedom Train in these little towns and on these little farms than the women.[39]

Recently, Danielle L. McGuire, in *At the Dark End of the Street: Black Women, Rape, and Resistance—A New History of the Civil Rights Movement from Rosa Parks to the Rise of Black Power,* argues that women's active participation in the civil rights movement was rooted in their organized resistance to sexual violence and appeals for protection of black womanhood.[40] Prior to being noted for her role in igniting the Montgomery bus boycott, Parks was an antirape activist. After meeting Recy Taylor from Abbeville, Alabama, who had been raped on September 3, 1944, by a gang of white men, Parks assisted in the founding of the Committee for Equal Justice. With strong community support, according to *The Chicago Defender,* she organized one of the "strongest campaigns" for equal justice. Eleven years later, this group became known as the Montgomery Improvement Association (MIA).[41] The formation of the MIA ultimately catapulted the Reverend Dr. Martin Luther King, Jr. into national leadership in the movement.

However, men of the movement made no connection between sexual violence perpetrated against American black women by white men, their appeals for the protection of black womanhood, and black women's activism in the movement for equality and justice. McGuire's overarching point is that sexual violence against black women and black women's resistance to this violence shaped the civil rights movement. She noted that between 1940 and 1975, sexual violence and interracial rape became one crucial battleground upon which black Americans sought to destroy white supremacy and gain personal and political autonomy. Civil rights campaigns in Little Rock, Arkansas; Macon, Georgia; Tallahassee, Florida; Washington, North Carolina; Birmingham and Selma, Alabama; and Hattiesburg, Mississippi, among other places, had roots in organized resistance to sexual violence and appeals for protection of black womanhood. Often the history of the civil rights movement is presented as a struggle between black and white men—the valiant leadership of King confronting intractable white supremacists like Eugene "Bull" Connor.[42] This representation of the civil

---

39. John Lewis with Michael D'Orso, *Walking with the Wind: A Memoir of the Movement* (New York: Simon & Schuster, 1998) 187.

40. McGuire, *At the Dark End of the Street,* xx.

41. Ibid., xvii and 6.

42. Ibid., xx.

rights chronicle conceals as much as it exposes. By inserting patriarchy and white supremacy, it shifts the narrative, and men are placed at its center.

THE DEVELOPMENT OF MARTIN LUTHER KING, JR.'S ATTITUDE TOWARD WOMEN

Before King and his attitude toward women can adequately be discussed, it is necessary to look into his childhood, to consider the way in which he was reared. He was brought up in a male-dominated culture, and gender roles and family life were defined in time-honored stipulations. The accepted wisdom of what constituted real masculinity and femininity were hardly ever examined, and the subordination of women pervaded all aspects of American institutional life. The mores of this culture influenced how King viewed and related to women. His most basic perception of and relationship with women began within the context of his family's home life and were cultivated by his experience with the black community in which he was reared. In this atmosphere, the young King encountered from childhood American black women who, despite being oppressed by the three "isms" of race, class, and gender, were nevertheless strong, self-assured, and imbued with a spirit far more resilient than that of many African American men.[43] Alberta Williams King gave her son his first real understanding of womanhood and motherhood. She had a calm but powerful impact on her husband and children. However, King knew and understood that his father, Martin Luther King, Sr., was without a shred of doubt the head of the household. King, Sr. was a resolute, patriarchal figure who declared, albeit in discreet ways, that biblical instruction prohibited women from appropriating male authority.[44] In his mother he found an attribute of caring that supported him whenever his father lacked patience, became easily incensed, uncompromising, and too heavy-handed as a disciplinarian. His mother demanded that the senior King exercise self-constraint when administering corporal punishment on their children. As King, Sr. reported: "Bunch insisted, though, as the children grew older that any form of discipline used on them by either of us be agreed upon by both. . . . [S]he was

43. King, *Stride Toward Freedom*, 18–19.

44. Clayborne Carson et al., eds., *The Papers of Martin Luther King, Jr.*, vol. 1, *Called to Serve: January 1929–June 1951* (Berkeley: University of California Press, 1994) 360; Baldwin, *There Is a Balm in Gilead*, 106; and Lawrence D. Reddick, *Crusader without Violence: A Biography of Martin Luther King, Jr.* (New York: Harper & Row, 1959) 51.

able to understand that even when I got very upset with them, it was only because I wanted them to be strong and able and happy."[45] Jennie C. Parks Williams, King, Jr.'s maternal grandmother, with whom he had a close relationship, hated to see him receive punishment from his father. King, Jr.'s sister, Willie Christine King, reported: "Whenever Daddy had to discipline M. L., grandmother always had a hug, kiss or kind word to help the hurt go away. She often told Dad that she hated to see him spank Martin because 'the child looked so pitiful' when he did."[46]

Alberta Williams King's role as a steady pillow of strength in the family was apparent to young King, who once stated, "Our mother has also been behind the scene setting forth those motherly cares . . . the lack of which leaves a missing link in my life." King, Jr. saw character traits in her that merited imitating—qualities such as love, compassion, and the capacity to listen to others. He also gained from her his deep pride and intense dislike for systems of oppression. These values carried over to inform King, Jr.'s attitude toward women in general.[47]

King demonstrated his appreciation to his mother for her instruction about history and self-respect when he was six years of age. As he asserted in _Stride Toward Freedom_, it was his mother who took him on her lap and told him about slavery and how it ended with the Civil War. She explained the divided system of the South—the segregated schools, restaurants, theaters, housing, the "white" and "colored" signs on drinking fountains, waiting rooms, lavatories—as social conditions rather than a natural order. Then, according to King, Jr., she uttered the words that almost every black child heard before he could yet understand the injustice that makes them necessary: "You are as good as anyone."[48] King, Jr. also garnered lessons from "Big Mama," Jennie C. Parks Williams, who gave him a strong sense of identity, self-esteem, and mission, as well as his aunt, Ida Worthem. The stories that they passed on to King, Jr., his sister Christine, and his brother

45. Martin Luther King, Sr., with Clayton Riley, _Daddy King: An Autobiography_ (New York: Morrow, 1980) 131.

46. Christine King Farris, "The Young Martin: From Childhood through College," _Ebony_ 41.3 (1986) 56–58; Coretta Scott King, _My Life with Martin Luther King, Jr._ (New York: Henry Holt, 1993) 91; Oates, _Let the Trumpet Sound_, 8; and Baldwin, _There Is a Balm in Gilead_, 110.

47. Carson et al., _Papers_, 1:360; Farris, "Young Martin," 56–58; Scott King, _My Life with Martin Luther King, Jr._, 76–77, 92; Baldwin, _There Is a Balm in Gilead_, 106–7; and King, _Stride Toward Freedom_, 19.

48. King, _Stride Toward Freedom_, 19.

Alfred Daniel (A. D.) gave all a sense of values and served a didactic purpose. Through these stories, King, Jr. and his siblings were informed about the values of family, church, and the larger community in which they resided.[49] Because of the interactions between him and the women who surrounded him during his childhood, King, Jr. respected the women in his immediate environment as more than cooks, housekeepers, and bearers of children. These women were powerful spiritual forces, protectors of family honor, and possessors of knowledge about the experiences of the past. Yet, how did King, Jr.'s early upbringing shape his attitude about women as he matured into a young man? His mother's influence on his early life, the nurturing he received from his grandmother and aunt, and the close relationship he had with his sister apparently made King, Jr. less apt to physically mistreat or speak disdainfully of women. Notwithstanding, that did not stop him from viewing women as sex objects as he matriculated through his collegiate and post-baccalaureate years. The religious and academic subcultures that fostered young King seldom challenged or confronted conventional gender values that improved men's lives while limiting the social possibilities of women.

In 1952, during his second year at Boston University, King met Coretta Scott, who was working on a graduate degree in music at the New England Conservatory. The future couple had numerous values in common—both were from the South, both had an affinity for music, both were grounded in their faith, and both wanted to bring an end to the lack of equality and freedom within their community. Scott, whose family had faced difficulties in Marion, Alabama, had "decided to become something of an activist. . . . Early on she decided that she would not marry a man unless he held an active and strong stance on racial matters."[50] As the couple dated and became serious about each other, Scott was faced with some pressing questions regarding her future professional aspirations, not because she was changing her mind but because King wanted his future wife to adhere to certain gender conditions. Prior to their marriage, Scott, who was studying concert performance, changed her major to music education. After a brief courtship, they were married in June 1953. King's idea of the roles that husband

---

49. Carson et al., *Papers*, 1:359; Baldwin, *There Is a Balm in Gilead*, 106–27.

50. Frederick L. Downing, *To See the Promised Land: The Faith Pilgrimage of Martin Luther King, Jr.* (Macon, GA: Mercer University Press, 1986) 171; Scott King, *My Life with Martin Luther King*, Jr., 58 and 67–72.

and wife should have in the home was influenced by his parents' example. As Coretta Scott King noted in her *My Life with Martin Luther King, Jr.*:

> Martin had, all through his life, an ambivalent attitude toward the role of women. On the one hand, he believed that women are just as intelligent and capable as men and that they should hold positions of authority and influence. But when it came to his own situation, he thought in terms of his wife being a homemaker and a mother for his children. He was very definite that he would expect whoever he married to be at home waiting for him. . . . At the same time, Martin, even in those days, would say, "I don't want a wife I can't communicate with." From the beginning, he would encourage me to be active outside the home, and would be very pleased when I had ideas of my own or even when I could fill in for him. Yet it was the female role he was anxious for me to play.[51]

Although King may not have wanted a wife with whom he could not communicate, he exhibited restrictive tendencies in that he wanted her to use her expertise and skill almost exclusively in the domestic sphere. Consequently, Coretta acclimated herself to the role of a minister's wife, believing "this is one of the most important roles that I can play."[52] Coretta Scott King's decision to give up her own aspirations for her husband was an act of selflessness. "As Martin was being made ready to be the leader and symbol of the Negro Movement," she noted, "so was I being prepared to be his wife and partner. . . . It was in Montgomery that I became aware of the contribution I could make in sustaining and helping my husband in what was to come."[53] Coretta King was an activist in her own right, as testified to by her husband. Referring to her knowledge of and participation in the struggle, King noted that "at many points she educated me." As he recounted, when they met, Coretta was already very concerned about all the change they were seeking to achieve in the movement. "I never will forget that the first discussion we had when we met was the whole question of racial justice, economic justice, and peace," King recalled. King also noted that during Coretta's college days, she had been deeply involved in movements dealing with such problems. "So I must admit—I wish I could say, to satisfy my

---

51. Scott King, *My Life with Martin Luther King, Jr.*, 73–74.

52. Ibid., 27, 83, 109, and 179.

53. Ibid., 109.

masculine ego, that I led her down this path," King conceded, "but I must say that we went down together."[54]

Although they may have gone down the path toward freedom and justice together, numerous questions have been raised about King's infidelity. Since the 1980s, several scholars have discussed King's marital transgressions, thus providing more information and insights from which to assess his attitude toward women. For example, David J. Garrow's *Bearing the Cross: Martin Luther Dr. King, Jr. and the Southern Christian Leadership Conference* asserts that Dr. King had "occasional one-night stands."[55] It was further contended that he not only had one-night stands but had significant relationships with three women. One woman with whom he had a long-standing affair became, according to Michael Eric Dyson, King's "de facto wife, a spousal equivalent upon whom he became emotionally dependent."[56] Notwithstanding the accusations regarding King's philandering, Coretta King asserts that she and her husband never had a serious conversation about his womanizing during the course of their marriage. "If ever I had any suspicions," she explained, "I never would have even mentioned them to Martin." In Coretta's judgment, such matters were "so trivial" and did not "have a place in the very high-level relationship we enjoyed."[57]

Coretta King, according to the Reverend Ralph Abernathy, "never seemed to be touched" by King's indiscretion: "She rose above all the petty attempts to damage their marriage by refusing to entertain such thoughts."[58]

54. Baldwin, *There Is a Balm in Gilead*, 144–45. To garner a better understanding and full discussion of Coretta Scott King's role as the supportive wife, see Scott King, *My Life with Martin Luther King, Jr.*; King, *Daddy King*; and Octavia Vivian, *Coretta: The Story of Mrs. Martin Luther King, Jr.* (Philadelphia: Fortress, 1970).

55. Garrow, *Bearing the Cross*, 375.

56. Dyson, *I May Not Get There with You*, 216–18. Other authors who have discussed King's philandering include Abernathy, *And the Walls Came Tumbling Down*, 434–75; Baldwin, *There Is a Balm in Gilead*, 155; Taylor Branch, *Pillar of Fire: America in the King Years, 1963–1965* (New York: Simon & Schuster, 1998) 197–207 and 518–33; Friedly and Gallen, *FBI File*, 66 and 623–26; David Garrow, *The FBI and Martin Luther King, Jr: From "Solo" to Memphis* (New Haven: Yale University Press, 1981); Oates, *Let the Trumpet Sound*, 265 and 283; Georgia Davis Powers, *I Shared the Dream: The Pride, Passion, and Politics of the First Black Woman Senator from Kentucky* (Far Hills, NJ: New Horizon, 1995) 145–62, 172–85, and 226–27.

57. Dyson, *I May Not Get There With You*, 216; and Garrow, *Bearing the Cross*, 374.

58. Abernathy, *And the Walls Came Tumbling Down*, 472–73. It must also be noted that Abernathy's book caused quite an uproar in the year of its publication because of the details contained in the book about King's sexual liaisons and unfaithfulness to Coretta Scott King.

For now, how Coretta King actually felt about the reports concerning King's marital indiscretions will have to wait until more primary documentation is found that reveals her true feelings about the matter. The revelations about King and his marital indiscretions, his absolute chauvinism, and even his insistence that Coretta not be involved in the movement, could not keep her from participating. Not only did she participate in civil rights marches, but she conveyed the core values of the movement to the world through song, worked with the Women's International League for Peace and Freedom, and on occasion spoke at antiwar rallies.[59] Like other women involved in the movement, Coretta King understood that its patriarchal structure, along with the "isms" of race, sex, and class, could not be transcended without women's active involvement. She comprehended that if the movement was to move forward and embrace all within the "beloved community" or the "world house," its patriarchal structures had to be demolished.

Notwithstanding, like his male colleagues, King's sexist beliefs were nurtured in a black religious culture that mostly depended on the work of women across the socioeconomic stratum, from the poor to the working and middle classes. These women poured themselves into the movement. They placed their skills and talents at its disposal. Like men who were active in the movement's vineyard, women too faced many of the same trials and tribulations. Since many black women who supported the movement attended church, were the employees of whites, and rented from white proprietors, their active participation in the boycotts incensed white property owners and homemakers. Because of their participation, the potential for retribution against them and their families, economic and otherwise, was immeasurable, thus making their actions all the more courageous. King's beliefs about women reflected the thoughtlessness and lack of concern among the majority of black men toward the dilemma of black women. Many black men before the 1970s combined the concerns of black communities in general, without carefully distinguishing between or considering the effects and intersection of class and gender on a person's racial status.

---

59. David L. Lewis, *King: A Critical Biography* (New York: Praeger, 1970) 288–90; Carson et al., *Papers*, 3:386; Oates, *Let the Trumpet Sound*, 381 and 331–40; and Scott King, *My Life with Martin Luther King, Jr.*, 12 and 91–92.

WOMEN, MOVEMENT LESSONS, AND THE GLOBAL IMPLICATIONS OF THE KING LEGACY

The struggle of black women for both racial freedom and gender equity have been represented in the historical narrative of blacks in America, even if their contributions were unnoticed or unacknowledged by black men. Near the end of the nineteenth century and in the early twentieth century, the National Association of Colored Women (NACW) provided American black women a base from which to fight stereotypes of black female immorality. Through their resources, the NACW fought against racial tyranny, initiated programs to uplift the race, and demanded racial and gender justice. King and the civil rights movement owed much to this legacy of struggle.

Although women had been in the forefront of bringing to bear the direct nonviolent tactics used in the movement in the 1950s and 1960s, they were all but ignored during the March on Washington for Jobs and Freedom. Anna Arnold Hedgeman, the only woman on the nineteen-member planning committee for the march, was outraged that no woman was to march with male leaders, speak at the Lincoln Memorial, or meet with President Kennedy after the march. The eighteen male members of the planning committee acquiesced to Hedgeman's pressure and agreed to a brief "Tribute to Women," to take place at the beginning of the Lincoln Memorial rally. However, not one of the women given the tribute would be allowed to add her voice on that day in August 1963.[60] Hedgemen felt that the last-minute "Tribute to Women" did not adequately recognize the contributions made by women pursuers of civil and human rights, such as Rosa Parks, Daisy Bates, Diane Nash, Gloria Richardson, and widows of slain civil rights activists Medgar Evers and Herbert Lee. Dorothy Height of the National Negro Council, Hedgeman of the National Council of the Churches of Christ, and attorney and activist Pauli Murray pleaded with A. Philip Randolph and other members of the march's leadership to include young people, the unemployed, and women on the roster of speakers. The inclusivity would have been reflective of "the solidarity of the human

---

60. Olson, *Freedom's Daughter*, 284. All of the "Big Six" organizers spoke at the March on Washington. They were James Farmer (Congress of Racial Equality), Martin Luther King, Jr. (Southern Christian Leadership Conference), John Lewis (Student Nonviolent Coordinating Committee), A. Philip Randolph (Brotherhood of Sleeping Car Porters), Roy Wilkins (National Association for the Advancement of Colored People), and Whitney Young, Jr. (National Urban League).

family,"[61] an expression King used often to communicate his idea of the beloved community. Further enunciating the concept, he said, "We are tied together in the single garment of destiny, caught in an inescapable network of mutuality."[62] Refusing to yield to their request, Murray charged that Randolph was guilty of sexual "tokenism." Height recalled, "We could not get women's participation to be taken seriously." It was not enough that Mahalia Jackson sang or that Daisy Bates was allowed to pledge support to male "fighters for civil liberties." The exclusion went deeper, Height argued, symbolizing men's failure to understand black women's economic needs. The statistics of the period showed the growing prevalence of mother-only families, but the male leadership believed that "if men were given enough, the women would be better off."[63] Murray was disturbed that black women, who clearly played an integral part in the movement, were not seen by the public or by black male leadership as leaders or policymakers. "Negro women need to face some hard questions," Murray wrote. "One thing is perfectly clear. The Negro woman can no longer postpone or subordinate the fight against discrimination because of sex to the civil rights struggle but must carry on both fights simultaneously. She must insist upon a partnership role in the integration . . ." Murray also believed that many male civil rights leaders "harbored medieval attitudes toward women."[64]

In the mid-1960s, the National Welfare Rights Organization (NWRO), an activist organization that fought for the welfare rights of people, especially women and children, gave poor and working-class women the wherewithal to seek the reform of welfare laws and to bring the matter of impoverishment to the attention of those on the national level who had the means to affect public policy. The organization had four goals: adequate income, dignity, justice, and democratic participation. Black American women have always fought gallantly for themselves and their race. While their labors greatly affected the freedom struggles of black Americans,

61. Martin Luther King, Jr. "The Ethical Demands of Integration," in Washington, _Testament of Hope,_ 117.

62. Martin Luther King, Jr., "Remaining Awake through a Great Revolution," in ibid., 269.

63. Dorothy I. Height, "We Wanted the Voice of a Woman to Be Heard: Black Women and the 1963 March on Washington," in _Sisters in the Struggle: African American Women in the Civil Rights-Black Power Movement,_ ed. Bettye Collier-Thomas and V. P. Franklin (New York: New York University Press, 2001) 88–90; Olson, _Freedom's Daughters,_ 284–89.

64. Olson, _Freedom's Daughters,_ 287.

women of the race seldom received recognition for their accomplishments. As Paula Giddings points out, the NWRO "had actually come up with the idea of a poor people's campaign before Dr. King did," and they "were peeved when Dr. King started to beat that drum without even acknowledging their efforts—or their knowledge of the issue." Johnnie Tillmon and her fellow activists were livid that the leaders of the Poor People's Campaign had disregarded welfare issues in their push to dramatize the plight of the poor.[65] Additionally, they were systematically excluded from the upper levels of formal leadership in the civil rights movement's organizations, as well as in the black church, in which black women outnumbered black men.

Even in the case of the SCLC, founded by King and others in 1957, the motto "To Redeem the Soul of America" exhibited chauvinistic tendencies around the question of women's leadership. Ella Baker, who had served in the civil rights movement as an organizer and strategist, worked with those in Montgomery before the boycott ended. She worked with two of King's aides, Bayard Rustin and Stanley Levison, and they discussed strategies and considered ways to transform the moments of mass rebellion into a genuine mass movement for social change. When in Montgomery, she often stayed with Parks, whom she met in 1946 when Parks attended a leadership workshop that Baker conducted in Jacksonville, Florida. Shortly before Parks kindled the Montgomery bus boycott, she attended a civil rights workshop led by Baker at Highlander Folk School.

Because of her exceptional skills, Baker was encouraged by SCLC board members to run the SCLC, and she agreed until they found an executive director. As one might expect, she confronted ministers weighed down by charismatic, top-down, and personality-driven leadership. From the beginning, there was tension between Baker and the male ministers. They ignored her exceptional leadership and her organizational and institution-building skills, and consigned her to performing basic secretarial duties. Additionally, her belief in the equality and the rights of women brought her into direct conflict with the chauvinist attitudes of the male ministers. As the Reverend C. T. Vivian stated, "she wasn't church."[66]

---

65. Giddings, *When and Where I Enter,* 312; and White, *Too Heavy a Load,* 214.

66. Grant, *Ella Baker,* 107 and 122. Baker clashed with SCLC's male cult of personality. See Gerda Lerner, *Black Women in White America: A Documentary History* (New York: Random House, 1972). Also see Adam Fairclough, *To Redeem the Soul of America: The Southern Christian Leadership Conference and Martin Luther King, Jr.* (Athens: University of Georgia Press, 1987).

Baker believed in a type of group-centered leadership that let individuals identify their leadership talents and that emboldened common, everyday people to perform uncommon deeds. Her belief in democratic leadership went against the hierarchical habits of black ministers. She criticized King's leadership style, which reflected the accepted practices in most black organizations, religious or otherwise, where authority was most open to men who belonged to the inner circle.[67] As Baker noted, "I . . . knew from the beginning that having a women be an executive of SCLC was not something that would go over with a male-dominated leadership." Further, she stated, "and then, of course, my personality wasn't right. . . . I was not afraid to disagree with higher authorities."[68] Dorothy Cotton and Septima Clark, both of whom served on SCLC's executive staff in the 1960s, also expressed similar sentiments. Cotton, who served as director of the Citizenship Education Program, said, "I did have a decision-making role but I am also very conscious of the male chauvinism that existed. Black preachers are some of the most chauvinistic of them all."[69] Clark, who supervised leadership training for SCLC, expressed a similar position:

> I was on the Executive Staff of SCLC, but the men . . . didn't listen to me too well. They liked to send me into many places, because I could always make a path in to get people to listen to what I have to say. But those men didn't have any faith in women, none whatsoever. They just thought that women were sex symbols and had no contribution to make. . . . Rev. Abernathy would say continuously, "Why is Mrs. Clark on this staff?" . . . I had a great feeling that Dr. King didn't think much of women either. He would say . . . Mrs. Clark has expanded our program. She has taken it into eleven deep south states. But I don't think that he thought too much of me, because when I was in Europe with him, when he received the Nobel Peace Prize in 1964, the American Friends Service Committee wanted me to speak. In sort of a casual way he would say, "Anything I can't answer, ask Mrs. Clark." But he didn't mean it, because I never did get the chance to do any speaking to

67. Lerner, *Black Women in White America*, 345–52; Grant, *Ella Baker*, 105–24; James Joy, *Transcending the Talented Tenth: Black Leaders and American Intellectuals* (New York: Routledge, 1996) 87–88; Lewis, *Walking with the Wind*, 114 and 182–89.

68. Ann Standley, "The Role of Black Women in the Civil Rights Movement," in Crawford et al., *Women in the Civil Rights Movement*, 195.

69. Fairclough, *To Redeem the Soul of America*, 49–50. Cotton asserts, "I'm always asked to take notes, I'm always asked to go fix Dr. King some coffee. . . . They were sexist male preachers who grew up in a sexist culture." See Garrow, *Bearing the Cross*, 376.

the American Friends Service Committee in London or any of the other groups.[70]

Clark maintained that her ability to criticize Dr. King and other male members of SCLC came from the influence of the National Organization of Women (NOW), which she joined in 1968. She admitted that while she worked for the SCLC from the early to mid-1960s, she was sightless to the sexism exhibited by the organization's male leadership. "In those days," she said, "I didn't criticize Dr. King, other than ask him not to lead all marches . . ." Clark further noted: "I supported him in every way that I could because I greatly respected his courage, his service to others, and his nonviolence. But in those days, of course, in the black church men were always in charge. The way I think about him now comes from my experience in the women's movement."[71]

Cheryl J. Sanders maintains that when the ethical and biographical works on King are carefully studied, there are some well-defined variations between black and white male assessments of his ethical leadership and legacy. African American male scholars have generally focused on King's "public triumphs and moral vision." However, they tend to "stumble over the question of his relation to women and attitudes toward female leadership."[72] By being hesitant to openly address the question of King's relations with women and his attitude toward female leadership, while endeavoring to present him as an advocate for the rights of women, they appear to present antithetical views. On the other hand, white male scholars seem eager to bring to the forefront King's "private sins and his struggles as bearer of the cross of America's conscience."[73]

The women activists of the Student Nonviolent Coordinating Committee (SNCC) experienced some of the same difficulties as those in SCLC. SNCC grew out of the student sit-in movement when student leaders gathered in Raleigh, North Carolina, at Shaw University, Ella Baker's alma mater, in April 1960. Baker, one of the initiators of SCLC, noticed a

70. Standley, "Role of Black Women in the Civil Rights Movement," 196.

71. Ibid.; Cynthia Stokes Brown, ed., *Ready from Within: Septima Clark and the Civil Rights Movement* (Trenton, NJ: Africa World, 1990) 77–79. Abernathy's book *And the Walls Came Tumbling Down* reveals very little about the contributions made to the movement and SCLC by Dorothy Cotton, Ella Baker, and Septima Clark. See Cheryl J. Sanders, *Empowerment Ethics for a Liberated People: A Path to African American Social Transformation* (Minneapolis: Fortress, 1995) 97–98.

72. Sanders, *Empowerment Ethics for a Liberated People*, 97–98.

73. Ibid.

month after the first sit-in that took place in Greensboro, North Carolina, which captured national attention, the rapidity with which sit-ins spread across the South. The consummate organizer and strategist, she decided that the student-sit movement needed coordination.[74] Baker invited student leaders to Raleigh for the purpose of capitalizing on the success of numerous sit-ins that took place across the South, where mostly black students refused to leave restaurants when refused service. She called on the more than two hundred student attendees to remain independent and self-directing, rather than collaborate and join forces with SCLC or any other civil rights organization. King issued a press statement on the opening day of the conference and described the time as "an era of offensive on the part of oppressed people." He encouraged the students to institute "some type of continuing organization" and "to delve deeper into the philosophy of nonviolence" and offered this counsel: "Our ultimate end must be the creation of the beloved community."[75] Baker, who had grown suspicious of leader-centered approaches to civil rights during her tenure with SCLC, especially among "glory-seeking black preachers," favored a grassroots model of dynamic and active local participation. Such a philosophy was at SNCC's core. "Strong people," Baker declared, "don't need strong leaders." Although sponsored by SCLC, Baker steered the students away from aligning themselves with the black clergy–dominated group. In her speech, "More Than a Hamburger," the promoter of decentralized leadership told the students to "think and act for yourselves. Hold onto your energy and your vision. Keep it pure. Keep it real."[76]

As the students moved toward formalizing their organization, it was decided that the first chair of the new organization would come from Nashville and the organization would be headquartered in Atlanta. Because of Fisk student Diane Nash's prominence and leadership position in the Nashville movement, many thought she would be elected its chair. However, her fellow collegian Marion Barry, Jr., a chemistry graduate student from Fisk University, was elected chair. It appears that the issue of gender came to the

74. Howard Zinn, *SNCC: The New Abolitionists* (Boston: Beacon, 1964) 32.

75. Clayborne Carson et al., eds., *The Papers of Martin Luther Dr. King, Jr.*, vol. 5, *Threshold of a New Decade, January 1959–December 1960* (Berkley: University of California Press, 2005) 426–27.

76. Lewis, *Walking with the Wind*, 108. Between 1962 and 1967 Baker was a staff member of the Southern Conference Education Fund. Throughout the 1970s, she was active in a number of social justice causes including the Third World Women's Alliance and the Women's International League for Peace and Freedom.

forefront as students prepared for the vote. According to John Lewis, the vote was taken while Nash was out of the room. Lewis was convinced that the timing was deliberate. "Diane was a devoted, beautiful leader, but she was the wrong sex," said Lewis. "There was a desire to emphasize and showcase black manhood."[77] Even Lewis's statement is charged with patriarchy and is reflective of a period when men held positions of authority rather than women. Even so, SNCC moved beyond patriarchy more than did the other male-dominated civil rights organizations, all of which exhibited an authoritarian and masculine culture.

From its beginning, the youngest civil rights organization, which reflected Baker's philosophy, insisted that everyone have an equal voice, irrespective of gender difference. It has been stated that many women in SNCC came to see the group as having a distinctive "feminine" ethos.[78] However, while SNCC women activists may have felt that the organization reflected a distinctive feminine ethos, they found that their experiences in the field were demonstrative of an earlier period when interracial rape was used to uphold white patriarchal power. To be sure, they came face to face with SNCC worker and freedom fighter Fannie Lou Hamer's affirmation that "a black woman's body was never hers alone."[79]

Hamer represented the embodiment of SNCC's civil rights ethos that favored grassroots leadership, where local leaders sustained the movement long after civil rights organizers had left the area. She became a field secretary with SNCC and in 1963 endured a brutal beating in Winona, Mississippi, that was sexualized. "As they ruthlessly beat her, Hamer felt them 'pull my dress over my head and try to feel under my clothes.'" As she attempted to "preserve some respectability through honor and disgrace," a white officer "walked over, took my dress, pulled it over my shoulders, leaving my body exposed to five men."[80] Hamer related her story on national television at the Democratic National Convention in 1964 and to congressional representatives investigating civil rights abuses in June of that same year.

Like Hamer, Dorothy Height, president of the National Council of Negro Women, and Jean Noble, president of Delta Sigma Theta, Inc., spoke

77. Harry S. Haffee and Tom Sherwood, *Dream City: Race, Power, and the Decline of Washington, D.C.* (New York: Simon & Schuster, 1994) 88; and Olson, *Freedom's Daughters*, 160–61.

78. Olson, *Freedom's Daughters*, 161.

79. McGuire, *At the Dark End of the Street*, xviii–xix.

80. Ibid., 194.

out against the sexualized violence in Southern institutions of imprisonment. Both women appeared on WNEW, one of New York's popular radio stations, to announce an exclusive report documenting "indignities to girl freedom demonstrators in Southern prisons." Height reported that a month earlier, leaders of twenty-four women's groups met to hear firsthand accounts of "brutality and sexual abuse" from civil rights demonstrators in the South. Jean Nobel related a story that she was told by one young woman who was "asked to strip naked and stand before male prisoners in the yard of the jail" and who was also among the many women forced to undergo "unsanitary and unmedical [sic] vaginal exams."[81] These sexual abuses were not unusual, as they had been taking place since the days of slavery. Five years before Hamer placed the contemporary sexual atrocities before the viewing public, there was the 1959 case of Betty Jean Owens, who was gang-raped by four white men in Tallahassee, Florida. King did address this particular case at an annual SCLC meeting in Tallahassee by praising student protesters for giving "hope to all of us who struggle for human dignity and equal justice." However, instead of addressing directly the sexual abuse of women, King exploited the chasm between rhetoric and reality to highlight the injustice of Jim Crow. "It is ironical that these un-American outrages occur as our representatives confer in Geneva to expand democratic principles. . . . It might well be necessary and expedient," King held, "to appeal to the conscience of the world through the Commission on Human Rights of the United Nations." Yet, unlike Audley "Queen Mother" Moore, leader of the Universal Association of Ethiopian Women, who had appeared in person before the Commission on Human Rights, King did not connect the interrelatedness of race, gender, and sex.[82]

However, by the mid-1960s, King, in his address before the 1965 meeting of the Women's International League for Peace and Freedom, began to see the fusion between the contributions made by women on the global front against numerous forms of oppression, especially in South Africa, where apartheid and sexism were interrelated.[83] Like black women in America, women of color in South Africa had to confront the "isms" of race and gender. They also relegated the issues of gender below the issues associated with racism. They feared that the South African power structure would use issues of gender to further divide and ultimately conquer

81. Ibid., 195–96.
82. Ibid., 172–73; Height, *Open Wide the Freedom Gates*, 158–59.
83. Baldwin and Al-Hadid, *Between Cross and Crescent*, 192–93.

the black community, thereby preserving the apartheid power structure.[84] According to an August 1994 article written by Lynn Norment, titled, "Women in South Africa," women constituted approximately 53 percent of South Africa's population; however, men were the dominant force and controlled the society's structures and institutions.[85] Gender discrimination against women was sustained by the patriarchal system in which laws, mores, and folkways were institutionalized along with classism.

Black South African women can and have benefited from King's ethic of liberation for the oppressed. Several black womanist scholars have suggested that his ethic of liberation is relevant for black women. In a larger sense, his system of moral standards and principles are applicable to women universally, especially when taking into consideration his concept of humans made in the divine image, or *imago Dei*; his proposition of love as grounded in justice and social change; and his communitarian vision for addressing gender inequities.[86] As global societies move beyond patriarchy and consider carefully and thoughtfully King's philosophy of liberation, one will find that King's message is applicable for the women of the world and can be used as a tool to fashion liberation in the "world house." Like women globally, black women in America during the modern civil rights movement experienced patriarchy and were placed at its margins by the movement's male structure, as well as the public's awareness.

In moving beyond the popular perception of male dominance, it must be recognized that although men presumably led the movement, black women foreshadowed King in focusing on issues that benefited the entire community. Robinson and the WPC were in the forefront of the Montgomery bus boycott. They and Parks gave King the platform from which to put into place and practice his ideology of nonviolence. It was the women on whose behalf the U.S. Supreme Court ruled that segregated seating on public conveyances were unconstitutional. After the trials, tribulations, and successes of the bus boycott, Baker planted the seed for the formation of SCLC. Hamer and other women of like disposition in the MDFP were in opposition to the Vietnam War prior to King's stance on this issue.[87] The

84. Baldwin, *Toward the Beloved Community*, 171.

85. Lynn Norment, "Women in South Africa," *Ebony* 49.2 (1994) 101.

86. Katie G. Cannon, *Black Womanist Ethics* (Atlanta: Scholars, 1988) 160–74; Baldwin, *Toward the Beloved Community*, 174; and Baldwin, *To Make the Wounded Whole*, 156–59.

87. Lee, *For Freedom's Sake*, 166.

idea of a poor people's campaign originated with the NWRO and its cadre of black women before King took steps to bring the idea to fruition in 1967.

Although King was chauvinist in his views toward women, the principles he espoused through the concept of the beloved community were not mutually exclusive and therefore included gender. He understood that the freedom of all oppressed people, including women, from injustice and exploitation also required the liberation of their oppressors. As expressed through the numerous metaphors he used to articulate a global concept of humanity, the liberation of both the oppressor and the oppressed is dependent upon both groups, and women cannot logically be excluded. In other words, all people share a mutual humanity and consequently they should be accorded basic human rights. This ethos represents, if not the centerpiece, then certainly a main element of the civil and human rights leader's philosophical position. Both a practitioner of liberation and nonviolence, King enacted a liberating nonviolence that caught the imagination of the world. Perhaps more than anyone in the twentieth century, King spoke for all people under the control of the oppressors, and his efforts were ultimately inclusive of race, class, and gender. His appeal transcended borders and his philosophy can serve people, including women, across the globe.

Because of technological advancements, the swiftness of communications, and the speed of information sources, globalization is increasing the world's awareness of women's issues across the globe. The rights of women, generally speaking, are acknowledged and recognized as part of a broader campaign for human rights and the eradication of social injustices. Organizations such as the United Nations and others dedicated to the eradication of human injustices have taken on the issues confronting women.[88] As Lewis V. Baldwin has noted, King envisioned and articulated such possibilities during the late 1960s, when he thought in terms of a revolution of human values and priorities. "I am convinced that if we are to get on the right side of the world revolution," said Dr. King in 1967, "we as a nation must undergo a radical revolution of values." He further noted, in the speech given at Riverside Church in New York exactly one year to the day before his assassination, that "a true revolution of values will soon cause us to question the fairness and justice of many of our past and present poli-

88. Candace C. Archer, "Women and Globalization," in *Women and Politics around the World: A Comparative History and Survey*, ed. Joyce Gelb and Marian L. Palley (Santa Barbara, CA: ABC-CLIO, 2009) 1:17–23; and "How Does Globalization Affect Women?," *The Globalization Website*, 1. Online: http://www.sociology.emory.edu/globalization/issues02.html.

cies. . . . A true revolution of values will soon look uneasily on the glaring contrast of poverty and wealth . . ." In summing up his "Break the Silence" discourse, King concluded, "every nation must . . . develop an overriding loyalty to mankind [humanity] as a whole in order to preserve the best in their individual societies."[89] These thoughts are just as applicable to women across the world today as they were then.

According to Mark M. Gray, Miki Caul Kittilson, and Wayne Sandholtz's "Women and Globalization: A Study of 180 Countries, 1975–2000," economic globalization has resulted in new opportunities and resources for women. Equally important, however, globalization promotes the diffusion of ideas and norms of equality for women; though some societies resist such notions, others gradually abandon rules and practices that have functioned to subordinate and constrain women.[90]

The lingering question is, has globalization liberated women from patriarchal control and the all-consuming dilemmas of poverty and economic inequality? Based on the evidence, women are still among those paid the lowest of wages worldwide. Globally, men are still the controlling transmitters of economic and political institutions. In 2005, women constituted less than 10 percent of World Bank and International Monetary Fund governors, and those consulted by the World Trade Organization in its Dispute Resolutions Body. Universally, men still constitute approximately 85 percent of those seated in the world's legislative bodies.[91]

Even so, the women's movement has made some progress since the First World Conference on Women in 1975. In February 2006, gender activists and policymakers convened in New York on the fiftieth anniversary of the United Nations Commission on the Status of Women (CSW) to assess its progress. Established in 1946 by the Economic and Social Council (one of the five organs of the U.N.), the commission is tasked with advancing women's interests. When the CSW was first established, women could vote in only thirty of the original fifty-one U.N. member states. Now, across the globe, women have secured the right to vote and, in most countries, to run for election. However, woman activists want more women in high office in international financial institutions like the World Bank and the

89. King, "A Time to Break Silence," in Washington, *Testament of Hope*, 231–44.

90. "Women and Globalization: A Study of 180 Countries, 1975–2000," *International Organization* 60.2 (2006) 3.

91. Elaine Coburn, "Globalization and Women," in *Gendered Intersections: A Collection of Readings for Women's and Gender Studies*, ed. Leslie Biggs and Pamela Downe (Black Point, NS: Fernwood, 2005) 3–4.

International Monetary Fund. Out of all policymaking areas, women are least represented in economics and finance, notes the Women's Environment and Development Organization (WEDO), an international women's lobbying group. Over the last few decades, the World Bank and International Monetary Fund have been designing economic reform programs in poor countries, but the lack of women in the formulation of those policies means "that the majority of the monetary, financial and trade policies being implemented worldwide . . . are gender blind, resulting in serious economic costs to society as a whole," reports the WEDO. At the World Bank and IMF, female representation among leadership staff is around 20 percent. While those institutions have the authority to alter the gender makeup of their staffs, they have little control over the boards, as the governors are appointed by individual member countries. At last, some progress was made in June 2011, when Christine Lagarde of France became the first woman to head the IMF. Previously, she was the first women to serve as France's minister of the economy and finance.[92]

Black women active in the movement for freedom, equality, and justice encountered difficulty in accepting the androcentric leadership style of its leaders, which emanated from and conformed to the black church tradition. However, this style of leadership was *antithetical* to King's ethos or core values as embedded in the concept of his "beloved community." Black women brought an inclusive vision to the black freedom struggle. They disapproved of "men who wanted to lead but were unable to confront their fears," and they were confident that "leadership came from actual work and commitment and was not preordained by sex." Fannie Lou Hamer appealed for a shared working relationship between black women and black men "in the interest of the family and future of our people."[93] Moving beyond the patriarchal male leadership of the movement, she and others comprehended that the "isms" of race, class, and gender were interrelated. They understood that if the principles and values of the beloved community were to be actualized from a global perspective, women would have to be included. As averred by Coretta Scott King and other notable women, freedom, self-determination, and peace in a global context are nothing if not women's issues, and they cannot be won without the active

92. Gumisai Mutume, "African Women Are Ready to Lead, but Social Beliefs and Attitudes Hinder Their Quest," in *Africa Renewal: Special Edition on Women 2012*, 14. Online: http://www.un.org/en/africarenewal/special-edition-women/ready-to-lead.html.

93. Janice D. Hamlet, "Fannie Lou Hamer: The Unquenchable Spirit of the Civil Rights Movement," *Journal of Black Studies* 26.5 (1996) 560–76.

involvement of women.[94] Black women believed that the male-dominated leadership paradigm caused problems rather than helped people reach the goals of the movement, and the same might be said of such a paradigm on the world scale.

Moving beyond the patriarchy of King and looking instead to his ethical discourse as centered in the "beloved community," one finds values and insights that can aid in elucidating the issue of female subordination and in addressing the unique encounters of oppressed women's issues and their need for liberation. Another foundational stone laid by King is the premise contained in the idea of the social nature of human existence. Simply put, "all life is interrelated." Therefore, men can never be what they should be until women are what they should be, and, consequently, there must be a move from gender inequality and exclusivity to gender equality and inclusiveness globally. While King did not live to see the flourishing of the women's movement, his ethos did speak to issues that were pertinent to women then and are pertinent to women now. The ethic of women's liberation is now, for the most part, an inclusive component of freedom, equal opportunity, and self-determination. Moreover, there is even an ethical responsibility to oppose evil and injustice in all of their multilayered forms. In moving beyond patriarchy, the ideas and social praxis of the world's most recognized leader of the 1950s and 1960s civil rights movement still has relevance for women across the globe.

---

94. Baldwin, *To Make the Wounded Whole*, 240.

PART TWO

A Global Quest for Common Ground

Martin Luther King, Jr. and the Power of
Interreligious and Intercultural Learning

4

On Racism and War as Global Phenomena

*Martin Luther King, Jr.
and the World Council of Churches*

Thomas A. Mulhall

First I think all of us must develop a world perspective if we are to survive. The American dream will not become a reality devoid of the larger dream of a world of brotherhood and peace and good will. The world in which we live is a world of geographical oneness and we are challenged now to make it spiritually one.

MARTIN LUTHER KING, JR.[1]

1. See Martin Luther King, Jr., "The American Dream," in James M. Washington, ed., *A Testament of Hope: The Essential Writings and Speeches of Martin Luther King, Jr.* (New York: HarperCollins, 1999) 209. Also see Martin Luther King, Jr., "The American Dream" (February 10, 1963), The Library and Archives of the Martin Luther King, Jr. Center for Nonviolent Social Change, Inc., Atlanta, Georgia; and Martin Luther King, Jr., *The Trumpet of Conscience* (New York: Harper & Row, 1968) 68.

MARTIN LUTHER KING, JR., and the World Council of Churches (WCC), the principal ecumenical Christian organization with over 560 million members in more than 110 countries, influenced one another in their efforts to bring an end to the Vietnam War and racism worldwide. Both recognized that what was happening in Vietnam was racist in nature. Member churches of the WCC were impressed by Dr. King's success in the civil rights movement, and at the Fourth Assembly, meeting in Uppsala, Sweden, in July 1968, delegates passed a resolution proposing a "Martin Luther King Institute for Nonviolent Social Change."

During the 1960s, King and the WCC appreciated the interconnectedness of reality that prevailed, a phenomenon known as globalization. This called for urgent dialogue to bring about a brotherhood of man. In a world that has become a global village, mankind faced a dilemma—what do we morally and ethically owe our fellow human beings? Dr. King recognized this challenge early in his public life. He popularized the term "beloved community," a phrase coined earlier by Josiah Royce, an ethicist who influenced the Fellowship of Reconciliation (FOR), an international peace and justice organization.

THE GLOBAL KING AND THE WORLD COUNCIL OF CHURCHES

No study of Martin Luther King, Jr. is complete without considering his international reputation. King was way ahead of his contemporaries when he suggested that "if we are to have peace on earth, our loyalties must become ecumenical rather than sectional. Our loyalties must transcend our race, our tribe, our class, and our nation; and this means we must develop a world perspective."[2] The contribution that King and the civil rights movement made to the easing of racial strife in the United States caught the imagination of the WCC. Members saw the potential for the application of nonviolent action to other areas of conflict in the world.

To reach a global audience, Dr. King built up an excellent working relationship with the WCC. Dr. Willem Visser't Hooft, General Secretary

2. King, *Trumpet of Conscience*, 68; Martin Luther King, Jr., *Where Do We Go from Here: Chaos or Community?* (Boston: Beacon, 1968) 190. Also see Martin Luther King, Jr., "A Christmas Sermon on Peace," Ebenezer Baptist Church, Atlanta, Georgia. The Canadian Broadcasting Corporation aired this sermon on December 24, 1967; King Center Library Archives (August 1967–December 1967).

of the WCC, acknowledged King's increasing influence in a letter after his Nobel Peace Prize award in Oslo in 1964. King responded, "Your encouraging words and your genuine expression of confidence give me new determination to carry on the struggle to make the brotherhood of man a reality." King pronounced the challenge before him as follows: "to work passionately and unrelentingly to discover the international implications of nonviolence; for in a real sense, there can be no justice without peace and there can be no peace without justice."[3] The WCC confirmed King's good standing when, in October 1965, Dr. Visser't Hooft wrote inviting him to be a participant and a speaker at the World Conference on Church and Society, to be held in Geneva, Switzerland, in July 1966. It would bring together about four hundred participants from the WCC member churches around the world. Dr. Visser't Hooft expressed his "high hopes that this Conference may result in a constructive contribution towards the solution of the urgent problems that confront our churches, the racial revolution being a major one."[4]

The timing of this invitation was significant. King was at the pinnacle of his career after the major legislative successes on civil rights in the United States. As the foremost black Christian leader there, he now had an opportunity to extend his international influence. The exchange of correspondence between King and the WCC revealed how the politics of the day, in this case the Vietnam War, intertwined with their pastoral roles. George D. Comnas, President of the American Club of Geneva, learned that Dr. King was to address the WCC and invited him in February 1966 to speak at a luncheon meeting about "your work in the field of civil rights." The invitation was later withdrawn due to controversial circumstances because a member of the American diplomatic mission in Geneva had expressed fears that King would speak out against the escalating war in Vietnam. Amid the turmoil Dr. Visser't Hooft intervened and the invitation was renewed.[5]

It transpired that King did not travel to Geneva, for in mid-July 1966, he sent a telegram advising that the riots in Chicago demanded that he

3. Martin Luther King, Jr. letter to Visser't Hooft (December 4, 1964), 42.11.08, WCC General Secretariat, Correspondence: Frequent 1938- Martin Luther King (1966–1970), WCC, Geneva, Switzerland.

4. Visser't Hooft letter to Martin Luther King, Jr. (October 27, 1965), 42.11.08, WCC General Secretariat, Correspondence: Frequent 1938- Martin Luther King (1966–1970), WCC, Geneva, Switzerland.

5. George D. Comnas letter to Martin Luther King, Jr. (April 29, 1966), 42.11.08, WCC General Secretariat, Correspondence: Frequent 1938- WCC, Geneva, Switzerland.

remain on the scene in the United States. King was disappointed that he could not attend the WCC conference. He said, "I am sure the Council will understand the pre-eminence of my responsibility to society in these revolutionary times."[6] These were momentous times, for a social revolution was taking place around the world. With decolonization, the old order was changing and new states were being born in Africa and Asia. Though King remained at home, his voice was broadcast throughout Europe during the WCC conference by CBS Radio. His speech, "A Knock at Midnight," was wide ranging and covered the role of the church in a "revolutionary age." King spoke of the conflict in Vietnam. He described it "as the evil of the war still before us." He proclaimed that church people can never endorse violence. King was driven by his conscience to declare that "we in the church must admit we have left men and women disappointed at midnight." King was equally blunt in making a point about South Africa, where fourteen million black men and women were segregated on 2 percent of their land and had "to use passes to walk the streets." Dr. King was quite direct in declaring, "The Dutch Reformed Church by supporting the status quo had left them standing there disappointed." King had prepared his taped speech with a view toward his European audience. His message was clear: the church must remember that "it is the conscience of the state." King indicted the church for its failure to act, and he demanded that it "recover its historic mission of truth, justice and peace."[7]

Dr. King's speech was a triumph. Dr. Visser't Hooft wrote in gratitude to CBS News in New York, praising the speech and King's magnificent communicative skills. In addition, representatives of the WCC conveyed their regard for King's work in a letter to him:

> The strike in Chicago has weighed heavily on the hearts of us all gathered in Geneva for the World Conference on Church and Society. The empty pulpit in the cathedral last Sunday was a vivid word of the Lord, reminding us that the needs of the world must take priority over the meeting of the churches.[8]

6. Martin Luther King, Jr. telegram to WCC (July 15, 1966), 42.11.08, WCC General Secretariat, Correspondence: Frequent 1938- WCC, Geneva, Switzerland.

7. WCC Sound Archives, MCW-66–048 (compact disc), Martin Luther King sermon delivered at the St. Pierre Cathedral in Geneva, Switzerland (July 17, 1966), "A Knock at Midnight," WCC, Geneva. This version is somewhat different from the one that appears in King's book *Strength to Love* (Philadelphia: Fortress, 1963) 56–66, and in Clayborne Carson and Peter Holloran, eds., *A Knock at Midnight: Inspiration from the Great Sermons of Reverend Martin Luther King, Jr.* (New York: Warner, 1998) 61–78.

8. WCC Board letter to Martin Luther King, Jr. (July, 1966), 42.11.08, General

Dr. Visser't Hooft confirmed that Dr. King's sermon had struck a chord at the conference and instilled enthusiasm into its members: "The stirring and sobering words of your sermon cut deeply into the key issues of our conference and have greatly encouraged us in our work. Christians from every corner of the world uphold you in their prayers." Furthermore, the example shown by Dr. King prompted this response: "from your deeds and words this week we have been taught again that Christians belong in the midst of conflict and crisis." The WCC recognized that the success of Dr. King's nonviolent action could be replicated elsewhere when the board indicated, "We are eager to learn from the civil rights movement's work in Chicago, for many countries are struggling with similar problems."[9]

King and the WCC shared significant common ground in their opposition to the Vietnam War and racism. The board explained that what was happening in Vietnam was part of a social revolution, and that the Vietnamese people should be free to determine their own future without foreign intervention. Dr. Eugene Carson Blake, who took over as WCC General Secretary in December 1966, was a great admirer of King and expressed similar concerns to him. The WCC considered the Vietnam War racist and was concerned that it was adversely affecting its outreach to Asia. Members agonized over the very thought of "white people killing people of color," noting that "this is not helping us in terms of our position in Asia."[10] King denounced the racist nature of the war in a similar fashion when he preached, "There is something strangely inconsistent about a nation and a press that would praise you when you say 'be nonviolent toward Jim Clark' but will curse and damn you when you say 'be nonviolent toward little brown children.'"[11] The WCC also thought that the conflict in Vietnam was bad for the United States. It detected in the conflict "a spurious type of

Secretariat, Correspondence: Frequent 1938- WCC, Geneva, Switzerland.

9. Ibid.

10. Eugene Carson Blake, transcript of interview (December 25, 1966), on *Face the Nation*, 995.1.03/14, WCC General Secretariat, Speeches 1966–1968, WCC, Geneva, Switzerland.

11 Martin Luther King , Jr., "Why I Am Opposed to the War in Vietnam," text of sermon at Ebenezer Baptist Church, Atlanta, Georgia (April 30, 1967), King Center Library and Archives, Atlanta, Georgia. See also David Halberstam quoting King in a chapter titled "When 'Civil Rights' and 'Peace' Join Forces." But, interestingly enough, Halberstam, despite evidence to the contrary, contends that King did "not particularly think of the war in Vietnam as a racial one." See the Halberstam chapter in *Martin Luther King, Jr.: A Profile*, ed. C. Eric Lincoln (New York: Hill & Wang, 1970) 207.

patriotism" that was "challenging the right of dissent and the open debate of public issues,"[12] a view King shared.

In October 1967, Dr. Blake invited Dr. King to preach the opening sermon at the Fourth Assembly of the World Council of Churches, which was to be held in Uppsala, Sweden, in July of the following year. His letter addressed King as a biblical preacher who would have a rapport with an international audience. Blake asked King to base the sermon on the theme of the Assembly: Revelation 21:5, "Behold, I make all things new." He advised King that his sermon should be theologically and exegetically sound as well as spiritually powerful, and that the invitation was based not primarily on King's role as a civil rights leader or as a Nobel Peace Prize winner, but rather was extended due to King's experiences of racial strife, poverty, and war in which God's purpose through the church is fully taken on board. Blake expressed the hope that King would stay as an adviser for the duration of the Assembly. If this was not possible, he would have "guest status" during his stay.[13]

Earlier, in October 1966, Dr. Blake had outlined the relevance of the ecumenical movement in relation to the world community. He urged, "if mankind is unable to find a way spiritually and politically to create a single community to match the hopes and control the dangers of the technological advances of our time, it is certain that civilization will destroy itself."[14] King and Blake were on a similar trajectory in terms of their thinking about the threats that faced an increasingly fragmented, materialistic, and violent world. The global "beloved community" was foremost in King's thoughts, and he refused to separate "the dream of our mission from the dream of the world." He asserted, "If we are to realize the American dream we must cultivate this world perspective."[15]

In December 1967, Dr. Blake acknowledged Dr. King's acceptance to preach in Uppsala the following July. In the interim, Blake and the Executive Committee of the WCC discussed possible action on the Vietnam War

12. Blake, transcript of interview (December 25, 1966), in *Face the Nation*, 995.1.03/14, WCC General Secretariat, Speeches 1966–1968, WCC, Geneva, Switzerland.

13. Eugene Carson Blake letter to Martin Luther King, Jr. (October 13, 1967), 42.11.08, WCC General Secretariat, Correspondence: frequent 1938- WCC, Geneva, Switzerland.

14. Eugene Carson Blake, "The Ecumenical Movement and Its Relation to a World Community," text of speech (October 1966), Westdeuctcher, Rurdfunk, 995.1.01/1, Blake, Eugene Carson Works 1966–69, WCC Geneva.

15. King, "The American Dream" (February 10, 1963); Washington, *Testament of Hope*, 210–11.

during their Geneva meeting in March 1968. But 1968 had arrived with little progress on the peace front. In December 1967, in "A Christmas Sermon on Peace," King had addressed the issue of how peace might be achieved in Vietnam. We see just how prophetic King was when he reminded U.S. and Canadian audiences that even though there may be political and ideological differences between people, "the Vietnamese are our brothers, the Russians are our brothers, the Chinese are our brothers; and one day we've got to sit down together at the table of brotherhood."[16]

Sadly, Dr. King did not make it to Uppsala, as he was assassinated on April 4, 1968. However, Dr. Blake's words to Mrs. Coretta Scott King confirmed his awareness of King's enormous influence: "I counted your husband as a friend and colleague, and I want you to know that in my judgment he was the outstanding minister in our Nation."[17] Church bodies issued numerous tributes following King's death. Below is the text of an appreciation issued jointly by three international Christian organizations based at the Ecumenical Centre in Geneva—namely, Dr. Eugene Carson Blake, General Secretary of the WCC; Dr. Marcel Pradervand, General Secretary of the World Alliance of Reformed Churches; and Dr. Andre Appel, General Secretary of the Lutheran World Federation:

> By international consensus Dr. King was a first citizen of the world. In the United States he was a main hope for a tormented nation. To the church he was the leading minister of Christ. For the unjustly used everywhere, he was a prime mover in the nonviolent campaign for justice, the peaceful way to peace. . . . we missed him then, we miss him now; but we heard, we hear.[18]

As noted earlier, the WCC recognized Dr. King's success in bringing about change by peaceful means at the Fourth Assembly in Uppsala, Sweden. The Martin Luther King Resolution proposed "A Martin Luther King Institute for Nonviolent Social Change" in these terms:

---

16. See King, "A Christmas Sermon on Peace"; and King, *Trumpet of Conscience*, 67–78.

17. Eugene Carson Blake letter to Mrs. Coretta Scott King (April 10, 1968). A telegram was also sent on April 5, 1968, by Blake, expressing sympathy and underlining "the rightness of his nonviolent commitment." 42.11.08, WCC General Secretariat, Correspondence: Frequent 1938–1970, WCC, Geneva, Switzerland.

18. *Approach: The Mission/Education Newsweekly* 2.13 (April 22, 1968), Philadelphia, Pennsylvania, WCC 42.11.08/2, Martin Luther King, WCC, Geneva, Switzerland.

> *Whereas* Dr. Martin Luther King bore witness in his own life, ministry and action to the New Testament gospel of love and nonviolence as the appropriate Christian means for social change;
>
> and *whereas* the Christian Church is today the legitimate bearer of this gospel of love and nonviolence in a world fraught with injustice, war, poverty, revolution and violence;
>
> *Be It Therefore Resolved* that the Fourth Assembly of the World Council of Churches, as a fitting memorial to Dr. Martin Luther King, initiate all in its member churches a two-year study of "Christian nonviolent methods for effecting social change," and that this study culminate in an ongoing program of research, study, training and action to be known as "The Martin Luther King Institute for Nonviolent Social Change."[19]

This was a fitting tribute to the life and work of King, who, as a Christian minister, was one of the greatest proponents for change through nonviolent means.

The Fourth Assembly of the WCC expressed confidence that the causes for which King stood would ultimately triumph. There was evidence of the deep feelings against racism and economic exploitation that would find expression in the Assembly.[20] King had condemned the Vietnam War from the early sixties on. It is likely he would have found acceptable the resolution adopted by the Assembly when it declared that "the mortal suffering of the Vietnamese people should at once be ended. The restoration of peace in Vietnam is of paramount importance to our member churches concerned as they are that mankind shall live reconciled in justice and peace." The resolution claimed that it was intolerable that Vietnam was the "symbol for our time of the misery of a developing people caught in world conflict."[21] King had indeed seen the racist nature of the Vietnam War, and he sought to resolve that and other international conflicts by peaceful means. The Uppsala program addressed both issues.

19. Rev. William A. Cooper, Earlham College, Richmond, Indiana letter to Eugene Carson Blake (September 11, 1968), 42.11.08/2, WCC General Secretariat, Correspondence Frequent 1938–1970, WCC, Geneva, Switzerland.

20. Eugene Carson Blake and Ernest A. Payne letter (July 6, 1968), 42.11.03, WCC General Secretariat, Correspondence Frequent 1938–1970, WCC, Geneva, Switzerland.

21. "Resolution on Vietnam," adopted by the Fourth Assembly, Uppsala, Sweden, July 4–14, 1968, Asia/Vietnam (not sorted), 41.3.115/5, WCC General Secretariat, WCC, Geneva, Switzerland.

THE WCC'S MARTIN LUTHER KING RESOLUTION

We now explore some of the practicalities involved in implementing the WCC's Martin Luther King Resolution on Nonviolence. Dr. Beverly Woodward of the International FOR staff argued that the assassination of Dr. King in 1968 led the WCC to pass the resolution. Although King and the wider freedom movement clearly provided only partial answers to the question of achieving significant social change, Woodward nevertheless claimed, "[he] had furnished a challenge."[22] It is essential to appreciate that King believed that in order to have peace in the world, "men and nations must embrace the nonviolent affirmation that ends and means must cohere." For King, the argument was quite clear: "You can't reach good ends through evil means, because the means represent the seed and end represents the tree."[23]

In September 1968, Wilmer A. Cooper, one of three members of the ad hoc committee on the King resolution, wrote to Dr. Blake urging action to explain ways in which the WCC could promote studies on nonviolent methods of achieving social change. Blake replied that there was a new WCC Program to Combat Racism, to be launched in 1969 in response to a 1968 mandate from the Fourth Assembly. Blake went on to indicate that he was chair of the committee to implement the program, which would include study, education, and action to effect social change through Christian nonviolent methods. The recommendations were to be ready for January 1969. Blake stated that this initiative indicated that the WCC had the resolution passed "in memory of Dr. King very much in mind." In conclusion, he wrote: "there is every reason for us to find ways of calling attention to the ecumenical significance of what he did."[24]

Cooper wrote to Dr. Blake again in July 1969, and he expressed his satisfaction with the response from Archbishop Ruben Josefson and the Swedish Ecumenical Council. Cooper again urged the WCC to take action on the King resolution. The Swedish Ecumenical Council saw nonviolent methods as having potential or action relevant in three types of conflict

22. Beverly Woodward, "Violence, Nonviolence and Human Struggle" (July 25, 1976), CCIA Archives 1977, Box P.354, International Fellowship of Reconciliation, WCC, Geneva, Switzerland.

23. King, *Trumpet of Conscience*, 70–71.

24. Eugene Carson Blake letter to Rev. William A. Cooper, Birmingham, England, (October 28, 1968), 42.11.08/2, WCC General Secretariat, Correspondence: Frequent 1938–1970, WCC, Geneva. At the time, Cooper was on sabbatical from Earlham School of Religion, Richmond, Indiana.

situations: to achieve social change in countries in Africa, Asia, and Latin America; to achieve social change in Europe and North America; and as a means of national defense against foreign aggression. Cooper was aware that the WCC was having difficulty in acquiring sufficient funding to get a program up and running. He suggested that some of the work could be farmed out to regional study groups in Bangalore or Rio Plate.[25]

KING, THE WCC, AND RACIAL JUSTICE ISSUES

Martin Luther King's use of nonviolent actions to dismantle segregation highly impressed the WCC, whose own limited efforts around this issue up to that point seemed grossly inadequate. As suggested earlier, the elimination of racism in the United States and worldwide was of primary importance to King. However, when asked for his opinion in March 1968 on the state of the civil rights movement, King confirmed that he saw the most powerful nation still staggering in confusion and bewilderment.[26] For its part, the WCC had been considering action on racism, and as early as 1954 had opposed racism based on race, color, or ethnic origin.

On March 21, 1960, South African police opened fire against demonstrators who were protesting against bylaws at the township of Sharpeville in the Transvaal. At least 69 black people were killed and 180 injured. In December 1960, the WCC convened a consultation with member churches in South Africa at Cottesloe, Johannesburg. In their response to the Sharpeville Massacre, delegates noted that in a period of rapid social change, the church had a special responsibility "for fearless witness within society." The WCC called for an enlightened response by the South African government to make the country more inclusive.[27] This resolution was too much for the Afrikaner Church to accept, and its members left the WCC after the consultation. The same theme was discussed at the New Delhi Assembly in 1961. The WCC called on Christians to encourage and support all efforts to bring about change through nonviolent means in order to construct a society permeated by justice and reconciliation. It was emphasized that

25. Ibid.

26. Washington, *Testament of Hope*, 313–14.

27. WCC Statements and Actions on Racism, 1948–1979, Program to Combat Racism, 4223.16.3, WCC, Geneva, Switzerland. For King's response to the Sharpeville Massacre, see Martin Luther King, Jr. letter to Claude Barnett (March 24, 1960), in Clayborne Carson et al., eds., *The Papers of Martin Luther King, Jr.*, vol. 5, *Threshold of a New Decade, January 1959–December 1960* (Berkeley: University of California Press, 2005) 399–400.

everyone has a unique contribution to make to the fellowship of human society; therefore, there was no reason for divided loyalties and efforts. The WCC statement found the expression "separate but equal" a contradiction in terms, for it was only "in community with others of diverse gifts that persons or communities can give of their best."[28] This was a direct indictment of U.S. practice at the time. Citing the two main players in the battle against apartheid, the WCC proclaimed, "We remind ourselves that the references to South Africa and the United States present a challenge to all our consciences, to do in our cities and churches all that we should for racial justice and Christian fellowship."[29]

The importance of the WCC's putting the United States in the same category as South Africa was far-reaching. To improve racial relations, the WCC accepted that the solution demanded radical change "in long established patterns of thought and action." Racism was again brought to the fore at the Mindolo Consultation (Zambia, 1964) when the WCC highlighted black awareness of white indifference to the plight of the oppressed in southern Africa. The question of violence became a very serious dilemma for many black Africans. As all peaceful measures tried by African political organizations over a period of many years to bring about an ordered change proved abortive, only one avenue remained open—that of violence. Those attending the consultation felt that if the urgency of the situation were not recognized, violence would increase.[30]

Then in 1966 the Conference on Church and Society laid the foundation for the Program to Combat Racism when delegates resolved the following: "It is not enough for churches and groups to condemn the sin of racial arrogance and oppression. The struggle for racial change in structures will inevitably bring suffering and will demand costly and bitter engagement." Dr. Blake accepted that the conference laid the foundation for a program to combat racism, but the consultation had no legislative power. Blake further reinforced his view of a role for the churches, to prevent them from becoming "merely a religious embroidery on a materialistic culture." He saw it as an imperative to show leadership to the rank and file and represent to them "what we understand the Gospel of Jesus coming into the world means."[31]

28. WCC Statement and Actions on Racism, 1948–1979.

29. Ibid.

30. Ibid.

31. Blake, transcript of interview, December 25, 1966, in *Face the Nation*, 995.103/14, WCC General Secretariat, WCC, Geneva, Switzerland.

As an answer to the racial crisis, Dr. King had already relayed this message on several occasions. As early as 1958, King had preached that "another thing the church can do to make the principle of brotherhood a reality is to keep men's minds and visions centered on God."[32] In 1968, however, the WCC accepted at Uppsala that "words and pious statements over many years were no longer enough."[33]

I contend that the successful campaigns of Dr. King and the civil rights movement inspired the WCC Consultation on Racism held in London on May 19–20, 1969. The adoption of the Martin Luther King Resolution on Nonviolence at Uppsala showed the commitment of the WCC to King's nonviolent methods and was no doubt a stimulus for this consultation. Therefore, this consultation had as a backdrop the Christian socialist principles promulgated by King for the eradication of injustice and the creation of the "beloved community." On November 14, 1966, at Frogmore, South Carolina, Dr. King, in a groundbreaking speech, called for "a restructuring of the very architecture of American society." He added that he was not going to be pigeonholed by advocating that "America move toward a Democratic Socialism" or that "we must be Communist or Marxist." Furthermore, he said, "God never intended for some of his children to live in inordinate superfluous wealth while others live in abject deadening poverty."[34]

Dr. King was no stranger to London when he stopped over during his trip to Oslo, Norway, where he received the Nobel Peace Prize in December 1964. King criticized Britain's immigration policy toward commonwealth citizens when he warned, "Immigration laws based on color were totally out of keeping with the laws of God and with the trends of the twentieth century."[35] King also called for economic sanctions against South Africa, for he believed the situation could not be ignored. In November 1967, King visited the University of Newcastle, where he received the honorary degree of Doctor of Civil Law. During the gathering, he expounded his views, asserting that "more and more I have come to realize that racism is a world problem."

---

32. Martin Luther King, Jr., "The Church and the Race Crisis" (October 8, 1958), King Center Library and Archives; and Lewis V. Baldwin, *The Voice of Conscience: The Church in the Mind of Martin Luther King, Jr.* (New York: Oxford University Press, 2010) 90 and 292 n. 201.

33. WCC Statements and Actions on Racism, 1948–1979.

34. Martin Luther King, Jr., Speech at Frogmore, South Carolina (November 14, 1966), King Center Library and Archives; Martin Luther King, Jr., "The Church and the Race Crisis," *Christian Century* 75.41 (October 8, 1958) 1141.

35. *The Times*, July 12, 1964, 6.

"There are three urgent and indeed great problems that we face, not only in the United States but all over the world today. That is the problem of racism, the problem of poverty and the problem of war," he stated. King was adamant that the world would never rise to its full moral, political, or even social maturity until racism was totally eradicated.[36] While it is accepted that whites in general exploited people of color throughout the world, a very important admission was made by the WCC as part of the rationale for an Ecumenical Program to Combat Racism: "We have also sadly to confess that churches have participated in racial discrimination. Many religious institutions have benefited from racially exploitative economic systems."[37]

The format of the Program to Combat Racism Consultation at Notting Hill in London was to invite forty-five participants, including four Roman Catholics, to meet with a group of twenty-five consultants who ranged from radical to conservative, persons who could be regarded as experts resulting from study and personal experience in racial conflict worldwide. Dr. Blake concluded that the final report would include attitudes and positions that challenged Christian assumptions and even the Christian faith at its depths.[38] The program was initiated to commit Christians to end discrimination based on race; to end the exploitation of man by man based on feelings of superiority; and, finally, to help the churches in the understanding of the Christian mission. Blake made it clear that race relations and racial understanding was a local responsibility everywhere; however, the WCC had a world responsibility to address these matters for two reasons. First, he saw race relations as part of the international problem of justice and peace. Second, he believed a world perspective could make a contribution to specific local racial confrontations and was required especially in those monoracial communities or nations where it is often believed that there is no problem of racism.[39]

The Notting Hill Consultation was chaired by George McGovern, a U.S. senator from North Dakota. He was moved by "a memorable and significant experience in human dynamics marked by love and anger, hope and despair." McGovern concluded that the central theme running throughout

36. World Speeches by the public orator and Dr. Martin Luther King, Jr. at a special Honorary Degree Congregation (November 13, 1967), University of Newcastle Archives.

37. WCC Statements and Actions on Racism 1948–1979.

38. WCC Program to Combat Racism, May 19–24, 1969, 4223.1.02, Notting Hill Consultation, WCC, Geneva, Switzerland.

39. WCC Program to Combat Racism, History of the Program to Combat Racism, 4223.17.1, WCC, Geneva, Switzerland.

the deliberations and recommendations of the consultation was that if racism was to be eliminated, it would require more than the private commitment of individual Christians: "Indeed, the entire church must be committed to an action program on a broad social, economic and political front aimed at the eradication of institutional racism in the society of man."[40]

South Africa was accorded particular attention, given its ruthless reputation on apartheid. Indeed, this was further consolidated in the consultation where it was recorded that the role of international finance in reinforcing racist regimes in southern Africa gave them a false sense of power and security through trade, investments, bank loans, and the role of gold in the international monetary system. It was further argued that racial discrimination and the police state stood in direct challenge to the ecumenical movement, and both were to be resisted; the churches in the ecumenical movement gave an absolute "no" to both of these phenomena. Thus, the WCC addressed problems at Notting Hill, London, where it was stated that as the developed Western and so-called Christian countries of the world obtained their wealth from centuries of exploitation, they now had a moral obligation to make restitution through the transfer of these material resources.[41]

Dr. King shared an analysis similar to that of the WCC on why there existed such global inequities, which led to war, poverty, and injustice. King insisted that "America today suffers from a kind of poverty of the spirit which stands in glaring contrast to her scientific and technological abundance.... We have learned to fly the air like birds and swim the sea like fish, but we have not learned the simple act of walking the earth like brothers."[42]

KING AND THE WCC: A FINAL WORD

In summary, the message of both the WCC and Dr. Martin Luther King, Jr. was clear—namely, that the churches as the chief moral guardians of the community had a responsibility to broaden horizons, challenge the status

40. World Council of Churches, Consultation on Racism, 4223.1.03, Notting Hill Consultation, WCC, Geneva, Switzerland.

41. WCC Consultation on Racism, Towards the Eradication of Racism, Program to Combat Racism, Notting Hill Consultation, 4223.1.02, Box II 6, Consultation Papers, WCC Geneva, Switzerland.

42. Martin Luther King, Jr., "Beyond Discovery, Love," address delivered at the International Convention of Christian Churches, Dallas, Texas (September 25, 1966), King Center Library and Archives; and Washington, *Testament of Hope*, 209.

quo, and change mores when necessary.[43] King and the WCC worked in tandem in seeking an end to both the war in Vietnam and racism. Both acknowledged a connection between racism, poverty, and militarism, and they accepted that the consequences were stark for the United States and the world if appropriate action was not taken. The Notting Hill Consultation called on the WCC to take action to tackle inequalities. The church had to realize that in the institutional world, "the closest approximation to love possible is justice."[44] Therefore, the WCC should decide on the application of economic sanctions against corporations and institutions that practiced blatant racism. Further, WCC member churches should lobby their governments for similar action. It was necessary for the WCC to support and encourage "reparations" to exploited peoples and countries, while acknowledging the churches' own involvement in the exploitation.[45] The WCC Central Committee made three major policy decisions in their Program to Combat Racism. First, members called for withdrawal of investments from South Africa. Second, they requested an end to bank loans to the South African government. Third, they asked for the termination of white emigration to South Africa. In addition, the WCC itself sold its holdings in corporations investing in South Africa, totaling 1.5 million in U.S. dollars.[46]

Dr. King would have been pleased with the decisions made at Notting Hill in 1969, a year after his untimely death. King was certainly aware of the changing world order when, in September 1966, he told his audience at the International Convention of Christian Churches where the future lay: "Those who have been on the oppressor end of the old order must go into the new age which is emerging with a deep sense of penitence, love and understanding. They must search their souls to be sure that they have moved . . . away from the deadening idea of white supremacy."[47]

43. Baldwin, *Voice of Conscience*, 51–100.

44. World Council of Churches Report on the WCC-Sponsored Consultation on Racism held in Notting Hill, London, May 19–24 1969, 4223.1.03/1, WCC, Geneva, Switzerland.

45. Ibid.

46. WCC Program to Combat Racism, History of PCR, 4223.17.1, WCC, Geneva, Switzerland.

47. King, "Beyond Discovery, Love." For a similar remark made more than a decade earlier, see Martin Luther King, Jr., "The Vision of a World Made New," in Clayborne Carson et al., eds., *The Papers of Martin Luther King, Jr., Volume 4: Advocate of the Social Gospel, September 1948–March 1963* (Berkeley: University of California Press, 2007) 181–84.

5

Forging Bonds and Obligations

*The Fellowship of Reconciliation, Nonviolence,
and Martin Luther King, Jr.*[1]

Paul R. Dekar

You don't have to ride Jim Crow,
You don't have to ride Jim Crow,
On June the 3rd
The High court said
When you ride interstate Jim Crow is dead,
You don't have to ride Jim Crow.[2]

---

1. This chapter draws on Paul R. Dekar, *Creating the Beloved Community: A Journey with the Fellowship of Reconciliation* (Telford, PA: Cascadia, 2005).

2. Johnny Carr, Donald Coan, Doreen Curtis, A. C. Thompson, and Bayard Rustin wrote this verse for the Journey of Reconciliation, discussed in this chapter.

INTRODUCTION

Early in the twentieth century, many African Americans challenged segregation in the South and all forms of racism in the United States. They recognized the importance of Gandhi's nonviolent movement for Indian independence for their own efforts to create the beloved community, the phrase by which Dr. Martin Luther King, Jr. articulated his dream of a society in which people respect differences, address conflicts nonviolently, dismantle oppressive structures, and live in harmony with the earth. Nurtured by diverse spiritual traditions that foster compassion, solidarity, and reconciliation, many African Americans traveled to India to meet Gandhi and other nonviolent activists. Gandhi inspired them and urged that they return to the United States to apply what they had learned in India in their work at home for social change.[3]

W. E. B. Du Bois (1868–1963), cofounder of the National Association for the Advancement of Colored People (NAACP) and editor of its journal, *The Crisis*, visited Gandhi in India. He subsequently developed ideas like truth force (*satyagraha*), the sacredness of all living creatures, nonviolent struggle for justice (*ahimsa*), and universal uplift (*sarvodaya*) in the movement to effect significant social change in the South. He insisted that only fair means can produce fair ends.[4]

Two Fellowship of Reconciliation (FOR) publications bridged Christian pacifism and North American activism and served as organizing manuals for the freedom movement. These were Richard B. Gregg's *The Power of Nonviolence* (1935), for which King wrote the foreword of a 1959 reprint edition, and *Nonviolence in an Aggressive World* (1940), by A. J. Muste (1885–1967), head of the FOR from 1940–1953. In his essay "Pilgrimage to Nonviolence," Dr. King mentioned FOR as crucial in his appropriation

---

3. Mark Shepard, *Gandhi Today: A Report on Mahatma Gandhi's Successors* (Arcata, CA: Simple Productions, 1987). M. K. Gandhi, *An Autobiography: The Story of My Experiments with Truth*, trans. Mahadev Desai (Boston: Beacon, 1957) 299; Gandhi, *Satyagraha in South Africa*, trans. Valji Govindji Desai, rev. ed. (Ahmedabad: Navajivan, 1950) 86–107; also, S. Chabot, "Submerged Diffusion and the African American Adoption of the Gandhian Repertoire," *Passages* 3 (2001) 32–56; John Vijay Prashad, "The Influence of Gandhi on the American Nonviolence Movement," http://www.littleindia.com/India/march02/ahimsa.htm; Sudarshan Kapur, *Raising Up a Prophet: The African American Encounter with Gandhi* (Boston: Beacon, 1992).

4. Ramashray Roy, *Self and Society: A Study in Gandhian Thought* (New Delhi: Sage, 1985) 167, cites *War without Violence: The Sociology of Gandhi's Satyagraha* (1939) by Gandhian Krishnalal Shridharani (1911–1960).

of Gandhian nonviolence and as an ally in the struggle for racial justice in the United States.[5] The balance of this essay explores FOR's role in the movement.

EARLY *FOR* EFFORTS AGAINST RACISM

FOR began in England on August 7, 1914, and in the United States in 1915. FOR grew out of Christian nonresistance, socialism, and social gospel teaching. The founders resolved as follows:

1. That Love, as revealed and interpreted in the life and death of Jesus Christ, involves more than we have yet seen, that it is the only power by which evil can be overcome, and the only sufficient basis of human society.

2. That, to establish a world-order based on love, it is incumbent upon those who believe in this principle to accept it fully, both for themselves and in their relation to others, and to take the risks involved in doing so in a world which does not as yet accept it.

3. That, therefore, as Christians, we are forbidden to wage war, and that our loyalty to our country, to humanity, to the Church Universal, and to Jesus Christ, our Lord and Master, calls us instead to a life service for the enthronement of Love in personal, social, commercial and national life.

4. That the Power, Wisdom and Love of God stretch far beyond the limits of our present experience, and that He is ever waiting to break forth into human life in new and larger ways.

5. That since God manifests Himself in the world through men and women, we offer ourselves to Him for his redemptive purpose, to be used by Him in whatever way He may reveal to us.[6]

The current Statement of Purpose reads as follows:

> The Fellowship of Reconciliation is composed of women and men who recognize the essential unity of all creation and have joined

5. Martin Luther King, Jr., *Stride Toward Freedom: The Montgomery Story* (San Francisco: Harper & Row, 1958) 96–97. Dekar, *Creating the Beloved Community.*

6. Jill Wallis, *Valiant for Peace: A History of the Fellowship of Reconciliation, 1914–1989* (London: Fellowship of Reconciliation, 1991) 7–8. Wallis focuses on the Fellowship of Reconciliation in England.

together to explore the power of love and truth for resolving human conflict. While it has always been vigorous in its opposition to war, FOR has insisted equally that this effort must be based on a commitment to the achieving of a just and peaceful world community, with full dignity and freedom for every human being.[7]

FOR was one vehicle of pacifism. In England in 1914, various libertarians and socialists formed the No Conscription Fellowship, which later became War Resisters' International (WRI).

Congress enacted conscription during World War I, World War II, the Korean War, and the war in Vietnam. FORUSA and WRI provided alternatives for conscientious objectors who served their country by means other than bearing arms. FOR's first generation also witnessed against conditions that generate war, including racism. FOR's first executive secretary, Edward F. Evans, visited "colored Harlem" and urged Christians to give attention to the race problem. Paul Jones succeeded Evans in 1919 and stressed that pacifism be related not to war alone, but to every aspect of life. Jones called for training in methods designed to eliminate conditions that engender racial hatred and violence and to promote racial inclusiveness.[8]

FOR activists organized interracial seminars and published newsletters with articles that adapted Gandhian ideas in their struggle for racial equality. In the 1920s, George "Shorty" Collins (1892–1991), Baptist minister on FOR's staff, was traveling field secretary especially in the area of race relations. In 1924, he toured Southern colleges and universities, where he advocated racial equality and integration of segregated campuses. In 1925, along with Juliette Derricotte, an African American Dean of Women at Fisk University, he represented FOR at a National Interracial Conference. His witness attracted people like Howard Thurman (1900–1981), for whom Collins represented "a radically new spirit in the relations between the races. It was through Shorty that I received confirmation of the fact that meaningful shared experiences among people are more binding than ideology or creed."[9]

7. See http://forusa.org/about/sop.

8. Edward F. Evans, "Christianity and the Race Problem," 1919. Swarthmore College's Peace Collection (SCPC) houses FOR's papers. Document Group [DG] 13, Section II, Series E, Box 16, General and Miscellaneous Papers; and John Dillingham, "Our Racial Caste System," *Fellowship* 2 (1936) 5.

9 In 1971Collins received the American Baptist Dahlberg Prize. Obituary, *Fellowship* 57 (June 1991) 23; Paul R. Dekar, *For the Healing of the Nations: Baptist Peacemakers* (Macon, GA: Smyth & Helwys, 1993).

Collins was the first of a succession of FOR staff working in the South. Howard Kester (1904–1977) succeeded him. Kester initiated interracial conferences and camps for African American children in Mississippi.[10] Kester left FOR's staff to head two change organizations: the Southern Tenant Farmers' Union and the Fellowship of Southern Churchmen. His successors in the role of southern secretary included Constance H. Rumbaugh and James Morris Lawson, Jr.

Rumbaugh was the third woman appointed to a FOR executive staff position. Before taking up her duties with FOR, she served southern Methodism in several home and overseas positions. Joining FOR staff on a half-time basis, she devoted the other half of her time to promoting a cooperative farm in Mississippi as a step in addressing the needs of sharecroppers.[11]

Born in Pennsylvania in 1928, Lawson refused to take either a student or ministerial deferment when conscripted during the Korean War. He served fourteen months in prison. After his release in 1953, he spent three years in Nagbur, India, where he studied Gandhi's life and principles, thereby preparing himself for the impelling intellectual, moral, and spiritual power that he and Martin Luther King, Jr. would receive from each other less than a decade later.

In 1955, Lawson returned to the United States and enrolled at the Graduate School of Theology in Oberlin, Ohio. He then moved to Nashville, Tennessee, where he also enrolled at the Divinity School of Vanderbilt University. As southern director of the Congress of Racial Equality (CORE), Lawson mentored students at Vanderbilt University, at the historic black institution Fisk University, and at other area institutions. Diane Nash, James Bevel, Bernard Lafayette, Marion Barry, John Lewis, and other participants in Lawson's workshops on nonviolent direct action challenged segregation by initiating sit-ins at Nashville stores.

As a result of these activities, Vanderbilt University expelled Lawson. Lawson became FOR's southern secretary. In 2006, Vanderbilt finally apologized for its treatment of Lawson. Lawson then served as a member

10. Oral history interview with Howard Kester, July 22, 1974. Online: http://crdl. usg.edu/people/k/kester_howard_1904_1977/. See also Howard Kester, *Revolt among the Sharecroppers* (New York: Covici, 1936) and Robert Francis Martin, *Howard Kester and the Struggle for Social Justice in the South, 1904–1977* (Charlottesville: University of Virginia Press, 1991).

11. Letter dated January 14, 1939, SCPC DG 13 Section II, Series A, Box 6, "Southern States." John M. Swomley, Jr., refers to the camps for "Negro" children in Mississippi in a draft "FOR History." SCPC DG 13 Section II, Series A-1, Box 2.

of its faculty for a few years, and he has been the recipient of many awards and honors from that institution.

From 1962–1974, Lawson served as pastor of Centenary Methodist Church in Memphis, Tennessee. To support striking sanitation workers, Lawson invited Dr. King to Memphis, where an assassin murdered King on April 4, 1968. In any case, Memphis actually became the focal point of the strongest joint effort between Lawson and King in the interest of civil rights, and especially economic justice concerns.

Other brilliant African Americans played key roles in FOR's emerging leadership of racial change, including James L. Farmer, Jr. (1920–1999),[12] one of the founders of CORE, and Bayard Rustin (1912–1987), who became head of WRI. Both of these men would also associate with Dr. King in a number of freedom crusades. Rustin visited India in 1948. He was a leading organizer of the March on Washington on August 28, 1963, when Dr. King gave his "I Have a Dream" speech.[13]

In the 1940s and 1950s, FOR staff members included Muste; Rustin; John M. Swomley, Jr. (1915–2010),[14] who, as FORUSA director in the 1950s, campaigned against universal military training; George Houser (b. 1916);[15] and Glenn Smiley (1910–1993). Under the influence of these figures, all of whom either supported or worked closely with King, FOR organized chapters around the country. Members focused on racism in employment, housing, and public schools, and on segregation in prisons and in the military.[16] In the legislative arena, FOR members lobbied Congress in support of an antilynching bill.

Members formed "peace teams" that conducted Race Relations Institutes in northern cities such as Boulder, Chicago, Cleveland, Dayton,

12. http://en.wikipedia.org/wiki/James_L._Farmer,_Jr.

13. http://en.wikipedia.org/wiki/Bayard_Rustin.

14. John M. Swomley, *Confronting Church and State: Memoirs of an Activist* (Amherst, NY: Humanist, 1997); Swomley, *Confronting Systems of Violence: Memoirs of a Peace Activist* (Nyack, NY: Fellowship, 1998); interview, June 1, 2002.

15. George M. Houser, *No One Can Stop the Rain: Glimpses of Africa's Liberation Struggle* (Cleveland: Pilgrim, 1989) and interview with Houser in Santa Rosa, California, on September 21, 2011. Houser highlights John Gunther (1901–1970), author of *Inside Africa* (New York: Harper, 1955), a book that fostered growing interest in the United States in Africa.

16. The military integrated Hispanics and Chinese Americans, but not Japanese Americans or African Americans. In 1948, President Harry S Truman integrated all the military services by Executive Order 9981. Filipinos served in the Navy, mainly as cooks and stewards, so their relationship differed from the experience of other ethnic groups.

Denver, and Indianapolis.[17] Beginning on Friday nights, a group would explore the reality of human unity. A scientist would demonstrate such unity in the fact that descendants of both Europe and Africa had similar blood types. This point was crucial because there were objections during World War II to the use of blood drawn from African Americans for white casualties. Saturday activities generally involved integrating establishments such as restaurants, theaters, or bowling alleys.

One day in June 1943, after a race riot in Detroit, Farmer and Swomley investigated whether FOR could help. Around 2 P.M., they entered the large Greenfield Cafeteria and proceeded though the line before anyone was aware that an African American had been served. The manager ordered a white busboy to stand beside their table. When Farmer finished eating, the busboy picked up his tray with its dishes and smashed them on the tile floor. Swomley spoke up, saying,

> What has happened to a Negro friend of mine is an illumination not only of a lack of respect for human beings, but multiplied thousands of times, is the cause of division in America, a cause of race riots and the failure to use the talents of people of color. God created us equally. We have the same organs, hearts, lungs, brain; the same physical, mental and spiritual capacities. Every war is therefore a civil war, because it is always a war against brothers and destroys something of our common heritage and humanity.

While Swomley spoke, there was dead silence. Boos and a few "bravos" followed.[18]

On another occasion, Bayard Rustin went to Boulder, where Marjie Carpenter, a white FOR member, was a student. The campus chapter of FOR organized a sit-in at the off-campus drugstore and sandwich shop. The demonstration led to making services available to everyone.

Recognizing the need to intensify resistance to racial injustice, the FOR appointed Bill Lovell as an additional field worker. Lovell organized FOR members to open up cafeterias and other public facilities on a non-discriminatory basis. James Farmer anticipated the postwar situation of the United States. As large numbers of African American veterans returned from fighting for freedom on foreign soil, they expected to be treated justly.

17. August Meier and Elliott Rudwick, *CORE: A Study in the Civil Rights Movement, 1942–1968* (Oxford: Oxford University Press, 1973).

18. Swomley, *Confronting Systems of Violence*, ch. 9; Swomley, "F.O.R.'s Early Efforts for Racial Equality," *Fellowship* 56 (1990) 7.

But Farmer and so many others knew that "no great and oppressive evil is ever truly wiped out until the people oppressed by that evil, together with their sympathizers, refuse to participate in and cooperate with that evil."[19]

Another nonviolent initiative was the Harlem Ashram. In 1940, the first white members issued a pamphlet that read,

> WE LIVE IN HARLEM BECAUSE:
>
> We regard the problem of racial justice as America's No. 1 problem in reconciliation, and most of our work concerns the Negro-white aspect of this problem.
>
> Living here makes it easy for us to contact Negro leaders.
>
> Harlem is the opinion-making center of Negro America, the Negro capital of the nation.
>
> Living here helps us who are white to get something of the "feel" of being a Negro in America.[20]

Three Christian African Americans joined the Harlem Ashram. A Hindu from India also joined the core group. The ashram included single men and women as well as families. Located at 2013 Fifth Avenue, near 125th Street, the ashram was near FOR's office at the time. Residents joined FOR, and FOR's Statement of Purpose provided a spiritual basis for the work.

The Harlem Ashram exemplified primitive Christian communism. Adopting voluntary poverty, all residents gave according to their ability and received according to their need. In prayer, each one submitted to group discipline in money matters. All gave to the common purse that portion of their income they were led to give and withdrew only what was needed. Members lived in solidarity with the wider Harlem community. They helped Southern African Americans migrating to the North find housing; investigated the use of violence by the police in strikes; created a credit union run by and for African Americans, Puerto Ricans, and other minority persons; organized neighbors into a cooperative buying club; and conducted play activities for children on the streets of African American and Puerto Rican neighborhoods.

Muriel Lester of the International Fellowship of Reconciliation (IFOR) visited the ashram and helped members develop a training course in "total pacifism." She encouraged members to "out-train the totalitarians, and to

19. "The Coming Revolt against Jim Crow," *Fellowship,* 11 (1945) 90.

20. September 9, 1942 brochure; Harlem Ashram papers; SCPC Collected Documents Group.

out-match their 'intrepidity, contempt for comfort, surrender of private interest, obedience to command' with a superior courage, frugality, loyalty and selflessness." One of the founders, Jay Holmes Smith, explained, "If we are not to go off 'half-cocked' in our nonviolent direct action campaigns, we must get the benefit of study of the history of such action and the best thought of pacifist sages, past and present."[21]

Harlem Ashram members organized a nonviolent direct action committee and a Free India committee. Among successful campaigns, they championed desegregation of New York City's YMCAs. In 1942, members undertook a two-week interracial pilgrimage from New York to the Lincoln Memorial in Washington, DC. Fourteen persons walked 240 miles in support of antilynching and anti-poll tax bills before Congress. On April 24, 1944, at a rally against poll taxes, FOR members distributed a broadsheet that read as follows:

> Here's our plan. Will you cooperate? We will throw a picket line around the Capitol area when the filibuster starts and we will walk as long as the senators talk. We're asking as many men and women of all races and creeds as can to make a continuous, disciplined and peaceful demonstration for the duration of the filibuster. . . . Are there 200 people to defend democracy at home and keep faith with the millions of men fighting fascism abroad?

Harlem Ashram members worked on other campaigns, including the wider March on Washington movement led by FOR member A. Philip Randolph of the Brotherhood of Sleeping Car Porters. Harlem Ashram members participated in demonstrations at the British consulate in New York City or in front of British agencies. Members promoted Puerto Rican independence, thus anticipating Martin Luther King, Jr.'s conviction that the Negro's freedom was inextricably linked to that of other peoples of color.

Another initiative concerned Irene Morgan, a twenty-seven-year-old mother of two living in Gloucester County, Virginia, who fell ill one Sunday in July 1944. An African American, she boarded a Greyhound bus for Baltimore, Maryland, to see a doctor and sat down four rows from the back of the bus in the section for "colored" people. A European American couple needed seats. The driver told Morgan to move farther back. Morgan refused. The bus driver summoned a sheriff and Morgan was arrested. Charged with resisting arrest and violating Virginia's segregation law, Morgan pleaded

21. J. Holmes Smith, "Non-violent Direct Action," *Fellowship* 7 (1941) 207.

guilty to the first charge and paid a $100 fine. She pleaded not guilty to the second charge. Found guilty, Morgan was fined $10. She refused to pay. Years later she explained, "When something's wrong, it's wrong. It needs to be corrected."[22]

The U.S. Supreme Court ultimately heard Morgan's case. On June 3, 1946, the court ruled that Virginia's law enforcing segregation in interstate travel on buses was illegal. However, the Supreme Court did not strike down all Jim Crow state laws. It only prohibited segregation on interstate buses and trains. The Morgan decision was later applied to interstate train travel, a significant outcome that sparked other efforts to desegregate busing and education in the South, including the 1954 *Brown v. Board of Education* decision and the Montgomery bus protest, during which Dr. King would be catapulted to national and international fame.

THE JOURNEY OF RECONCILIATION (1947)[23]

Long before King emerged to prominence, FOR members persistently used nonviolent strategies to challenge segregation in interstate travel. One initiative was to organize Freedom Rides in the United States. In 1945, George Houser and Bayard Rustin, who together had succeeded Farmer in the race relations position, proposed an action that became the most daring FOR and CORE undertaking: the Journey of Reconciliation.

The idea was to test whether bus and train companies would honor the Morgan decision. The journey would also test the reaction of bus drivers, passengers, and police. Finally, participants sought to develop techniques to deal creatively with conflict situations.

Over time, Houser and Rustin floated several ideas, developed action plans, and engendered debate. While the NAACP was prepared to offer legal assistance, in principle it opposed this kind of direct action. Thurgood

22. Lea Setegn, "Irene Morgan," *Richmond Times-Dispatch*, February 13, 2002. Pauli Murray, *States' Laws on Race and Color* (Cincinnati: Woman's Division of Christian Service, 1951).

23. September 17, 1946, SCPC DG 13, Section II, Series A-4, Racial-Industrial Department, 1943–47. George Houser and Bayard Rustin, *We Challenged Jim Crow! A Report on the Journey of Reconciliation, April 9–23, 1947* (New York: FOR and CORE, 1948). A gifted musician, Rustin composed the song quoted at the beginning of this chapter. Also, CORE papers, Box 1, SCPC Collected Documents Group. Participants recalled the journey in a 1995 PBS documentary titled *You Don't Have to Ride Jim Crow!*, directed by journalist and filmmaker Robin Washington.

Marshall headed NAACP's legal department at the time. He warned, "a disobedience movement on the part of Negroes and their white allies, if employed in the South, would result in wholesale slaughter with no good achieved." Rustin responded in an article in the April 1, 1947, issue of *The Louisiana Weekly*:

> I am sure that Marshall is either ill-informed on the principles and techniques of nonviolence or ignorant of the process of social change.
>
> Unjust social laws and patterns do not change because supreme courts deliver just decisions. One needs merely to observe the continued practice of Jim Crow in interstate travel, six months after the Supreme Court's decision, to see the necessity of resistance. Social progress comes from struggle; all freedom demands a price.
>
> At times, freedom will demand that its followers go into situations where even death is to be faced. Resistance on the buses would, for example, mean humiliation, mistreatment by police, arrest, and some physical violence inflicted on the participants.
>
> But if anyone at this date in history believes that the "white problem," which is one of privilege, can be settled without some violence, he is mistaken and fails to realize the ends to which men can be driven to hold on to what they consider their privileges.
>
> This is why Negroes and whites who participate in direct action must pledge themselves to non-violence in word and deed. For in this way alone can the inevitable violence be reduced to a minimum.[24]

Though Houser and Rustin were prepared to include women in another test of the Supreme Court decision, they decided that only men should take part in this first freedom ride. The team included eight European Americans and eight African Americans. White participants included Houser and seven other European Americans—namely, Louis Adams, Methodist minister from North Carolina; Ernest Bromley, Methodist minister from North Carolina; Joseph Felmet of the Southern Workers Defense League; Homer Jack, Executive Secretary of the Chicago Council Against Racial and Religious Discrimination; James Peck, editor of the Workers Defense League *News Bulletin*; Igal Roodenko, New York horticulturist; and Worth Randle, Cincinnati biologist. In addition to Rustin, African American volunteers included Dennis Banks, Chicago musician; Andrew Johnson,

24. See Jervis Anderson, *Bayard Rustin: Troubles I've Seen: A Biography* (New York: HarperCollins, 1997) 115; Raymond Arsenault, *Freedom Riders: 1961 and the Struggle for Justice* (Oxford: Oxford University Press, 2006) 37.

Cincinnati student; Conrad Lynn, New York attorney; Wallace Nelson, freelance lecturer; Eugene Stanley of A. and T. College, Greensboro, North Carolina; William Worthy of the New York Council for a Permanent Fair Employment Practices Commission; and Nathan Wright, a church social worker from Cincinnati.

Houser and Rustin described what followed:

> From April 9–23, 1947, an interracial group of men, traveling as a deputation team, visited fifteen cities in Virginia, North Carolina, Tennessee, and Kentucky. More than thirty speaking engagements were met before church, NAACP, and college groups. The Morgan decision was explained and reports made on the buses and trains in the light of this decision. The response was most enthusiastic.[25]

In the last line, it would be appropriate to substitute "sometimes" for "most." Several times on the journey officials arrested members.

In a North Carolina court, Judge Henry Whitfield found that Rustin and Andrew Johnson had violated the state's Jim Crow bus statute. He sentenced them to thirty days on a chain gang, but added that he found the behavior of the European American men even more objectionable. He told Igal Roodenko and Joseph Felmet, "It's about time you Jews from New York learned that you can't come down here bringing your niggers with you to upset the customs of the South. Just to teach you a lesson, I gave your black boys thirty days, and I give you ninety."

On the buses, there were no acts of violence. At least on this occasion, police and bus drivers acted in a considerate manner. One officer, when pressed for a reason for his refusal to sit beside an African American, stated, "I'm just not Christian enough, I guess." The most extreme negative reactions were verbal, but without profanity. Typical was a young Marine who said, "The KKK [Ku Klux Klan] is coming up again, and I guess I'll join up."

The Journey of Reconciliation garnered a great deal of publicity. In their report, Houser and Rustin observed that the one word that most universally described the attitude of police and white and black bus riders was *confusion*. Most passengers were apathetic and did not register their feelings or want to get involved. African American passengers tended to follow the dominant reaction of the other riders. Generally, they showed fear first, then caution. Some were empowered and moved forward on the buses. Houser and Rustin concluded that the bus companies were attempting to circumvent the intentions of the Supreme Court in the Irene

25. Houser and Rustin, *We Challenged Jim Crow!*.

Morgan decision by a reliance on state laws, company regulations, and subtle pressures.

The Journey of Reconciliation was remarkable in many ways. It exposed the need for nonviolent direct action, without which the Jim Crow pattern in the South would not have been broken; convinced many African Americans that they were not alone in their struggle for racial justice; and contributed to changes in the way African Americans would be treated in prison.

Nearly two years after the Journey of Reconciliation, Rustin surrendered to a court order in Hillsboro, North Carolina, to serve the thirty-day sentence the state had imposed upon him for his role in the journey; he was released after twenty-two days for good behavior. He served his time at a prison camp in Roxboro, where he wrote a series of articles. In his "Twenty-Two Days on a Chain Gang," published by the *New York Post*, Rustin reported,

> To me the most degrading condition of the job was the feeling that "I am not a person; I am a thing to be used." The men who worked us had the same attitude toward us as toward the tools we used. At times the walking bosses would stand around for hours while we worked, seeming to do nothing—just watching, often moving from foot to foot or walking from one side of the road to the other. It was under these conditions that they would select a "plaything." One boy, Oscar, was often "it." Once the bored gun guard ordered Oscar to take off his cap and dance. With a broad smile on his face, he warned Oscar, "I'll shoot your heart out if you don't." As the guard trained his rifle on Oscar's chest, Oscar took off his cap, grinned, and danced vigorously. The guard and the walking boss screamed with laughter. Later most of the crew told Oscar that they hated him for pretending that he had enjoyed the experience. But almost any of them would have reacted the same way.[26]

Rustin's account of what he saw contributed to the dismantling of this system of punishment.[27] Houser and Rustin received the Jefferson Award of the Council Against Intolerance and called for more grassroots organizing to generate a mass movement. In 1948, they initiated a Fellowship Appeal for Intergroup Reconciliation and a Pledge Brotherhood Campaign. The latter initiative enlisted thousands of individuals—more than forty

26. Bayard Rustin, *Down the Line: The Collected Writings of Bayard Rustin* (Chicago: Quadrangle, 1971) 44.

27. Ibid.

thousand in 1951 alone—who committed themselves to racial reconciliation by forming interracial campus groups, bringing a friend of another
racial group to one's place of worship, and other actions. FOR and CORE
publications gave ideas to encourage people to put their pacifist principles
into practice.

Rustin's conversations with admirers and followers of Gandhi in India
strengthened his commitment to *satyagraha*. Years later, Devi Prasad recalled, "The Dr. Martin Luther King phenomenon had not yet started, but
we got a very profound impression that Bayard was doing Gandhi's work in
North America."[28] Rustin epitomized FOR activity on behalf of civil rights
in the years prior to the rise of King, and this helps explain why Rustin
would later serve King in an advisory capacity.

Houser became convinced that the freedom struggle in the United
States had broader significance, especially for Africa. With the exception
of South Africa, Ethiopia, and Liberia, a failed state, the continent was still
under colonial rule. Houser supported the struggle against apartheid in
South Africa. He wanted to visit South Africa, but the government initially
did not grant him a visa. Nor did the British give him a visa to visit East
Africa; they were dealing with the Mau Mau uprising in Kenya. The French
government did issue Houser a visa to visit Senegal, from which he continued to Gold Coast (before it became Ghana). He met Kwame Nkrumah
(1909–1972), leader of the struggle for independence and first president of
Ghana. In Nigeria, Houser met Benjamin Nnamdi Azikiwe (1904–1996),
who in 1960 became the country's first president. Houser continued on
to Cameroon, Gabon, Congo-Kinshasa, and Angola. Ultimately, Houser
did receive a two-day clergy visa that enabled him to visit Johannesburg,
South Africa, in 1954. Among those with whom he had discussions was
Arthur Blaxall, then head of IFOR's South African office.[29] South African
police detained Houser in Port Elizabeth for being with Joe Matthews, at
the time head of the Cape branch of the African National Congress and son
of Zachariah Keodirelang "ZK" Matthews (1901–1968), a prominent black
academic then "banned" from political activity.[30]

28. Anderson, *Bayard Rustin*, 131.

29. Vera Brittain, *The Rebel Passion: A Short History of Some Pioneer Peace-makers*
(Nyack, NY: Fellowship, 1964) 195–200.

30. The government arrested Matthews in December 1956 and charged him with
treason. It withdrew the case the next year. See Nelson Mandela, *No Easy Walk to Freedom* (London: Heinemann, 1965) 261. See also Houser interview of Matthews: http://
africanactivist.msu.edu/asearch.php?keyword=z.%20k.%20matthews.

Returning to North America, Houser met with FOR staff and then took a six-month leave of absence, after which he resigned from FOR's staff. In 1953, he helped found Americans for South African Resistance (AFSAR), which later became the American Committee on Africa (ACOA); he served as its executive director from 1955 to 1981. Dr. King would also become involved with the ACOA, making financial contributions and signing appeals, petitions, letters, and declarations in support of antiaparthied efforts in South Africa and anticolonial activities throughout the African continent.

MONTGOMERY BUS BOYCOTT (1955–1957)

The 1954 Supreme Court decision in the *Brown v. Board of Education* case set the stage for a series of actions that would significantly alter the tripartite system of personal, economic, and political oppression. In Orangeburg, South Carolina, a group of African Americans petitioned for integrated schools. Glenn Smiley, FOR's national field secretary and a European American Texan by birth, went to Orangeburg to investigate. He reported that fifty-three people had signed the petition, but that all but twenty-three withdrew their names when European Americans retaliated by stopping milk and bread deliveries to the homes of petitioners, foreclosing mortgages, and taking other actions. This in turn sparked a boycott by African Americans, who refused to buy and drink milk, buy and eat bread, or purchase Coca Cola. FOR provided food and clothing to those affected.

A year later, Dr. Martin Luther King, Jr. emerged as an articulate champion of nonviolence. Several of King's closest mentors, including Howard Thurman, had studied Gandhian nonviolence. In 1935, four African Americans, including Howard Thurman and his wife, Sue Bailey, went to Burma, Ceylon (Sri Lanka), and India. Gandhi told the delegation that the greatest enemy the religion of Jesus had in India was Christianity. Hearing this, Thurman understood that Christians must do more than recite Christian ideals. He urged the group to return to the United States and apply what they had learned in India to their struggle. In 1944, he created an interracial congregation in San Francisco, the Church for the Fellowship of All Peoples, which embodied many of the ingredients of what was Thurman's and later King's ethic of love and community.

Other prominent African Americans met with Gandhi in India, including Benjamin Elijah Mays, dean of Howard University's School of Religion and future president of Morehouse College, and Dr. Channing

H. Tobias, Director of the Phelps-Stokes Foundation. Especially because of the closeness of the Thurman and Mays families to Dr. Martin Luther King, Jr., the importance of these visits by African Americans to the land of Gandhi cannot be understated. Largely because of mentors like Thurman and Mays, King knew of Gandhi before he studied at Crozer Theological Seminary and Boston University.

Two other African Americans influential in King's journey to non-violence also visited India—namely, Mordecai Wyatt Johnson (1890–1976) and James Morris Lawson, Jr. From Paris, Tennessee, Johnson studied at the University of Chicago and at Rochester Theological Seminary. There, Johnson studied the key social gospel principles of theologian Walter Rauschenbusch (1861–1918), a teacher whose writings later influenced King.

In 1926, Johnson became the first African-American president of Howard University in Washington, DC. In 1948, Johnson went to India and, upon his return, preached a sermon in Philadelphia in which he explained how Gandhi had forged *satyagraha* into a vehicle for social change. He argued that Gandhian nonviolent action could be useful in the struggle to improve race relations in the United States, and he called for the progress of all based on the idea of *sarvodaya*. King was present when Johnson spoke on Gandhi in Philadelphia in 1951.

In his essay, "Pilgrimage to Nonviolence," Dr. King wrote that Johnson's message electrified him. King left the meeting and bought half a dozen books on Gandhi, including *Gandhi: Portrayal of a Friend* (1948), by E. Stanley Jones. King later told Jones, "It was your book on Gandhi that gave me my first inkling of nonviolent noncooperation. Here, I said to myself, is the way for the Negro to achieve his freedom."[31]

After the arrest of Rosa Parks on December 1, 1955, for sitting in the white or front section of a Montgomery city bus and for refusing to move when so ordered, E. D. Nixon, district leader of the Brotherhood of Sleeping Car Porters, organized a meeting. Uneducated, he felt an action such as a boycott required other leadership. During the meeting, Nixon, after underscoring the need for courageous and uncompromising action, deferred to a relative newcomer to the city, Martin Luther King, Jr., as a potential

---

31. King, *Stride Toward Freedom*, 96; E. Stanley Jones, *A Song of Ascents: A Spiritual Autobiography* (Nashville: Abingdon, 1968) 260. King told Jones's daughter Eunice Mathews that *Portrayal* was the book that "triggered his decision to use Gandhian nonviolent methods." David Scott Cooney, "A Consistent Witness of Conscience: Methodist Nonviolent Activists, 1940–1970," PhD diss., Iliff School of Theology and the University of Denver, 2000.

leader of the boycott. King was quickly nominated for the leadership role, and he accepted with some hesitation, while declaring nonetheless that he was prepared to face the consequences of standing up to the white power structure; he got to his feet and said, "No one is going to call me a coward in public and get away with it."[32]

Early in the Montgomery boycott, FOR asked Glenn Smiley to go to Montgomery to investigate whether FOR could play a role. Smiley met Dr. King for the first time on February 14, 1956, and spent two hours alone with him. Smiley returned two weeks later. He attended meetings of the Montgomery Improvement Association and spent several hours with King, Ralph Abernathy, and other leaders. Smiley was prepared to spend a significant amount of time there. Recalling his initial meetings with King, Smiley reported that Dr. King asked him to teach movement leaders all he knew about nonviolence, to seek out others in churches and other community groups committed to nonviolence, to help build bridges between African Americans and European Americans, and to gather "intelligence" about what whites were thinking.[33]

Smiley assured Dr. King that he would assist without attempting to run the movement, and without acting as if FOR had all the answers. In a letter to John Swomley, at the time FOR's executive director, Smiley reported, "I am seeking to arrange a meeting between [Southern] liberal whites and the Improvement Association." He mentioned the Reverend Andrew Turnipseed in Mobile and the Reverend Dan Whitsett, both FOR members. Smiley continued, "The White Citizens Council has started a program to print posters for merchants to put in their windows, indicating membership in the White Citizens Council," which "will precipitate a massive buyers' strike here [by blacks] and the lines will be even more clearly drawn." Smiley indicated that "whites are scared stiff and Negroes are calm as cucumbers." He described a mass meeting with "2,500 people laughing, crying, moaning, shouting, and singing. . . . Not once was there an expression of hatred toward whites."[34]

In February, the executive committee of FOR's governing board made the following recommendation:

32. Swomley, *Confronting Systems of Violence*, 111; Richard Deats, *Martin Luther King, Jr.: Spirit-Led Prophet: A Biography* (New York: New City, 1999) 43–52. Swomley and Deats both served as FOR staff.

33. "Smiley Tapes: Training in Nonviolence," FOR headquarters, Nyack, New York (c. 1990).

34. Swomley, *Confronting Systems of Violence*, 113.

The role of the FOR in the South might be to contribute to the following:

1.) Maintaining the solidarity of those who resist segregation;

2.) Building and maintaining communication, especially where it has been interrupted;

3.) Encouraging the church to give stronger leadership for integration by:

   a.) FOR might get a group of distinguished clergymen to send a letter to ministerial associations in the South urging them to merge or integrate white and Negro associations;

   b.) FOR should ask a staff member or bring someone on to the staff temporarily to keep in touch with the situation in Montgomery, Tuscaloosa and Birmingham, Alabama [where there were also civil rights efforts and repression of blacks]; and Orangeburg, South Carolina;

   c.) FOR might set up a workshop or institute somewhere in Tennessee such as Nashville, to which whites and Negroes from the Deep South might come to discuss and work out how to be militant and at the same time not break communication.[35]

An African American member of FOR's staff, Wilson Riles, joined Smiley along with a support committee that included Margaret McCulloch, a white professor teaching at an African American college in Memphis, and Clarence Jordan, cofounder of the interracial Koinonia Community in Georgia. Regrettably, Bayard Rustin was not part of these efforts. Some years earlier, Rustin had left FOR's staff after a homosexual incident. Concerned that this could become the focal point of negative publicity about and opposition to the Montgomery bus boycott, A. J. Muste sought assurances that there would be no further incidents. Given the attitudes of the day toward gay men, Rustin could extend no such guarantee.

Rustin's photograph hangs at Shadowcliff, home of FOR's national offices in Nyack, New York. FOR recently rereleased *Rustin, the Singer*, a compact disc including the words that open this chapter: "You don't have to ride Jim Crow." The songs reflect Rustin's musical interests and gifts, as well as his philosophical and spiritual contribution to the freedom movement.

---

35. Ibid.; National Council minutes, SCPC; and tapes.

During the Montgomery bus boycott, Smiley, Riles, and other FOR members assisted the campaign as they could. They raised funds, built bridges with white leaders, offered training sessions, distributed materials such as Gregg's *The Power of Nonviolence*, and publicized the movement in FOR's magazine, *Fellowship*, and in brochures and other literature. Also, FOR raised money for bombed churches and produced a film, *Walk to Freedom*, based on the Montgomery campaign.

Notably, several hundred thousand copies of a comic book titled *Martin Luther King and the Montgomery Story* circulated. It sold for ten cents a copy in English and Spanish editions. FOR recently reprinted the publication in English and Spanish. In Iran, a Farsi translation circulated, and in Egypt an Arabic translation; both were widely distributed.

FOR sought to adapt lessons from Montgomery elsewhere. A pamphlet titled "Freedom, the South, and Nonviolence" offered "a practical solution to a problem confronting the entire nation." The pamphlet summarized how nonviolent resistance operates at its best by showing how activists acted directly against the evil practices that they were protesting.

FOR members did not seek to overcome or humiliate their opponents, but rather to win them to understanding and friendship. FOR activists rejected violence of deed and of spirit. They quoted Dr. King, who insisted, "Don't ever let anyone pull you down so low as to hate them. We must use the weapon of love."[36]

Dr. King, James Lawson, Ralph Abernathy, and Dr. Charles Radford Lawrence II (1915–1986) were key African American FOR leaders. Dr. Lawrence was an eminent African American sociologist and committed Christian pacifist, as was (and still is) his wife, Margaret. An Episcopalian, he served as a lay member of the House of Deputies. For several years, he chaired that body and was only the third layperson (and the first African American) to hold that position. A champion of racial inclusion, he also appointed women to legislative leadership positions and supported the ordination of women. Dr. Lawrence succeeded at making the Episcopal Church more racially diverse. He was also an early advocate within the Episcopal Church for ending South Africa's apartheid policies. In 1985, the church voted to divest its portfolio of stock in firms continuing to work in South Africa.[37]

36. King, *Stride Toward Freedom*, 106.

37. See the Episcopal Church's description of Lawrence's activities and involvement: http://www.episcopalarchives.org/Afro-Anglican_history/exhibit/leadership/lawrence.php.

On May 12, 1956, at Morehouse College in Atlanta, Georgia, Lawrence, along with other FOR leaders—Muste, Smiley, Swomley, a Mississippi writer named Will D. Campbell (1924–2013), and Methodist pastor James Thomas—participated in a crucial meeting. Smiley wrote that of all the accomplishments of that meeting, most important was the realization that racism was a problem "that was 'ours' and not just 'mine' and it seemed to me that we began to accept individual responsibility for collective action in this field." Some years later, James Thomas, who had become the United Methodist bishop of Iowa, wrote Swomley that he had recently been on a commencement program with Dr. King's wife, Coretta Scott King:

> My mind went back to that day in 1956 when you and I met with Martin Luther King, Jr. and a number of others on the campus of Morehouse College. Your presence there was, in my judgment, crucial. I will always believe that much of what we discussed that day became a foundation for the nonviolence movement that was so effectively led by Martin during his ministry in Montgomery and Atlanta.[38]

Upon reflection, Swomley concluded that the meeting at Morehouse College was the spiritual beginning of the Southern Christian Leadership Conference (SCLC), the organization that Dr. King went on to found and lead. Its goal was no less than to "redeem the soul" of the United States, a goal also pursued, in various ways, by Rustin, Houser, Smiley, and many others who had worked with FOR.

At the successful conclusion of the Montgomery bus boycott, Alfred Hassler, editor of *Fellowship*, invited Dr. King to send a statement acknowledging the role of FOR, and specifically of Glenn Smiley, in the bus boycott that FOR could use in its fund-raising efforts. King declined. He wrote that "if we do it for one, we will be faced with the problem of having to do it for all." Hassler responded with understanding, acknowledging that "we have all felt it has been a privilege to have participated to the degree that we have been able in your movement and our only concern was to let our members know that this participation had been of some significance."[39]

---

38. Bishop James S. Thomas to John Swomley (n.d.), housed at FOR headquarters, Nyack, New York.

39. Martin Luther King, Jr., letter to Alfred Hassler in Clayborne Carson et al., eds., *The Papers of Martin Luther King, Jr.*,vol. 4, *Symbol of the Movement, January 1957–December 1958* (Berkeley: University of California Press, 1997) 111.

Nonetheless, in 1958, Dr. King joined FOR. He signed the Statement of Purpose with its revolutionary vision of a world of justice, peace, and freedom. From 1958–1968, King was on the national advisory committee. He supported many FOR campaigns by agreeing to sign petitions, broadsides, and calls for action that appeared in leading newspapers. As the war in Vietnam escalated, King became a leading voice among its opponents. He came under constant surveillance by the Federal Bureau of Investigation; J. Edgar Hoover called the civil rights leader "a traitor to his country and to his race."[40]

Dr. King took a special interest in Africa and in 1962 cochaired, with Zulu chief Albert Luthuli, the campaign "An Appeal for Action against Apartheid," which called for December 10—Human Rights Day—to be a day of worldwide protest against the apartheid regime in South Africa. Three years later, on December 10, 1965, Dr. King was keynote speaker at a Human Rights Day rally at Hunter College in New York, during which he gave his longest public proclamation against South African apartheid.[41]

REFLECTIONS

Where do habits of peace rather than fear, of love rather than hate, come from? A story from Gandhi's youth shows how an ordinary person inculcated positive values in himself.

Arun Gandhi, one of the Mahatma's grandchildren, shared that as a boy, Gandhi was rambunctious. This led his parents to retain Rumbha, an unlettered woman, as a nanny. Young Gandhi formed an attachment to her that continued into his mature years. Realizing that Gandhi was afraid of real or imagined dangers, Rumbha told stories from sacred texts and Indian history and gave Gandhi a talisman. She advised him that, when afraid, he should chant the name of Rama, a popular Hindu deity. She assured him this would help relieve his fear.

Gandhi used the name of Rama as a mantra. He repeated it every time he was overwhelmed with fear. He found this extremely comforting, not simply because it was the name of Rama that he was repeating, but because the exercise of repeating the name of someone in whom he had faith distracted him from any object of fear. As Gandhi grew and enlarged the scope

---

40. Deats, *Spirit-Led Prophet*, 119.

41. Houser, *No One Can Stop the Rain*, 266. For King's involvement in the anti-apartheid movement, see Lewis V. Baldwin, *Toward the Beloved Community: Martin Luther King, Jr. and South Africa* (Cleveland: Pilgrim, 1995) 32–40.

of his vision for a different world, he believed the mantra could be the name of anyone or anything in which a person had faith.[42]

What impresses me about this story is how an ordinary person, Rumbha, helped Gandhi overcome fear and in turn shaped Gandhi's lifelong pursuit of *satyagraha* through nonviolent action, or *ahimsa*. Largely, those who joined Gandhi in his Salt March and other campaigns were people of remarkable courage, uncowed like Rumbha in the face of powerful opposition.

Elsewhere, remarkable people have similarly said *no* to fear and *yes* to peace. For example, the protests of the Mothers of the Plaza de Mayo—Argentine women whose children disappeared under a military dictatorship between 1976 and 1983 contributed to Argentina's return to democracy. Workers who formed the Solidarity movement in Poland in 1980 faced Soviet tanks, claimed their rights, and in 1989 contributed to the collapse of the Soviet empire.

To say *no* to fear and *yes* to peace is no guarantee that one will not suffer. In 1968, Dr. Martin Luther King, Jr., who championed nonviolent campaigns in Montgomery, Birmingham, and elsewhere during the mid-twentieth century, went to Memphis, Tennessee, on behalf of striking sanitation workers. There, on April 4, 1968, an assassin murdered Dr. King. But his dream of a global beloved community did not die with him. Two months later, on June 19, over fifty thousand people gathered at the Lincoln Memorial in Washington, DC, to conclude the Poor People's Campaign that Dr. King had helped organize.

FOR was but one player both in the background to the civil rights movement of the 1950s and 1960s and in confronting the United States—and indeed the world—with the need to address basic economic, political, and social problems that could no longer be ignored. Not every campaign was a success, and although the era was by no means free of violence, there could have been far more violence, especially by resisters, than was the case, thanks to the nonviolent initiatives of peace and justice activists.

On November 10, 1998, the General Assembly of the United Nations proclaimed the first decade of the twenty-first century and the third millennium (2001–2010) as the International Decade for the Promotion of a Culture of Peace and Non-Violence for the Children of the World.[43] The

42. Arun Gandhi, "Who Influenced Gandhi?," in *Nonviolence for the Third Millennium: Its Legacy and Future*, ed. G. Simon Harak (Macon, GA: Mercer University Press, 2000) 15.

43. For the text of the resolution adoped by the U.N. General Assembly, see http://www.undemocracy.com/A-RES-53-25.

action plan for the decade proposed eight spheres of activity in which to work for the promotion of a culture of peace: to reinforce a culture of peace through education; to promote economically and socially sustainable development; to promote the respect of all human rights; to ensure equality between women and men; to support democratic participation; to develop comprehension, tolerance, and solidarity; to support participative communication and the freedom of movement of information and knowledge; and to promote international peace and safety. One detects here echoes of the same concerns raised by Dr. King in a world context.

The General Assembly entrusted the United Nations Education, Scientific and Cultural Organization with coordination of the activities within the United Nations system to promote a culture of peace, as well as liaison with other groups. FOR produced a resource manual, "Celebrating the Decade for a Culture of Peace and Nonviolence, 2001–2010," which I used as a training tool in Memphis, Tennessee, where I lived from 1995 to 2008.

Memphis is the home of the sons and daughters of garbage collectors whose demand for a living wage in 1968 attracted Dr. King to the city. A living wage is the minimum hourly income necessary for a worker to meet basic needs such as housing, clothing, and nutrition. A living wage differs from a minimum wage in that the latter is set by law and may generally fall short of requirements of a living wage.

In 2005, full-time workers employed by the City of Memphis, and subsequently workers employed by Shelby County, formed the Workers Interfaith Network to advocate for a living wage. Then city mayor Dr. Willie Harenton and Shelby County mayor A. C. Wharton, the first African Americans elected to their respective positions, were adamant that to grant such a wage would bankrupt the city and county. Workers received threats. At stake were their jobs and their own and their families' safety. Participants in the campaign did not flinch. They did not give in to fear.

In 1995, I joined the delegation that first approached Mayor Harenton to support a living wage proposal. I indicated that I had come to Memphis with a dream, namely, that people not regard Memphis as the city where Dr. Martin Luther King, Jr. died, but rather as the city where Dr. King's dream for economic justice was increasingly becoming a reality. I proposed that the city, upon passage of a living wage ordinance, erect signs at every major point of entry into the city, including the airport, welcoming people to Memphis as a place where Dr. King's dream is alive.

The mayor greeted the living wage proposal with incredulity. Nevertheless, in 2007, the campaign came to a successful conclusion. Shelby County quickly followed. While neither the city nor the county have posted signs to this effect, full-time city and county workers have benefited tremendously. The Workers Interfaith Network has subsequently spearheaded a similar campaign to ensure that staff at the University of Memphis and other institutions of higher learning receive a living wage.

In Hamilton, Ontario, where I presently live, a Culture of Peace committee coordinates myriad activities—including recognition of September 21st as an annual International Day of Peace[44]—in six areas: respect of all life; rejection of violence; sharing with others; listening to understand; preserving the planet; and rediscovering solidarity, especially with the marginalized.

In Greece, Egypt, Gaza, Colombia, and elsewhere, a surge of nonviolent campaigns is unfolding. Those in the struggle beckon us all to strive for a better future for our children and grandchildren—saying *no* to fear and *yes* to a world at peace. A number of organizations, including FOR, employ a strategy proposed by Gandhi in the 1920s. Civilian teams from all parts of the world are targeted to work in a particular location with local people, to create safe space for nonviolent action. They engage international awareness using information nights and urgent action notices. They model cross-cultural and cross-gender cooperation.[45]

Among the many voices affirming the inspiration of Dr. King in their lives, Rosa Parks visited Hamilton, Ontario, on January 22, 1989. The occasion was a celebration of Dr. King's life organized by Stewart Memorial Church, a historic African American congregation founded by ex-slaves who came to Canada in the 1830s. Parks explained that, more than any other qualities, Dr. King made African Americans believe in themselves. King dreamed of a beloved community and encouraged leaders to carry on the work they felt called to do, and he continues to inspire nonviolent activists seeking a world free of personal, economic, and political oppression.

Similarly, author Alice Walker remembers how, during later campaigns, she went to bed praying for the safety of Dr. Martin Luther King, Jr. Each morning she awoke stronger because he was still with the movement:

---

44. See http://www.cultureofpeace.ca/values.htm.

45. Paul R. Dekar, "Protective Accompaniment in Colombia," *Baptist Peacemaker* 30 (2010) 10–11; Gianne Broughton, "Non-violent Methods for Protecting Vulnerable Populations: An Analysis of Experience, with Real-Life Examples and Directions for Encouragement" (March 2012, *Quaker Concern* 38, 2).

It was Martin King, more than any other single person, who exposed the hidden beauty of black people in the South, and caused us to look again at the land our fathers and mothers knew. The North is not for us. We will not be forced away from what is ours. Martin King, with Coretta at his side, gave the South to black people, and reduced the North to an option. And, though I realize the South belonged to me all the time, it has a newness in my eyes. I gaze down from the plane on the blood-red hills of Georgia and Alabama and finally, home, Mississippi, knowing that when I arrive the very ground may tremble and convulse, but I will walk upright, forever.[46]

Active during the Nashville sit-ins, Congressman John Lewis recently recalled:

Dr. King is responsible for me doing the things that I have done. He inspired me to act on the beliefs and values that burned within me. By his words and his deeds, he taught me that we can change the world through nonviolent protest. It was Dr. King who led me to Mohandas Gandhi, James Lawson, and a life founded on the principles of nonviolence.[47]

Martin Luther King, Jr. called love the supreme unifying principle that brings together Hindus, Muslims, Christians, Jews, Buddhists, and all people in the work of building a new world together, as Student Nonviolent Coordinating Committee militants put it. Dr. King demonstrated that this principle outweighs that which divides us. His message of goodwill and compassion toward all people can still serve to bring people together to effect healing and to overcome division, hate, and suspicion wherever they are found. As Dr. King stated in his 1964 Nobel Peace Prize lecture, "we will not build a peaceful world by following a negative path. . . . We need to make a supreme effort to generate the readiness, indeed the eagerness, to enter into the new world which is now possible, 'the city which hath foundations, whose builder and maker is God'" (Heb 11:10).

46. Alice Walker, "Coretta King: Revisited," in *In Search of Our Mothers' Gardens: Womanist Prose* (San Diego: Harcourt Brace Jovanovich, 1984) 156–57.

47. Gretchen Sullivan Sorin et al., *In the Spirit of Martin: The Living Legacy of Dr. Martin Luther King, Jr.* (Atlanta: Tinwood, 2001) 50.

6

The Hospitality of Receiving

Mahatma Gandhi, Martin Luther King, Jr., and Interreligious Learning[1]

John J. Thatamanil

You are here to find out the distress of the people of India and remove it. But I hope you are here also in a receptive mood, and if there is anything that India has to give, you will not stop your ears, you will not close your eyes, and steel your hearts, but open up your ears, eyes, and most of all your hearts to receive all that may be good in this land. . . . If I have read the Bible correctly, I know many men who have never heard the name of Jesus Christ or have even rejected the official interpretation of Christianity who will, probably, if Jesus

1. This chapter could not have been written without the support of Lewis V. Baldwin. Also of great help were email conversations with Vivek Pinto, author of *Gandhi's Vision and Values: The Moral Quest for Change in Indian Agriculture* (New Delhi: Sage, 1998). Baldwin proved to be an invaluable aid on matters pertaining to King, and Pinto on matters pertaining to Gandhi. I also owe an enormous personal and intellectual debt to Rev. James Lawson, who was one of King's close colleagues and a guide on questions of nonviolence theory and practice. I treasure our lunchtime conversations in Nashville, Tennessee, about King and the civil rights movement. Naturally, none ought to be held responsible for what remains incomplete or mistaken in these reflections.

came in our midst today in the flesh, be owned by him more than any of us. I therefore ask you to approach the problem before you with open heartedness and humility.

MAHATMA GANDHI[2]

CHRISTIAN FASCINATION WITH THE life and work of Mohandas K. Gandhi is an enduring and ongoing phenomenon. This attraction is likely rooted in Gandhi's deep love for the life and teachings of Jesus, in particular the Sermon on the Mount, and the sense that Gandhi's self-sacrificial life has a Christ-like character. He too, like Martin Luther King, Jr. a generation later, is one who gave his life for his friends and even his enemies.

Christian curiosity about Gandhi long predated his death, and Gandhi enjoyed many friendships with Christians, including missionaries. An abiding fruit of his encounters with missionaries are the many addresses that Gandhi delivered to them at their request. One senses in these invitations and missionary writings a certain puzzlement about this ardent lover of Jesus who took no interest in conversion. Conversation *yes*, but conversion *no*.

Christian theologians are privileged to have access to a number of the Mahatma's addresses to missionaries. Sadly, they are rarely read despite the theological treasures they contain. In these addresses, a striking theme is sounded time and again; namely, a humble and earnest call for receptivity. Gandhi pleads with his interlocutors to demonstrate a spirit of openness, and, more specifically, an openness to receiving from India. However commendable it may be that missionaries come to give—to remove "the distress of the people of India"—something is missing in the characteristic posture of missionaries, and that is a willingness to receive.

INTERRELIGIOUS RECEPTIVITY: WELCOMING WISDOM FROM OTHER TRADITIONS

In what follows, I wish to suggest that the African-American community, under the leadership of Martin Luther King, Jr. and others, answered this poignant invitation to learn from India in their openhearted reception of

2. Mohandas K. Gandhi, *Gandhi on Christianity*, ed. Robert Ellsberg (Maryknoll, NY: Orbis, 1991) 36.

the theory and practice of nonviolent resistance from Gandhi himself.[3] It would behoove us to think of this reception of *satyagraha*—Gandhi's name for the power of nonviolent resistance—as an exemplary act of *interreligious learning and receptivity*, indeed one of world historical significance.

In what follows, I will present the urgency and power of Gandhi's call for what I call "the hospitality of receiving." I shall then suggest that we must look to the African-American reception and performance of nonviolence as itself a moment of interreligious receptivity. I conclude with a preliminary investigation of the theological convictions and resources that enabled Martin Luther King, Jr. to answer Gandhi's call and so to become a hospitable recipient of Gandhian wisdom. What should be clear throughout these reflections is the global horizon of King's deliberative life, a life marked by his readiness to learn from and be transformed by a Hindu reading of Jesus.

For the moment, let us stipulate that interreligious receptivity is the capacity for and practice of receiving resources from the repertoire of insights and practices of a tradition other than one's own. Such receptivity is an ethical and religious virtue that accords to one's neighbors and their traditions genuine respect. Other traditions are not celebrated as variations of one's own but are instead appreciated for the richness of their concrete practices and intellectual claims. Such receptivity is also rooted in a theological humility about one's own tradition. Even if maximal claims are made about the salvific power of what is disclosed in one's own tradition, it is nonetheless the case that the hospitable recipient believes that genuine learning is possible in and through encounter and conversation with religious neighbors.

Paying attention to critical moments of interreligious receptivity matters, especially in this historical moment, when far too often religious traditions and the civilizations that they putatively fund are taken to be

---

3. Sudarshan Kapur has demonstrated that far too often studies of the civil rights movement focus narrowly on King's "discovery of Gandhi" and in doing so adopt an "elitist approach to a story which should involve the preparation of an entire people." He argues instead that "it is the experience of the African-American people and the possibilities of their prior knowledge of and experience with Gandhian methodology which are largely missing from earlier approaches to this story." See Sudarshan Kapur, *Raising Up a Prophet: The African-American Encounter with Gandhi* (Boston: Beacon, 1992) 2. My focus on King in this chapter is not meant to be a return to an older elitist approach. I intend only to explore the resources that fueled King's particular capacity for interreligious receptivity. Kapur is right. We must ask larger questions about the religious resources that empowered the African-American community to learn from Gandhi.

impermeable and reified entities that are bound to clash and predestined to undying hostility. Attention to moments of interreligious receptivity can give the lie to this dominant narrative and even problematize the very idea of syncretism as the illegitimate conflation of ideas and practices from across religious traditions. What if our traditions have always been porous to each other? What if traditions are often enriched and even transfigured by what they receive from external sources? Might our very understanding of tradition undergo modification as we observe critical moments of inter-religious receptivity?

Admittedly, few have thought to ask whether the African-American reception of nonviolent resistance is a moment in the history of interreligious receptivity. At the time, the exigency of overcoming segregation focused attention on questions of "race" and not "religion." Moreover, King and others understood the civil rights movement as part of a larger revolutionary moment in which the darker skinned peoples of the world were emancipating themselves from their erstwhile colonial masters. Hence, interracial postcolonial solidarity, not interreligious receptivity, was foremost in his mind and so also on the minds of those who study that historical period.

Finally, King's core work can be understood as one of transplanting Gandhian nonviolence into the welcoming soil of African American churches.[4] In the midst of such work, it is unsurprising that Gandhi was depicted largely as a singular disciple of Jesus and the greatest Christian of the twentieth century. King and others had neither the time nor the inclination to attend to the Indic elements of Gandhi's thought. Nonetheless, I contend that the willingness to learn from and practice nonviolence as understood by Gandhi, and the further willingness to understand Jesus himself as a *satyagrahi*, or as the exemplary practitioner of nonviolent love, is itself an exercise in interreligious receptivity even when not formally theorized as such.

In our present early twenty-first-century context, we would do well to recognize the civil rights movement as a moment of interreligious

---

4. Kapur suggests as much when he concludes his book by asserting that King "provided a bridge between . . . Gandhi-inspired activists and church-centered followers of Jesus." See ibid., 165. Kapur has in mind the decades of long preparatory work of such activists as A. Philip Randolph, Bayard Rustin, and others whose earnest study of Gandhi prepared the ground for King's own work—a work that could only come to full fruition, in Kapur's estimation, when it was transplanted from "the dry bed of secularism" into the rich religious heritage of the black church (163).

receptivity and learning. Although it is widely known that King marched alongside and worked with Abraham Joshua Heschel and admired the work of Thich Naht Hanh, the following question has yet to be sufficiently pondered: what enabled King, his teachers, and his colleagues to learn from, be transformed by, and hold in reverence a non-Christian figure like Mahatma Gandhi? There is ample historical evidence to suggest that King's devotion to Gandhi was hardly uncontroversial in his own time. Indeed, King was chastised for his dedication to Gandhi and his Christian faith called into question by prominent figures[5] precisely because of that very public devotion. Given such opposition, it is worth asking about the animating sources of King's own theological openness. Why was King able to engage so readily in the hospitality of receiving?

Given the relative novelty of this question, I cannot aspire to offer herein a comprehensive answer, most especially because King was not alone in this capacity for receptivity. Rather than treating King as an exception, his capacity for interreligious receptivity must be placed alongside an exploration of the life and work of figures like Benjamin E. Mays, Howard Thurman, and James Lawson, who were also deeply open to interreligious learning. Indeed, insofar as these figures were themselves products of the black church, one must ultimately ask a broader question: what features of mid-twentieth century African-American church life made it such a rich and supportive matrix for interreligious learning? The following brief survey of King's attitudes about religious diversity is meant to be a comparative theologian's partial and preliminary exploration of a larger project that can be carried forward only by specialist scholars of African-American religious life.

Comparative theology has been defined in a number of ways. Francis X. Clooney defines it as "deep learning across religious borders." For Clooney, comparative theology "marks acts of faith seeking understanding which are rooted in a particular faith tradition but which, from that foundation, venture into learning from one or more other faith traditions. This learning is sought for the sake of fresh theological insights that are indebted to the newly encountered tradition/s as well as the home tradition."[6]

---

5. This was most certainly the case with white Southern Baptist leaders, one of whom accused King of rejecting "the cardinal tenets of biblical Christianity for the heathen philosophy of Mahatma Gandhi." See Bill J. Leonard, "A Theology for Racism: Southern Fundamentalists and the Civil Rights Movement," *Baptist History and Heritage* 34.1 (1999) 63.

6. Francis X. Clooney, *Comparative Theology: Deep Learning across Religious Borders* (Malden, MA: Wiley-Blackwell, 2010) 10.

Comparative theology is thus the work of studying and learning from the wisdom and practices of one's religious neighbors so that a more encompassing knowledge of ultimate reality and the world's relation to ultimate reality might be gained. Although King, his teachers, and peers did not theorize their own study of Gandhi as a moment of interreligious learning and hence as a kind of comparative theology, insofar as they learned from Gandhi and therefore from Hindu and Jain traditions which inspired him, genuine interreligious learning took place. It must also be borne in mind that Gandhi himself learned deeply from his study of Christian texts and traditions. When King and others subsequently studied Gandhi, they learned from a Hindu reading of Christian traditions which is not a reduplication of what Christians *already knew* about their own tradition. These Christians learned to receive their own tradition back again but afresh as it had been performed and transformed by a Hindu.

Why should comparative theologians take interest in such processes of interreligious transmission? The answer is relatively straightforward: an appreciation of Gandhi's learning from Christians and Christian learning from Gandhi suggests that the kind of work done in comparative theology is hardly an *ex nihilo* form of creativity. Interreligious flows that generated *satyagraha* in Gandhi's own thought and praxis and the further reception of that praxis in the King-led civil rights campaigns is material evidence that "deep learning across religious borders" has already taken place both in the lives of individuals and in global cultural flows to vast, indeed planetary, good effect. Hence, the current academic practice of comparative theology is neither the only modality of interreligious learning nor the most important. Comparative theology is often consequent to other culturally pervasive flows of information and practice—the transmission of yoga, Zen, and vipasanna, for example—and is perhaps best understood as reflection upon, support for, and sometimes critique of other primary processes of interreligious learning and mutual transformation. Perhaps such learning as comparative theologians seek will seem less novel, less exceptional, and less questionable if we would attend to the work of figures like Gandhi and King, who have demonstrated the deep power and promise of interreligious learning.

GANDHI'S URGENT CALL FOR THE HOSPITALITY OF RECEIVING

We can be helped in appreciating the importance of receptivity by turning to Mohandas Gandhi's many conversations with Christian missionaries in India. But first, a foundational query: Why should Christians adopt a posture of receptivity toward persons from other religious traditions? Gandhi's words as presented in the epigraph go a long way toward answering this question: "You are here to find out the distress of the people of India and remove it. But I hope you are here also in a receptive mood, and if there is anything that India has to give, you will not stop your ears, you will not close your eyes, and steel your hearts, but open up your ears, eyes, and most of all your hearts to receive all that may be good in this land." One hears in the Mahatma's plaintive appeal a profound pain that bespeaks wounding. Time and again, Gandhi argues that Christian missionaries are present in India with an orientation that is empty of mutuality. They seek to give but without receiving. But this posture is an unsustainable contradiction.

Here is Gandhi again addressing missionaries: "The powers of God should not be limited by the limitations of your understanding. To you who have come to teach India, I therefore say, you cannot give without taking. If you have come to give rich treasures of experiences, open your hearts out to receive the treasures of this land, and you will not be disappointed, neither will you have misread the message of the Bible."[7]

You cannot give without taking, without receiving. Here Gandhi speaks a fundamental human truth: the one who seeks to give without receiving does neither. Authentic giving requires receptivity. Those who seek to give must stand prepared to receive, as any giving that comes from on high, for an attitude of asymmetrical condescension demeans and does not enrich. If you give in such a way that suggests that you have nothing to receive, then you do not in truth give. Instead, you violate.

Consider the gesture of holding the hand of someone whom you wish to console. In the very act of extending your hand, you render yourself vulnerable, as the lives of both Gandhi and King illustrated. Will the one who is in need grasp your extended hand? Will your desire to give be accepted? And there is more—when you grasp the other's hand, you receive also the touch of the other. Here it becomes impossible to tell any longer who comforts and who is comforted. In the mutuality of the embracing

---

7. Gandhi, *Gandhi on Christianity*, 41.

hands, both give and both receive. In touch and in life, it is impossible that one alone should do the giving and the other alone the receiving.

Is such mutuality possible in interfaith relations? Gandhi, like King, asserts that it is not only possible but mandatory. The missionary cannot truly give without receiving. In fact, Gandhi suggests that any reading of the Bible that disposes one towards an attitude of nonreciprocal giving is sure to be a misreading of that resource. One cannot simply appeal to John 14:6 and assert that the "I am" saying—"I am the way, the truth and the life, no one comes to the Father but by me"—forecloses on the possibility of receiving healing wisdom from religious neighbors. In the same address to Christian missionaries, the Mahatma says, "You want to find men in India, and if you want to do that, you will have to go to the lowly cottages—not to give them something, but maybe to take something from them. A true friend as I claim to be of the missionaries of India and of the Europeans, I speak to you from the bottom of my heart. I miss receptiveness, humility, willingness on your part to identify yourself with the masses of India."[8] Gandhi invites Christian missionaries to give themselves in solidarity to India's poorest and serve them in love but also in expectancy, with an open heart that looks to receive as well as to give. Interestingly, Gandhi does not presume to tell Christians just what we might receive from Hindus when we so open our hearts. That is our work and not his. Gandhi plainly believes that without the virtues of receptivity, humility, and solidarity, the missionary enterprise is compromised because it violates the dignity of those whom it seeks to serve.[9]

8. Ibid., 37.

9 Has this call for humble receptivity been heard in Christian theology and, in particular, among Christian theologians who work in interreligious dialogue? By and large, Gandhi's call has gone unheard. One exemplary argument on behalf of hospitality, including the hospitality of receiving, comes from the Pentecostal theologian Amos Yong, although Yong does not derive his theology of hospitality from Gandhi. What is most striking about Yong's work is his claim that "Jesus characterizes the hospitality of God in part as the exemplary recipient of hospitality. From his conception in Mary's womb by the power of the Holy Spirit to his birth in a manger to his burial (in a tomb of Joseph of Arimathea), Jesus was dependent on the welcome of others." The argument of this chapter is indebted to Yong's fine book *Hospitality and the Other: Pentecost, Christian Practices, and the Neighbor* (Maryknoll, NY: Orbis, 2008) 101.

KING, NONVIOLENCE, AND INTERRELIGIOUS RECEIVING

The power of Gandhi's call might be felt with clarity if we come to appreciate the tremendous promise of interreligious receptivity as manifest in the life of King and in the civil rights movement. There is no better argument for receptivity than a demonstration of its power in action.

To assert that King's reception of Gandhian praxis and reflections is a case of interreligious learning hardly seems controversial, and yet, that case has yet to be made. King famously asserted that he had learned to see Jesus differently as a result of his encounter with Gandhi. Put otherwise, he learned from Gandhi what he did not already know about Jesus. King received his own tradition anew as mediated back to him by a Hindu. In a more extended treatment, it would also be possible to show, if only by suggestion, that some features of King's understanding of the practice of nonviolence as both means and ends is rooted partly in Gandhi's own understanding of *karma yoga*, which can be defined as action freed from attachment to the fruits of action. The primary question to be explored herein is this: What features of King's own theology made such learning possible? Ultimately, that is a question about King's theology of religions or theology of religious pluralism.

Theology of religious pluralism asks about the meaning of my neighbor's faith for mine.[10] Theologians of religious pluralism inquire also about the status of religious diversity as such. Is religious diversity a positive good—a promise to be received—or a problem to be solved? Conversations in theologies of religious pluralism have, in their contemporary incarnation, focused centrally on the question of the parity of religious traditions as measured by their saving efficacy. Christian theologians ask whether it is possible to affirm that salvation takes place outside of Christianity and the degree to which access to God's saving power is made available in other religious traditions.

Over the course of the last fifty years, there has been a steady shift on the part of Christian theologians away from rigorous forms of exclusivism, which maintain that "outside of the church there is no salvation," toward inclusivist and even pluralist positions. Inclusivists have typically appealed to a part-whole logic which maintains that the fullness of God's saving

---

10. The best single introduction to theology of religious pluralism remains Paul Knitter's *Introducing Theologies of Religion* (Maryknoll, NY: Orbis, 2002).

presence and power is revealed in Jesus the Christ but that partial and even salvific disclosures of God are available in other religious traditions. Pluralists have gone further and argued that religious traditions must be regarded as on par in bringing about ultimate transformation from self-centeredness to reality-centeredness, with no tradition exceeding the other in any decisive fashion. Repudiating a part-whole logic that would rank order traditions, they insist that each tradition affords equal and independent access to saving truth and power.

Where does Martin King stand on this question? Fruitful and productive work remains to be done to survey King's writings on the relationship between Christianity and other religious traditions, to elicit therefrom his nascent theology of religious pluralism.[11] Here, I broach that question but in a distinctive key by asking, What features of King's theology made it possible for him to function as a hospitable recipient of religious wisdom from other traditions? This way of framing the question is more exigent than rank ordering traditions on a soteriological scale because the capacity to receive marks a more decisive repudiation of religious isolationism and self-sufficiency than an abstract, fair-minded, and charitable assertion of the relative parity of religious traditions. After all, one might well posit the relative equality of traditions while remaining indifferent to or uninterested in the distinctive goods of those traditions. Indeed, a pluralism which asserts that religious traditions are mere variations on a theme and so different paths to the same destination may impede appreciation of enriching difference.

Despite the presence of pluralist elements in King's theology, I argue that King's theology of religious pluralism is best characterized as an "open inclusivism." By "open inclusivism," I mean that King confessed that God's revelation in Jesus Christ represents the fullest disclosure of divinity available in the world's religions while remaining open to learning from other traditions. Put otherwise, his is an inclusivism that actually *includes new insights and practices* from other religious traditions and so materially learns from them. King's version of inclusivism does not hold that because the fullness of divine disclosure takes place in Jesus the Christ, Christians have nothing new to learn. His inclusivism is, therefore, qualitatively different from a hierarchical or self-sufficient version in which one's own tradition

11. Lewis V. Baldwin has taken important steps in addressing this subject in his *Voice of Conscience: The Church in the Mind of Martin Luther King, Jr.* (New York: Oxford University Press, 2010) 201–16.

is said already to contain all that can be known of religious truth. Perhaps, then, one criterion for measuring the adequacy of any theology of religious pluralism is not its willingness to pronounce the world's religious traditions as in some abstract sense "equal"—it is after all hard to see how one might weigh traditions as totalities—but rather in the capacity of those who hold to such theologies to demonstrate a deep interreligious receptivity marked by learning from a tradition other than one's own. To any theology of religious pluralism, the following question might be posed: Does this theology enable its advocates to receive wisdom from another tradition and be transformed thereby?

When thinking about the relationship between Gandhi, King, and the civil rights movement at large, one oft-repeated quotation comes to mind: "Nonviolent resistance had emerged as the technique of the movement, while love stood as the regulating ideal. In other words, *Christ furnished the spirit and motivation, while Gandhi furnished the method.*"[12] King's assertion might be taken to imply that Gandhi's contribution was merely instrumental rather than substantive—a means rather than an end. On this account, the most important spiritual resources for nonviolent resistance come from the Christian tradition rather than from Gandhi's own religious milieu.

We see also in much discourse of the time a tendency to read Gandhi entirely in Christian terms and to depict him as the greatest Christian of the twentieth century. Without a doubt, calling Gandhi a Christian was meant as a blessing—and the epigraph of this chapter indicates that Gandhi would have received it as such. He himself suggests that Christ would receive as his own those who are not Christian. Gandhi, an avid reader of the Gospels, is likely to have had in mind John 10:16, a verse to which King alluded at times when defending the power of religious pluralism and also Gandhi's importance as a Christlike figure: "And other sheep I have, which are not of this fold: them also I must bring, and they shall hear my voice" (KJV). Hence, Gandhi is prepared to assert about others what some, in particular King, explicitly asserted of him. In his famous Palm Sunday sermon about the Mahatma, King cites this very verse, claiming that Jesus "is saying in substance that 'I have people dedicated and following my ways who have not become attached to the institution surrounding my name. . . . And my influence is not limited to the institutional Christian church.'"[13] The import

12. Martin Luther King, Jr., *Stride Toward Freedom: The Montgomery Story* (San Francisco: Harper & Row, 1958) 85. Emphasis added.

13. Clayborne Carson et al., eds., *The Papers of Martin Luther King, Jr.*, vol. 5,

of King's claim is that among the followers of Jesus must be included his non-Christian disciples.

But these two propositions taken together hardly support the case that King and other leaders of the civil rights movement were engaged in inter-religious learning. If Gandhi offers only a method to implement what Jesus called for, and if Gandhi himself is among the greatest of Christians, how can learning from him be characterized as interreligious? To respond effectively to this problematic query, one must show that King moved beyond these formulaic assertions and came to understand that in Gandhi we have a non-Christian who was nonetheless illumined by the presence of God while remaining self-avowedly non-Christian, and also that King learned with and from Gandhi that *satyagraha* was no mere method. Both of these propositions are readily demonstrable.

That King's understanding of Gandhi is not reductionist becomes evident in the preacher's preparedness to impute to the Mahatma another more remarkable verse: "Verily, verily, I say unto you, he that believeth on me, the works that I do, shall he do also. And greater works than these shall he do because I go unto my Father" (John 14:12). King prepares a foundation for claiming that Christians have much to learn from Gandhi because Gandhi's works *exceed* the works of the Christ—a bold claim indeed. Perhaps readers would do well not to read uncharitably King's famous assertion about Gandhi as a great Christian. There is reason to believe that there is more going on in such claims than is apparent at first glance:

> And I believe these two passages of scripture apply more uniquely to the life and work of Mahatma Gandhi than to any other indi-vidual in the history of the world. For here was a man who was not a Christian in terms of being a member of the Christian church but who was a Christian. And it is one of the strange ironies of the modern world that the greatest Christian of the twentieth century was not a member of the Christian church. And the second thing is, that this man took the message of Jesus Christ and was able to do even greater works than Jesus did in his lifetime.[14]

King makes clear herein that Gandhi is no son of the church; he does not intend surreptitiously to baptize the Mahatma. Secondly, he directs

---

Threshold of a New Decade, January 1959–December 1960 (Berkeley: University Of California Press, 2005) 146–47; and Martin Luther King, Jr. letter to Dr. Harold E. Fey (June 23, 1962), 2–4. Document housed at the Library and Archives of the Martin Luther King, Jr. Center for Nonviolent Social Change, Inc., Atlanta, Georgia.

14. Carson et al., *Papers*, 5:147–48.

and prepares his Christian listeners to learn from Gandhi what they do not already know from following the Christ. He argues compellingly that the power of nonviolent resistance as taught by Jesus was enacted and vindicated on an unprecedented social scale by Gandhi. Gandhi dramatically demonstrates the wide social applicability of nonviolence by leading millions to freedom in a way that Jesus never did.

What then are we to make of King's apparent claim that Gandhi offers only a method for putting into practice what Jesus taught? Readers of King's language about nonviolent resistance as a method miss the genuine import of King's claim. To begin with, civil rights leaders like King and James Lawson knew with absolute clarity that it was inadequate to speak of nonviolent resistance as a means to an end. When one reads the writings of King, a common pattern presents itself: almost immediately after sentences in which King speaks of nonviolent resistance as a method, a strong corrective note is proffered cautioning readers that nonviolence must not be understood instrumentally. In Gandhi's thinking, means and ends can never be separated. One cannot use nonviolence as a means to some other extrinsic end. Nonviolence is both the means and the desired end.

King and Lawson fully appreciated this truth. And hence, soon after the above passage in which Gandhi is said to offer a method, King writes: "nonviolence in the truest sense is not a strategy that one uses simply because it is expedient at the moment; nonviolence is ultimately a way of life that men live by because of the sheer morality of its claim."[15] Elsewhere, in speaking of his "pilgrimage to nonviolence," King writes:

> The experience in Montgomery did more to clarify my thinking on the question of nonviolence than all of the books that I had read. As the days unfolded I became more and more convinced of the power of nonviolence. Living through the actual experience of the protest, nonviolence became more than a method to which I gave intellectual assent; it became a commitment to a way of life.[16]

If it is true then that Gandhi offers more than a means, more than an instrumental method to implement Jesus's teaching, how then are we to understand the relationship between Gandhi and Jesus? Here, it is critical to let King speak in his own voice and at length:

15. King, *Stride Toward Freedom*, 89.

16. Martin Luther King, Jr., "Pilgrimage to Nonviolence," in *A Testament of Hope: The Essential Writings and Speeches of Martin Luther King, Jr.*, ed. James M. Washington (San Francisco: HarperCollins, 1991) 38.

As I delved deeper into the philosophy of Gandhi my skepticism concerning the power of love gradually diminished, and I came to see for the first time its potency in the area of social reform. Prior to reading Gandhi, I had about concluded that the ethics of Jesus were only effective in individual relationships. The "turn the other cheek" philosophy and the "love your enemies" philosophy were only valid, I felt, when individuals were in conflict with other individuals; when racial groups and nations were in conflict a more realistic approach seemed necessary. But after reading Gandhi, I saw how utterly mistaken I was. Gandhi was probably the first person in history to lift the love ethic of Jesus above mere interaction between individuals to a powerful and effective social force on a large scale. Love for Gandhi was a potent instrument for social and collective transformation.[17]

The deep significance of this familiar proclamation has yet to be fully appreciated for the lessons it can teach about interreligious giving and receiving. I contend that King must be read herein as asserting that Christians receive from Gandhi not merely a new method, but a new understanding of Jesus and so perhaps even a new Christology. The Christ who is made known to Christians by Gandhi's work is Jesus the ideal *satyagrahi*, the ideal practitioner of nonviolent resistance understood as the power of truth—*satya* understood as truth, and *graha* understood as force. King asserts that Christians did not have this Jesus prior to Gandhi's creative reading and enactment of his teachings. Prior to Gandhi, Jesus's Sermon on the Mount was understood largely as advancing a limited ethic applicable only to person-to-person encounter.

There is also a shared resonance in the way that Gandhi and King understand the meaning of Jesus's death; both move away from a focus on substitutionary atonement—the teaching that Jesus dies as a substitute sacrifice for human sin—as both find it unappealing and unpersuasive.[18] The

17. King, *Stride Toward Freedom*, 96–97. It is worth noting here that King specialists have called into question King's narrative of his own discovery of Gandhi in seminary. The general consensus has shifted, and most argue that King's appreciation for Gandhian nonviolence was far more gradual and a later, post-Montgomery phenomenon. This question of timing and gradually unfolding appreciation does not bear on my contention that King learned how to understand Jesus anew and afresh under Gandhian inspiration.

18. On this point, Gary Dorrien has demonstrated that King followed his Boston University teacher A. C. Knudson and held that "merit and guilt belong to individuals; they cannot be transferred from one person to another. Moreover, it is immoral to punish one person for the sins of another." Dorrien cites King on this point as saying, "Christ's death was not a ransom, or a penal substitute, or a penal example; rather it was

cross is understood instead as an act of nonviolent political resistance to the powers of violence and ultimately a sign that those principalities can never triumph over the power of love.

What matters here is not whether King is correct in asserting that no political account of Jesus as engaged in nonviolent resistance was available before Gandhi. What is incontestable is King's claim that Gandhi was the first to demonstrate and embody that vision on a mass sociopolitical scale and so vindicate any political reading of Jesus that might have been available prior to Gandhi. That a Hindu should be the first to accomplish this revolutionary work is what strikes King as remarkable. To assert the Christianness of Gandhi then is not so much an attempt to baptize him after the fact, but is, instead, an act of affirmation that a Hindu understood and performed the true meaning of Jesus's life and teachings more deeply than any Christian had heretofore done.

How Gandhi generated his own Christology would take yet another chapter and indeed books to lay out. That story, too, would be a tale of interreligious giving and receiving. Simplistically stated, Gandhi, in framing his program of nonviolent resistance, took the Jain notion of *ahimsa*, or noninjury, and the idea of *karma yoga*, which derived from his reading of the Bhagavad Gita, and wedded to both a creative reading of the Sermon on the Mount. For Gandhi, Jesus's life and death on the cross perfectly exemplify suffering love lived both as means and end. In Jesus's life, as interpreted by Gandhi, nonviolent love is the way that births a new social order marked by nonviolent love.

In King's considered estimation, "Gandhi was probably the first person in history to lift the love ethic of Jesus above mere interaction between individuals to a powerful and effective social force on a large scale. Love for Gandhi was a potent instrument for social and collective transformation." This remarkable claim suggests that King recognized that Gandhi gives Christians more than a new method; he gives a *new Jesus*, whose redemptive work lies not just in the private atonement of individual persons from personal sin but in the collective redemption of the social order itself. What

---

a revelation of the sacrificial love of God intended to awaken an answering love in the hearts of men." See Gary Dorrien, *The Making of American Liberal Theology: Crisis, Irony, and Postmodernity, 1950–2005* (Louisville: Westminster John Knox, 2006) 152. Mohandas K. Gandhi long held to the selfsame position and found the notion of substitutionary atonement morally incoherent and distasteful. Here we have a case not of influence but of resonance. Perhaps King's rejection of traditional theories of atonement prepared him for a Gandhian reading of the cross.

I am arguing here is that's King's recognition of Gandhi as offering a new understanding of Jesus's life and work is a historically profound instance of interreligious learning, a moment of hospitable receptivity.

At this juncture, a critical question must be posed: What features of King's theological orientation made it possible for him to receive what Gandhi had to teach him? Why was he prepared to assert that Gandhi performed greater deeds than Jesus himself? Any attempt to answer these questions must begin by noting that King's preparedness to learn from Gandhi was a source of controversy. The most telling evidence of this friction is discernible in the public criticism that King received for being involved in the founding of a Gandhi Society in America. For taking this step, he was publically chastised by no less a figure than Dr. Harold Fey, editor of *The Christian Century*. In fact, Fey went so far as to call into question the sincerity of King's Christian faith because of his devotion to Gandhi. King's public interest in and love for the life and teachings of Gandhi did not come without cost. That is why King's unpublished response to Dr. Fey, in the form of a letter, is noteworthy and worth citing here at length:

> As far as my Christology goes, I believe as firmly now as ever that God revealed himself uniquely and completely through Jesus Christ. . . . One's commitment to Jesus Christ as Lord and Savior, however, should not mean that one cannot be inspired by another great personality that enters the stage of history. . . . While I firmly believe that God reveals himself more completely and uniquely in Christianity than any other religion, I cannot make myself believe that God did not reveal himself in other religions. I believe that in some marvelous way, God worked through Gandhi, and the spirit of Jesus saturated his life. It is ironic, yet inescapably true that the greatest Christian of the modern world was a man who never embraced Christianity. This is not an indictment on Christ but a tribute to Him—a tribute to his universality and His Lordship. When I think of Gandhi, I think of the Master's way in the words of the fourth gospel: "I have other sheep that are not of this fold."[19]

Many features of this King's response are noteworthy because we see in them the stirrings of theological resources for receptivity. First, King's openness to Gandhi was not impeded by, and nor did it require King to surrender, his conviction that "God revealed himself uniquely and completely in Jesus." King is unwilling to relinquish this evangelical axiom. But crucially, King does not believe that God has revealed himself *only* in Jesus.

19. King letter to Fey (June 23, 1962) 3.

Here King's discourse is inclusivist in character. It is "the spirit of Jesus" that "saturated" Gandhi's life.

Martin Luther King, Jr. makes a decisive step that many mainline Christian theologians and church bodies have since taken, though largely only after his passing.[20] Well before it was theologically popular to do so, King affirmed that divine revelation is available in other religions. King asserts herein both the power of spirit in Gandhi's individual life as well as the presence of revelation in other religions. Other religions as such are repositories of revelation; it does not just happen to visit or grasp extraordinary individuals like Gandhi alone. Hence, it seems reasonable to suppose that King would hold that Gandhi, and presumably other non-Christians, are not inspired despite the religious traditions to which they belong but precisely by them. Affirming *both* these propositions entails that Gandhi's religious life would have to be understood from within its own context and as inspired by indigenous resources and not just the spirit of Jesus. King did not insist on this point but would, it seems, be open to such a claim.

To begin with, King is quite clear that Gandhi is not a Christian. He is prepared to recognize Gandhi as a *Hindu follower of Jesus*. While contemporary theologians may not hold this to be an especially noteworthy valorization of religious difference, King's openness to the possibility and indeed the reality of non-Christian Jesus followers is a theological advance with important ramifications, especially for any viable future theology of mission. King's openness to non-Christian Jesus followers suggests that the goal of mission need not be the conversion of persons from other traditions to one's own. Instead, all persons might understand themselves as invited to share membership in what King called "the beloved community." King's body of writing and preaching shows that he understood the beloved

20. By way of juxtaposition, it is noteworthy that the Catholic Church's shift toward inclusivism found history-making expression a full three years later on October 28, 1965, in the Vatican II document *Nostra Aetate*, or "The Declaration on the Relationship Between the Church and Non-Christian Religions." That document maintains that "the Catholic Church rejects nothing that is true and holy in these religions. She regards with sincere reverence those ways of conduct and of life, those precepts and teachings which, though differing in many aspects from the ones she holds and sets forth, nonetheless often reflect a ray of that Truth which enlightens all men. Indeed, she proclaims, and ever must proclaim Christ 'the way, the truth, and the life' (John 14:6), in whom men may find the fullness of religious life, in whom God has reconciled all things to Himself." King's creativity on questions of revelation in other religions predates *Nostra Aetate* and stands at the cutting edge of the best theological thinking of the day. The entirety of this key document is available on the Vatican's Web site: http://www.vatican.va/archive/hist_councils/ii_vatican_council/documents/vat-ii_decl_19651028_nostra-aetate_en.html.

community, from the first and throughout his public career, as an *interreligious community* and not just an interracial one. In the beloved community, differences, including religious ones, are not erased, but they are no longer a cause for suspicion, rancor, or enmity.

King was prepared to recognize Gandhi's discipleship as an authentic way of following Jesus Christ. Indeed, King says far more; he speaks of Gandhi as "the greatest Christian of the modern world." If that is true, if Christ can be followed to the full, even unto death, without entering the church, then several convictions that have traditionally prevented Christians from adopting a posture of hospitality toward other religious traditions can also be called into question. These include the claims of the following sort: "True reception of Jesus the Christ requires becoming a member of the church, which is the body of the Christ." In any case, King is prepared to move toward an encompassing posture of hospitality and receptivity precisely because he sees nothing deficient or problematic in Gandhi's desire to follow the Christ *as a Hindu!* King was prepared to reject the notion that faithful discipleship requires conversion, wherein conversion is understood to be leaving the religion of one's birth and embracing another.

Intriguingly, this kind of openness toward non-Christians seems precisely to echo Gandhi's own stance toward and advice to missionaries. In Gandhi's recounting of an encounter with a South African chaplain, the Mahatma reports that he appealed to the Gospels and argued, "It is not he who says 'Lord, Lord' . . .who enters the Kingdom of Heaven, but he that doeth his will. I reminded him, 'I am conscious of my weaknesses, and try to fight them—not in my own strength but in the strength of God. Is that enough or do you wish me to repeat parrot-like that Jesus has cleansed me from all sin?' He stopped me and said, 'I understand what you mean.' So I say that instead of wanting to find out how many heads you count as Christian, work away . . . silently among the people and let your work be the silent testimony of your worth. What do you want to convert them for?"[21] Gandhi advises his Christian interlocutor to adopt toward non-Christians the very position that King seems to have adopted toward Gandhi. Conversion to Christianity is not the goal but rather a faithful following of the divine will. King's focus on creating an interreligious beloved community is arguably a fulfillment of Gandhi's own desires and aspirations.

Perhaps King was able to focus resolutely on creating "a world-wide fellowship," one that did not seek to erase religious difference by way of

21. Gandhi, *Gandhi on Christianity*, 33.

conversion because of his conviction that the world's religious traditions were oriented toward the selfsame reality best understood as love:

> This call for a world-wide fellowship that lifts neighborly concern beyond one's tribe, race, class, and nation is in reality a call for an all-embracing and unconditional love for all men.... When I speak of love I am not speaking of some sentimental and weak response. I am speaking of that force which all of the great religions have seen as the supreme unifying principle of life. Love is somehow the key that unlocks the door which leads to ultimate reality. This Hindu-Moslem-Christian-Jewish-Buddhist belief about ultimate reality is beautifully summed up in the first epistle of Saint John: "Let us love one another; for love is God and everyone that loveth is born of God and knoweth God. He that loveth not knoweth not God; for God is love...."[22]

Here, King articulates a theological perspective that seems most akin to the family of positions that has come to be known as pluralism. The heart of the pluralist position, as noted earlier, is that the world's religious traditions are diverse and independent ways of accessing ultimate reality. Most importantly, pluralists customarily insist that no tradition affords more complete or efficacious access to ultimate reality than any other.

In this particular statement, King does not claim that any tradition affords richer access to ultimate reality than any other. Hence, it might be read as indicative of a certain pluralist leaning. However, there is insufficient information to ascertain where precisely King stands. He does not explicitly specify that all traditions offer equally efficacious access to ultimate reality, as is suggested in Gandhi's idea of *sarva dharma sambava,* or "the equality of all religions."[23] King stipulates only that all alike are oriented to ultimate reality understood as love, and all alike insist that love can be accessed by love alone. No more can be said. What is distinctive to King's approach is his performative emphasis; not doctrinal correctness but only fidelity in love affords access to love itself.

Given the lack of a fulsome and explicit statement from King, it may be impossible to ascertain whether this latter position marks a departure from his earlier inclusivist position. King may have shifted away from the inclusivist position he held in 1962 to the more pluralist position articulated

22. This selection is from King's milestone sermon, "A Time to Break the Silence," delivered at Riverside Church in New York on April 4, 1967, precisely one year before his assassination. See Washington, *Testament of Hope,* 243.

23. Baldwin, *Voice of Conscience,* 202.

here. Further investigation of King's papers is required before a claim of transition can be sustained. Moreover, he may have held both convictions together. It is possible to hold without contradiction both the pluralist conviction that all religious traditions are rightly oriented to ultimate reality while maintaining that ultimate reality is disclosed most completely in Jesus the Christ. Put otherwise, one can be pluralist on the question of theological ontology while being an inclusivist on questions of revelation and epistemology.

What is clear, at any rate, is that by some combination of inclusivist and pluralist intuitions, King arrived at a theological posture of hospitable receiving. King was confident that God is at work in the lives of neighbors of other faiths. His conviction that revelation takes place outside the church justifies the hope that others possess riches from which Christians have much to learn. What is striking about King's stance is his capacity to be a hospitable receiver even as he maintained that the fullness of God's disclosure was available in Jesus the Christ. If Martin Luther King, Jr. is right, that it is only in the twentieth century that Christians have come fully to appreciate Jesus as an embodiment of nonviolent love, and if, furthermore, Christians learned that lesson most capaciously from a Hindu, then even Christians who confess the finality and unsurpassability of God's revelation in Jesus Christ need not adopt a posture of self-sufficiency toward other religious traditions. It may be that Christians will only know what it means to confess the Christ when the Christ is given away and received anew from persons of other religious traditions.

King's openness to learning from Gandhi, at personal cost, remains striking today. Even on the contemporary theological scene, few Christian leaders defend the possibility that non-Christians might receive something precious, transformative, and even salvific from Christian quarters *while remaining non-Christian.* Fewer still suggest that non-Christians have much to teach Christians, even about their own tradition, because the resources of other traditions may illumine one's home tradition precisely in their very difference. On the contrary, the standard posture remains that those who receive from the Christian tradition must, if the work of reception is genuine and complete, cease to be non-Christian. The normative posture is that you, the non-Christian, not only need to receive this or that vital Christian good, but you must relinquish your religious identity in the very act of receiving. But how can giving that seeks to erase the otherness of the other be characterized as hospitable? King's openness to the reality of non-Christian followers of Jesus opens up the possibility of a giving that does not require that others cease to be who they are. Thus, a close reading of King has the promise to unfold new conceptions of mission and conversion. Conversion can be understood not as movement into a new religious tradition but as entrance into the beloved community.

The exchange between Gandhi and King is a profound and multidirectional movement marked by the hospitality of receiving. First, Gandhi received generously from Henry David Thoreau, Leo Tolstoy, and others from within the Christian tradition. In turn, King received a great deal from Gandhi, perhaps because he was able to see Gandhi as a fellow disciple of Christ, *albeit a Hindu disciple.* Were King himself a scholar of Indian religious traditions, he would have recognized that what he received from Gandhi was a transformed understanding of Jesus as the ideal *satyagrahi*; he might see that that Christology includes and is enriched by fundamental Jain and Hindu notions and practices. Therefore, it is possible credibly to hold that King received from Gandhi a new Christology that was shaped in part by religious riches alien to the Christian tradition—riches that enlivened Christian reflection and practice. Furthermore, King's work of hospitality demonstrates that even Christians who are wholeheartedly committed to affirming the plenitude of God's self-disclosure in Christ can be open to hospitable receiving. He shows that there need be no bar between searching faith and interreligious learning. Even traditionalist Christians can confess that God has disclosed God's self most fully in the Christ and yet also believe that one's Hindu neighbor may see dimensions of that fullness that Christians have not yet appreciated.

Depth of piety need never become an obstacle to the hospitality of receiving. How could it, as authentic faith demands the work of welcoming wisdom whatever its source? These lessons offered by King remain very much ours to learn.

7

Mohandas K. Gandhi and Martin Luther King, Jr.'s Bequest

Nonviolent Civil Resistance in a Globalized World[1]

Mary Elizabeth King

Until we have wrung justice and until we have wrung our self-respect from unwilling hands and from unwilling pens, there can be no cooperation. . . . Cooperation is a duty only so long as government protects your honour, and non-cooperation is an equal duty when the government, instead of protecting, robs you of your honour. That is the doctrine of non-cooperation.

MOHANDAS K. GANDHI[2]

1. At the request of the editors, aspects of this chapter are derived from research contributing to Mary Elizabeth King, *Mahatma Gandhi and Martin Luther King, Jr: The Power of Nonviolent Action*, 2nd ed. (Paris: UNESCO, 1999).

2. *The Hindu*, August 13, 1920.

Along with the march as a weapon for change in our nonviolent arsenal must be listed the boycott. Basic to the philosophy of nonviolence is the refusal to cooperate with evil. There is nothing quite so effective as a refusal to cooperate economically with the forces and institutions which perpetuate evil in our communities.

MARTIN LUTHER KING, JR.[3]

IN THE FIRST HALF of the twentieth century on the Indian subcontinent, a body of knowledge and experience developed on how to organize effective mass movements of citizen action. Often through word of mouth, pulsing westward from India, knowledge and information on such nonviolent resistance spread. Within eight years of India's gaining independence in 1947, civil disobedience, fasting, vigils, and alternative institutions—methods used by Mohandas Karamchand Gandhi in the Indian independence struggles—had become more evident than previously in the southern United States. A 1955–1956 Montgomery citywide action against racially segregated public buses created an opportunity for relaying knowledge from India directly and intentionally into the United States. When the Montgomery bus boycott started, seasoned professional practitioners of nonviolent action, some of whom had studied in India, descended on Alabama's capital city and began to share with the black community the theories and methods of nonviolent direct action honed in the Indian struggles.

Transmitting ideas, strategies, and tactics from India's fight for independence twelve thousand miles away, these individuals also helped to shape the leadership of the young and newly arrived pastor Martin Luther King, Jr. (no relation to the author). They were able to give him a practical and theoretical grounding in a technique of fighting for social and political change that had been effective in India and which also derived from Gandhi's experiences of working for twenty-one years in South Africa. Bayard Rustin and James M. Lawson were among the professionals who would tutor King over the next few years, as he became the exemplar for a U.S. movement that would signally be able to unify itself, possess aspects of planning and strategy, and exert nonviolent discipline. Both plans and spontaneous challenges would cumulatively build, until the civil rights

3. Martin Luther King, Jr., "Nonviolence: The Only Road to Freedom," *Ebony*, October 1966, 31–32.

movement coalesced across the southern United States, during the decade between the 1955 Montgomery bus boycott and the passage of the 1965 Voting Rights Act.

In the decades following King's assassination in 1968, the knowledge that he had helped propagate throughout the southern U.S. black community and the nation as a whole for a crusade of peaceful change swelled throughout the world. On every continent since, people have drawn upon his words and example as they have learned how to fight for social and political change without violence—the aspect of his leadership most readily identifiable and the major anchor of his place in world history. King's sharing of the technique of nonviolent civil resistance has helped to breach barriers of disbelief and skepticism across the globe, as this method of active struggle has increased in importance in the twenty-first century.

AN IMPORTANT DEVELOPMENT OF THE TWENTIETH CENTURY

Nonviolent resistance is a general term for a technique of using dozens of identifiable forms of action or tactics—in an active response in which those who have chosen the technique take action that does not rely on violence. The methods used in civil resistance, although universal, derive from specific histories and traditions, and they are continually being modified. Each social movement improvises with adaptations and new technologies. By 1973, scholar Gene Sharp, in his three-volume trilogy *The Politics of Nonviolent Action,* had identified 198 different methods used by nonviolent campaigns, a tally that continually expands as virtually every movement devises distinctive forms of action drawn from its particular culture and history. (Methods may also be thought of as sanctions or tactics.) Sharp's work cumulatively has shown that nonviolent action is one response to the question of how to act effectively in wielding political power. Most methods can be classified under three broad categories: protest and persuasion, noncooperation, and nonviolent intervention.[4] The technique employs strategies for applying nonviolent sanctions to bring about the results sought. Nonviolent strategy in the initial phase tries to protest or persuade the

4. Gene Sharp, ed., *Waging Nonviolent Struggle: Twentieth Century Practice and Twenty-First Century Potential* (Boston: Porter Sargent, 2005) 51–65, updating Gene Sharp, *The Politics of Nonviolent Action: Power and Struggle,* vol. 1 (Boston: Porter Sargent, 1973).

adversary of the validity of the nonviolent group's point of view. Sequencing is important, because if the opening actions fail to dissuade or induce, nonviolent challengers subsequently turn to noncooperation, and, failing progress, to the more interventionist methods. The moves and countermoves of nonviolent struggle generally proceed along a trajectory of communicating the severity of the grievance as part of the process of prevailing upon the target group to make alterations.

Civil resistance, another name for the same technique, does not mean the absence of violence, which can be produced by assorted causes. The technique holds no inference of passivity—which alters nothing and may even signify submission to aggressive violence. Nor does it allude to the values of tolerance or the virtues of nonviolent interaction that are celebrated in modern political thought and often correspond to civil society. More exactly, it stands as a way of achieving social and political justice, particularly when the social contract has broken down or institutionalized political systems fail to work. Depending on its purpose, the technique of nonviolent action contains within it the stuff of possible eventual reconciliation, because it is not seeking to accomplish its goals by wounding or harming the adversary, except politically.

Violence can change the character of a conflict from one of asymmetry, in which nonviolent challengers are unarmed against the military superiority of security systems provisioned with strategic weapons—a situation that can sometimes be advantageous for the nonviolent protagonists—to an eventually symmetrical affray in which both sides utilize violent weaponry, offering the winning position to the bellicose attackers with military hardware.

From the late eighteenth century until the present day, the technique of nonviolent civil resistance has been broadly used in such struggles as trans-century movements on both sides of the Atlantic to abolish slavery, raise wages, battle for tenant and land rights, and secure independence from imperial rule. The development of workers' rights and the realization of collective bargaining was largely advanced through marches, boycotts, and strikes. One of the most remarkable transnational nonviolent movements of the modern age was the women's suffrage movement of the first two decades of the twentieth century.[5] Another twenty years and women

5. Fred Halliday, "Hidden from International Relations: Women and the International Arena," in *Gender and International Relations*, ed. Rebecca Grant and Kathleen Newland (Buckingham, UK: Open University Press, 1991) 162.

were enfranchised in countries from Uruguay to Austria to the Netherlands to Turkey to Germany and to Ceylon.

In the twentieth century, nonviolent struggle was chosen with unprecedented frequency by men and women who were seeking to improve working conditions, reform governments, defeat dictators, prevent genocide, thwart invaders, and resist military occupations and coups d'état. The nonviolent civil resistance technique that helped to end imperial rule in India and to bring down legalized racial discrimination in the United States is as much indicative of the twentieth century as are its two world wars. As the twentieth century came toward its close, *national* nonviolent revolutions brought the communist order to an end in the Eastern bloc and began the dissolution of the former Soviet Union. Mass mobilizations in the twenty-first century have continued to disintegrate dictatorships, as can be seen in the Arab Awakening.

Another broad defining development of the twentieth century was recognition of fundamental human rights for a large proportion of the world's population. Entitlements now deemed universal human rights had in many instances first been fought for and institutionalized through nonviolent struggles. Codification of internationally recognized human rights is in large part a consequence of anticolonial, civil rights, democracy, and women's suffrage movements that deliberately avoided the use of violence in pursuing their tangible goals. The human rights project itself is an outgrowth of nonviolent resistance. Choosing options that relied neither on violent responses nor passivity, ordinary individuals reshaped their societies through methods selected precisely because they do not seek to realize their goals through injury, threat of physical assault, or inflicting death.

Martin Luther King, Jr. is often associated with "principled nonviolence," an approach based on moral constructions, in contrast to "pragmatic nonviolence," resting on grounds of practicality. In real life, these are not separate and independent paths, with one avenue soaring to the high ground of ethics and nobility of purpose and the other sunk in the slough of calculated and mechanistic measures focused on what will work in the concrete. The two contexts can be complementary. Scholars are increasingly documenting that most nonviolent struggles have been organized by people and groups without a philosophical commitment to the principles of nonviolence as a creed and who instead chose the technique as the most effective for their circumstances. It can now be readily seen across the world that the decision to choose nonviolent action most often involves pragmatic choices, made on the grounds of what is sensible or will bring the most enduring results, and much less so a question of principled or moral opposition to violence. Although nonviolent action can be stripped to its essential powers and understood solely as a strategic targeting of action strategies and tactics, its proponents often *want* to fight within an ethical framework, partly due to a philosophical and strategic assessment that the means affects the ends.

Generally with meager resources, the protagonists in nonviolent mobilizations have relied on themselves. In some cases they were pacifists. Still other pacifists were offended by embarking on active struggles and promoting the taking of action. Some believed in nonresistance. This is one reason why it is inaccurate to view nonviolent action as equivalent to pacifism. Overwhelmingly, the people, groups, and societies who have chosen civil resistance in recent eras were folk who believed that the results would be more beneficial and enduring if they eschewed violence and fought with an alternative technique. The vast majority were motivated by a perception that the long-term structural outcome of their challenge would be more advantageous if they could win their rights or alter their condition without using violent insurrection, armed struggle, or guerrilla warfare.

Rather than denouncing violence, today's nonviolent protagonists often seek a realistic way to make their condition more just, without creating new instances of injustice. Frequently interacting with other forms of power, the nonviolent technique has over the course of time developed as a rational way to pursue social justice without deepening the dispute or grievance. It has repeatedly proved to be the only workable option when every other approach has failed or when any other method will make things worse. Nothing is ignoble about choosing the nonviolent option for utilitarian reasons—intrinsic to civil resistance are popular participation in making decisions, maximal inclusivity, regard for human rights, the pursuit of justice, concern for political legitimacy, and reverence for life.

A growing perspective sees nonviolent sanctions as offering a practical substitute for violent struggle which may in time replace deadly conflict. Yet this would require the readiness of an effective alternative method for engaging in conflict that is not reliant on violence. In this trajectory of thought, civil resistance is seen as a technique that might progressively be substituted for the use of armed force, if organized around particular needs and specific conflicts. Armed force has been important and necessary for societies in areas such as defense and policing, and nonviolent action is often chosen by those who would be willing to employ violent tactics under some other circumstances. The holders of this perspective seek to build knowledge and enlarge the comprehension of nonviolent struggle so that it might be more frequently and productively pursued as an alterative. This outlook is based on a presumption that only if a rigorous and efficient substitute has been dependably developed can armed force be realistically renounced.

Civil resistance employs economic, political, psychological, and social power in a conflict, but is not equivalent to verbal or purely psychological persuasion. Much more is involved than nonviolent communications. With nonviolent conflict, it is more desirable that the adversary change from within—having become persuaded of the strength of the dissenters' perspective, the cost of not remedying the situation, or the loss of its own power—and adjust or yield to the nonviolent challengers' view. Where such an alteration exists as a possibility, it is essential for the nonviolent challengers to communicate clearly the grievance or injustice, because it preserves their energy, psychological potency, and forbearance—significant assets that need to be preserved in planning for nonviolent struggle. At the most fundamental level, one cannot expect the target group to change in the desired way unless the wrong to be changed is made utterly clear. This is one reason why communications are vitally important in a nonviolent campaign.

The technique of nonviolent struggle does not assume that human beings are inherently "good." Civil resistance does not refer to conflict resolution, although this might be one of many outcomes of a nonviolent struggle. Methods of conflict resolution are more consensual in their properties than is the technique of nonviolent resistance, and thus are not appropriate for addressing all conflicts at every phase. To suppose that every severe conflict can be negotiated or "resolved" is as analytically weak a conjecture as is the notion that violence represents the "strongest" force. Conflict resolution approaches call for collaborative attitudes, yet conciliation, mediation, and compromise strategies fail as realistic choices if the grounds of distress and anguish are so profound or egregious that shifts are necessary in the positions of the opposing sides in order to create the circumstances that allow for consideration of settlements or solutions. Also, in going to the roots of deep, elemental issues, where grave injustices are involved, the encouragement of methodologies primarily based on compromise may not be advantageous in principle, achievable, or even pertinent. To be sure, contemporary political thought accentuates peaceful alternatives to war through arbitration, compromise, conciliation, dialogic methods, diplomacy, mediation, and negotiations. Each such approach rests on specific bodies of truth, experience, and specific literatures, and these methodologies represent an improvement over the presumed "superiority" of military responses. Allocation of resources for continuing study of the prevention, management, and resolution of conflict is imperative. Yet apart from the fact that the actual resolution of an acute conflict remains rare (most are reduced, demoted, or contained), these choices do not represent the full spectrum of alternatives to violent struggle. If such intercessionary and conciliation-based approaches are considered without respect for the substantial corpus of knowledge on the historic technique of nonviolent struggle, they are unlikely to contribute appreciably to a diminution of reliance on violent strategies.

Conflicts sometimes demand full threshing before attaining the stage of probing for options of resolution. Some strife results from harm of such acuity that no solution is possible until the causal origins of the conflict have been fully faced. Peace can remain unfit for mention in some strife until the depths of despair, humiliation, and anguish have been addressed to the satisfaction of the aggrieved, which may be one or both or several parties.

When the parties in a dispute possess severely unbalanced power, the lesser or weaker side may find it impossible to obtain a hearing apart from carrying out a nonviolent struggle, which can balance the sides in an otherwise lopsided relationship. Civil resistance strategies may be the *only* way to undermine the power of an adversary, equalize the sides, and reach parity. They may be the sole route to negotiations in acute conflicts between two unevenly matched sides. In fact, without employing nonviolent struggle, negotiations may eventuate, but be unproductive on their own. Negotiating can be futile without fundamental power shifts and modifications having occurred in the target group's own awareness of its vulnerability to popular consent. Nonviolent resistance may be in such instances the *only* way to reach negotiations, a point that King would articulate with lasting discernment in 1963 in his "Letter from Birmingham Jail," about which more will be said in this chapter.

Although the practice of nonviolent action reaches back to times prior to recorded history, rigorous theoretical analysis of the subject began approximately four decades ago. Some achievements have been lost to the possibility of analysis, and how many struggles have gone unchronicled can never be known. The understandings of power manifested by civil resistance are complex and cannot be reduced to a simple opposition of violence or nonviolence, which work in different ways. Elements of the theoretical comprehension of the power of nonviolent action had made some inroads into the U.S. black community as early as the 1920s, as African American leaders were becoming aware of the Indian subcontinent's freedom struggles, perceiving the Indian strategies for resistance to colonialism as applicable to societal conditions in the United States.

HOW KING LEARNED FROM INDIA

Martin Luther King, Jr. first heard about the type of power used by Mohandas K. Gandhi as a student at Morehouse College in Atlanta, Georgia, which he entered at age fifteen in the autumn of 1944. The courtly president of the college, Benjamin E. Mays, was international in outlook and had traveled to India in 1936 to meet with Gandhi. In his campus-wide Tuesday morning lectures, Dr. Mays would often mention the Indian independence struggles against British colonialism.

While at Morehouse, King was assigned to read *Civil Disobedience*, an essay by the New England transcendentalist Henry David Thoreau. On his first reading, King was struck by Thoreau, a captivation readily conveyed in King's writings and speeches. In 1958, he would write of Thoreau's essay, noting that he had been "fascinated by the idea of refusing to cooperate with an evil system," and that he was so deeply moved that he reread the work several times, his "first intellectual contact with the theory of nonviolent resistance."[6] King was intrigued by Thoreau's assertion that a creative minority could inspire a moral revolution. In 1962, King recalled his fascination:

> During my early college days I read Thoreau's essay on civil disobedience for the first time. Fascinated by the idea of refusing to cooperate with an evil system, I was so deeply moved that I re-read the work several times. I became deeply convinced then that non-cooperation with evil is as much a moral obligation as is cooperation with good. No other person has been more eloquent and passionate in getting his idea across than Henry David Thoreau.

6. Martin Luther King, Jr., *Stride Toward Freedom: The Montgomery Story* (New York: Harper, 1958) 91.

As a result of his writings and personal witness we are the heirs of a legacy of creative protest. It goes without saying that the teachings of Thoreau are alive today, indeed, they are more alive today than ever before. Whether expressed in a sit-in at lunch counters, a freedom ride to Mississippi, a peaceful protest in Albany, Georgia, a bus boycott in Montgomery, Alabama, it is an outgrowth of Thoreau's insistence that evil must be resisted and no moral man can patiently adjust to injustice.[7]

The question of the degree of popular deference or obedience to the nation-state is at the core of numerous present-day conflicts; hence, virtually all movements of civil resistance bear some debt to Thoreau. King and the U.S. civil rights movement were no exception.

In 1948, at the age of nineteen, King entered Crozer Theological Seminary in Chester, Pennsylvania. As a seminarian, he was intensely focused on the redemptive power of love. In pondering the three revealed religions, Judaism may be considered the religion of the will of God and obedience, Islam the religion of the majesty of God and humility, and Christianity the religion of the love of God and reciprocal love.[8] In a sense, Christianity needs only one word: *love,* expressed as "God is love." Gandhi, on the other hand, saw God as Truth. God, Truth, and love were for Gandhi all pervasive, penetrating everything, and one. Truth for Gandhi was not what could be counted or proved. Truth or God, for Gandhi, was "the search for realizing the truth of human unity." Yet he also often spoke of love and thought it stronger than anger or fear, because it was more intelligent and could lead to resolution of conflict rather than to destructiveness.

At Crozer, King was developing his understanding of *agape* love, which he saw as inseparable from justice, a conception that would sustain him for the rest of his life. In favoring the Greek word *agape*, King meant love in its sense of goodwill toward humanity, asking nothing in return. As with Gandhi, so, too, with King, love was not weak, sweet, or sentimental; rather, it was a source of power and energy. It allowed for differentiation between the person and the practices to be changed, because an interpretation of *agape* allows love for a person who does evil while hating the deed. Making a distinction between the wrong and the wrongdoer was also one

7. Martin Luther King, Jr., "Thoreau: A Centenary Gathering," *Massachusetts Review* 4 (1962), as cited in Mary Elizabeth King, *Mahatma Gandhi and Martin Luther King, Jr.,* 216–17.

8. Gerardus van der Leeuw, *Religion in Essence and Manifestation: A Study in Phenomenology* (London: Allen & Unwin, 1938) 597–649.

of Gandhi's touchstones, separating the person from the malice. The capacity to differentiate between the individuals who were implicated and the system that they administered or represented was essential for Gandhi, because it permitted conflict to be conducted on a depersonalized basis, without the corrosion resulting from personal animosity or hostility. Actions that resulted in counter-hatred, he believed, only increased animosities.

One Sunday afternoon in Philadelphia, King, the young seminarian, heard a sermon preached by the president of Howard University, Mordecai Wyatt Johnson. For twenty years Dr. Johnson had been speaking and preaching about the life and thinking of Gandhi. King writes that Johnson's message was "so profound and electrifying that I left the meeting and went out and bought half a dozen books on Gandhi's life and works."[9] Johnson encouraged young African Americans to study Gandhi because of the kinship he saw between the situation in the United States for black people and the struggle of the Indians against the British. As early as 1930, Johnson had proposed that Gandhi's theories and methods deserved "the Negro's most careful consideration."[10] In 1949, Johnson had spent forty days in India, meeting with individuals who had worked with Gandhi.

King's reading of Gandhi—a Hindu from childhood albeit an eclectic seeker of insights from faiths other than his own—resolved his own ideas about a philosophy based on *agape* love: "As I delved deeper into the philosophy of Gandhi my skepticism concerning the power of love gradually diminished, and I came to see for the first time its potency in the area of social reform."[11] Gandhi thus helped King integrate his Christian ministry with social and political action. He had previously thought that anything involving politics was incompatible with his Christian ministry. Reading Gandhi helped him resolve this dilemma:

> Love for Gandhi was a potent instrument for social and collective transformation. It was in this Gandhian emphasis on love and nonviolence that I discovered the method for social reform that I had been seeking. . . . The intellectual and moral satisfaction that I failed to gain from the utilitarianism of Bentham and Mill, the revolutionary methods of Marx and Lenin, the social-contract theory of Hobbes, the "back to nature" optimism of Rousseau, and

9. Ibid., 96.

10. Quoted in George Schuyler, "Views and Reviews," *Pittsburgh Courier*, March 29, 1930, 10; cited in Sudarshan Kapur, *Raising Up a Prophet: The African-American Encounter with Gandhi* (Boston: Beacon, 1992) 86, 187 n. 24.

11. King, *Stride Toward Freedom*, 97.

the superman philosophy of Nietzsche, I found in the nonviolent resistance philosophy of Gandhi. I came to feel that this was the only morally and practically sound method open to oppressed people in their struggle for freedom.[12]

Mohandas K. Gandhi had in 1893 traveled from India to work in South Africa with a law firm in Natal, where he first encountered blatant prejudice against people of dark complexions. Gandhi was not a systematic pacifist; he was an autodidact, who, with brilliant yet intuitive strategic intelligence, claimed that he could show a way to discover Truth by taking action in society. He conducted what he called "experiments"—to learn how to fight for one's rights, against injustice, an end to the caste system, lifting the oppression of women—and to do so without further deterioration. His fundamental conviction was that violence worsens the possibilities for lasting, intergenerational settlements. Historian Judith M. Brown contends that Gandhi, self-taught and not a trained thinker, should be viewed as a "pilgrim figure," whose life experiences as a social and political activist had forced him to contemplate major philosophical and political questions and deep human dilemmas.[13] Gandhi would speed the collapse of British imperialism, as such systems in general became dispirited and enervated. He may be credited with accelerating the disintegration of most forms of European colonialism. Gandhi was assassinated on January 30, 1948, the year that King was graduated from Morehouse College.

Starting in the 1920s, historian Sudarshan Kapur has shown that the ideas of Gandhi were traveling from India to the United States, as the African American news media reported on the Indian struggles. Through research in the morgues of black-owned newspapers, Kapur has shown that reporters were eagerly covering the Indian campaigns from the 1920s onward. Writing about the "little brown man" in India, they covered his fights against colonialism and for independence, his struggles against the caste system and poverty, and his efforts to reconcile Hindus and Muslims.

By the 1930s and 1940s, via ocean voyages and later propeller airplanes, prominent black leaders were traveling to India. Interaction was occurring between the black community in the United States and the Indian independence struggles, as Kapur documents, through a constant flow of black college presidents, professors, pastors, and journalists who journeyed

12. Ibid.

13. Judith M. Brown, ed., *Mahatma Gandhi—The Essential Writings*, Oxford World's Classics (Oxford: Oxford University Press, 2008) vi.

to India in order to meet Gandhi, and to study how to forge mass struggle with nonviolent means. Upon returning to the United States, they conveyed news of the various struggles through black-owned newspapers, churches, and lecture halls. They wrote articles, preached, gave lectures, and passed key documents from hand to hand for study by other black leaders.[14] The visitors included Howard Thurman, dean of the Rankin Chapel at Howard University. By the 1950s, James M. Lawson and Bayard Rustin had traveled to India, about whom more will be said.

Although Martin Luther King, Jr. would become the person most responsible for advancing and popularizing Gandhi's ideas in the United States—persuading black Americans of the value of the ideas and practices coming from India for effectively ending white racial domination—he was not the first and was one of many who brought this knowledge from India. Indeed, for decades prior to the emergence of King on the national stage, leading figures in the U.S. black community were voyaging to India to learn how to link the moral qualities of nonviolence that they admired with Gandhi's techniques for social and political struggle. By the time of the Montgomery bus boycott, for thirty years or more African American leaders had been talking about a "black Gandhi" for the United States. One woman called it "raising up a prophet," the source of the title of Kapur's book.

The young King was intrigued by reading Thoreau and Gandhi, yet he had not actually studied Gandhi seriously. A friend, J. Pius Barbour, remembered that the young seminarian argued on behalf of Gandhian methods at Crozer and "always contended that no minority can afford to adopt a policy of violence." King would clarify, "Just a matter of [arithmetic], [doctor]."[15] Hence, King started out with a stance based on numerical calculations—any minority would be outnumbered if it chose a policy of violence. Once King started to read Gandhi in 1950 and 1951, he became particularly fascinated by the 1930 Salt March and Gandhi's use of fasting, which had potential for penetrating the defenses of an obdurate opponent.

The Salt Laws of the British Raj penalized the poorest Indians, taxing a natural resource that was vital; they made it illegal for anyone to prepare salt from sea-water, so as not to deny London revenues from its colonies. The Salt March challenging the tax was to be part of a year-long

14 Kapur, *Raising Up a Prophet*, passim.

15. J. Pius Barbour, "Meditations on Rev. M. L. King, Jr., of Montgomery, Ala.," *National Baptist Voice* (March 1956), cited in Clayborne Carson et al., eds., *The Papers of Martin Luther King, Jr.*, vol. 3, *Birth of a New Age, December 1955–December 1956* (Berkeley: University of California Press, 1997) 16–17.

civil-disobedience movement in 1930 and 1931, embarked upon as part of the political program of the Indian National Congress (INC) for independence. The Congress passed a resolution delegating to Gandhi the responsibility for organizing the endeavor, Bombay was to be the headquarters, and activities were planned for every province. The laws were also emblematic of an unpopular foreign government.

Gandhi tried first to persuade the British through documentation, information, and argumentation. On March 2, 1930, ten days before the actual start of any action, Gandhi wrote to the British Viceroy in India, Lord Irwin, summarizing the grievances and advising the colonial authority of the planned actions. Ten days later, hearing no response, on March 12 Gandhi set out on the 241-mile march from Ahmedabad to the sea coast at Dandi, having selected seventy-nine adherents from all walks of life to accompany him. All were seasoned, trained for the ardors of twenty-four days on foot, and prepared to endure provocations to their nonviolent discipline without retaliation.

A large group of journalists accompanied the marchers, who, by the time they reached the sea, numbered in the tens of thousands. Surrounded by an international press corps, Gandhi stooped, filled his container with sea water, and set about to make salt. He called upon the entire nation to violate the Salt Laws. The next day, in India's six hundred thousand villages, people took out their pots and pans and proceeded to disobey the Salt Laws by evaporating sea water, in a militantly nonviolent campaign. A national boycott of imports, particularly of British goods, was in place. Women turned out in huge numbers, including large processions solely of women in various cities.[16] The reporters saw to it that reports spanned the globe of the sixty thousand Indians who were jailed in consequence. If the British did not have a change of heart, they would be forced to change, without a spirit of vengeance or revenge. A firsthand contemporary narrative by one of the marchers who set out with Gandhi, Krishnalal Shridharani, notes:

> [N]o less than 17,000 women . . . underwent various terms of imprisonment. . . . Thousands [of people] were wounded and hundreds killed. Despite this "reign of terror," the people of India displayed a remarkable degree of restraint and non-violent discipline. What is more important, slaughter and mutilation failed to repress the movement or intimidate the people. On the contrary,

16. Krishnalal Shridharani, *War without Violence* (New York: Harcourt Brace, 1939; expanded paperback version published in Chowpatty, Bombay: Bharatiya Vidya Bhavan, 1962) 123.

it exhausted the government itself. . . . After a full year of struggle, the government gave in and began negotiating with the Congress high command. Gandhi and the members of the Working Committee of the Congress were released from jail and the former was invited to Delhi.[17]

After direct negotiations with Lord Irwin, Gandhi permitted a truce and ended the civil disobedience campaign. The principal conditions were granted in a treaty called the "Gandhi-Irwin Pact" of 1930, as further talks ensued. Reading about it twenty years later, King was enthralled. He saw that no government or system could persist if the people cease to obey it. The idea implanted itself: one can refuse to submit to any government, laws, or customs that treat any group as inferior.

The more that King read Gandhi, the less he doubted the validity of a philosophy based on love, which was central to his preparation for the Christian ministry.[18] Yet an all-encompassing commitment to a purely nonviolent method for social and political change, associated by many with the life of King, had to wait until after the success of the Montgomery bus boycott.

A TECHNIQUE RATHER THAN COLLECTION OF BELIEFS AND PRINCIPLES

To be effective and successful, understanding the basic theories and methods is important, even vital, because nonviolent civil resistance is a form of power, knowledge of which greatly improves its prospects for success.[19] It utilizes economic, political, psychological, and social weapons. Whether one is opposing tyranny, fighting for democracy, pressing for human rights, opening closed structures, opposing military occupations, reforming systems, combating bureaucracy, or defending one's way of life, the method's use of power is more complex than military force or coercion based on domination. It can pull the legitimacy away from a repressive government and undermine the bulwarks that support it. It attacks the *power* of the opponent, not its well-being or the survival of its members.

17. Ibid., 126.

18. King, *Stride Toward Freedom*, 96.

19. See, for example, Gene Sharp, *Social Power and Political Freedom* (Boston: Porter Sargent, 1980).

That Gandhi and King both possessed deep religious faith has misled some into thinking that nonviolent action refers to spirituality or religion. A commitment to foreswear violence may be religiously based, but not necessarily. Nonviolent civil resistance is linked to religion for some practitioners, yet the technique of nonviolent civil resistance itself is not connected to religion. What constitutes a nonviolent movement are not the convictions held by participants, but the actions they take. Movements are composed of persons of innumerable persuasions. Gandhi often said that nonviolence was as "old as the hills," and, indeed, this kind of power shows up throughout history. Militantly committed to opposing what he saw as evil, Gandhi accepted the fact that many of those around him had tactically adopted nonviolence. He himself borrowed customary cultural traditions, perceiving the resonance that they would have for the Indian populace. Reaching back in time, he revived forms of mass collective action from bygone India in formulating his techniques, including a nineteenth-century indigo revolt, movements against landlords, and campaigns of tax resistance—peasant rebellions that had won support from élites. He was also writing about struggles elsewhere, such as the Hungarian nationalist struggle against the Hapsburgs from 1849 to 1867.[20] He followed closely the Russian Revolution of 1905 and its use of the general strike.[21]

Scholars believe that even prior to 1906, while still in South Africa, Gandhi had worked out the principles of power that would govern his experiments for the next four decades. Self-trained and lacking formal learning apart from his preparations in London for practicing the law, Gandhi had figured out at a very early stage of his life that any ruling power needed to secure cooperation, whether willing or coerced, from its subject population. Gandhi's writings from South Africa show that even prior to his first collective nonviolent action there in 1906, at the Empire Theatre in

20. M. K. Gandhi, "Benefits of Passive Resistance, Notable Instance," [from Gujarati] *Indian Opinion* (September 7, 1907), in *The Collected Works of Mahatma Gandhi* (hereafter *CWMG*), ed. K. Swaminathan, 100 vols. (New Delhi: Ministry of Information and Broadcasting, Government of India, 1958–1984) 7:184.

21. Observing events in Russia, Gandhi writes that the Russian people "have found another remedy which, though very simple, is more powerful than rebellion and murder. The Russian workers and all the other servants declared a general strike and stopped all work. They left their jobs and informed the Czar that, unless justice was done, they would not resume work. . . . It was quite impossible to exact work from people by force. It is not within the power of even the Czar of Russia to force strikers to return at the point of the bayonet. . . . We, too, can resort to the Russian remedy against tyranny." M. K. Gandhi, "Russia and India," [from Gujarati] *Indian Opinion* (November 11, 1905), in *CWMG*, 5:8.

Johannesburg, to protest a law of the colonial government that would require all "Asiatics" to carry registration cards, he had grasped a fundamental understanding that popular cooperation can be withdrawn. Thousands went to jail over this statute, and by 1914 the government would withdraw the act. Hence, while still in his early thirties, Gandhi had become familiar with a concept of group action as a method of struggle and viewed nonviolent resistance as a technique, and not a bricolage of beliefs or convictions. Gandhi's writings disclose that he had become aware that such an approach was not reliant on an ethical or moral orientation of either the challengers or the target group. He was attentively studying events around him in South Africa, as well as in Bengal, China, England, Ireland, and elsewhere in Africa, drawing correlations for his own efforts.

The evidence is unmistakable that even before departing from South Africa in 1914 to return to India the following year, Gandhi had embraced a consent theory of power in which all systems rely on such cooperation.[22] In 1905, Gandhi articulates this insight: "For even the most powerful cannot rule without the co-operation of the ruled."[23] If the people themselves were to cease conforming to the unspoken contract by which they are ruled, the power of a reigning government would shrink.[24] Faced with organized withholding of obedience, a state might collapse. By the time he wrote *Hind Swaraj* (Indian Home Rule) in 1909, Gandhi was forthrightly saying that India's independence was reliant on the Indians, in that British rule depended on their cooperation. "The English have not taken India; we have given it to them," Gandhi declared. He added: "They are not in India because of their strength, but because we keep them. . . . [I]t is truer to say that we gave India to the English than that India was lost. . . . The sword is entirely useless for holding India. We alone keep them. . . . We

22. According to Gene Sharp, "by 1905 Gandhi had already grasped the essentials of the theory of power which views all governments as constantly dependent upon the obedience and cooperation of the ruled." Gene Sharp, *Gandhi as a Political Strategist, with Essays on Ethics and Politics* (Boston: Porter Sargent, 1979) 27. See esp. chapter 2, "Origins of Gandhi's Use of Nonviolent Struggle," 23–41.

23. M. K. Gandhi, "Russia and India," *Indian Opinion* (November 11, 1905), in *CWMG* 5:8.

24. A starting point for studying this stream of thought is Étienne de la Boétie, *Oeuvres complétes d'Étienne de la Boétie* (Paris: J. Rouam, 1892). See Sharp, *Gandhi as a Political Strategist*, 11. Also see Roland Bleiker, *Popular Dissent, Human Agency and Global Politics*, Cambridge Studies in International Relations 70 (Cambridge: Cambridge University Press, 2000).

shall get nothing by asking; we shall have to take what we want . . ."[25] Expressing his ideas about freeing India from British colonial domination, he rebutted the advocacy of armed insurrection being promoted by zealous anarchists across the subcontinent. He realized that the British were well schooled in crushing nineteenth-century violent revolts and could put down any violence. Certainly by 1909, if not before, Gandhi saw that broadly based withdrawal of cooperation from the British Raj would wither its ability to govern. A trifling number of colonial officers were British. Indians staffed the civil service, law courts, police, and army. Millions more were professionals in banking, teaching, and health care. The contractors, building trades, merchant classes, and shopkeepers were Indian. The costs of the governmental apparatus of colonialism were borne by Indian taxes. By 1920, the Indian National Congress had accepted Gandhi's program of nonviolent noncooperation.

The number of human beings who would die in Gandhi's quarter-century of active engagement against the imperial power of the British appears high, by Richard Gregg's tally:

> In the Indian struggle for independence, though I know of no accurate statistic, hundreds of thousands of Indians went to jail, probably no more than five hundred received permanent physical injuries, and probably not over eight thousand were killed immediately or died later from wounds. No British, I believe, were killed or wounded. Considering the importance and size of the conflict and the many years it lasted, these numbers are much smaller than they would have been if the Indians had used violence against the British.[26]

Yet, as Gregg notes, this figure is a fraction of what would have resulted if the promoters of armed insurrection had prevailed.

THE CONNECTION BETWEEN MEANS AND ENDS

To understand Gandhi and his influence on King, one must grasp his profound rejection of conventional views that one's method can be separated from the results achieved. Gandhi was not simply arguing that a good

25. M. K. Gandhi, *Hind Swaraj, or, Indian Home Rule* (Ahmedabad: Navajivan, 1938; orig. 1909) 35–36 and 90.

26. Richard Gregg, *The Power of Nonviolence*, 2nd ed. (London: James Clarke, 1960) 100.

purpose does not justify morally bankrupt or violent means. He was repudiating any differentiation between the methods used and the goal. To Gandhi, and later for King, the means of action—the measures, or tools—should embody the aim. The means and ends might be protracted over time but they could not be split into two—they are one and the same. The forms of struggle should reveal the goal. Gandhi was more flexible on his ends than he was on the means. Today's nonviolent mobilizations reject the notion that the ends justify the means on both moral and strategic grounds. The overall strategy for a movement is tied to a sequencing of particular nonviolent methods. In theory, if a group's actions, step by step, are consistent with the ultimate goal, they improve the chances of producing intermediate successes along the way to larger objectives

For King, the "first principle" for the civil rights movement was that "the end represents the means in process and the ideal in the making."[27] Having studied Gandhi's rejection of variance between the method and the goal, he, too, adopted the perspective that the measures used should embody the purpose. With his own ethical framework coinciding with many of Gandhi's views, King thought it impossible to use destructive means and achieve constructive results. Both believed that it was important at the onset of a struggle to reach out to the opponent and attempt persuasion before going on to more coercive measures. Similarly, if possible, reconciliation was important in completion. This would be highly unlikely with *ad hoc*, improvisational spontaneity—it meant preparation, planning, and discipline.

King wanted the technique to work for the betterment of all the parties: "We do not wish to triumph over the white community. That would only result in transferring those now on the bottom to the top. But, if we can live up to nonviolence in thought and deed, there will emerge an interracial society based on freedom for all."[28] King worried that successes by the civil rights movement might lead to gloating. He warned against becoming "victimized with a philosophy of 'black supremacy'" and developing "a psychology of victors," regarding such a possibility as a danger and betrayal of the movement's basic goals.[29] He wanted "to win the victory

27. Martin Luther King, Jr., "Love, Law, and Civil Disobedience" (1961), in *A Testament of Hope: The Essential Writings and Speeches of Martin Luther King, Jr.*, ed. James M. Washington (San Francisco: Harper & Row, 1986) 45.

28. Martin Luther King, Jr., "Our Struggle," *Liberation* 1 (April 1956) 6, as cited in Mary Elizabeth King, *Mahatma Gandhi and Martin Luther King, Jr.*, 284.

29. Martin Luther King, Jr., "Give Us the Ballot: We Will Transform the South" (1957), in Washington, *Testament of Hope*, 200.

over the conflict situation, to persuade the opponent, not to triumph over him."[30] Gandhi, too, advised against triumphalism and shaming the target group. This reflected Gandhi's persisting hope that the opponent could be reached in such a way that conversion occurred—in which the attitudes and feelings of the adversary would have been won over. Such an outcome is extraordinarily rare, but for Gandhi and King it remained the ideal. Each step, thought King, should reflect the type of community envisioned. To achieve a nonviolent community, one must pursue one's objectives nonviolently. This congruity is an essential part of King's goal of what he called the beloved community.

Furthermore, nonviolent movements have often tended to lead to democratic outcomes, which may illustrate a connection between means and ends. A search for consensus, the building of unity, endless debates, and a culture of personal participation in making the decisions required for civil resistance all strengthen the likelihood of strong democratic governance. When people and groups contribute to developing goals, articulating grievances, and selecting messages and slogans, it creates a psychological expectation and lays the groundwork for the strengthening or later formation of democratic institutions.

A SHARED VIEW OF COWARDICE AS WORSE THAN VIOLENCE

Although Gandhi was adamantly opposed to submitting to oppression and injustice, if an individual were unable to summon the wherewithal to resist nonviolently, he would counsel a personal resort to violence rather than acquiescence. More than once, speaking of individual choice, he expressed the view that "cowardice is worse than violence."[31] He thought it preferable to speak with enmity honestly than to be hypocritical and avoid confrontation out of cowardice. Along with his fellow citizens, Gandhi was concerned about Indian masculinity and the colonial disparagement of some Indian men as weak and "unmanly." Gandhi's formulations were disputed by some in the Muslim community in India, because they were interpreted

---

30. Martin Luther King, Jr., 1957, seven note cards, no specific date or audience given, as cited in Mary Elizabeth King, *Mahatma Gandhi and Martin Luther King, Jr.*, 247.

31. Letter from M. K. Gandhi (April 18, 1932), in *CWMG*, 55:248.

as cowardice or unmanliness.[32] Historian Judith M. Brown explains that "his fear of cowardice tapped into one of the most sensitive cultural areas of Indian responses to imperial ideology. For Gandhi, real strength lay in moral and physical courage, sustained by constant physical and moral self-discipline, which found its highest manifestation in non-violent resistance to wrong. But in extreme conditions he felt that violent resistance was better than cowardly inaction."[33]

In 1920, in an article titled, "The Doctrine of the Sword," Gandhi writes:

> I do believe that when there is only a choice between cowardice and violence, I would advise violence. . . . I would rather have India resort to arms in order to defend her honor than that she should in a cowardly manner become or remain a helpless victim to her own dishonor. But I believe that nonviolence is infinitely superior to violence, forgiveness is more manly than punishment. . . . Let me not be misunderstood. Strength does not come from physical capacity. It comes from an indomitable will.[34]

"Anything is better than cowardice," Gandhi told an African American delegation visiting India in 1946, twenty-six years later. "It is violence double distilled."[35]

Gandhi also wanted to avoid the inaccurate and misleading connotations of the nineteenth-century term *passive resistance*, still in use in his day by English speakers. As he analyzed the situation, the fundamental choices were between the taking of action and passively doing nothing, because inaction left the oppression or injustice unchallenged, altering nothing. Action might be violent or nonviolent, and he would resolutely advise the choice of nonviolent action, but if the only action one could take was violent he thought this more desirable than doing nothing out of cowardice. Gene Sharp stresses, ". . . it is crucial to understand that the basic dichotomy

32. B. R. Nanda, *Gandhi: Pan-Islamism, Imperialism, and Nationalism in India* (Bombay: Oxford University Press, 1989) 290.

33. Judith M. Brown, "Gandhi and Civil Resistance in India, 1917–47: Key Issues," in *Civil Resistance and Power Politics: The Experience of Non-Violent Action from Gandhi to the Present*, ed. Adam Roberts and Timothy Garton Ash (Oxford: Oxford University Press, 2009) 49.

34. Gandhi, *Young India*, August 11, 1920, as cited in Mary Elizabeth King, *Mahatma Gandhi and Martin Luther King, Jr.*, 18.

35. Interview with Louis Fischer, biographer of Gandhi, in *Harijan*, August 4, 1946, as cited in Mary Elizabeth King, *Mahatma Gandhi and Martin Luther King, Jr.*, 228.

of social and political behavior is between action and inaction, rather than between nonviolence and violence."[36]

Martin Luther King, Jr. absorbed Gandhi's viewpoint, maintaining, "If the only alternative is between cowardice and violence, it is better—as Gandhi said—to use violence." As a student at Crozer Theological Seminary, King had felt that the problem of segregation could only be solved through "armed revolt." At that point, he reduced the Christian love ethic to "individual relationships," believing that it could not work in "social conflicts." A serious reading of the Gandhian ethic convinced King that the love ethic could be lifted from "individual relationships" to the sphere of "social transformation." "This Gandhi helped us to understand," King asserted, "and for this we are grateful a decade after his death."[37]

Noticing that the Montgomery bus boycott affected not solely the white racist oligarchy of the city, King saw that the black community was unexpectedly transformed:

> Everyone must realize that in the early days of the protest there were many who questioned the effectiveness and even the manliness, of nonviolence. But as the protest has continued there has been a growing commitment on the part of the entire Negro population. Those who were willing to get their guns in the beginning are coming to see the futility of such an approach.
>
> The struggle has produced a definite character development among Negroes. The Negro is more willing now to tell the truth about his attitude to segregation. In the past, he often used deception as a technique for appeasing and soothing the white man. Now he is willing to stand up and speak more honestly.
>
> Crime has noticeably diminished. . . . There is an amazing lack of bitterness, a contagious spirit of warmth and friendliness. . . . We did not anticipate these developments. But they have strengthened our faith in nonviolence. Believing that a movement is finally judged by its effect on the human beings associated with it, we are not discouraged by the problems that lie ahead.[38]

36. Sharp, *Politics of Nonviolent Action*, 1:65.

37. Martin Luther King, Jr., "His Influence Speaks to World Conscience," *Hindustan Times*, January 30, 1958, as cited in Mary Elizabeth King, *Mahatma Gandhi and Martin Luther King, Jr.*, 211.

38. King, "We Are Still Walking," *Liberation* (December 1956), as cited in Mary Elizabeth King, *Mahatma Gandhi and Martin Luther King, Jr.*, 245.

Traditional views held violence to be manly. Gandhi and King were aware of criticism that nonviolent struggle was "weakness." Each knew that civil resistance required and would affect the banishing of fear.

KING LEARNS FROM GANDHI: THE MONTGOMERY BUS BOYCOTT

Martin Luther King, Jr.'s theology was undoubtedly the major force shaping his life; he derived imperatives to nonviolent action from Scripture. His comprehension of fundamental strategies for organizing a movement, however, came from a study of Gandhi's national campaigns for India's independence. Serious contemplation of Gandhi's record began in Montgomery, soon after King had newly taken up his ministry there. On April 14, 1954, Martin Luther King accepted the invitation of the Dexter Avenue Baptist Church in Montgomery and became their pastor. Soon thereafter, the U.S. Supreme Court handed down *Brown v. Board of Education*, the first of its five landmark decisions ruling segregation in public schools unconstitutional.

Within a few short years of India's outlawing untouchability as unconstitutional, the black citizens of Montgomery launched a boycott. It was the first immediately recognizable nonviolent method to be collectively employed in what would come to be called the civil rights movement. The term *boycott* dates to 1880 in County Mayo, Ireland, when Captain Charles Cunningham Boycott, an appointed English land agent for Lord Erne, forced eleven tenants off the baron's land, and in consequence, the Irish peasant and merchant classes shunned and socially ostracized him. Blacksmiths declined to shoe Boycott's horses, laundresses refused to wash his laundry, shopkeepers would not serve him, and his servants resigned.[39]

Rosa Parks, a seamstress active in the National Association for the Advancement of Colored People (NAACP), was arrested on December 1, 1955, for refusing to yield her seat on a public conveyance to a white man. The Women's Political Council had previously been advocating boycotting as a means of resistance to racial segregation on Montgomery's buses for some time. Jo Ann Robinson, a leader in the council since 1950, worked

---

39. Joyce Marlow, *Captain Boycott and the Irish* (New York: Saturday Review, 1973) 136–42. Also see Clarence Marsh Case, *Nonviolent Coercion: A Study in the Methods of Social Pressure* (New York: Century, 1923) 305, as cited in Gene Sharp, *Methods of Nonviolent Action*, vol. 2, *The Politics of Nonviolent Action* (Boston: Porter Sargent, 1973) 220.

through the night to organize this action of economic noncooperation. King was elected unanimously to lead the Montgomery Improvement Association (MIA), the boycott organization. The city's black community learned how to use nonviolent sanctions such as boycotts through regular nightly "mass meetings," sessions usually held in churches. These sessions were preceded by congregational singing of freedom songs, not for worship in the traditional sense, and followed by training. Often involving role playing, such assemblies prepared the nonviolent challengers with practical applications of theoretical bases for action and taught them how to preserve nonviolent discipline if violently attacked.

The target in Montgomery was one city's bus system. The boycott's success—acknowledged when the Supreme Court ruled, on November 13, 1956, that local laws requiring segregation on buses were unconstitutional—lifted hopes for similar abolition of other discriminatory practices in the South. Remembered for the exquisite unity of the city's black populace during meticulously implemented civil resistance, the boycott set the parameters of strategic nonviolent action for the civil rights movement as a whole, which within one decade would undermine the legal supports for the racial caste system of the United States. It happened the way that King had hoped, commensurate with consistency between means and ends. "The tension in Montgomery is not between seventy thousand white people and fifty thousand Negroes," King declared. "The tension is at bottom a tension between justice and injustice," between "the forces of light and the forces of darkness." "And if there is a victory," King continued, "it will not be a victory" for fifty thousand Negroes in Montgomery or sixteen million Negroes in America, "but a victory for justice, a victory for good will, a victory for democracy."[40]

At 9:30 P.M. on January 30, 1956, a stick of dynamite exploded on the porch of the parsonage of the Dexter Avenue Baptist Church. Rushing home to his family, King found his wife, Coretta, and their firstborn, Yolanda, unharmed. Once confident that they were safe, King turned to find his black neighbors, outraged, shoving the police and city officials, including the mayor and police commissioner, who had stopped by that night. Some neighbors, frightened and alarmed by the attempted killing of the pastor and his family, had retribution in mind. Many were carrying

---

40. Martin Luther King, Jr., "Non-Aggression Procedures to Interracial Harmony," address delivered to executives of the Home Mission Societies of Christian Friends, Green Lake, Wisconsin (July 23, 1956), in Carson et al., *Papers*, 3:326.

arms. At that moment, the grandson of slaves peered out from the thick darkness surrounding the portico of his bombed-out residence, raised his hand for silence, and looked into the eyes of his distressed kindred. "Don't get your weapons," he implored the crowd. "He who lives by the sword will perish by the sword. . . . We are not advocating violence. We want to love our enemies. . . . I did not start this boycott. I was asked by you to serve as your spokesman. . . ." His voice quivering, he reassured his listeners that if anything happened to him it would not cut short the boycott, because he was not indispensable: "[I]f I am stopped this movement will not stop. If I am stopped our work will not stop. For what we are doing is right."[41]

King's sincerity and the resilience of his faith affected his listeners so that they set aside their talk of retaliation and returned home. The perpetrators who might have killed his wife and baby were misguided, in King's mind, and caught up in collective evil. Across the United States, the public marveled, observing how he had been able to rise above loathing and hatred. It was, if not Martin Luther King's greatest oration, his finest hour. The spirit of the full mass movement yet to unfold was impressed on observers the world over. To the extent that there is a precise moment at which the nonviolent parameters for the decade-long American struggle were drawn, it would coincide with this moment, when the reluctant young leader was recognized to have stature beyond his twenty-seven years.

What is noteworthy is that in 1956, having learned only the rudiments of nonviolent struggle, King was nonetheless thinking globally, insisting that nonviolent resistance was "an important method," a "method that I would like to recommend," and "a method that all of the oppressed peoples of the world must use if justice is to be achieved in a proper sense." King went on to note that the "technique of nonviolence" is "not a method of submission or surrender," but "a method that is *very* active in seeking to change conditions . . ."[42]

The framework for the U.S. civil rights movement of the 1960s as one of strategic nonviolent action was engendered by the Montgomery bus boycott, and it was derived from Gandhi. "While the Montgomery boycott was going on," King said, "India's Gandhi was the guiding light of our technique

41. Joe Azbell, "Blast Rocks Residence of Bus Boycott Leader" *Montgomery Advertiser*, January 31, 1956, as cited in Carson et al., *Papers*, 3:115.

42. "Non-Aggression Procedures to Interracial Harmony," in Carson et al., *Papers*, 3:321–28.

of nonviolent social change."[43] Even so, the formation of a politically so-phisticated and all-encompassing creed would have to await a renewed encounter with the serious study of nonviolent struggle.

King was neither generative nor original in creating the nonviolent strategies that he promoted, but he was an apt student and able to absorb, study, learn, modify, and teach his understanding of the technique, which would ultimately encourage other movements on the world stage in the decades to come. In so doing, he became one of history's most influential agents for propagating knowledge of the potential for constructive social change without resorting to violence. How he himself learned the theory and practice of nonviolent civil resistance is a reminder that this method is neither intuitive nor spontaneous, but a logical system that must be learned. Comprehension and preparation are frequently essential elements in explaining the emergence of a nonviolent mobilization.

TUTORIALS IN GANDHI'S STRATEGIES

Upon moving to Montgomery, the Kings kept a pistol in the parsonage. Even in its cities, the southland of the United States retained rural char-acteristics. Aspects of the frontier mentality persisted, and the South had inherited from the brutal practices of slave overseers a tolerance of weap-onry. Furthermore, in an agrarian society, guns were always available for hog killings, hunting game for food, or to put a horse out of its misery; learning to shoot was often a rite of passage into adulthood.

After the bombing of the parsonage, floodlights were installed to il-luminate the grounds at night, and sentries were posted. King allowed his watchmen to carry pistols and shotguns, and to bring them inside the par-sonage, as his church's trustees had insisted that his guards be armed. He applied to the county sheriff for a permit to carry a pistol.[44] King portrayed these initiatives as a matter of self-defense and, when asked whether these were compatible with a nonviolent movement, responded that they implied no intention to harm anyone unless he and the security teams were first attacked with violence.

43. Martin Luther King, Jr., "My Trip to the Land of Gandhi," *Ebony*, July 1959, in Washington, *Testament of Hope*, 23.

44. David J. Garrow, *Bearing the Cross: Martin Luther King, Jr., and the Southern Christian Leadership Conference* (New York: William Morrow, 1986) 62.

Later, becoming uncertain about this decision, King began to feel that there was a contradiction between leading a nonviolent movement and permitting the use of arms to protect himself and his family. Despite an avowal that he had banned guns after conversing with Coretta about this predicament, two months into the boycott visitors reported that King's bodyguards had an "arsenal."[45]

Among King's earliest callers was Bayard Rustin, a black socialist and Quaker who had spent twenty-eight months in jail as a conscientious objector during World War II. In the 1920s, he had been a disciple of A. Philip Randolph, founder and head of the Brotherhood of Sleeping Car Porters, one of the earliest black labor unions of the United States. Randolph had threatened a march on Washington, planned for June 1941, which, although called off, had compelled President Franklin D. Roosevelt to issue an executive order banning racial discrimination in the defense industries. Joining with other black leaders in 1947, Randolph had pressured President Harry S. Truman to issue an executive order desegregating the armed services. The 1941 blueprint for a march on Washington was the precursor for the 1963 national march on Washington, in which Rustin would play a major role behind the scenes. As early as 1942, Rustin had presciently written an essay asserting that only with nonviolent direct action could Jim Crow be ended.[46] He was active in the Congress of Racial Equality (CORE), founded by James Farmer and based on strict Gandhian theories and methods, and until 1953 had worked for the Fellowship of Reconciliation (FOR), a pacifist organization that had come into existence around the time of World War I. It is still actively teaching what it terms "militant nonviolence."

At the time Rustin called on the Dexter parsonage, he was employed by the War Resisters' League in New York. In 1948, he had been invited by the Indian National Congress, the political party that aligned itself with Gandhi, for some time to study Gandhi's campaigns. Rustin's exposure in India led to his being sent to Montgomery to advise King, because sympathetic onlookers believed that the young minister lacked experience in the technique of nonviolent struggle.[47] He was among a group of activists,

45. King, *Stride Toward Freedom*, 141; Glenn E. Smiley to John Swomley and Alfred Hassler, February 29, 1956, as cited in Carson et al., *Papers*, 3:14 n. 60.

46. Bayard Rustin, "The Negro and Nonviolence," *Fellowship* (October 1942), in Bayard Rustin, *Down the Line: The Collected Writings of Bayard Rustin* (Chicago: Quadrangle, 1971) 8–12.

47. Bayard Rustin, interview, in Howell Raines, *My Soul Is Rested: Movement Days in the Deep South Remembered* (New York: Putnam, 1977) 53.

communists, pacifists, reformers, radical Christians, and socialists who were elated by King and believed that he could take the fight for justice to a new order of magnitude unlike anything the United States had seen since the abolition of slavery. The forty-four-year-old Rustin, seventeen years King's senior, would go on to help King to develop flinty self-discipline and build the Montgomery boycott into a mature, political usage of nonviolent collective action. He decided to work for King full time. The War Resisters League let him leave for this assignment.[48] He hoped the city-wide campaign could become the basis for a broad-based mass mobilization across the South.

When Rustin first arrived in Montgomery on February 21, 1956, King was away, and he noticed the sentinels patrolling the King home, a round-the-clock detail of armed black security officers. After King returned, Rustin called at the parsonage on February 26, divulged his controversial past, and listened as King responded that the boycott needed as much help as it could obtain.[49] Rustin was alarmed that a gun was lying in a chair in the living room during his meeting.[50] He later recollected:

> Now, quite contrary to what many people think, Dr. King was not a confirmed believer in nonviolence, totally, at the time that the boycott began. . . . [I]t was gradually over several weeks that Dr. King continuously deepened his commitment to nonviolence, and within six weeks, he had demanded that there be no armed guards and no effort at associating himself with any form of violence. . . . I take no credit for Dr. King's development, but I think that the fact that Dr. King had someone around recommending certain

48. Not everyone in New York viewed Rustin with unadulterated admiration. Associated in the 1930s with the Young Communist League, he had three years earlier been convicted in Pasadena, California, for homosexual activity. Rustin's plans were condemned by some who feared that stigma from his personal and political history would hurt King. A. Philip Randolph and A. J. Muste, the Christian pacifist leader of FOR, approved of Rustin's working for King. The initial recommendation that Rustin join King had been made by Lillian Smith, author of the famed antilynching novel *Strange Fruit*, which roiled the 1940s, and she was one of the first white Southerners to support King publicly. See Mary Elizabeth King, *Mahatma Gandhi and Martin Luther King, Jr.*, 119–20.

49. Jervis Anderson, *Bayard Rustin: Troubles I've Seen: A Biography* (New York: HarperCollins, 1997) 185.

50. Bayard Rustin, interview with T. H. Baker (June 17, 1969), Lyndon Baines Johnson Library, Austin, Texas, as cited in Carson et al., *Papers*, 3:14 n. 60; Rustin interview in Raines, *My Soul Is Rested*, 53.

readings and discussing these things with him was helpful to bring up in him what was obviously already there.[51]

This was unsuitable for a Gandhian leader, as Rustin recalled spelling out for King: "If in the heat and flow of battle a leader's house is bombed and he shoots back, then that is an encouragement to his followers to pick up guns. If, on the other hand, he has no guns around him, and his followers know it, then they will rise to the nonviolent occasion."[52] The black community in Montgomery, as elsewhere in the South, was armed, and not everyone was amenable to hearing of justice as correcting that which would work against love. Rustin was properly concerned that the young exemplar of militant nonviolence might falter without deeper foundations.

Rustin was, however, intrigued by twenty-three dispatch centers that were organized in Montgomery, where the resisters could find rides in black sections of town. Beside pooled taxis and borrowed automobiles, three other transportation methods functioned: hitchhiking, driving of domestic servants by white employers, and walking. King introduced Rustin to a man whose work demanded that he walk seven miles a day and another who daily trod fourteen miles.[53] When King despaired of finding more vehicles to help those on foot, Rustin telephoned A. Philip Randolph for guidance. Randolph told Rustin to go to Birmingham, where black steelworkers could earn enough to own two cars, and ask them to donate their second cars, which they did.[54]

Rustin found King to have sound instincts, an aptitude for blending his religious faith with shrewd strategic planning, and a handle on the sheer persistence required for nonviolent resistance. While plying King with books and bidding him to analyze Gandhi, Rustin formed an enduring alliance with the young pastor, managed his correspondence, composed freedom songs for the nightly mass meetings, arranged car pools, wrote working papers and news releases, raised funds, secured legal assistance, and set up bail.[55]

Rustin's interpretation of a kernel of Gandhian strategy helped King and other leaders realize that they should not consider arrests and jailings as burdensome, but as momentous opportunities. When you go to jail,

51. See Raines, *My Soul Is Rested*, 53.

52 Anderson, *Trouble I've Seen*, 188.

53. Bayard Rustin, "Montgomery Diary," in Rustin, *Down the Line*, 57.

54. Anderson, *Trouble I've Seen*, 189.

55. Ibid., 189 and 195.

Rustin demonstrated with clapping hands, make it into a party! This is your chance to make a testament. Go to jail joyfully. Sing, clap, and chant! Don't wait to be rounded up. Walk with a light step, deliberately and happily, toward the waiting paddy wagons. This is the instant to show the earnestness of your goals and be persuasive. King was able to take this crucial morsel of perception and imbue the civil rights movement with an appreciation of how jailings might penetrate the psychological defenses of the onlooker.[56]

Rustin was clear-thinking and possessed atypical insights that he was not afraid to express. Despite his astuteness, some soft-spoken Southerners experienced Rustin as an abrasive Northerner. His detractors soon outnumbered his admirers.[57] Objections reached A. Philip Randolph in New York, who telegraphed Rustin that he should return. Instead, Rustin went to Birmingham, for a short time, and continued to advise King.[58]

King's tutorials proceeded under someone equally competent. Glenn E. Smiley was a white, Texas-born Methodist minister who, along with Rustin, was a field secretary with FOR in the 1940s and was imprisoned as a conscientious objector during World War II. Among the few seasoned professional trainers in nonviolent direct action in the United States, he had organized three and a half months of sit-ins against the 350-seat Bullock's Tea Room in Los Angeles in the 1940s, ending the establishment's policy of racial discrimination.[59] Committed and painstaking, Smiley considered Rustin his "American guru," and the two men initially overlapped in Montgomery in early 1956. Both FOR veterans were concerned that King's understanding was not sufficiently deep enough for a national leader of a nonviolent mass movement. Arriving on February 27, 1956, two months into the boycott, Smiley wrote in a report to FOR concerning King:

> He had Gandhi in mind when this thing started, he says. Is aware
> of the dangers to him inwardly, wants to do it right, but is too
> young and some of his close help is violent. King accepts, as an
> example, a body guard, and asked for a permit for them to carry

56. Ibid., 4 and 185–96. See also Daniel Levine, *Bayard Rustin and the Civil Rights Movement* (New Brunswick: Rutgers University Press, 2000) 122.

57. "Even the shrewd and intelligent help of Bayard Rustin verged on a kind of manipulation I disliked," said Harris Wofford, Jr. "Steeped in Gandhian lore . . . Rustin seemed ever-present with advice, and sometimes acted as if King were a precious puppet . . ." See Harris Wofford, *Of Kennedys and Kings: Making Sense of the Sixties* (Pittsburgh: University of Pittsburgh Press, 1980) 115.

58. Anderson, *Trouble I've Seen*, 185–96 and 198.

59. Glenn Smiley, "A Pebble Thrown into the Pond," *Fellowship* (June 1989) 8.

guns. This was denied by the police, but nevertheless, the place is an arsenal. King sees the inconsistency but not enough. . . . The whole movement is armed in a sense. . . . At first King was asked merely to be the spokesman of the movement, but . . . he has really become the real leader and symbol of growing magnitude. . . . Soon he will be able to direct the movement by the sheer force of being the symbol of resistance.[60]

Smiley recalled that King had asked him to "teach him everything [Smiley] knew about nonviolence, since by his own admission he had only been casually acquainted with Gandhi and his methods."[61] The new resident tutor wondered in writing why God had laid hands on someone so young, so inexperienced, and so good.[62] Smiley noticed that King rarely used the word *nonviolent* and seemed to prefer the nineteenth-century term *passive resistance*, which Gandhi had discarded as misleading half a century earlier. In 1907, Gandhi offered a small prize through his journal in South Africa, *Indian Opinion*, for the best proposal of a single word to express his principles of Truth and Love as the forces of power and change. With small alteration, Gandhi chose *satyagraha*, literally meaning holding onto Truth, firmness in Truth, a relentless search for Truth.[63] Gandhi explained the Sanskrit origins: "Truth (*satya*) implies love, and firmness (*agraha*) engenders and therefore serves as a synonym for force."[64] The term is used in India both for Gandhi's experiments in nonviolent action and to describe individual struggles using such methods. For the modern reader in English, *satyagraha* may be best understood as a concept equivalent to nonviolent direct action or nonviolent resistance.

First Rustin and then Smiley systematically reintroduced King to Gandhi's thinking through books on nonviolent struggle. Among the works

60. Glenn Smiley to Muriel Lester, February 28, 1956; Glenn Smiley to John Swomley and Alfred Hassler (editor of *Fellowship*), February 29, 1956, as cited in Adam Fairclough, *To Redeem the Soul of America: The Southern Christian Leadership Conference and Martin Luther King, Jr.* (Athens: University of Georgia Press, 1987) 25.

61. Glenn Smiley, *Nonviolence: The Gentle Persuader* (Nyack, NY: Fellowship of Reconciliation, 1991) 5.

62. Glenn Smiley to Muriel Lester, February 28, 1956; Glenn Smiley to Alfred Hassler (editor of *Fellowship*), February 29, 1956, as cited in Fairclough, *To Redeem the Soul of America*, 24–26.

63 B. R. Nanda, *Mahatma Gandhi: A Biography* (New Delhi: Oxford University Press, 1958) 95.

64. M. K. Gandhi, "The Advent of Satyagraha," in *Satyagraha in South Africa*, trans. Valji Govindji Desai (Ahmedabad: Navajivan, 1928) 109.

was *The Power of Nonviolence* by Richard Gregg (quoted earlier), a white Southerner and a Quaker, who spent four years in India studying Gandhi's methods while he was alive. In exquisite prose, he wrote to interpret Gandhi for Western readers. Gregg soon began corresponding with King. Another volume that King closely analyzed was *War without Violence*, by Krishnalal Shridharani (also cited above), one of the original seventy-nine adherents who trained with Gandhi for the 1930 Salt March and walked with him to the seacoast, where they prepared salt from seawater.[65] Smiley termed Shridharani's book "a tiny pebble . . . thrown into the pond," from which "the resulting ripples and waves" had not "reached the distant shores of our planet."[66] Originally published in 1939, based on Shridharani's doctoral dissertation at Columbia University, and abounding with picturesque details, it is a contemporaneously written, firsthand analysis of Gandhi's strategic theories and methods. It was often passed hand to hand. During the 1940s, this work was avidly studied by U.S. black leaders. A. J. Muste, among the twentieth century's most influential pacifists, was among numerous other readers.[67]

Regardless, some of King's security men, deacons and lay leaders of the Dexter Avenue Baptist Church, insisted that King carry a gun. More than three months into the boycott, Rustin reported to colleagues in FOR that even though King rejected violence, he had found "considerable confusion on the question as to whether violence is justified in retaliation to violence directed against the Negro community."[68] The question of armed self-defense kept surfacing, and whether, if attacked, retaliation was appropriate. King carried his gun for a period of time but started to feel uncomfortable with the practice, and he confided in Smiley regarding his doubts. King asked him when he should give it up, to which Smiley responded, "When the gun gets too heavy, you will put it down."[69] King's ambiguous

65. Shridharani, *War without Violence*.

66. Smiley, "Pebble Thrown into the Pond," 8.

67. Ibid. In 1941, James Farmer, then with FOR and soon to found CORE, met and consulted Shridharani, whom he remembered as a *brahmin*, and whose firsthand account of the Salt March stimulated the advocates around FOR. James Farmer, "On Cracking White City," in Raines, *My Soul Is Rested*, 28.

68. Bayard Rustin, "Report on Montgomery, Alabama" (March 21, 1956), cited in Carson et al., *Papers*, 3:20 and 514.

69. Glenn Smiley to Martin Luther King, Jr., in James M. Lawson, Jr., interview with the author, Los Angeles, California (February 27, 1996), as cited in Mary Elizabeth King, *Mahatma Gandhi and Martin Luther King, Jr.*, 125 n. 78. Lawson learned firsthand of this interchange from Smiley.

ruminations about armed self-defense and violence as a possibly necessary response would soon harden into an outright disavowal of violence.

In March 1956, Rustin returned to New York. Writing to Rustin, King noted the intensification of the boycott and asked his help on its behalf in New York. King was aware that alterations were occurring in his own mind. "When I went to Montgomery as a pastor," he recalled, "I had not the slightest idea that I would later become involved in a crisis in which nonviolent resistance would be applicable." King also recounted that when the bus protest began, his mind, "consciously or unconsciously," drifted back to Jesus' Sermon on the Mount, "with its sublime teachings on love," and also "the Gandhian method of nonviolent resistance." King increasingly articulated the power of nonviolent action, and civil resistance ultimately became not merely "a method" to which he "gave intellectual assent" but, more importantly, "a commitment to a way of life."[70] Gandhi's works "deeply fascinated" him, and he wrote that the "whole Gandhian concept of *satyagraha*" had become profoundly significant to him.[71] King now acknowledged the moral value of what Gandhi had taught the world.

"TWELVE MONTHS OF GLORIOUS DIGNITY": 381 DAYS OF BOYCOTT

As previously noted, the U.S. Supreme Court ruled on November 13, 1956, that local statutes requiring racial segregation on buses were unconstitutional. In the same way that nightly mass meetings in churches had prepared the black community in Montgomery on the importance of nonviolent discipline, so as not to give a pretext for harsh retaliation, meetings were now set up to prepare the boycotters for their return to public transportation. Most churches erected bus simulations to allow the playing of roles of hostile whites who refused to accept the court's ruling. King was disappointed that not one white organization in the capital city similarly sought to prepare white citizens. The bus integration order at last arrived on December 20, having been received from the clerk of the court in Washington, and mass meetings were scheduled for that night at several black churches. "We seek an integration based on mutual respect," King told the

70. King, *Stride Toward Freedom*, 101.

71. Martin Luther King, Jr., "Pilgrimage to Nonviolence," *Christian Century* 77 (April 13, 1960) 440.

ebullient crowd, warning that "twelve months of glorious dignity" would have been squandered if violence were to be utilized. "We must now move from protest to reconciliation," he said.[72] After the meeting, King asked his fellow clergy to spread out two by two and ride the buses for a few days, to reinforce the willpower needed to avoid retaliation to any slurs or abuses. Smiley rode twenty-eight buses on the first day and witnessed three violent actions against black passengers. Notwithstanding the restraint of the black community, state-condoned terror groups soon rose again and the Ku Klux Klan flagrantly marched. Still, the nonviolent discipline held tight.

In the midst of the boycott, King studied and became interested in Gandhi's formulation of a *constructive program*, which attempted to address long-term, intergenerational problems. The question for Gandhi was how to achieve major change in the existing social and political order without relying on traditional approaches that had failed in the past. He did not want to emphasize strategies that centralized power; his ideal was direct democracy, and he believed that democracy's best guarantor was in decentralization and deconcentration. Part of Gandhi's eighteen-point constructive program was the creation of decentralized institutions that could serve as the infrastructure for a just society. Perhaps most significant, Gandhi saw the constructive program as a way of actualizing a new social reality in the midst of the old—while still bowed down by injustice or oppression, people could begin to create more equitable organizations and achieve self-sufficiency in the process. The building of alternative, or parallel, institutions could lessen dependency on the opponent, enabling the building of a new order in the midst of the old. Under the influence of such views, King writes in *Stride Toward Freedom*, "The constructive program ahead must include a campaign to get Negroes to register and vote."[73] Gandhi saw the constructive program as the basis for a national strategy of noncooperation, something that King was not thinking about, but helped by study of Gandhi, King was by the mid-1950s clearly beginning to look at the power potential of voter registration. Parallel institutions also provide a way to withdraw some of the bases of an opponent's power. This approach would be utilized in the 1964 organizing of credit unions, cooperatives, and a parallel political party, which were developed in the Mississippi Freedom Summer by the Student Nonviolent Coordinating Committee (SNCC) and

72. Martin Luther King, Jr., "Statement on Ending the Bus Boycott," in Carson et al., *Papers*, 3:487.

73 King, *Stride Toward Freedom*, 222.

the Congress of Racial Equality (CORE). Such alternative institutions allowed black Mississippians to circumvent the jurisdiction of white oligarchies in pursuit of social justice while also withdrawing cooperation from racist structures.

The success of the Montgomery campaign led the young pastor to embark on a process of rediscovery, instigated by the specialists in civil resistance with whom he was working, and through continuing inquiry to comprehend the theories and techniques disclosed in Gandhi's writings in a deeper way. King's pilgrimage had begun as an intellectual exercise, combining theological study with conviction in the social responsibility required of Christians. No longer viewing nonviolent struggle as an arithmetical calculation for an outnumbered minority as noted earlier, King's views intensified in graduate school, and he located nonviolent struggle within a larger theological spectrum. He now began serious engagement with the politics, strategic thinking, and tactics of nonviolent struggle. Through Gandhi, King would learn how to stand face to face with power.

REDISCOVERY: "GANDHI FURNISHED THE METHOD"

Many in the National Baptist Convention, the denominational body with which King and his church were affiliated, viewed nonviolent action as ill-mannered. Others in the convention, such as its president, Joseph H. Jackson, felt threatened by King and thought he might harm their own standing and prestige; a great number were plainly cold to him. Some favored a "separate but equal" society, in which they could dominate. A small group within the convention backed King, but others didn't even want him formally to address the denomination.[74] The Baptist decentralized structure, with each congregation electing its minister, meant that any testy black Baptist ministers would have been hard to rally under the best of circumstances. The NAACP, and its leader Roy Wilkins, considered King an interloper, often frankly mocking his advocacy of nonviolent resistance.

---

74. By 1961, King, then thirty-two, would be removed as an officer of the National Baptist Convention USA due to his leadership in the civil rights movement. See J. H. Jackson, *A Story of Christian Activism: The History of the National Baptist Convention, U.S.A., Inc.* (Nashville: Townsend, 1980) 483–85; Charles H. King, "Quest and Conflict: The Untold Story of the Power Struggle Between King and Jackson," *Negro Digest* (May 1967) 6–9, 71–79; William D. Booth, "Dr. L. Venchael Booth and the Origin of the Progressive National Baptist Convention, Inc.," *American Baptist Quarterly* 20 (2001) 72–90.

They wanted nothing that might challenge their preeminence and were opposed to the creation of another organization.

Even so, Rustin and Smiley were discussing the future with King, and began planning for the establishment of what would be called the Southern Christian Leadership Conference (SCLC). They considered it crucial to sustain the momentum from Montgomery and build upon it to create a strategy for the American South as a whole.

On New Year's Day, 1957, King, along with the Reverend C. K. Steele of the Tallahassee, Florida, bus boycott, which had occurred conterminously with the Montgomery campaign, and the Reverend Fred L. Shuttlesworth, a pivotal figure in Birmingham, mailed approximately one hundred invitations for a meeting at Ebenezer Baptist Church, in Atlanta, scheduled for January 10 and 11, three weeks after the Montgomery boycott's completion. There, working papers were provided by Rustin and Ella J. Baker, who, when she had been national field secretary and director of field offices for the NAACP, had worked to strengthen the Montgomery chapter. A spate of bombings at four churches and two parsonages forced King to return to Montgomery, so Coretta Scott King and Shuttlesworth presided, with Rustin and Baker at hand.[75] To Rustin, the session was historic:

> Sixty Negro leaders had come from 29 localities of 10 Southern states for the first session of the Negro Leaders Conference on Nonviolent Integration. . . . Leaders struggling with economic boycotts and reprisals in South Carolina were standing in a corner exchanging views with "strong men" from the Mississippi Delta, who are forced to carry on their work at night, underground. The first person to take the floor was a man who had been shot because he had dared to vote.[76]

Upon King's return, the gathering learned that no one had been hurt in the six bombings. As the meeting closed, Rustin recalled, King "spoke movingly on the power of nonviolence."

In response to King's resolve in specifying that the word *Christian* be part of the name of the group being formed, the Southern Christian Leadership Conference was born. King was elected president, a post he would hold until his death in 1968. Its motto, "To Redeem the Soul of America," reflected its base among church leaders and commitment to bring about

75. Garrow, *Bearing the Cross*, 86.

76. Bayard Rustin, "Even in the Face of Death," *Liberation* (February 1957), in Rustin, *Down the Line*, 101.

redemptive nonviolent change. A series of meetings would follow in various cities.

King had in Montgomery come to believe that nonviolent strategies held potential for improving reconciliation and, thus, realization of "the beloved community."[77] He had become the principal interpreter for the Southern black community of theories and methods absorbed from study of the Indian independence struggles. He was able to communicate within a biblical ethos the knowledge of the specific powers of nonviolent civil resistance that Gandhi had developed in South Africa and India. King in 1957 said as much: "Non-violent resistance had emerged as the technique of the movement, while love stood as the regulating ideal. Christ furnished the spirit and motivation, while Gandhi furnished the Method."[78] Moreover, as the black-owned newspapers in Atlanta, Pittsburgh, New York, and elsewhere reported on the unity and determination of the Montgomery boycott, they were kindling the spirits of African Americans across the South and rousing the energies of black leaders of all political outlooks across the nation.

JAMES M. LAWSON, JR.: "WE DON'T HAVE ANYONE LIKE YOU!"

In February 1957, King met another individual who would affect both his theoretical and technical grasp of nonviolent action. At a speaking invitation at Oberlin College in Ohio, King met a black Methodist minister named James M. Lawson, Jr., who was spending a year at Oberlin in preparatory study for his ministry. King learned that Lawson had served thirteen months in U.S. federal prison for refusing to cooperate with conscription during the Korean War. During Lawson's imprisonment, the Board of Missions of the Methodist Church successfully petitioned the court for him to be appointed to them, and they assigned him to teach at Hislop College in Nagpur, India. Lawson told King that he had decided while in college that he would become a Methodist minister and go south to work to end segregation and racism. Already an ordained deacon, study at Oberlin was

77. Martin Luther King, Jr., "The Power of Nonviolence," in Washington, *Testament of Hope*, 12.

78. Clayborne Carson et al., eds., *The Papers of Martin Luther King, Jr.*, vol. 5, *Threshold of a New Decade, January 1959–December 1960* (Berkeley: University of California Press, 2005) 423; King, *Stride Toward Freedom*, 85.

part of Lawson's plan. Engrossed by Lawson's background, King noted that they were both aged twenty-eight. King exclaimed, "Don't wait! Come now! You're badly needed. We don't have anyone like you!"[79] At that moment, Lawson made a commitment to King.

Virtually unknown to countless numbers of those who have studied Gandhi and King, Lawson is, as much as anyone, their connector—a human bridge linking knowledge from India to the U.S. civil rights movement and beyond to contemporary struggles. Lawson had arrived at Nagpur, in Maharashtra, at the crossroads of India, in 1953, five years after Gandhi's death. He spent the next three years teaching at Hislop College, a Presbyterian institution subsequently affiliated with Nagpur University. Meeting numerous individuals who had worked with Gandhi and learning firsthand of the *satyagraha* campaigns from participants, Lawson visited sites of the independence struggles. More than once he met with Jawaharlal Nehru, India's first prime minister. Lawson would soon make the most of these experiences.

After Lawson met King in 1957, he contacted A. J. Muste, still at the helm of FOR. Muste offered Lawson a job as southern field secretary of FOR, and by January 1958, Lawson was settled in Nashville. Upon arrival, he discovered that Glenn Smiley, national field director of FOR, had arranged for him to conduct a full schedule of workshops—including one to occur early that year at the first annual meeting of the Southern Christian Leadership Conference (SCLC) in Columbia, South Carolina. At the South Carolina session, King made an enthusiastic introduction of Lawson as FOR's new regional representative and commented on the assistance given by individuals associated with FOR in Montgomery. "Be back promptly at 2:00 pm," King declared, "for Brother Lawson's workshop on nonviolence!" Several minutes before the agreed time, King seated himself in the first pew, waiting eagerly for the three-hour session to commence. Lawson recalled,

> Martin did that at every SCLC meeting as long as he lived. He would ask me to conduct an afternoon workshop, usually two or three hours, and he would arrange for it to be "at-large" so that everyone could attend, with nothing else to compete. He put it on the schedule himself. A few minutes early, he would show up and sit alone, as an example, in the front row.[80]

79. James M. Lawson, Jr., interview with the author, Los Angeles (February 27, 1996), as cited in Mary Elizabeth King, *Mahatma Gandhi and Martin Luther King, Jr.*, 132.

80. Ibid., 190 n. 37.

The target in Montgomery had been limited, and along with effective and enduring results, the boycott left no residual bitterness. It offered evidence that similar eradication of other discriminatory practices might be feasible. Hearing reports of anticolonial movements occurring in Africa, where in 1960 seventeen nations reached independence from colonial rule, and knowing that news of Montgomery had girdled the globe, during the next four years students in black Southern colleges and universities—typically in isolation from each other, or in small groups—contemplated what steps they should take.

On February 1, 1960, after a rambling discussion among themselves, four first-year students attending North Carolina Agricultural and Technical State University in Greensboro made their decision. Joseph McNeil and Ezell Blair, who roomed together, and their friends Franklin McCain and David Rich, determined that they would sit down at a "whites only" lunch counter. They would request service and when refused would remain sitting; when asked to leave, they would refuse to comply. The action is called a "sit-in," although it is unlikely that the four students were familiar with the name of this particular nonviolent method. Rather, it was called a "sitdown" in the local newspaper reports of the time.[81]

Although not known until after the Greensboro sit-ins began, students elsewhere in the South had been preparing for such activity, and unrelated individual protests had occurred. In the winter of 1958 and spring of 1959, the Nashville Christian Leadership Conference, the first SCLC affiliate, had embarked on a major nonviolent direct-action campaign aimed at the discrimination practiced by downtown stores and restaurants. Preparations had been comprehensive, including workshops for students attending institutions of higher learning in the city.

Throughout the fall of 1959, the Reverend James M. Lawson, Jr. led weekly Monday evening meetings in which he used a systematic approach to analyze with interested students the theories and techniques that he had studied in India. His workshops scrutinized the writings of Gandhi, King, and Thoreau, as well as the Bible. In a byproduct of these workshops, test cases were instituted, including small sit-ins for practice and role-playing.[82] Lawson's workshops lasted for several months before news broke on February 1 of the Greensboro sit-ins. When Lawson took a phone call from North

81. See, for example, Mary Elizabeth King, *Freedom Song: A Personal Story of the 1960s Civil Rights Movement* (New York: William Morrow, 1987) 268.

82. Lawson, interview with the author (February 27, 1996).

Carolina informing him of what was happening in Greensboro, seventy-five Nashville students moved into action with the largest, most disciplined and influential of the sit-in campaigns of 1960.[83] In working with Lawson, calm and self-effacing, the Nashville students were not only receiving training from one of King's instructors, they were able to benefit from his direct acquaintance with Gandhi's experiments. For their part, they brought grit, discipline, skills, training, and youth to the escalating drama.

With the national focus on Greensboro, the sit-ins occurring in Nashville, Tennessee; Norfolk, Virginia; and Rock Hill, South Carolina, appeared to come together in a form of spontaneous combustion. Sweeping through the Southland, thousands of students moved into action. "Unjust laws exist," Thoreau said. "Shall we transgress them at once?"[84]

As a chain reaction involving the awakening of hundreds of Southern black college students occurred, increasingly joined by whites, the sit-ins provided a base and regional reach for what was becoming a mass movement. Precisely as King and his advisers had yearned, unrelated scenes of action were cohering and uniting. Sitting-in offered a means for bold, energetic, and youthful leaders to engage in this climactic moral struggle, while also demonstrating that both the young and nonviolent direct action could be effective. Within two months, thirty-five thousand students had "sat down." By the end of 1960, some seventy thousand students had participated in sit-ins. Approximately thirty-six hundred had been arrested, most going limp in noncooperation, forcing police to carry them to waiting vehicles.[85]

Schooled in meticulously formulated interpretations of what it means to be both nonviolent and Christian under Lawson's tutelage, the Nashville students' readings and immersion gave the local movement a distinguishing characteristic. Throughout the short decade of the civil rights movement, Nashville would remain resolutely committed to disciplined nonviolent struggle and students would demonstrate courage, cohesion, and strategic genius.

83 Milton Viorst, *Fire in the Streets: America in the 1960s* (New York: Simon & Schuster, 1979) 107.

84. Henry David Thoreau, "Resistance to Civil Government," in *Aesthetic Papers*, ed. Elizabeth P. Peabody (Boston: 1849; reprint ed. *Annals of America*, Encyclopaedia Britannica, 1976) 543.

85. See Mary Elizabeth King, "Civil Rights Movement: Methods of Nonviolent Action," in vol. 1 of *The Oxford International Encyclopedia of Peace*, ed. Nigel Young (Oxford: Oxford University Press, 2010).

As a consequence of the sit-ins, a second Southern civil rights organization came into being—the aforementioned Student Nonviolent Coordinating Committee (SNCC). Just as Ella J. Baker had aided SCLC's beginning in 1957, she was the catalyst for SNCC three years later. The granddaughter of slaves and originally from Norfolk, Virginia, she had worked with the NAACP and lived in New York for many years. Baker called a regional meeting of student sit-in leaders for a Southwide Student Leadership Conference, at Shaw University in Raleigh, North Carolina, April 15–17, 1960. By then working with SCLC, she was able to persuade King to allocate $800 for the costs of the assembly, with the keynote address given by Lawson and the benediction by King.[86]

The sit-in leaders decided to form their own coordinating committee of comparable activists, and in the next few weeks a statement of purpose circulated across the South in draft form for comment. Lawson integrated the additional ideas that were recommended and wrote the final version:

> We affirm the philosophical or religious ideal of nonviolence as the foundation of our purpose, the pre-supposition of our faith, and the manner of our action. . . . Through nonviolence, courage displaces fear; love transforms hate. Acceptance dissipates prejudice; hope ends despair. . . . Justice for all overthrows injustice. The redemptive community supersedes systems of gross social immorality. . . . Nonviolence nurtures the atmosphere in which reconciliation and justice become actual possibilities.[87]

The declaration stated that "each member of our movement must work diligently to understand the depths of *nonviolence*." SNCC was entirely organized and run by young people—apart from having as senior advisers Baker, James Lawson, and history professor Howard Zinn of Spelman College in Atlanta. From this point onward, it became difficult to view

---

86. Lawson's call for militant nonviolent struggle against racism was afterward interpreted by some as a move to supplant King as the voice for the movement, which Lawson utterly rejects. He recalls King as deferring to him on the technique of nonviolent resistance and has said that they were both at ease with the speaking arrangements in Raleigh. He also criticizes the notion that King wanted to submerge the emerging student movement under SCLC, to make it a submerged wing. "Maybe some had this thought," Lawson recalled, "but certainly not Martin—he and I both wanted the students to do whatever they wanted." Lawson, interview with the author.

87. James M. Lawson, Jr., "Statement of Purpose (dated May 14, 1960)," *The Student Voice* 1.1 (June 1960) 2.

King and SCLC without seeing SNCC in the background, just as it would be unsound to consider SNCC without taking SCLC into account.

KING'S "LETTER FROM BIRMINGHAM JAIL"

By 1963, SCLC was directing demonstrations at desegregating the restaurants of downtown department stores in Birmingham, an Alabama industrial city in which so many unsolved bombings had sought to intimidate black citizens that the city was called "Bombingham."

Walking in a small march in April 1963, King was arrested by authorities. Behind bars, he penned his "Letter from Birmingham Jail," a response to eight Alabama religious leaders who had argued that the movement's goals were ill-advised and that it should be aiming at litigation and negotiations. In replying, King acknowledged that nonviolent action can sometimes produce negotiations: "You may well ask, 'Why direct action? Why sit-ins, marches, etc.? Isn't negotiation a better path?' You are exactly right in your call for negotiation. Indeed, this is the purpose of direct action. Nonviolent direct action seeks to create such a crisis and establish such creative tension that a community that has constantly refused to negotiate is forced to confront the issue. It seeks so to dramatize the issue that it can no longer be ignored."[88] King's missive justifies civil disobedience, is the most significant single document written during the civil rights movement, and is still in circulation across the world. King's words address a quandary: seeking compromise and negotiations is a reasonable principle in settling disputes that are not comprised of deep-seated questions of beliefs, ominous issues of social inequity, or egregious historical wrongs. Yet in circumstances of severe and protracted long-term grievance and injustice, to reach negotiations may be a pyrrhic victory. Some nonviolent movements have made the facile and false presumption that achieving negotiations means reaching one's goal. Not so. The 1960s U.S. civil rights movement avoided this trap, such that uneducated sharecroppers in isolated plantation economies appreciated that nonviolent struggle would be the only way to reach the stage of negotiations with what they called the "power structure."[89] King's 1968

88. Martin Luther King, Jr., "Letter from Birmingham Jail" (April 16, 1963), in *Nonviolence in America: A Documentary History*, ed. Staughton Lynd and Alice Lynd (Maryknoll, NY: Orbis, 1995) 254.

89. Awareness of "power structures" and the interlocking directorates of corporations and government spread across the South from the work in the research department

death in Memphis, Tennessee, would occur after he had traveled to the city to shore up a local sanitation workers' strike, as a favor to local clergy, who were hoping that his being there would bring the mayor to start bargaining. No one, however, was operating under the illusion that meaningful negotiations could take place without the pressures exerted by collective nonviolent action.[90]

AFRICA INFLUENCED KING; KING AFFECTED AFRICA

By the late nineteenth century, Africans were challenging colonial practices and imperial powers by their tax resistance, seeking improvements to working conditions for laborers, disputing the lack of channels for representation, and contesting the forcible alienation of settled peoples from their traditional ancestral lands. Defying colonial dominion through a variety of demonstrations and processions, their marches enjoyed great popularity. Kings, paramount chiefs, educated African élites, newspaper reporters, and individuals from all strata participated in nonviolent action. Often elaborately planned, such popular contention took the form of petitions, boycotts, deputations, and parades. Tax resistance was admired:

> In West Africa, the hut, or house, tax required residents to pay the British government for shelter that they owned. In Sierra Leone and Ghana, this levy resulted in eventual rebellions following prolonged protest and negotiation. In Sierra Leone, for example, Governor Frederic Cardew passed the tax on 14 December 1896. Three days later, the tribal chiefs of the Temne people wrote to the district commissioner, Captain William Sharpe, appealing to him to ask the governor not to "make war to us." All the chiefs had unanimously decided not to pay the tax.[91]

By the mid-twentieth century, Nigerians with leadership from journalist Nnamdi Azikiwe, and in the Gold Coast (later Ghana) with guidance

---

of the Student Nonviolent Coordinating Committee (SNCC), headed by Jack Minnis. SNCC used this tool of analysis widely, with indebtedness to political scientist Floyd Hunter for his work on power structures.

90. Michael K. Honey, *Going Down Jericho Road: The Memphis Strike, Martin Luther King's Last Campaign* (New York: Norton, 2007).

91. Desmond George-Williams, *Bite Not One Another: Selected Accounts of Nonviolent Struggle in Africa*, ed. Mary E. King, Nonviolent Transformation of Conflict—Africa (Geneva: University for Peace, 2006) 29–30. See http://www.upeace.org/library/documents/nvtc_bite_not_one_another.pdf.

from Kwame Nkrumah, were using nonviolent methods to press for independence and the end of European colonialism. In Ghana, Kenya, and
Zambia the nationalist calls for self-rule and freedom from British rule
manifested themselves in largely nonviolent movements that sought free
elections. Julius Nyerere of Tanzania, Kenneth Kaunda of Zambia, and
Chief Albert Luthuli of South Africa would later state their indebtedness
to the work of Mohandas K. Gandhi. When he received the Gandhi Peace
Prize in New Delhi on January 27, 1996, Nyerere said, "Gandhi's unique-
ness is in his life and in the strategies he advocated and adopted as matters
of principle."[92] Kaunda called Gandhi's an ideal that "brought perfection
to all qualities. I was struggling to develop self-discipline, austerity . . . and
practical wisdom. . . . So it was according to the principles of nonviolence
on the Gandhi model that the final stages of the freedom struggle in Zambia were conducted."[93]

The African nonviolent struggles would entice King's attention. Following the Montgomery success, King was invited by the incoming government of Ghana and its leader, Kwame Nkrumah, to attend the independence
celebrations of the new nation emerging from British colonial rule. Protracted nonviolent struggle had been pursued in the Gold Coast in seeking
free elections. On March 2, 1957, the Kings departed from New York along
with Congressman Adam Clayton Powell, Jr., A. Philip Randolph, and U.N.
Undersecretary Ralph J. Bunche, who had won the 1950 Nobel Peace Prize.
The plane landed in Lisbon, Dakar, and Monrovia. While in Monrovia,
King met with Romeo Houghton, president of the Bank of Liberia. On
March 4, the group disembarked in Accra, capital of the Gold Coast. The
next day, King held an impromptu news conference during a ceremony at
the University of Ghana and later attended the final session of the Gold
Coast Legislative Assembly. On March 6, King and his party joined the
crowd at midnight in the Accra polo grounds to witness the Union Jack
being replaced by the official flag of the new nation of Ghana, and later
observed the opening of Ghana's Parliament and attended a formal reception at Christiansborg Castle.

Whether or not the King party was aware of it, the Christiansborg
Castle had been the scene of an episode that, in February 1948, enflamed

92. Julius Nyerere, "And Then Gandhi Came," address delivered in New Delhi, India
(January 27, 1996).

93. For an important reference to Kaunda's admiration for Gandhi, see George M.
Houser, *No One Can Stop the Rain: Glimpses of Africa's Liberation Struggle* (New York:
Pilgrim, 1989) 108.

already prevalent anticolonial sentiments. Soldiers returning home to the Gold Coast after fighting on behalf of the British in World War II, members of the Ex-Servicemen's Union, organized a demonstration to submit a list of their grievances to the governor. The complaints included joblessness, lack of educational opportunities, and political exclusion from the affairs of the nation. As two thousand unarmed protesters marched peacefully to the castle, a white police officer ordered his subordinates to open fire.[94] When the riflemen disobeyed the order, the officer seized a rifle from a policeman and started shooting into the throng of petitioners, killing three men. A committee created to scrutinize the disturbances in Accra and other cities in that year recommended the drafting of a new constitution to increase African participation in government.

King was taken with the appearance of Nkrumah and his cabinet wearing prison caps to their inauguration ceremony, depicting the fact that they had only recently been arrested by the colonial government for their pursuit of free elections and activities supporting a Pan-African movement. W. E. B. Du Bois, the African American political philosopher, was a leading figure in the movement and had helped to organize Pan-African Congresses in Paris, London, and Brussels in 1919 and the early 1920s. The congress in Manchester, England, in 1945, was the most momentous of these gatherings insofar as participants included Nkrumah, Obafemi Awolowo of Nigeria, Jomo Kenyatta of Kenya, and Hastings Banda of Malawi, all of whom would feature in achieving independence for their countries.

In June 1949, Nkrumah had formed the Convention Peoples Party (CPP), comprised largely of young political professionals. He spearheaded a campaign of "positive action" to engage laborers and people from diverse backgrounds in nationwide boycotts and strikes. In the booklet "What I Mean by Positive Action," Nkrumah explains positive action as "a civil disobedience campaign of agitation, propaganda and as a last resort the constitutional application of strikes, boycotts, and non-cooperation based on the principles of absolute nonviolence."[95] The purpose, among other aims, was to pressure the colonial government into summoning a constituent assembly that would lead to full self-governance for the country. When Nkrumah declared January 5, 1950, for the start of positive action, the people

94. Dennis Austin, *Politics in Ghana, 1946–1960* (Oxford: Oxford University Press, 1964) 47, as cited in George-Williams, *Bite Not One Another*, 39. This was an early example of civil resistance in post–World War II Africa, providing "auspicious conditions upon which Kwame Nkrumah could build."

95. Cited in George-Williams, *Bite Not One Another*, 41.

had been primed for it through newspapers, public assemblies, and rallies. Nkrumah's push for independence was in harmony with the conclusions of the Fifth Pan-African Congress in Manchester in 1945 on the value of mass popular action in colonial struggles, including boycotts, civil disobedience, and strikes. The positive-action drive began with a boycott of British products. Extensive strikes and work slowdowns occurred across Gold Coast industries. The response of the colonial authorities was to impose a state of emergency and a harsh curfew. In spite of forewarning against any violence, some skirmishes occurred, with resultant deaths of two policemen. Feeling the concentrated pressure from the strike actions, British authorities arrested Nkrumah, who would become Ghana's first prime minister, and other leaders of the CPP. While incarcerated, elections were conducted in which Nkrumah and his party won.

King recalled, "When I looked out and saw the prime minister there with his prison cap on that night, that reminded me of that fact, that freedom never comes easy. It comes through hard labor and it comes through toil."[96] The following day, March 7, unwell and bedridden, King was visited by Anglican priest Michael Scott on the Achimota College campus, where the Kings stayed while in Ghana. By March 10, King was able to be present for Father Scott's sermon at the Sunday service in the Anglican Cathedral in Accra.

Also in attendance at the independence ceremony was U.S. Vice President Richard Nixon. Introducing himself to the vice president, King compared the struggle of the Ghanaians to his own. He said, "I want you to come visit us down in Alabama where we are seeking the same kind of freedom the Gold Coast is celebrating."[97] King's visit to Ghana offered inspiration, but also a caution. Nkrumah warned King at the independence celebration that Ghana "would never be able to accept the American ideology of freedom and democracy fully until America settles its own internal racial strife."[98] On March 12, 1957, the Kings left Accra and flew to Kano, in northeast Nigeria, for a brief interlude.

In the days and weeks after returning home, King invoked Ghana's experience as decisive, emphasizing how it had resulted from the employment

96 Clayborne Carson et al., eds., *The Papers of Martin Luther King, Jr.*, vol. 4, *Symbol of the Movement, January 1957–December 1958* (Berkeley: University of California Press, 2000) 163.

97. "M. L. King Meets Nixon in Ghana," *Pittsburgh Courier*, March 16, 1957.

98. Kevin Gaines, *African-Americans in Ghana* (Chapel Hill: University of North Carolina Press) 82.

of nonviolent action and "continual agitation, continual resistance."[99] He preached about his trip in his first sermon after returning to Montgomery, outlining his indebtedness to Gandhi and citing the history of Ghana's independence movement as rooted in nonviolent struggle.[100] King would adopt Nkrumah's term "positive action" as a synonym for nonviolent resistance.

Still in the midst of the cold war and forewarned by Nkrumah, King used the experiences on his trip to Africa as an argument for the moral necessity of racial integration in the United States. He maintained that progress in desegregation was how the African nations would judge the United States in its conflict with the Soviet Union and the global war of public opinion. Pro-segregation U.S. politicians often bragged of their staunchly anticommunist views, allowing King to use the imagery of the red menace as a rhetorical weapon.[101] In turn, the success of King's tactics in the Montgomery bus boycott would be cited in the development of Ghana's nationalist movement and South Africa's 1950s Defiance Campaign against segregated public facilities.[102]

SOUTH AFRICA'S PROTRACTED HISTORY OF NONVIOLENT STRUGGLE

Indeed, the most prolonged history of African nonviolent action was in South Africa. It is worth briefly chronicling this long engagement. While in Natal, Gandhi honed the concept of *satyagraha* in 1907 and initiated experiments that would become influential with early leaders of what would become the African National Congress (ANC). The ANC emerged seamlessly in 1923 out of its progenitor, the South African Native National Congress, a group formed in 1912 while Gandhi was still working in Natal. The ANC was influenced by Gandhi in its work against racial discrimination and held to a policy of nonviolent action through the mid-twentieth century. In 1950, the ANC adopted civil disobedience in reaction to the recently elected Afrikaner nationalist government's apartheid program. The

---

99. G. Pascal Zachary, "Freedom for Blacks First Rang in Ghana," *San Francisco Chronicle*, February 11, 2007. Online: http://www.sfgate.com/opinion/article/Freedom-for-blacks-rang-first-in-Ghana-1957-2650162.php.

100. Martin Luther King, Jr., "The Birth of a New Nation," in Carson et al., *Papers*, 4:162.

101. Gaines, *African-Americans in Ghana*, 88.

102. Ibid., 80.

Defiance Campaign against Unjust Laws was initiated by the ANC during a conference in Bloemfontein, South Africa, in 1951, calling for national action based on noncooperation with unjust laws. Albert J. Luthuli, a Zulu chief and the ANC president (1952–1960), spoke of his indebtedness to Gandhi and in 1960 became the first African to receive a Nobel Peace Prize for his insistence that the antiapartheid struggle remain nonviolent.

The Defiance Campaign reached its high point in 1960, when a breakaway group, the Pan-Africanist Congress (PAC), called on Africans to surrender without passbooks at police stations, an act of defiance that resulted in the police killing sixty-nine people in Sharpeville on March 21. In South Africa, it was not unusual for the police to respond to protest, even nonviolent protest such as this, with deadly force. In the ensuing emergency, the ANC and PAC were outlawed by the apartheid government. From 1912 until 1960, the assumption had been widespread that civil resistance might end apartheid, but this changed with the Sharpeville Massacre. In 1960–1961, the ANC leadership set up an armed wing, Umkhonto we Sizwe (Spear of the Nation, or MK). Once this attempt at organized violence was commenced, military struggle came quickly to dominate the thinking of those ANC and allied Communist Party members, who remained active in the new conditions of clandestinity. According to former ANC member and historian of ANC strategy Howard Barrell: "[The ANC] considered armed struggle important enough in 1960–61 to deploy almost all its most gifted organizers from political to military roles. This undermined its capacity either to mount further civil resistance or to solidify the political base on which revolutionary armed struggle is commonly thought to depend."[103] King wanted to travel to apartheid South Africa and applied for a visa to visit in 1965 "to exchange cultural and human rights concerns." But King's application was rejected.[104] That year represented the nadir of the ANC's fortunes as state repression mopped up all but a handful of its domestic organizations. Introduction of a regulation that half the curriculum should be taught in Afrikaans stimulated demonstrations in June 1976 at Soweto, when police fired into a crowd of fifteen thousand children. By year's end, 575 had died, but a spirit of militant resistance had been reborn.

103. Howard Barrell, unpublished version of paper, Fletcher Summer Institute (June 21, 2011), Fletcher School of Diplomacy, Tufts University, Boston, Massachusetts.

104. Martin Luther King, Jr. letter to the South African Embassy, New Orleans, Louisiana (February 9, 1965); Mark A. Uhlig, ed., *Apartheid in Crisis* (New York: Vintage, 1986) 39; Lewis V. Baldwin, *Toward the Beloved Community: Martin Luther King, Jr. and South Africa* (Cleveland: Pilgrim, 1995) 98–99.

The United Democratic Front (UDF), "a nonracial, nonviolent, and legally constituted movement," launched itself in 1983, initially coordinating 565 organizations, including religious groups, professional associations, student organizations, trade unions, women's groups, and youth groups, with 700 affiliates under its umbrella at its peak.[105] With the decentralized structures of the UDF purposely difficult for the state to repress, the front was able to channel the energies of youths, workers, and other social groups into nonviolent action. Campaigns of noncooperation, with innumerable rent and consumer boycotts, proved so effective that the apartheid government imposed a partial state of emergency in 1985. Historian Janet Cherry remembered, "Inside South Africa, the vast majority of leaders and members supported the ANC and its armed struggle—or its moral right to take up arms in a 'just war'—however, we understood that we could be much more effective in mobilising people against the state through mass action, and that the use of violence would undermine our organisations and render them vulnerable."[106] This point echoed the thinking of both Gandhi and King.

As a countrywide state of emergency was imposed in 1986, limiting publicly assertive methods of protest and persuasion (marches, parades, vigils), mass demonstrations largely disappeared, although funerals presented opportunities for processional mourning in the thousands. UDF-affiliated networks of neighborhood groups continued to use the less visible methods of noncooperation and nonviolent intervention (consumer and rent boycotts, tax resistance), working through locally led street committees whose leaders went unrecognized. Noncooperation was hard to make illegal. By 1989, the Mass Democratic Movement took over from the UDF and organized a Defiance Campaign of once more visible mass marches. A campaign of coordinated hunger strikes pressed for the release of political prisoners.

Without military bases inside the country, the armed wing was never a threat to the state. In a paper subtitled, "How a Military Mindset Retarded the South African Freedom Struggle," Barrell suggests that "an iconography of violence" derived from the ANC's armed struggle, which developed in civil resistance inside South Africa in the 1980s, paradoxically helped

105. Kurt Schock, *Unarmed Insurrections: People Power Movements in Nondemocracies* (Minneapolis: University of Minnesota Press, 2005) 59.

106. Janet Cherry, personal communication (e-mail from Port Elizabeth, February 19, 2007), as cited in Mary Elizabeth King, *A Quiet Revolution: The First Palestinian Intifada and Nonviolent Resistance* (New York: Nation, 2007) 319, 445 n. 109.

"advance a struggle by nonviolent means." It had a powerful mobilizing effect domestically while also helping the ANC abroad in its quest for recognition. But, he adds, over time there evolved

> inside South Africa (and in some more insightful quarters of the ANC in exile), a gradual realization—to which many were disinclined—that armed struggle was not sufficient to get rid of apartheid. By the late 1980s, some would be suggesting *sotto voce* the revolutionary heresy that armed struggle might not even be *necessary* to do so. What was driving this trend, besides the failure of the ANC's armed struggle? It was the patent success that civil resistance began to have in exacting far greater costs on the government and the economy. . . . The civil resistance represented by the UDF and MDM was the most significant force of any generated by South Africans in the defeat of apartheid. They mustered unprecedented pressures on the apartheid state at the levels at which the latter was, relatively, weakest—the political and economic. Armed struggle, on the other hand, which was narrowly conceived and conspiratorial, engaged the state at the level at which it was, comparatively, strongest—the military.[107]

In 1990, the ANC was unbanned and armed struggle suspended. At long last the government entered into talks, leading to a negotiated settlement and the 1994 South African elections that would end apartheid after nearly a century of struggle.[108]

Gandhi and King both learned from and were beholden to African collective nonviolent struggles, thereby reciprocally emboldening their respective movements. Africans derived inspiration from King long after his African sojourn. Kenya's Wangari Maathai—2004 Nobel Peace Prize winner and activist for women's mobilization and environmental preservation, and opponent of corruption in politics—later recalled King's "Free at last" as a rallying cry in Kenya's 1963 independence from Britain.[109] In a news

---

107. Barrell (June 21, 2011), Fletcher School of Diplomacy. Emphasis in original. "MDM" refers to Mass Democratic Movement, late 1980s. Barrell adds that the limitations of the ANC's armed struggle can be easily demonstrated. U.S. intelligence reports of insurgent attacks and contacts at the height of the Iraq insurgency in the mid-2000s indicated some five thousand incidents a day at times; in the entire thirty years of the ANC's armed struggle, Umkhonto we Sizwe did not manage half that number. Ibid.

108. See Tom Lodge, "The Interplay of Non-Violent and Violent Action in the Movement against Apartheid in South Africa, 1983–94," in Roberts and Ash, *Civil Resistance and Power Politics*, 213–30.

109. Amitabh Pal, "Interview with Wangari Maathai," *The Progressive* 69.5 (May 2005). Online: http://progressive.org/wangari_maathai_interview.html.

release of October 10, 1997, the National Union of Sierra Leone Students stated: "We have never used AK-47 rifles to demonstrate against the junta because we believe in the ideals of Martin Luther King Jr. by using nonviolent means for our voices to be heard by the whole world."

KING'S VISIT TO INDIA

Martin Luther King, Jr.'s best-known international trip was to India in 1959. Once SCLC was underway, other professionals came into King's circle. The educator Harris Wofford started writing letters to King when the boycott reached the front pages of major newspapers in December 1955. He was subsequently a U.S. senator from Pennsylvania and years later head of Americorps, the national volunteer service corps that formed during the Clinton administration. Along with his wife, Clare, Wofford had visited Gandhi's Sevagram home in 1949, and in 1951 the Woffords had published *India Afire*, a book interpreting Gandhi's nonviolent resistance. From an East Tennessee family, Wofford had done something inconceivable in his day. In 1954, he became one of the first whites to earn a law degree from Howard University, an institution established in nineteenth-century Washington, DC, for freed slaves and others who had bought their way out of bondage.

In December 1956, with King preoccupied in studying Gandhi at the behest of Rustin, Smiley, and the author Richard Gregg, with whom King was corresponding, Wofford was able to arrange a grant from the Christopher Reynolds Foundation in New York. The small, private philanthropic foundation awarded $5,000 for a study tour in India. King received a formal invitation from the Gandhi Memorial Trust.[110] Not until 1959, however, would he be able to embark.

Prior to the journey, King had written, "I firmly believe that the Gandhian philosophy of nonviolent resistance is the only logical and moral approach to the solution of the race problem in the United States."[111] Now

110. The grant went through the American Friends Service Committee; the Gandhi Memorial Trust (Gandhi Smarak Nidhi) issued its invitation through diplomatic channels. King, "My Trip to the Land of Gandhi," in Washington, *Testament of Hope*, 24–25. See also Wofford, *Of Kennedys and Kings*, 116.

111. Martin Luther King, Jr. letter to George Hendrick (February 5, 1957), Martin Luther King, Jr. Papers, Special Collections, Mugar Memorial Library, Boston University, Boston, Massachusetts; as cited in Mary Elizabeth King, *Mahatma Gandhi and Martin Luther King, Jr.*, 210.

he was able to retrace some of Gandhi's steps, visiting places where he had lived, as well as leading public prayers and holding meetings of his own. He met with freedom fighters from the Indian independence struggles and gave an address on All-India Radio. Contact with Gandhi's life experiences revived King's determination.

"The aftermath of hatred and bitterness that usually follows a violent campaign was found no where in India," King wrote expansively. He attributed the absence of hostility on the part of the Indians toward the British to the possibilities of civil resistance. King states, "I left India more convinced than ever before that the method of nonviolent resistance is the most potent weapon available to oppressed people in their struggle for freedom and dignity."[112] King noticed that the Indian newspapers had covered Montgomery well and found that "Indian publications perhaps gave a better continuity of our 381-day bus strike than did most of our papers in the United States."[113] After visiting India, King presciently wrote that "nonviolent resistance *when planned and positive in action* can work effectively even under totalitarian regimes."[114] "Positive in action" was Nkrumah's term, also adopted by Zambia's Kenneth Kaunda and other African leaders.

Persuaded that "there is no basic difference between colonialism and segregation," King saw them each as part of "the same tragic doctrine of white supremacy."[115] His articulation of this linkage strengthened the connections between the descendents of Africans in North America and those attempting to throw off the last vestiges of colonial rule across the world. His trips to Africa and India helped him to be influential with the rest of the world. Importantly, for the spread of its comprehension, King concluded that nonviolent struggle was a strategy that could be taught, and he became its most potent propagator, spreading knowledge of nonviolent action across cultures and peoples—interpreting, propounding, representing, and teaching the knowledge that had come from East to West.

---

112. Martin Luther King, Jr., *The Autobiography of Martin Luther King, Jr.*, ed. Clayborne Carson (New York: Warner, 2001) 134. (King to G. Ramachandran, May 19, 1959, letter in Martin Luther King, Jr. Papers, Boston University, as cited in Mary Elizabeth King, *Mahatma Gandhi and Martin Luther King, Jr.*, 212.)

113. King, "My Trip to the Land of Gandhi," in Washington, *Testament of Hope*, 25.

114. Ibid., 26. Emphasis in original.

115. Garrow, *Bearing the Cross*, 118.

BROADENING THE GLOBAL KNOWLEDGE OF
NONVIOLENT ACTION

In the years since King's death, scholarship and understanding have accelerated, with striking applications to bring about reform, rights, transitions to democracy, and the lifting of military occupations. Civil resistance has been used with coherence to achieve political and social change by peoples and societies in differing cultures and political systems, with some impressive results, as well as a number of failures. In the contemporary era, this phenomenon has gained growing respect as a potentially formidable strategic force by policy makers, political analysts, strategic-studies specialists, peacemakers, and international scholars of many disciplines.

Notwithstanding the record of results, the need for greater learning, education, and public attentiveness is a major challenge of the twenty-first century. Perhaps because of difficulties in comparative political analysis or linguistic barriers in understanding the history of ideas, major gaps exist in the historical analysis of nonviolent struggle despite the accomplishments achieved using the technique. Countless indigenous nonviolent struggles for justice have gone unrecorded and are not available for analysis. The first extensive documentation on the national movements of nonviolent resistance against Hitler did not appear until 1989, when Jacques Semelin analyzed the Czech, Danish, Dutch, and Norwegian unarmed resistance to the Nazis during World War II.[116] While scholarship concerning nonviolent action was at one time buried in obscure corners of political theory, the situation changed with the results wrought by national movements of the former Eastern bloc, which stirred public and academic interest.

Ordinary citizens in the Eastern bloc nation-states under communist rule after World War II, some as part of the Soviet Union, others occupied by the Soviet army at the close of World War II, took up nonviolent methods in the 1980s. Starting carefully, they would eventually reform their party-state governments, and assert individual liberties, as national nonviolent movements grew across Eastern Europe and into the Soviet Union, often undetected in the rest of the world. Activist intellectuals, academicians, artists, authors, editors, playwrights, theologians, and writers whose clandestine writings drove the spread of nonviolent resistance throughout the Eastern bloc generally made *practical* arguments for choosing nonviolent

---

116. Jacques Semelin, *Unarmed against Hitler: Civilian Resistance in Europe, 1939–1943*, trans. Suzan Husserl-Kapit (Westport, CT: Praeger, 1993).

means to assert their subject nations' independence from the Soviet Union, rather than moral refutations of violence, although they often said that they wanted the results to be ethical.

Trace elements of King's influence can be found in almost any civil resistance movement that one plumbs. Scholar activists such as historians Jacek Kuroń and Adam Michnik in Poland, Christian Führer in East Germany, and Valcláv Havel in what became the Czech and Slovak republics introduced nonviolent resistance as a practical means of resistance against Soviet totalitarianism, often citing King to make their arguments.

Poland's case is illustrative. With Soviet troops occupying Poland after World War II, and its population diminished to twenty-four million from the pre-war thirty-five million, knowledge of how to fight without bloodshed was quietly shared in Poland through an underground press of illegal publications and books, called *samizdat* (Russian for "self-published"). By the mid-1980s, some two thousand regular samizdat publications were circulating, some numbering in the tens of thousands of copies. Prior to Poland's Solidarity (Solidarność) Union coming to world attention, during the 1970s, committees of scholars and academicians worked together with Roman Catholic laity and theologians. Jacek Kuroń and Adam Michnik were members of the first group without sanction from a communist regime to organize independently in the Eastern bloc. In scrutinizing Poland's history of resistance, Kuroń concluded that "the most effective form of resistance is based on solidarity."[117] Knowledge of resistance techniques spread. A Catholic periodical published translations of Gandhi and King. Hunger strikers explicitly cited Gandhi and King as their influences.[118]

In June 1980, after an explosion in the Lenin shipyard in Gdańsk caused the deaths of eight laborers, instead of walking out of the shipyard as would be customary in a strike, the workers opted for a sit-down strike. That is, they created a new nonviolent method, an extended work stoppage during which laborers occupy the workplace. Kuroń acted as spokesperson for the strike committee, until the regime severed the telephone lines and placed him and Adam Michnik behind bars. Solidarity was in short order recognized by the party-state as the self-described first "independent, self-governing union" in an Eastern bloc communist country, with a right to

117. Jacek Kuroń, "Overcoming Totalitarianism," in *The Revolutions of 1989*, ed. Vladimir Tismaneanu (London: Routledge, 1999) 198–201.

118. Jan Zielonka, *Political Ideas in Contemporary Poland* (Aldershot, UK: Avebury, 1989) 95.

strike. Its membership exceeded ten million by late September 1980; it enlisted 80 percent of the Polish workforce. A large number of historians, like
Kuroń and Michnik, stood behind Solidarity, meaning that what counted
was not a principled opposition to violence, but concern that the new union
should avoid the meaningless losses that had accompanied bloody rebellions of the nineteenth century, when the Poles sought to remain intact
from both German and Russian predations. Having studied those revolts,
they wanted no more romanticized spilling of Polish blood.

The Polish communist party-state placed Solidarity under martial law
for seven years in 1981, but the union persisted. Michnik, later editor of
Poland's second-largest daily newspaper, *Gazeta Wyborcza* (Election Ga-
zette), in 1985 writes in *Letters from Prison and Other Essays* that the ethics
of Solidarity and its rejection of armed force "has a lot in common with the
idea of nonviolence as espoused by Gandhi and Martin Luther King, Jr."
From Gdansk prison he penned, "The ethics of Solidarity is based on the
. . . premise: that there are causes worth dying for. Gandhi and King died
for the same cause as the miners in Wujek [striking workers killed three
days after the Polish government's imposition of martial law in 1981] who
rejected the belief that it is better to remain a willing slave than be a victim
of murder."[119] Solidarity had not set out to topple the state or to take power.
Instead, it sought reforms to the existing communist system, a free trade
union to improve life for workers, broader rights and freedoms, and the
opening up of civil society.

Polish roundtable talks began in February 1989 between the government and Solidarity. Although the fall of the Berlin Wall is often cited as the
instant when the unraveling of the Soviet Union began, the moment when
the Eastern bloc began its self-liberation can more accurately be pinpointed
as February 6. The Polish negotiations between the formerly jailed and erstwhile jailers began nine months before the communist party-state in East
Germany, on November 9, announced that all East German citizens could
travel out of the country at will, without official permission. Four months of
roundtable talks led to agreement between the party-state and Solidarity, as
the negotiators restructured Poland into a democracy. In December 1990,
Lech Wałęsa was elected president of Poland—the first non-Communist
leader in Eastern Europe in nearly forty years. These talks, rather than
the sundered Berlin Wall, mark the start of success for the Eastern bloc's

---

119. Adam Michnik, *Letters from Prison and Other Essays* (Berkeley: University of
California Press, 1987) 89.

upheavals and the dissolution of the Soviet Union, which began with the Baltic states' quests for independence.

Within weeks of the outset of Poland's crucial negotiations, a movement for independence began in Hungary, led by party reformers. On May 2, 1989, Hungarian soldiers, commanded by reformers within the communist apparatus, removed the barbed wire fence along the Hungarian and Austrian border, cutting through the iron curtain and allowing Hungarians, East Germans, and others to "exit" to the West.

In the East German Pastors' Movement, on thirteen consecutive Mondays in late 1989 and early 1990, demonstrators holding candles poured from the Nikolai Church and other Protestant sanctuaries in Leipzig. Starting in 1982, the Reverend Christian Führer had protected those who gathered for "prayers for peace," in which any were welcome, and by 1983 the first demonstration emerged from the Nikolai Church.[120] Eventually five million would participate in candlelit processions, despite the dreaded secret police.

In Czechoslovakia, when police brutality disrupted a student demonstration on November 17, 1989, it was the start of the "Ten Days." Massive demonstrations filled Prague's Wenceslas Square, as the party-state started to split and divide. On November 27, Day Ten, 80 percent of the nation's labor force partook in a nationwide general strike, after which a citizen pro-democracy group and the government began discussions leading to a democratic transition of power. The playwright Valcláv Havel, whose *Living in Truth* had been formative in the Velvet Revolution, was elected president.

The Baltic States of Estonia, Latvia, and Lithuania progressed toward independence from the Soviet Union at varying speeds. The most stirring of innumerable "calendar events" memorializing events of history was the four hundred-mile human chain called the "Baltic Way," which stretched from Estonia to Latvia to Lithuania. Held on August 23, 1989, as many as two million participated, holding hands while singing national songs in their call for independence from the Soviet Union.

Twenty years after Solidarity began the largest mass strikes in European history in its fight for free trade unions in Poland, the phenomenon of national nonviolent mobilization coursed into Serbia, Georgia, and Ukraine in the Balkans and Caucasus. Nonviolent struggles for democratic

---

120. See Steven Pfaff, "The Politics of Peace in the GDR: The Independent Peace Movement, the Church, and the Origins of the East German Opposition," *Peace and Change: Journal of Peace Research* 26.3 (2001) 280–300.

freedoms in Serbia and Ukraine assailed the heart of power, as movements with youthful vanguards sculpted their states into democracies. Serbia's youth-led Otpor! (Resistance!) organization was catalytic in what has since been termed the Bulldozer Revolution, and galvanized the country's eighteen political parties to unify in bringing down the dictator Slobodan Milošević in 2000. This was dramatic enough, but what is more, Otpor also gave technical assistance to similar movements in Georgia on the Black Sea and Ukraine. A youthful galvanizing group in Georgia, called Kmara (Enough), was trained by Otpor and was instrumental in deposing Eduard A. Shevardnadze in 2003, in Georgia's Rose Revolution. Pora (It's Time!) became the galvanizing force behind Ukrainian civil resistance, and was trained by both Otpor and Kmara. In Ukraine, in what was dubbed the Orange Revolution, citizens confronted electoral fraud and activated a peaceful handover of power to the movement's presidential candidate in 2004–2005. These three spearheading youth organizations produced fundamental changes in the popular perception of what might be accomplished through citizen action and were similar in many ways to the Student Nonviolent Coordinating Committee of Martin Luther King, Jr.'s era. They helped to turn taught theories into national mobilizations.[121] In this regard, their activities were very much in the tradition of Gandhi.

Inside the fifteen former republics that comprised the Soviet Union, Russia became independent in 1991. Boris N. Yeltsin was the first popularly elected president of the Russian Federation, following nonviolent resistance against an attempted military coup directed at Mikhail Gorbachev. Armenia, Azerbaijan, and Belarus's struggles were ineffective, and Kyrgyzstan's Tulip Revolution is of unsure outcome.

At the same time that Solidarity in Poland was fighting to survive martial law, Chile's nationwide "No" Campaign against General Augusto Pinochet's dictatorship began with "days of protest" in 1983, eventually resulting in a 1988 plebiscite on his presidency that restored democracy.

In 1986, in the Philippines, a series of massive demonstrations (which have bestowed the name "people power" on nonviolent movements in which significant numbers participated) brought down the Ferdinand Marcos dictatorship. FOR lecturers had taught social ethics there for two decades. Over its radio station in 1986, *Radio Veritas*, the Roman Catholic

---

121. For details on the nonviolent struggles of the Eastern bloc, see Mary Elizabeth King, *The New York Times on Emerging Democracies in Eastern Europe* (Washington, DC: Time Reference, 2009).

Church urged Filipinos to come to Epifano de los Santos Avenue (known as EDSA) to demonstrate. As crowds surged to the hundreds of thousands, singing opposition anthems with nuns and priests leading prayer vigils, Radio Veritas broadcast transcripts from Gandhi and King's writings around the clock.

Predominantly nonviolent African mass mobilizations have riveted global audiences, first in watching South Africans end *de jure* apartheid in 1994. Zimbabwe's ongoing struggle against rigged elections, unconstitutional trials, and human rights abuses subsequently has held international attention. An eleven-year civil war in Nepal ended in 2006 after nineteen days of mass demonstrations united the Nepalese against their king, and the monarch relinquished absolute control and restored the parliament. The two-year Pakistani lawyers' movement in 2009 restored the chief justice to the high court's bench.

From the 1980s into the twenty-first century, the televised spectacle of dictatorships hemorrhaging has mesmerized viewers, as the populace refused to obey tyrants, bringing down authoritarian regimes. In 2011, preponderantly nonviolent, pro-democracy revolutions in Tunisia and Egypt were among successful movements of civil resistance that have ended dictatorships in the Arab Awakening. Dalia Ziada, among Egypt's many bloggers, was asked whether wisdom had been diffused through histori cal accounts, readings, and training programs to play any role in Egypt's nonviolent revolution in Tahrir Square, which ended nearly thirty years of Hosni Mubarak's regime. She explained:

> People mistakenly assume that Egypt's revolution was spontaneous. But we had been studying and learning for ten to fifteen years through study groups and nonviolent workshops, especially in 2007–2008. These workshops exposed us to cases of nonviolent action and they inspired us. I learned about the U.S. civil rights movement and translated a comic book on Martin Luther King into Arabic and distributed it through my blog and also in print. It was passed around widely. At first people didn't understand what nonviolent resistance was or why it was important, but gradually, the knowledge empowered people and helped all of us believe that we could do this.[122]

122. The author thanks Vanessa Ortiz, an official of the U.S. Agency for International Development, for her account of Ziada's words to the Woodrow Wilson Center, Washington, DC. Vanessa Ortiz, personal communication with the author (March 16, 2011, Washington, DC). For more on the comic book, see http://daliaziada.blogspot.com/2009/05/can-comic-book-about-mlk-change-middle.html.

Notwithstanding government repression, nonviolent upheavals have also challenged the governments of Bahrain, Syria, and Yemen, while smaller protests broke out in Oman, Sudan, Iraq, Algeria, and Morocco. Some of these movements have been awkwardly implemented. Importantly, a region thought to be saturated with the ideologies of violent insurrection, armed struggle, and guerrilla warfare has shown that the technique for mass action that Gandhi and King helped to form has become virtually universal.

Even as nonviolent movements in the contemporary era have been able to alter, transform, or topple authoritarian regimes partly due to knowledge of theory and praxis contributed by Gandhi and King, there have also been failures. In 1989, extensive Chinese student struggles occurred for political reforms, as the young sought greater freedoms of speech and news media, and democratic elections. They used the methods of hunger strikes, walkouts from classrooms, boycotts of university classes, sit-ins, marches, and other demonstrations. At one point, three thousand went on hunger strike. In May 1989, demonstrations of hundreds of thousands occurred in more than one hundred cities. Their approach, however, was without coordination and strategy, and they relied on improvisation, with deadly results. Military actions ordered by the communist party-state in Tiananmen Square and elsewhere in Beijing during a June 3–4 assault resulted in twenty-six hundred persons being killed and more than seven thousand wounded, including civilians and soldiers, according to educated estimates.[123] Exact figures have never been released, and the Chinese government blocks mention of the event on the Internet. The repercussions from this failure of civil resistance were severe.

Other mobilizations are also of uncertain results. While the 1979 revolution in Iran had been a largely nonviolent example of regime change, thirty years later in 2009, Iran underwent massive nationwide nonviolent demonstrations. After President Mahmoud Ahmadinejad won reelection over reformist candidate Mir-Hossein Mousavi in an election widely considered fraudulent, hundreds of thousands marched in Teheran. Adopting the color green as exemplifying change, the challengers in the "Green Wave" seeking ballot-box reform painted their fingers and faces and dressed in the color of reform. The regime's reprisals were severe. On August 5,

123. Joshua Paulson, "Uprising and Repression in China—1989," in Sharp, *Waging Nonviolent Struggle*, 266.

Ahmadinejad was sworn in for a second term. Protests have persisted on major holidays, with Iranian youth organizing and prominent politicians such as Mousavi and Mohammed Khatami, a reformist ex-president, holding rallies. In Burma, too, attempted prodemocracy mobilizations in 1989 and 2007 were met with violent government crackdowns. The leader, Aung San Suu Kyi, who for years could not be referred to by name inside the country and was called "The Lady," in April 2012 became an elected member of parliament.

INTERNATIONAL NONVIOLENT ACTION AND WORLD PEACE

Martin Luther King, Jr. was in St. Joseph's Infirmary, Atlanta, for exhaustion and a viral infection—the apparent cost exacted by intelligence surveillance efforts and the pressures of learning that Attorney General Robert F. Kennedy had formally approved wiretaps by the Federal Bureau of Investigation—when it was reported King would receive the 1964 Nobel Peace Prize.[124] King's remarks in Oslo that December tied the nonviolent struggle of the U.S. civil rights movement to the whole planet's need for disarmament. Noting that the most exceptional characteristic of the move ment was the direct participation of masses of people in it, and stressing Gandhi's introduction of the "[nonviolent] weapons of Truth, soul force, non-injury and courage," King's remarks also were his strongest bid for the use of nonviolent resistance on issues other than racial injustice. International nonviolent action, he said, might be utilized to let global leaders know that beyond racial and economic justice, individuals across the world were concerned about world peace: "I venture to suggest [above all] . . . that . . . nonviolence become immediately a subject for study and for serious experimentation in every field of human conflict, by no means excluding relations between nations . . . which [ultimately] make war . . ."[125] Telling journalists that he would donate the prize money to the movement, he returned home to engross himself in plans for the fifty-four-mile march from Selma to Montgomery, which would be the last major surge of direct action

124. Gary M. Pomerantz, *Where Peachtree Meets Sweet Auburn: The Saga of Two Families and the Making of Atlanta* (New York: Lisa Drew/Scribner, 1996) 334–35.

125. Martin Luther King, Jr., "The Quest for Peace and Justice," address of December 11, 1964, upon receiving the 1964 Nobel Peace Prize, in *Peace*, vol. 3, *1951–1970*, ed. Frederick Haberman (Amsterdam: Elsevier, 1972) 338–43.

for the movement. After this major event, the movement would turn to tools of political and economic organizing, including mock ballots and the development of alternative political parties and social institutions—among the most advanced methods of nonviolent struggle.

Across the world, people who are familiar with few or no details about the civil rights movement know about Martin Luther King, Jr. He had not sought leadership for himself; it was thrust upon him. Once entrusted, he drew upon his full moral stature, of which he possessed more than possibly any other U.S. figure of the twentieth century. In time, he became the greatest force for nonviolent action in the Western world.

Strains between sometimes competing groups or disparagement from the jealous had little relevance for King's eminence, and it was inconsequential, as critics in the movement mocked, that King had been jailed only thirteen different times and was locked up for at most thirty-nine days. Notwithstanding his own invariable preoccupation with his personal shortcomings, King had the ability to accept others as they were and was ready to accommodate arrogance, rebelliousness, and egotism from some with whom he worked. His equanimity was remarkable in the midst of a true people's movement staffed by impetuous and occasionally mutinous individualists. He understood more than he spoke. He was not the tamed and desiccated civil hero as sometimes portrayed in the United States around the time of his birthday, celebrated as a national holiday.

The rapidity with which alterations occurred not only in the South but across the nation in attitudes, laws, mores, statutory programs, and values can obstruct the perception that for most of King's short lifetime he was struggling for the simplest, most straightforward recognition of full citizenship for African Americans. Often he was attacked for moving too slowly or for not fulminating with outrage and militancy. King would not accept the rejectionism of separatists among the Black Power, Black Panther, and Black Muslim adherents in the movement. He well understood "Black Power" and the psychological yearning for a sense of identity that solemnized African origins. He himself was well aware that three-fourths of the inhabitants of the globe were people of color.[126] His quest, however, had been for strategies that left no hostility and offered eventual peace and reconciliation. Indeed, usually without notice or press releases, the blatant signs, physical barriers, and customary accessories of racial discrimination quietly came down in the United States.

126. King, *Stride Toward Freedom*, 220.

King sought a sophisticated though no less decisive form of resistance by creating a moral paradox for the white South. Although Black Power had as many meanings as ears that heard it—and regardless of positive aspects of asserting ethnic self-esteem—it was often used to hint or threaten a display of force, altercation, or reprisal. To King, this was not strategically sound. His ethical framework and his practical goals converged in nonviolent struggle into political astuteness. Well-sequenced nonviolent sanctions can place adversaries in a quandary that they cannot solve through violence. He created a dilemma for a white South that was mostly Christian, conservative, and satisfied with its morals and manners. King hoped to make white Southerners confront the incongruity of racial superiority as something anti-Christian. If they could be brought to see the disjuncture between their principles of civility, courtliness, and Christianity on the one hand, and the uncivilized barbarity that they sanctioned on the other, they might change themselves. In draping the demand for upheaval in the cloth of a beloved community, King prepared them for the inevitabilities of change as more compatible with their own values and less threatening. This is partly why he wanted no declarations of victory and sought to deflect any triumphalism. Mutual respect, he believed, could protect against white citizens feeling defeat or humiliation, while, as noted, the black community could avoid temptation from "the psychology of victors."

In 1966, two years after the 1964 Civil Rights Act outlawed discrimination in education, employment, and public accommodations, and one year following the 1965 Voting Rights Act's prohibited the states from denying the ballot on account of race or color, King's grip on a strategic approach was strong:

> This is no time for romantic illusions about freedom and empty philosophical debate. This is a time for action. What is needed is a strategy for change, a tactical program which will bring the Negro into the mainstream of American life as quickly as possible. So far this has only been offered by the nonviolent movement.
>
> Our record of achievement through nonviolent action is already remarkable. The dramatic social changes which have been made across the South are unmatched by the annals of history. Montgomery, Albany, Birmingham and Selma have paved the way for untold progress. Even more remarkable is the fact that this progress occurred with a minimum of human sacrifice and loss of life.[127]

127. King, "Nonviolence: The Only Road to Freedom," 56.

The entire region was emancipated by the civil rights movement. Relationships between white and black Americans were transformed by the civil rights movement and its exemplification in King. State-backed vigilante networks were enervated and depleted. The collusion of police and sheriffs with terror organizations atrophied. Psychological fear—with which Southern blacks had long grappled, manifesting internalized bondage—tapered. The South as a region was able to reverse its secession from the Union. The stigma suffered by the southland in the eyes of the rest of the nation and world was lifted. The least developed part of the country was freed to pursue prosperity.

King was able to create a way for the Southern sense of honor and history to be transformed into regional pride based on overcoming the perversity of racial injustice. He laid the groundwork for the South to reform itself into a region of dignity and racial amity, a project still in progress. He understood that mutual degradation often accompanies oppression, and that the oppressor and oppressed both undergo pain. His magnanimity allowed him to see that white Southerners were hoisted on their own petard, as their strong sense of liberty, individual rights, community obligation, and Christian fellowship led them in one direction, while they were being driven in another by a tyranny of ancestry, a contorted view of honor as linked to defeat in the Civil War, and the legacy of a cruel racial caste system. King's choice of nonviolent struggle let him take full advantage of this dichotomy. When he asked, "Will you pray with us?" he widened the dilemma. Although initially discomforting, King saw that white Southerners could be led to reject brutality by virtue of their deep cultural and historic beliefs, ultimately allowing them to accept societal change without bitterness. Rather than placing blame, his notion of a beloved community created a neutral place where the grappling could continue over how to understand the past, perhaps in such a way that everyone could win. The preoccupations of white Southerners with their families' defeats in the Civil War—the unrepentant "lost cause" of the Confederacy—could be exchanged for a repudiation of the segregationist past and pursuit of a thriving future. Ultimately, King provided a watchtower that could be seen worldwide rising above acquiescence and submission.

CONCLUSION

Nonviolent action was not just moral or ethical to King, it was the "only road to freedom."[128] After the end of the Montgomery bus boycott, he said, "The choice is no longer between violence and nonviolence. It is either nonviolence or nonexistence."[129] He was making the same point, in nearly identical language, in his final address at Memphis, on April 3, 1968, the night before he was killed. After the 1975 signing of the Final Act of the Helsinki Accords, the term *civil rights* fell into the background as *human rights* replaced it and became the prevailing phrase.

Contemporary studies express less certitude in the predictability of success with nonviolent action than did Gandhi or King in their lifetimes. Planning is wanting. Preparation is too often inadequate. Failures occur. Yet empirical evidence now substantiates civil resistance as more effective than struggles that employ violent measures. Scholars have shown that democratic transitions differentiated by violent action are less likely to result in sustainable democracy than those characterized by nonviolent civil resistance. In other words, the consolidation of democratic norms and values may partly be a consequence of the choice of methods rather than the other way around.[130] The evidence is strong that countries experiencing popular nonviolent struggle are more likely to sustain human rights and democracy, once established, than when violence has been used. In plain words, civil resistance is more successful than cases in which citizens use paramilitary or terrorist means to achieve their objectives. Campaigns of nonviolent resistances have "partial to full success" upward of 90 percent of the time, while endeavors utilizing violent methods were successful only 50 percent of the time, and, in the case of failure, often incur tighter controls and greater repression.[131]

The practice of nonviolent action as it developed during the twentieth century into a means of projecting immense and effective political power is indebted to both Gandhi and King for some of its fundamental discernments. Were King alive today, he would be pleased to observe that

128. Ibid., 30.

129. King, *Stride Toward Freedom*, 224.

130. Adrian Karatnycky and Peter Ackerman, *How Freedom Is Won: From Civic Resistance to Durable Democracy* (New York: Freedom House, 2005).

131. Maria J. Stephan and Erica Chenoweth, "Why Civil Resistance Works: The Strategic Logic of Nonviolent Conflict," *International Security* 33 (2008) 7–44. See also idem, *Why Civil Resistance Works* (New York: Columbia University Press, 2011).

oppressed peoples are absorbing alternative ways to fight without violence faster than the tyrants and oppressors are coming up with new ways to repress.

Notwithstanding the fact that nonviolent action has ascended in political significance on every continent since King's death, and it is no longer possible to focus on geopolitics without attention to people's movements that seek to recapture their dignity, civil resistance has remained underdeveloped as a technique. Comparatively insignificant efforts have been made to increase our comprehension of its logic, systems, and how it works. Minimal research and planning has been invested to support its study, development, and fine-tuning. This stands out against the vast assets allocated in developing and improving military and security studies, and the investments in refining the practices and procedures of representative democracies.

8

A Network of Mutuality

Martin Luther King, Jr., Interdependence, and Ethics

Roy Money

We are tied together in the single garment of destiny, caught in an inescapable network of mutuality. And whatever affects one directly affects all indirectly. For some strange reason I can never be what I ought to be until you are what you ought to be. And you can never be what you ought to be until I am what I ought to be. All I am saying is this: that all life is inter-related, and somehow we are all tied together.

MARTIN LUTHER KING, JR.[1]

I STILL REMEMBER THE Sunday service at Ebenezer Baptist Church in the spring of 1964. I had started college and was drawn into civil rights actions in Atlanta through a campus religious organization. I had read about

1. Martin Luther King, Jr., "Remaining Awake through a Great Revolution," in James M. Washington, ed., *A Testament of Hope: The Essential Writings and Speeches of Martin Luther King, Jr.* (New York: HarperCollins, 1991) 269.

the Reverend Martin Luther King, Jr. but had not heard him speak. His powerful voice lifted up the alternative of a beloved community to that of segregation and discrimination, and he spoke convincingly about the possibilities for creative action even in the darkest of hours. It was a watershed moment for me, full of inspiration to believe in the possibility of justice for all and to embrace the challenge of its realization. The following years were an eventful time for many of us as we tried to address the national disgrace of racism, poverty, and war. It was of course a time of great challenge for Rev. King as his rhetoric found both a wider national audience as well as broader concerns than segregation in the South. Four years later he was no longer with us, but the legacy of his words and actions is enduring.

The epigraph is from one of King's most famous speeches, "Remaining Awake though a Great Revolution," one version of which was his last sermon, delivered at the National Cathedral in Washington, DC, on March 31, 1968—just days before he was assassinated in Memphis. Similar words are found in King's 1963 "Letter from Birmingham Jail" and his 1958 "Pilgrimage to Nonviolence" essays. In all these texts, King asserts a fundamental level of interdependence in the workings of the world and an ethical principle that follows from it.

Many people have written about Rev. King's speeches and sermons from the perspective of his academic education and the black church tradition in which he grew up. His influences are not always easy to identify because he was essentially a preacher and activist rather than a writer. Though he had a PhD in systematic theology, was the recipient of twenty honorary degrees, and was the author of six books and numerous essays, King's communicative style was fundamentally inspirational rather than scholarly. In his sermons, he made extensive references to many authors in philosophy and secular literature as well as the Bible, but many of his sources are not known, as is characteristic of the homiletic tradition.

Here I concern myself primarily with King's language of interdependence as expressed repeatedly in variations on two phrases: "a network of mutuality" and "the interrelatedness of life." Many individuals have identified a variety of influences on King's thinking. In addition to summarizing what others have written, I will suggest some additional sources that seem especially relevant to his language of interdependence, and I will also explore the rich history of similar language in Buddhist literature as a way to provide a wider and more global context for understanding these concepts.

It is difficult to examine King's language without encountering controversies about his unacknowledged sources. This has been dealt with in various ways, certainly some more responsibly than others. My interest is not with intellectual originality but with a convergence of themes and ideas in King's language, and the legacy of that language. Whatever the source of his ideas, what may have been his most important contribution to the world was his skill in "exploring and dramatizing ideas in action rather than writing."[2] King was aware of the way that technology had greatly reduced the importance of distance and created a "geographical oneness," and he thought that it was very important to have a world perspective. Modern science and technology had transformed the globe into "a world-wide neighborhood," "a world house," and for him the challenge was to transform that into "a world-wide brotherhood."[3]

Repeated trips to Africa and to India beginning in 1957 and 1959 convinced King of the inseparability of anticolonial struggles abroad and the civil rights struggle in the United States. By 1963, King had already established friendships with Kwame Nkrumah, the first prime minister of Ghana; Tom Mboya, the Kenyan independence leader; Premier Ben Bella of the new Algerian Republic; and a number of Gandhi's followers and admirers in India.[4] King's notion of interdependence was partly based on a world-wide freedom struggle that found encouragement in the awareness that others were on the same path. And, aside from the moral debt owed to those who had suffered from Western exploitation, King believed that it was in our (Western) self-interest to assist these struggles because "if we don't learn to live together as brothers we will be forced to perish together as fools."[5]

It seems likely that in his trips to Africa and India, King became more familiar with non-Western concepts that parallel the idea of a network of mutuality. For example, here is a 1929 statement on interdependence by Mahatma Gandhi that makes the point:

2. Richard King, *Civil Rights and the Idea of Freedom* (New York: Oxford University Press, 1992) 109.

3. King, *Where Do We Go from Here?*, 171; Washington, *Testament of Hope*, 209.

4. Lewis V. Baldwin, *To Make the Wounded Whole: The Cultural Legacy of Martin Luther King, Jr.* (Minneapolis: Fortress, 1992) 247–49; Lewis V. Baldwin, *Toward the Beloved Community: Martin Luther King, Jr. and South Africa* (Cleveland: Pilgrim, 1995) 12; Washington, *Testament of Hope*, 25.

5. King, *Where Do We Go from Here?*, 171; Washington, *Testament of Hope*, 620. King made this point repeatedly and in various terms throughout his public life.

> Interdependence is and ought to be as much the ideal of man as self-sufficiency. Man is a social being. Without interrelation with society he cannot realize his oneness with the universe or suppress his egotism. His social interdependence enables him to test his faith and to prove himself on the touchstone of reality.[6]

King spoke often of the national liberation struggles in Africa, and it seems unlikely that the cultural traditions of these nations were unknown to him. No doubt the communalism of African cultures was historically influential in shaping black church understandings of community and solidarity as reflected in the characterization of pre-1950s black religious leaders incorporating an "organismic conception of reality."[7]

The theology of Personalism was clearly one important source of influence for Rev. King's language of interdependence. King claimed Personalism as his basic philosophical position in "Pilgrimage to Nonviolence," and there is an indication that he went to Boston University for the purpose of studying Personalism.[8] The legacy of Personalism that King generally talked about was its affirmation of a personal God and of the dignity of persons, but within the latter theme there was an emphasis on the interrelatedness of social reality.[9] However, the sensibility of Personalism is probably one that was already familiar to King from his lifelong informal education, since the culture surrounding the black church included both of those elements.[10] The language of interrelationality in Personalism was convenient for communicating with white liberal audiences, and that was a critical part of King's work as a leader of the civil rights movement.

Another important influence for King's language were the sermons of the liberal Baptist minister Harry Emerson Fosdick. In terms of King's signature "network of mutuality" metaphor, Keith Miller indicates a likely source[11] in one of the sermons of Fosdick, where he enumerates four factors to account for the tragedies of life; of the last of these, "the intermeshed relationships of life," Fosdick writes:

---

6. Mahatma Gandhi, *Young India*, March 21, 1929.

7. Henry J. Young, *Major Black Religious Leaders, 1755–1940* (Nashville: Abingdon, 1977) 13.

8. Rufus Burrow, Jr., *Personalism: A Critical Introduction* (St. Louis: Chalice, 1999) 77.

9. Ibid., 12.

10. Keith D. Miller, *Voice of Deliverance: The Language of Martin Luther King, Jr., and Its Sources* (New York: Free Press, 1992) 55–62.

11. Ibid., 116.

We are interrelated. We flow into one another. We are members
one of another, and as individuals and nations our woes, problems
and tragedies spill over from one into the other's life. We are intermeshed in an inescapable mutuality.[12]

The idea of an inescapable network of mutuality provides more speci-
ficity to the idea that we are all in this together. There is, of course, no mention of Fosdick's source for this language in his sermon text. Sermons are
exercises in direct communication that can sometimes benefit from attention to particular references, but the rhetoric of delivery is primary.

An awareness of global interdependence was developing rapidly in
the 1950s due both to accelerated political and economic changes and new
technologies of communication. Parallel language to that of Fosdick and
King was also used by Henry Nelson Wieman in *Man's Ultimate Commitment*. Wieman was a Process theologian following in the legacy of Alfred
North Whitehead, and the following passage amplifies Fosdick's ideas
above:

> Perhaps nothing now happening is more fateful for the future
> of the life of man than the swift and irresistible tightening of the
> bonds of interdependence among all peoples, all cultures, all the
> faiths and nations and classes and races on the earth. . . . In this
> tight global community not only are the misery and welfare of
> each major division of humanity determined by what the other
> divisions do; every individual human being is likewise dependent
> upon millions of others, not only for material goods, but also for
> his sense of security or insecurity, for his happiness or distress,
> his achievement or frustration. . . . No longer can any people or
> any individual go its own way regardless of others. Henceforth
> the whole of humanity must find a way of life which all can live
> together.[13]

Man's Ultimate Commitment was published in the same year (1958) as
Fosdick's *Riverside Sermons*. It seems they were both responding to a newly
emerging language for thinking about reality in terms of more relational
dynamic processes. Wieman and Fosdick and King all recognized the relevance of the language, but it was Rev. King who was able to communicate
it most widely.

12. Harry E. Fosdick, *Riverside Sermons* (New York: Harper, 1958) 252–53.

13. Henry N. Weiman, *Man's Ultimate Commitment* (Carbondale: Southern Illinois
University Press, 1958) 44–45.

In King's writing there are two different strands to the language of interdependence: first, the global and easily observed manifestations that King often linked to the freedom struggles in Africa and Asia and to the economic disparities with the Western nations that these efforts sought to correct, and second, the more fundamental social relationality for which King cited Personalist theology and John Donne and Martin Buber. King seems to acknowledge that he did not fully understand the phenomenon, because he writes that "we are *somehow* all tied together" and "*for some strange reason* I can never be what I ought to be until you are what you ought to be" (emphasis mine).[14] But even though he may not have understood why this was true, he sensed that it was true.

It is notable that both phrases, "the interrelated structure of reality" and "network of mutuality," parallel a Whiteheadian perspective that introduced modern alternatives to the prevailing mechanistic orientation of Western philosophy. It may seem counterintuitive to connect King with Whitehead because King's PhD dissertation was a critique of Henry Wieman and Paul Tillich's conception of God as impersonal. However, King had a highly developed intellectual curiosity and is reported to have asked for a copy of Tillich's *Systematic Theology* while serving time in jail.[15] Though King's theology was largely that of his father, he was very much interested in the ideas of the times.

King's inspiration for these concepts may indeed have been through his socialization in an African-American religious community and his trips to India and Africa, but he was adept at choosing evocative language and imagery from Western ideas and culture. He wanted to build a mass movement of black people, but he also needed to communicate effectively with white people in the United States. By making references to Western philosophy and literature, King was able to validate and vindicate the civil rights struggle by making it more integral to the American experience.[16]

Whitehead's Process Philosophy—a philosophy of organism— was part of the context for the development of systems of thinking by

14. King, "Don't Sleep through the Revolution."

15. See Taylor Branch, *Parting the Waters: America in the King Years, 1954–63* (New York: Simon & Schuster, 1988) 363; and Clayborne Carson et al., eds., *The Papers of Martin Luther King, Jr.*, vol. 5, *Threshold of a New Decade, January 1959–December 1960* (Berkeley: University of California Press, 2005) 532.

16. Fredrik Sunnemark, *An Inescapable Network of Mutuality: Discursivity and Ideology in the Rhetoric of Martin Luther King, Jr.* (Goteborg, Sweden: Acta Univeritatis Gothoburgensis, 2001) 247.

organismic biologists and ecologists in the 1920s and 1930s, and was subsequently expressed by the development of cybernetics in the 1940s and 1950s.[17] One of the cornerstones of such systems of thinking is the idea of reality as a dynamic network of relationships. It represented a shift to the study of integrated wholes whose properties could not be reduced to their constituent parts. The development of cybernetics was initially concerned with mathematics and computers, but it was embraced by individuals in the social sciences as well. Gregory Bateson was one of the foremost members of the latter group; he wrote: "I think that cybernetics is the biggest bite out of the fruit of the Tree of Knowledge that mankind has taken in the last 2000 years."[18] One of the central features of cybernetic thinking is the understanding of the feedback process as a way for systems to self-regulate as well as to go out of control. Feedback, of course, involves a process of mutual causality or interdependence.

There is no doubt that King was aware of cybernetics. In "Remaining Awake through a Great Revolution,"[19] King refers to the triple revolution taking place in the world, the first being "a technological revolution, with the impact of automation and cybernation." This is a reference to "a triple revolution" included in a joint statement by thirty-two writers and activists that was published in 1964 as part of a collection of political essays, including one by Rev. King on nonviolence, in *Seeds of Liberation*.[20]

This new paradigm of knowledge has found more recent expression in developments such as complexity science, fractal math, and network theory, all of which have more visibility to the current generation than cybernetics. But probably the most influential factors introducing these ideas to contemporary culture have been the development of ecology and the phenomenon of the Internet. Regarding the latter, the science writer

17. Fritjof Capra, *The Web of Life* (New York: Anchor, 1996) 43.

18. Gregory Bateson, *Steps to an Ecology* (New York: Ballantine, 1972) 481–82. An equally important source for exploring this topic is volume 12, issue 1–2 of *Cybernetics & Human Knowing: A Journal of Second-Order Cybernetics, Autopoiesis, and Cybersemiotics* (2005). This work highlights Bateson's concern for the links between human ways of knowing and our experienced worlds.

19. See Washington, *Testament of Hope*, 269; Clayborne Carson and Peter Holloran, eds., *A Knock at Midnight: Inspiration from the Great Sermons of Reverend Martin Luther King, Jr.* (New York: Warner, 1998) 207; King, *Where Do We Go from Here?*, 168; Baldwin, *To Make the Wounded Whole*, 253.

20. See Paul Goodman, ed., *Seeds of Liberation* (New York: George Braziller, 1964).

Thomas Gleick has written about how we are "inescapably connected,"[21] and newspaper columnist Thomas Friedman has written about how "the world has gone from connected to hyperconnected"—what King would call "a world-wide neighborhood"[22] indeed.

Of course, most of this new awareness has occurred since Rev. King's assassination, but its relevance is that it shows a fuller articulation of what was then emerging as a new way of thinking about the world. Though King was first and foremost a black Baptist preacher who believed that the inter-relational structure of reality was something God had made, he nonetheless seemed to sense a new paradigm that has become increasingly important in conventional language as well as in the realm of scientific research.

Usually King's language stressed the social dimension of the new paradigm of interdependence, and he often mentioned its basis in technological and political developments. However, many native cultures throughout the world had—and still have—a strong sense of a more fundamental inter-connectedness of life that includes the natural world as well as the human world. These indigenous beliefs point to an ontological reality obscured by the spread of reductionism and individualism in European cultures.

This non-European awareness of interrelatedness found a well-developed articulation in the philosophy of Buddhism, which anticipates the process philosophy of Alfred North Whitehead. The Buddhist literature on interdependence goes back to Shakyamuni Buddha's concept of "interdependent arising" and his statement that whoever understands the concept of "interdependent arising" understands his teachings.[23] While there is no evidence that King was directly influenced by Buddhist literature in his appropriation of the language of interdependence, this literature nonetheless provides a well-formulated context for thinking about it.

Ethan Nichtern has written about the concept of interdependence as consisting of five levels.[24] Perhaps the most self-evident are community and society. The first level refers to the relations we have with multiple individuals in families, neighborhoods, organizations, and towns, where the scale is

21. Thomas Gleick, "Inescapably Connected: Life in the Wireless Age," *New York Times Sunday Review*, August 13, 2011.

22. Thomas Friedman, "A Theory of Everything (Sort of)," *New York Times Sunday Review*, August 13, 2011; King, *Where Do We Go from Here?*, 167.

23. Dalai Lama, *The Four Noble Truths*, trans. Geshe Thupten Jinpa, ed. Dominique Side (London: Thorsons, 1997) 12.

24. Ethan Nichtern, *One City: A Declaration of Interdependence* (Boston: Wisdom, 2007) 29–53.

intermediate between interpersonal relations and international ones, and the latter level to the interdependent global realities that we read or hear about in the news every day. These are the ones that Rev. King's language most often addressed. As he wrote in his "Letter from Birmingham City Jail" on April 16, 1963:

> Moreover, I am cognizant of the interrelatedness of all communities and states. I cannot sit idly by in Atlanta and not be concerned about what happens in Birmingham. Injustice anywhere is a threat to justice everywhere. We are caught in an inescapable network of mutuality, tied in a single garment of destiny. Whatever affects one directly affects all indirectly.[25]

It is not that everyone is affected in the same way, but that individual effects are continually accumulating, interacting, and propagating as influences on others who reside at different locations in the web of relationships. Injustice represents a form of separation and contracted possibilities for everyone. Social divisions usually result in a fear of losing privileges for those who have more, as well as concern for survival and equity for those who have less. And the maintenance of these privileges and divisions consumes important resources that affect the possibilities of social community for each of us.

We cannot really escape the effects of social problems, even if they do not directly encompass our individual life or our national interests; withdrawal into an insular, individualistic or nationalistic identity is a denial of our fundamental interconnectedness and interdependence. Cultural conditioning may obscure the network of our mutuality, but the consequences of this interconnection are ultimately inescapable.

As Rev. King put it, the need to outlaw poverty goes beyond material concerns to the quality of our mind and spirit:

> [W]e cannot preserve self without being concerned about other selves. Nothing could be more disastrous and out of harmony with our self-interest than for the developed nations to travel a dead-end road of inordinate selfishness. We are in the fortunate position of having our deepest sense of morality coalesce with our self-interest. . . . The agony of the poor impoverishes the rich: the betterment of the poor enriches the rich. We are inevitably our

---

25. See James M. Washington, ed., *I Have a Dream: Writings and Speeches that Changed the World* (San Francisco: HarperSanFrancisco, 1992) 85; Martin Luther King, Jr., *Why We Can't Wait* (New York: New American Library, 1964) 77.

brother's keeper because we are our brother's brother. Whatever affects one directly affects all indirectly.[26]

Two additional levels of interdependence that Nichtern identifies are the interdependence of self and the interdependence of relationships. The interdependence of self is typically referred to as the Buddhist teaching of "no self," which demonstrates that the concept of self does not denote an independent entity but a complex configuration of feelings, thoughts, and actions that are continually changing in response to our relational experience. If the entity referred to as "self" is an aggregate of interdependent processes, it is naturally interdependent with what is not the "self," whether they are persons or other living or non-living things. As Zen master Yasutani Roshi is reported to have said, "The fundamental delusion of humanity is that I am here and you are out there."[27]

Lastly, Nichtern refers to what he calls "universal interdependence," which broadly equates to the concept of emptiness in Buddhist literature. This concept follows from the impermanence of all things, the understanding that nothing has an essence or independent existence. The concept of interdependent arising posits reality as a dynamic process where nothing exists independently but everything, mental and physical, is part of a complex web of interactions that is in continuous transformation, and the only thing that is truly real is the momentary *now* of experience. Nothing is without a cause, but since the causes are multiple and interactive, nothing is predetermined.

Even a brief discussion of Buddhism and the concept of interdependence would be incomplete without the mention of Indra's net. Indra's net was a metaphor first articulated in the third century Avatamsaka Sutra to illustrate concepts of interdependence and emptiness. This net was thought to be infinite in extent, with a jewel in each node that reflected all the other jewels. In more recent times, Indra's net has provided a physical image for the interconnectedness of complex networks ranging from the functioning of the human brain[28] to ecological systems.[29]

26. King, *Where Do We Go from Here?*, 180–81.

27. Cited in Robert Aitken, *The Mind of Clover: Essays in Zen Buddhist Ethics* (New York: North Point, 1984) 169.

28. See Annellen Simpkins and Alexander Simpkins, *The Dao of Neuroscience* (New York: Norton, 2009) 25; Robin Robertson, *Indra's Net: Alchemy and Chaos Theory as Models of Transformation* (Wheaton, IL: Quest, 2009) 137.

29. See Taigen Dan Leighton, "Now the Whole Planet Has Its Head on Fire," in *A*

Indra's net became central to Chinese Buddhism, as it provided a powerful image for the scholarly abstractions of Indian Buddhism. One contemporary Zen master, Thich Nhat Hanh, who collaborated with Martin Luther King, Jr. in expressing opposition to the war in Vietnam, has used this imagery extensively to convey Buddhist teachings in vivid and easily accessible prose. Thich Nhat Hanh coined the term *interbeing* to give fresh expression to the concepts of interdependence and interpenetration found in the Avatamsaka Sutra. Successive generations of Buddhist scholars have written numerous commentaries on the doctrine of interdependent arising, but for a Buddhist it is not a theory to believe but an experience to be realized. Thich Nhat Hanh writes:

> As we meditate on the interdependent nature of all things, we can penetrate reality easily, and see the fears, anguish, hopes, and despair of all beings. . . . The interdependent nature of all beings is not a philosophical game removed from spiritual and practical life. In bringing to light the interdependence of all phenomena, the meditator comes to see that the lives of all beings are one, and he or she is overcome with compassion for all. When you feel this love you know that your meditation is bearing fruit. Seeing and loving always go together. Seeing and loving are one.[30]

And, in a similar vein, the late Robert Aitken, influential American Zen master, has written the following:

> We may not realize it, but we are all dwelling in the original realm . . . a vast multidimensional net of unknown magnitude that is exquisitely dynamic—the mutual interdependence of all things and their mutual intersupport, the nature of our world. As philosophy this net forms a beautiful coherence. As experience it is the containment of all beings by me, by the *me* of you, and there are countless numbers of us.[31]

Though the quotations above provide a conceptual overlay for a Buddhist awareness, it is important to note that the words point to a personal experience that is not reducible to words. It is essentially perceptual and preconceptual.

Buddhist Response to the Climate Emergency (Boston: Wisdom, 2009); Leslie Paul Thiele, *Indra's Net and the Midas Touch* (Cambridge: MIT Press, 2011).

30 Thich Nhat Hanh, *The Sun My Heart* (Berkeley: Parallax, 1988) 72.

31. Robert Aitken, "Case 1: Chao-Chou's Dog," in *The Gateless Barrier: The Wu-Men Kuan (Mumonkan)* (New York: North Point, 1991) 14.

It seems relevant to note here the close friendship that developed between Rev. King and Thich Nhat Hanh after they met in May 1966 in Chicago. They discussed their common efforts to address social problems from their different religious perspectives and issued a joint statement about the "real enemies of man that lie within the human heart."[32] Thich Nhat Hanh was evidently an influence on King's subsequent controversial opposition to the Vietnam War in January 1967, and in the same year King nominated Hanh for a Nobel Peace Prize.

If we are inherently interdependent, why don't we live cooperatively together? How is it that oppression becomes so persistent and occludes our postulated fundamental interrelatedness? How do we account for the evils of racism and economic injustice and war and the developing environmental calamity, short of the conventional fallback to a flawed human nature? For King, injustice is a result of individuals choosing a path contrary to the will of God. It is the will of God that individuals cooperate in the creation of a beloved community, accepting responsibility for each other as children of God.[33] There is here the sense that humans are fundamentally social beings and can only realize their authentic identity through community with others, but ignorance and moral blindness inexorably lead to passive acquiescence, or active participation, in destructive social forces. As Rev. King often said, "for some strange reason" he could not be what he should be until others are what they should be. "This is the way God's universe is made," King continued, "this is the way it is structured."[34]

For Buddhists, there is a different understanding of evil but a common understanding that ignorance and an associated moral blindness are at the heart of the problem. For the Dalai Lama, all Buddhist philosophy rests on two basic principles: understanding the interdependent nature of reality, and applying that understanding to do our best to help others.[35]

32. Martin Luther King, Jr. and Thich Nhat Hanh, "Joint Statement," prepared under the auspices of the International Committee of Conscience on Vietnam, Nyack, New York (1966), housed in the Library and Archives of the Martin Luther King, Jr. Center for Nonviolent Social Change, Inc., Atlanta, Georgia; Lewis V. Baldwin, ed., "In a Single Garment of Destiny": A Global Vision of Justice—Martin Luther King, Jr. (Boston: Beacon, 2012) 207 and 213.

33. Walter E. Fluker, They Looked for a City: A Comparative Analysis of the Ideal of Community in the Thought of Howard Thurman and Martin Luther King, Jr. (Lanham, MD: University Press of America, 1989) 113.

34. Carson and Holloran, Knock at Midnight, 208.

35. Dalai Lama, Four Noble Truths, 7.

The proposed ethical life is based on an understanding about the nature of reality. Of course, "understanding the interdependent nature of reality" is problematic both because the interdependent nature of reality is not an objective fact evident to all, and because people may disagree as to its meaning. While there are many developments in modern science that point toward such a view of the physical and social world, for Rev. King this was fundamentally a spiritual proposition. Likewise for many Buddhists, it is an understanding grounded in a spiritual awareness, as captured in the previous passages by Thich Nhat Hanh and Robert Aitken.

For Buddhist scholar David Loy, Buddhist enlightenment occurs when the individual no longer confronts the world as object but experiences herself as an integral moment in the unfolding process of reality.[36] When the boundaries between self and other, and self and the natural world, become more diffuse and interpenetrated, there is little distinction between helping others and helping self:

> To wake up is to realize that I am not in the world, I am what the world is doing right here and now. When Shakyamuni became enlightened, the whole world awakened *in* him and *as* him. The world begins to heal when we realize that its sufferings are our own.[37]

For Loy, embracing our interdependence is not only central to individual enlightenment but also to addressing the urgent problems of our world. This includes finding ways to confront the institutionalized forms of what in Buddhist literature are referred to as the three poisons: greed, ill will, and delusion. In traditional Buddhist religious practice, the challenge for an individual is to transform these qualities into generosity, compassion, and wisdom. Loy has been instrumental in identifying the social implications of these qualities. In particular, he points to the way in which individual qualities of greed, ill will, and delusion are encouraged and promoted by social factors and institutions such as consumerism, financial profiteering, racism, militarism, and the misinformation characteristic of much our education system and the media.[38]

In January 2006, the Buddhist Peace Fellowship (BPF) published a document that addresses these issues directly. Titled, "A Declaration of

---

36. David Loy, *The Great Awakening* (Boston: Wisdom, 2003) 184.

37. Ibid., 198.

38. David Loy, "Bursting the Bubbles," *Insight Journal* 33 (2010) 7.

Interdependence: A Call to Transform the Three Poisons for the Sake of All Sentient Beings," it states:

> Every person on the planet has the full capacity to wake up from the mistaken notion that we are separate from each other. Each of us is connected interdependently with all others, including those who disagree with us. This understanding leads to a reverence for the preciousness of all sentient life.[39]

Though this statement is founded on Buddhist principles that go back twenty-five hundred years, it is of note that the BPF itself was founded in 1978 at the encouragement of the Fellowship of Reconciliation (FOR), which had first brought Thich Nhat Hanh to the United States in 1966. The FOR was closely involved with Rev. King's Montgomery boycott work and did extensive nonviolence trainings throughout the South. In 1979, the FOR established an annual King Peace Prize in his honor. So the legacy of King was implicated in the founding of BPF ten years after his assassination, and in its 2006 Declaration of Interdependence. The intertwining of Buddhism and Martin Luther King, Jr. and the BPF exemplifies this very process of interdependence that King spoke about.

King's message has been restated by the Dalai Lama in his call for the development of "a sense of universal responsibility—of the universal dimension of our every act and of the equal right of all others to happiness and not to suffer . . . the fundamental oneness of the human family."[40] We are called to understand that even small acts can have repercussions in the larger universe, and just as we are individually connected to that web of relations, so countless others are implicated in our individual lives. King's message about awakening to our "inescapable network of mutuality" continues to manifest itself in appeals to a wider awareness of our interrelatedness, especially now as a planetary environmental crisis further exacerbates the social crises of world poverty and hunger. In discussing the developing climate crisis and its many associated dire consequences, Naomi Klein, in words that recall King's own challenge to humanity, explains that what is needed is "an alternative worldview embedded in interdependence rather

39. For the full text, see http://www.rochesterbpf.org/A%20Declaration%20of%20 Interdependence.pdf.

40. Dalai Lama, *Ethics for the New Millennium* (New York: Riverhead, 1999) 162–63. King expressed this idea of the essential oneness of all humanity in various terms. See King, *Where Do We go from Here?*, 190; Washington, *Testament of Hope*, 629–33; and Martin Luther King, Jr., *Strength to Love* (Philadelphia: Fortress, 1981) 27–29.

than hyper-individualism, reciprocity rather than dominance and coopera-tion rather than hierarchy."[41]

As suggested previously, King's use of language is what distinguished him most from other civil rights movement leaders. He had the ability to craft language that was powerfully evocative and that transcended both race and class, so that it was instrumental in mobilizing the nation to begin a redemptive process to rectify centuries of racial oppression. King's rhetoric has helped inspire people throughout the world to lift neighborly concern beyond one's tribe, race, class, and nation and embrace the whole planet.[42]

My initial contact with Rev. King's vision and work happened during a critical period in my life. Subsequent experience enabled me to see his language in a broader context that he himself pointed to—"a network of mutuality." In this web of interconnections, every action we take has con-sequences that propagate out in complex and unpredictable ways. Waking up to a fuller awareness of this process is in the interest of everyone in the world because it means living life more fully and wisely.

41. Naomi Klein, "Capitalism vs. the Climate," *The Nation*, November 28, 2011.

42. King, *Where Do We Go from Here?*, 190; King, *Strength to Love*, 26–35; Washing-ton, *Testament of Hope*, 629–33; King, *Why We Can't Wait*, 77.

PART THREE

Linked in a Single Garment of Destiny

Martin Luther King, Jr., Nation-Building,
and the Challenges of an Interdependent World

9

What Method for the Oppressed?

Martin Luther King, Jr.'s Contribution to Nation-Building in the Caribbean

Noel Leo Erskine

I have often talked late at night and over into the small hours of the morning with proponents of Black Power who argued passionately about the validity of violence and riots. They don't quote Gandhi or Tolstoy. Their Bible is Frantz Fanon's *The Wretched of the Earth*. This black psychiatrist from Martinique . . . argues in his book—a well-written book, incidentally, with many penetrating insights—that violence is a psychologically healthy and tactically sound method for the oppressed.[1]

THE MODERN CIVIL RIGHTS movement led by Martin Luther King, Jr. during the 1950s and 1960s was important for Caribbean people in their understanding of nation-building and their efforts to win political independence

---

1. Martin Luther King, Jr., *Where Do We Go from Here: Chaos or Community?* (Boston: Beacon, 1968) 55.

from their colonial masters. Two pertinent questions inform this claim. First, at what point during the civil rights movement did King adopt and embrace an international perspective, believing that the movement had relevance for Caribbean nations? Second, did nations in the Caribbean view King and the work of the civil rights movement as integral to their own identity and growth? In short, we ask: How did Caribbean nations view the civil rights movement as it unfolded in the United States, and how were they affected by it?

Although King traveled to Ghana with Jamaican Prime Minister Norman W. Manley and others as early as 1957 to attend and participate in that nation's political independence celebrations,[2] and expressed an early desire to visit India, it is quite clear that the early vision for the civil rights movement and its commitments were to improve race relations between black and white people in the southern United States. Further, it should be noted that King initially provided leadership to a Southern organization, the Montgomery Improvement Association (MIA), which had no global connections. The name of the organization indicates that its reach and focus were local as it sought to address issues of racism and segregation in Montgomery engendered by the refusal of a local citizen, Rosa L. Parks, to obey the bus segregation laws. The black community in Montgomery protested against the arrest of Mrs. Parks by local police when she refused to comply with the order of the bus driver to sit in the back of the bus in order to accommodate a white male passenger, who, according to Montgomery's laws, was entitled to her seat. David J. Garrow captures the ethos and mood of Rosa Parks:

> Mrs. Parks was neither frightened nor angry. "I was thinking that the only way to let them know how I felt I was being mistreated was to do just what I did—resist the order," she later recalled. "I had not thought about it and I had taken no previous resolution until it happened, and then I simply decided that I would not get up. I was tired, but I was usually tired at the end of the day, and I was not feeling well, but then there had been many days when I had not felt well. I had felt for a long time, that if I were ever told to get up so a white person could sit that I would refuse to do so."[3]

2. Coretta Scott King, *My Life with Martin Luther King, Jr.* (New York: Avon, 1969) 164.

3. David J. Garrow, *Bearing the Cross: Martin Luther King, Jr. and the Southern Christian Leadership Conference* (New York: William Morrow, 1986) 12 .

This spirit of no surrender would reverberate throughout the so-called dark world, giving the most progressive-minded people in Jamaica, Haiti, Trinidad, and other parts of the Caribbean a special sense of pride.

COMBINING FAITH AND LEADERSHIP: THE KINGIAN ETHIC

Martin Luther King, Jr., a new pastor in Montgomery, Alabama, was drafted by fellow pastors and community leaders to lead the Montgomery Improvement Association. It is also worth noting that local clergymen in Montgomery were on both sides of the issue of racial equality and segregation of local transportation and other institutions in Montgomery, depending, of course, on the color of their skin. In 1956, the mayor of Montgomery, W. A. Gayle, called a meeting of his citizens' committee, along with members of Montgomery City Bus Line, to meet with the Montgomery Improvement Association, led by King. Members of the mayor's delegation included the Reverend Henry Parker, pastor of First Baptist Church; the Reverend E. Stanley Frazier, minister of St. James Methodist Church; and the Reverend Henry Russell of Trinity Presbyterian Church. King spelled out the goals of the Montgomery Improvement Association as articulated in the meeting with the mayor and his committee. King requested (*a*) a guarantee of courteous treatment for black people in Montgomery who routinely rode the buses; (*b*) that passengers be seated on a first come, first served basis, with black people being seated from the back of the bus; and (c) the employment of black bus operators in predominantly black routes. The mayor's committee would not agree to black people being hired to operate buses in predominantly black neighborhoods. This forced King's delegation to modify their request, and to ask instead that the bus company take applications from blacks for possible vacancies that would occur in the future. These efforts in Montgomery were closely watched by people throughout the Caribbean, especially those who felt a keen sense of identification with the struggles of blacks in America, and particularly those in the American South.

Mayor W. A. Gayle of Montgomery included white preachers on his committee not only because he was dealing in negotiations with members of that city's black clergy, but also because he knew that their theological position upheld the imperative to save souls rather than meddle in politics. It is of interest that in this meeting with the mayor's committee, King and his committee did not ask that segregation in public transportation be eradicated. Instead, they petitioned for a more humane system of bus segregation. It was precisely at this point that the Reverend Dr. Frazier from the Methodist Church in Montgomery made it clear that, from his reading of the Bible, black clergy were leading the black community down the wrong path by encouraging and assisting it in its boycott of city buses. Frazier pointed out that it was shameful that black clergy would participate in and lead the boycott against a bus company of Montgomery, and not devote that time to the preaching of the gospel of Christ.[4] Interestingly enough, this tendency to disconnect the gospel from any resistance to social evil had long characterized the approaches of white missionaries in their outreach to peoples of African descent, not only in the United States but in the Caribbean and across the African continent.

The world of white people in Montgomery was quite different from that of black people, as evidenced by the different approaches to civil rights articulated at the mayor's meeting by white and black clergy. If the white clergy in Montgomery summed up their understanding of Christianity in terms of personal and private redemption, black people, led by black clergy, held to a social gospel interpretation. Black preachers in Montgomery fully understood that the teachings of Christ had social and political implications for the question of segregation and racism, a message seldom heard in the Caribbean at that time. Montgomery's blacks were willing to put their bodies at risk in the struggle, as a way of effecting change in public accommodations and transportation. The black clergy, led by King, were not willing to accept a gospel that sanctioned their oppression and victimization. Recalling Rev. Frazier's suggestion that the leadership of the Montgomery Improvement Association divorce spiritual and religious concerns from political issues, King stated:

> He [Frazier] made it clear . . . that the job of the minister . . . is to lead the souls of men to God, not to bring about confusion by getting tangled up in transitory social problems. He moved on to a brief discussion of the Christmas story. In evocative terms he talked of "God's unspeakable gift." He ended by saying that as we move into the Christmas season our hearts and minds should be turned to the babe of Bethlehem; and he urged the Negro ministers to leave the meeting determined to bring this boycott to a

---

4. Martin Luther King, Jr., *Stride Toward Freedom: The Montgomery Story* (New York: Harper & Row, 1958) 116–17.

close and lead their people instead "to a glorious experience of the Christian faith."[5]

The Montgomery bus boycott not only provided the impetus for the rise of other civil rights campaigns across the American South, but it also inspired freedom movements in the wider world. King's goal, which involved the building and emergence of "an interracial society based on freedom for all," clearly struck a responsive chord in the hearts and minds of people in the Caribbean. The Montgomery Improvement Association became the Southern Christian Leadership Conference (SCLC) in 1957, thus taking on a regional focus that would ultimately extend to the national and the international arenas. Some of the values of the SCLC were transported to the Caribbean, especially the fight for justice, economic empowerment and equality, human indignity, and the emergence of a beloved community.

CARIBBEAN ISSUES AND KING'S SOCIAL AGENDA

Caribbean people did not see the need for racial integration during the 1950s and 1960s, and most church people would have agreed with Rev. Frazier that church leaders should not be actively engaged in social and political matters. A great deal of the way Caribbean people understood the world was informed by the teachings of missionaries from the United States and by African traditions as expressed in the communal values of slave religion. The values and practices of Caribbean people, as they relate to race and poverty, are often played out with a bias toward Euro-American or African identities. Often an answer to issues of poverty or Caribbean identity is sought in African-derived religions. But there are also occasions when Caribbean people turn to Pentecostal expressions of the Christian faith for answers to intransigent poverty, and in an attempt to make sense of an identity shaped in the nexus between the United States and Africa. In such settings, King's social gospel was not easily and readily understood in all of its dimensions.

I recall an incident that occurred in Jamaica circa 1962, while I served as pastor of Baptist churches on the island. The government of Jamaica, in an attempt to remove squatters from lands owned by the government, had the homes of poor people bulldozed and surrounded the land with police in order to prevent residents from returning to their yards. As a pastor, with

5. Ibid., 116.

five churches on the island, I addressed the topic from a Kingian perspective in a sermon at Sunday morning worship. In my sermon, I pointed out that the government was insensitive to the needs of the poor and had failed to practice the love ethic of Jesus. Half of my congregation protested that they came to church on Sunday with a desire to escape issues of class and economic inequality. The people were emphatic that they had come to church to hear about Jesus, not about injustices in the world. What is interesting in Caribbean culture is that many of those who shared this worldview were influenced not only by missionary theology in the islands but also by local religious groups, such as the Rastafari and the Revival church—communities that felt helpless to effect change in the socioeconomic spheres and thereby withdrew from political engagement. What is of interest here is that if on the one hand the refusal to engage social and political issues is motivated by Euro-American worldviews, on the other hand it is supported by indigenous religions.

The other side of the issue finds its credence in the teachings of the preeminent teacher of racial pride and uplift, Marcus M. Garvey. Scholars such as Barry Chevannes in *Betwixt and Between*; Rex Nettleford in *Inward Reach, Outward Stretch*; and Hernández Hiraldo in *Black Puerto Rican Identity and Religious Experience* point out that there is an African ethos that suffuses Caribbean identity, which is expressed in the embrace of racial pride. These scholars contend that an African ethos of cooperation, racial uplift, self-reliance, and communal values represented in the thought of scholars like Marcus Garvey critiques the earlier teachings of missionaries from North America.

VOICES FROM THE CARIBBEAN

Oscar Lacroix, a parish priest from Guadeloupe, writes in support of protecting Caribbean identity from the encroachment of imperial and colonial influences handed down from the United States and Europe. Among the imported values are

> a general context of valorization of western patterns and of the white man, and a depreciation of the black man and all that is indigenous; because everything was imported, a mentality of dependence and passivity, opposed to all creativity and initiative. A Gospel brought by . . . missionaries who apart from some fortunate exceptions, put forward their theological culture, language

of the faith . . . a frequent policy of compromise between church authority and civil powers . . .[6]

Although Father Lacroix writes from the French-speaking community of the Caribbean, his claims have currency throughout the Caribbean and speak to theological claims embraced by Caribbean churches that were indoctrinated by European and North American missionaries. It is interesting that in a meeting of the Caribbean Conference of Churches, Father Lacroix begins with criticism of the valorization of Western ways of thinking and the assumed superiority of views held by white people. He reminds us that this is a part of the history of plantation slavery throughout the Caribbean and of the inclination among Caribbean people to imitate white people and to internalize the idea of a self inferior to other selves. Father Lacroix calls for a reversal of values in which the superior/inferior assessment of humanity in the Caribbean is discarded and a new humanity is allowed to emerge. The Caribbean Conference of Churches was held in three regions of the Caribbean, and the subtext was a call for the emergence of a new humanity, one that renounces the white/black and master/slave portrayal of Caribbean humanity.

In this regard, the conference put forth a challenge that Martin Luther King, Jr. had consistently presented to the entire world. What is of interest for our purposes is that Father Lacroix did not suggest integration or accommodation to Western ways of thinking or with white people as a possible way forward. The challenge was for Caribbean people to "decolonize their thinking" and build a Caribbean identity that did not include or depend on North American ways of thinking. Ashley Smith, a theologian from Jamaica who spoke at the same conference, articulates the first planks of an incipient nationalism that remembers Marcus Garvey:

> De-colonization is a form of spiritual rebirth and not merely an external political process. It connotes change in the relationship between peoples resulting from a transformation of the dominated peoples' consciousness of their own status as human beings, their strength to bring an end to their domination and subjugation, their ability to decide on the quality and direction of their future. . . . Political decolonization is merely one manifestation of the change in a dominated people's perception of their world and

6. Oscar Lacroix, "How the Church Conceives of Her Mission in the French West-Indies," in *Out of the Depths*, ed. Idris Hamid (San Fernando, Trinidad: Rahaman, 1977) 232

their place in that world. Basic to the change in people's perception of reality is their understanding of the dynamics of power—the source of power, the symbolization of power and the exercise of it[7]

Informing Smith's assessment of the way forward was certainly not the teachings or the principles of the civil rights movement as articulated by King in the early period, but the influence of Marcus Garvey, the preeminent evangelist of African identity and ideals in the Caribbean. It is clear that the central challenge that Caribbean people confronted in the 1950s and 1960s was not racial integration or the overthrow of Jim Crow laws that encouraged and enforced segregation, but the overthrow of imperialist policies and a lifestyle of dependence fostered by colonialism. Many Caribbean nations were dissatisfied with flying colonial flags and singing national anthems of their colonial masters. Nation-states like Barbados, Trinidad, and Jamaica were eager to lower the Union Jack and hoist their own national flags, sharing the sentiment of Paul Gilroy: "There ain't no black in the Union Jack."

THE TEACHINGS OF MARCUS MOSIAH GARVEY

Marcus Garvey, Jr., the son of Marcus Mosiah Garvey, pointed out that through the teachings and advocacy of his father, the Caribbean had its civil rights movement as early as the 1920s and 1930s, and was thus poised to contribute to the movement led by Dr. King in the United States in the 1950s and 1960s. Garvey, Jr. highlighted for us what he considers the essential teachings of the Garvey movement, some of which were embraced by King and black liberation theology. The first principle is that of black awareness, the need for people of African descent to know their history, their culture, and their heritage. Garvey, Jr. observed that the cardinal principle of "Garveyism" is this: "Black people, know yourselves." Knowledge of self involves a sociological and educational task, as both Garvey and King knew. The sociological task includes an assessment of black institutions, the means of production including ownership of land, and the place occupied by blacks as the marginalized in the economic order.[8] The principle of black awareness has been invaluable for the journey to political independence

---

7. Ashley Smith, "Mission and Evangelism in an age of Decolonization," in ibid., 115.

8. Marcus Garvey, Jr., "Garveyism: Some Reflections on Its Significance for Today," in *Marcus Garvey and the Vision of Africa*, ed. John Henrik Clarke with Amy Jacques Garvey (Baltimore: Black Classic, 2011) 375.

throughout the Caribbean, as it includes the notion of being awakened to one's circumstance and identity. To be aware and awakened means that one is able to take action informed by reflection on one's history and culture, to forge a new direction and determination to effect change. A crucial aspect of this awareness of one's world and identity is the knowledge of the self-world. For Marcus Garvey, and for the King of the late 1960s as well, it was of primary importance that as people of African descent restore the image of the lost self that was stolen during slavery, they recall and remember their heritage. A central question Garvey addressed to people of African descent across the globe may be paraphrased thus: where do you stand in relation to Africa? For Garvey, the principle of black awareness and awakening was integrally related to this question. Black awareness and black awakening have to do with black people's affirmation of an African past and an African future. Bob Marley captures the teaching of Marcus Garvey in his song "Exodus": "We know where we're going; we know where we're from. Exodus, movement of Jah people."

It is clear that the first principle of black awareness, which for Garvey really meant African awareness, would not have been embraced by King throughout most of his life. King had philosophical and theological problems with the essentializing of the black experience. Throughout most of the movement, King's ultimate goal was not black community, because he felt that this could pose a problem and be understood as a way to keep segregation in place. Advocating the replacement of white community with black community would be understood as a reversal of values, the replacement of white supremacy with black supremacy. King was not pressing for a black nationalism but, instead, for something new and beyond black and white that at the same time included both. This new reality King called the beloved community. "We must all learn to live together as brothers, or we will perish as fools," he declared. He added: "We are tied together in a single garment of destiny, caught in an inescapable network of mutuality. And whatever affects one directly affects all indirectly. . . . This is the way God's universe is made; this is the way it is structured."[9]

9. Martin Luther King, Jr., "Remaining Awake through a Great Revolution," in *A Testament of Hope: The Essential Writings and Speeches of Martin Luther King, Jr.*, ed. James M. Washington (New York: HarperCollins, 1986) 269

KING AND GARVEY IN PROPER CONTEXT

If the early Martin Luther King, Jr. articulated an easy optimism that pointed in the direction of a community in which the sacredness of each person is respected, he had not yet, like Garvey, asked about African consciousness or an African awakening as a way of dealing with the issues of power and justice that are integral to authentic community. It is clear that throughout the Caribbean, an understanding of power influenced by Garvey and fired by the question of where one stood in relation to Africa resulted in the articulation and the embrace of black power. While King had problems with the term *black power*, he seems to have embraced the concept:

> The plantation and the ghetto were created by those who had power, both to confine those who had no power and to perpetuate their powerlessness. The problem of transforming the ghetto, therefore, is a problem of power confrontation of the forces of power demanding change and the forces of power dedicated to preserving the status quo. Now power properly understood is nothing but the ability to achieve purpose. It is the strength required to bring about social, political and economic change.[10]

Although the concept of power seems to function in similar ways for King and Garvey, Garvey, Jr. reminds us that there are conceptual moves that Garvey would make that King would not entertain. For Garvey, the notion of race pride was an indispensable aspect of power for black people. Garvey lived in a world and time in which whiteness as an ideal was elevated and blackness was denigrated. A world in which to be born white was to be socially privileged and to be born black was to be marginalized, and in which there were inequalities in economic and racial terms, made many black people dissatisfied and impatient with their condition. It was in this context that Garvey insisted that black people should view their world, including God, through an African lens. He was completely against miscegenation, as he believed this was a way to destroy the black race:

> Take down the pictures of white women from your walls. Elevate your own women to that place of honor. They are for the most part the burden-bearers of the race. Mothers! Give your children dolls that look like them to play with and to cuddle. They will learn as they grow older to love and care for their own children and not neglect them. Men and women, God made us as his perfect creation.

10. Ibid., 246.

He made no mistake when he made us black with kinky hair. It was Divine Purpose for us to live in our natural habitat—the tropical zones of the earth. Forget the white man's banter that he made us in the night and forgot to paint us. That we were brought here against our will is just a natural process of the strong enslaving the weak. We have outgrown slavery, but our minds are still enslaved to the thinking of the Master Race. Now take these kinks out of your mind instead of out of your hair.[11]

Garvey understood the importance of black symbolism in building authentic black community. Because of this, he reminded black people that the God who is perfect created them as perfect with beautiful noses, lips, and woolly hair. Additionally, he handed out black dolls to parents in the black community, an action in keeping with his claim that it would help young mothers love their children.

Much work needs to be done on the possible impact of Marcus Garvey on the teachings and life of Martin Luther King, Jr. While it is clear that throughout most of his life King was committed to the building of an integrated society, toward the end of his life he began to sound more like Garvey as he called on black communities to support black institutions. It is quite clear that after 1966, King began to take a fresh look at his dream for America, and he concluded with Malcolm X that the likelihood of the dream morphing into a nightmare was a real possibility. Like Garvey and Malcolm, King began to learn of the intransigence of racism, and, as his "Letter from Birmingham City Jail" (1963) made clear, he had lost confidence in the willingness of the white middle class to turn back the tide of racism. Like Garvey, King began to instruct black people to become self-reliant and proactive in developing their own businesses. According to King, black people should be willing to withdraw economic support from Coca-Cola, Sealtest Milk, and Wonder Bread, which King observed were not invested in treating all of God's children fairly.[12] It is also clear that although King began to sound like Garvey, he had not given up on the beloved community as the goal of the movement he led. Black people and white people needed to share power and work toward economic justice. "We've got to strengthen black institutions," King asserted. He added: "I call upon you to take your money out of the banks downtown and deposit your money in TriState bank—we want a 'bank-in' movement in Memphis. . . .

11. Garvey, Jr., "Garveyism," 377.

12. Washington, *Testament of Hope*, 283.

You have six or seven black insurance companies in Memphis. Take out your insurance there."[13] Interestingly enough, Garvey went further than King, advancing a vision that highlighted the need for a black nationality:

> No Negro, let him be American, European, West Indian or African, shall be truly respected until the race as a whole has emancipated itself, through self-achievement and progress, from universal prejudice. The Negro will have to build his own government, industry, art, science, literature, culture, before the world will stop to consider him. . . . The race needs workers at this time, not plagiarists, copyists and mere imitators, but men and women who are able to create, to originate and improve, and thus make an independent racial contribution to the world and civilization.[14]

It is worth noting that unlike in the United States, there is no overt racial discrimination throughout the Caribbean. There is no history of Jim Crow or of lynching; schools, restaurants, theaters, and public transportation are open to all people. One source further elaborates the point:

> Cases of rape of white women are unknown, and we have the testimony of an ex-governor of Jamaica [who was white] as to the safety of white women, anywhere at any time. White, brown, and black meet in the same churches in which pews, at a price, can be obtained by one and all. Graves of whites, browns, and blacks are seen side by side in cemeteries. The declaration of fundamental rights proclaimed by Cuba . . . may be taken as indicative of the legal situation in the Caribbean: "All Cubans are equal before the law. The Republic recognizes neither personal exexmptions nor privileges. All discrimination because of sex, race, color or class, or other affronts to human dignity is declared illegal and punishable."[15]

Although these claims were made by Eric Williams in the 1940s, who wrote then as a professor at Howard University, they remained true throughout the Caribbean until recently. If anything, they were even more closely observed in Cuba under the watchful eye of Fidel Castro, who is no longer in power. Williams, who became prime minister of Trinidad and

13. Ibid.

14. A. Jacques Garvey, *Garvey and Garveyism* (Kingston, Jamaica: United Printers, 1963) 23

15. Eric Williams, *The Negro in the Caribbean* (New York: Negro Universities Press, 1942) 62–63

Tobago, points to the different understandings of color throughout the Caribbean:

> The Haitians consider themselves "blacks," not Negroes. It is diffi-
> cult, too, for the American Negro to realize that the term "colored"
> signifies a distinct group in the Caribbean. . . . The English islands
> spoke of the "people of color"; in the French they were "gens de
> couleur"; in the Spanish "gente de color." One is not a mulatto
> in Cuba or Puerto Rico—one might be "pardo," or "Moreno," or
> "trigueno," indicating different shades of brown.[16]

Williams' analysis of race relations in the Caribbean may help us understand why the civil rights movement led by Dr. King did not kindle the
imagination of the Caribbean people, nor result in mass protest movements
throughout the Caribbean. Williams further points out that if one drop
of "Negro" blood makes one a "Negro" in the United States, in Caribbean
nations it is the shade of one's skin. While the question of one's relationship
to white prestige may be important for the emergent middle class, it is not
possible for the black masses at the bottom of the racial and political pyra-
mid. In the 1950s and 1960s, it was not unusual to see black men who studied in American or European universities return home to the Caribbean
with white wives. This provided instant access to the middle class. It was
often said that the next best thing to being white is to marry white. But this
was not available to the black masses that Garvey represented. As Williams
notes, "The middle class elite in the Caribbean is Christian or free-thinking,
while the masses still cling to ancient beliefs and rites; the 'voodoo' of Haiti,
the 'Shango' of Trinidad, the 'pocomania' of Jamaica. . . . The main aim of
the Caribbean colored middle class is to forget their African origin."[17] And
yet it does not matter how hard they try—the black middle class, whether
in the United States or in the Caribbean, cannot sever their history from
the triangular relationship between Africa, the Caribbean, and the United
States, a relationship rooted in the memory of Africa.

16. Ibid.
17. Ibid., 64

AFRO-CARIBBEAN LEADERS, BLACK NATIONALISM, AND THE CIVIL RIGHTS MOVEMENT

It is precisely at this point that Roy Innis, former national chairman of the Congress of Racial Equality (CORE) and one of the leaders of the "new black power wing of the civil rights movement," pointed out in an article in the *New York Times* in 1966 that civil rights workers in the United States were turning to black power as articulated by Caribbean workers in CORE and the Student Nonviolent Coordinating Committee (SNCC). Innis explained that when he joined CORE in 1963, he was shunned by many members, who saw him as a threat to their dream of racial integration because he was an avowed black nationalist in the tradition of Marcus Garvey. His goals were not in keeping with the integrationist key, articulated throughout CORE, to desegregate schools in New York State and to implement the Civil Rights Act of 1964. Innis, who was born in the nation of St. Croix in the Caribbean, put it this way:

> A big factor was that CORE kept trying to get New York to really desegregate its schools—a lot of busing and all that—and when it didn't happen and CORE people saw it wouldn't happen, they began to change their thinking. And then there was the Civil Rights Act of 1964—they had been working for it all these years, and thought it would solve everything, and it didn't. Then, there was all those civil rights killings in the South and the fact that Southern juries would not convict people for them, and there was the Vietnam War and the war on poverty—a lot of idealistic integrationists left the civil rights movement to work in the peace movement and on poverty, and that made it easier for me to get elected late last year. When Stokely Carmichael [chairman of the Student Nonviolent Coordinating Committee] started talking about black power on the civil rights march in Mississippi last month, I was caught by surprise. Then I realized that the same thing that was happening in New York CORE was happening all over the country. Maybe they were not calling themselves "nationalists" but they were thinking much the same way.[18]

If we are unable to spotlight a strong Caribbean influence in the integrationist key of the civil rights movement, it is clear that this is quite different in the black power philosophy that informed the civil rights movement

18. Gene Roberts, "Negro Nationalism a Black Power Key," *New York Times*, July 24, 1966, 51.

during the summer of 1966, when both CORE and SNCC embraced black power philosophy. Innis, who called attention to the disillusionment among civil rights workers with the traditional values of the movement, migrated to the United States from St. Croix when he was about thirteen years old. Stokely Carmichael came to the United States from Trinidad when he was about eleven; and Lincoln Lynch, the associate national director and chief theoretician of CORE, migrated from Jamaica at twenty-one.[19] Through the black power arm of the civil rights movement, three Afro-Caribbean leaders made their impact by citing the importance of black consciousness and their influence on the movement:

> Carmichael, Lynch and Innis cited their West Indian background, and Lincoln Lynch was quoted as saying: "I was shocked when I came here and found that the word 'black' was almost a cuss word with the American Negroes. . . . It must have something to do with the adjustment [we West Indians] make when we come here." The three West Indian seekers of Black Power said that their "stance on black consciousness was alienating middle-class Negroes [in America] and white supporters in Congress and in the public in general." Further, "They were tired of unenforced laws and felt that many middle-class Negroes [in America] were trying to escape their race"[20]

According to these black power advocates, what is needed "is for Negroes to reject integration as the major aim and to band themselves into a racially oriented mass movement, and to use political power and economic boycotts to win complete economic and political control of Northern ghettos and Southern counties in which they are in the numerical majority."[21] The flexing of economic and political muscle is the way forward, because, according to these race leaders, this is the way for black power to confront the white power structure. "If this fails, most black power leaders agree, the answer is armed revolt against whites."[22] Lynch and Carmichael pointed out that although people are poor in Jamaica and Trinidad, they are proud of being black and they have political power.

---

19. Ibid.

20. Harold Cruse, *The Crisis of the Negro Intellectual* (New York: William Morrow, 1967) 427.

21. Roberts, "Negro Nationalism," 51.

22. Ibid.

Although all three leaders from the Caribbean point to the success of Marcus Garvey in the United States and in the Caribbean, they fail to note that Garvey was successful among the poor and unemployed masses and that his policies and philosophy of black power failed miserably among the middle class in the Caribbean and the United States. The black middle class in the Caribbean prevented Garvey from establishing institutions or centers of black power there. It is interesting that much of the success that Garvey had came in the United States and not in the Caribbean. Harold Cruse is correct in pointing out how unrealistic the black power proposal advocated by Innis, Carmichael, and Lynch was with "the proviso that if white America refuses to comply with black people's demands for change in the social and economic spheres, then armed revolt would be an appropriate response." The "Garveyite success was in the United States, but Garveyism, left 'not much to be seen in the islands in the way of concrete organization.' Thus, today we have West Indian nationalists in the United States but no nationalist movement in the black West Indies. Hence, in West Indian terms, 'political independence' is 'integrationism.'"[23] I agree that Innis, Carmichael, and Lynch went beyond Garvey in suggesting armed revolt in response to any failure of the white power structure to meet their economic and political goals of power sharing. While Garvey was an advocate of economic and political power, insisting that black people needed their own governments, schools, and businesses—and ran for political office in Jamaica—he was not an advocate of armed revolt. The black power advocates from the Caribbean were closer to Malcolm X, whose roots went back to Garvey but who drew on the teachings of Elijah Muhammad and could articulate an understanding of black power that would not necessarily exclude violence. "'We have to be prepared to pay the price to get what we want,' said Mr. Lynch. This kind of talk, which amounts to the 'freedom at a price' doctrine of the late Malcolm X, is arousing the interest of nationalists, a development that is delighting black power advocates."[24] In contrast, Garvey and King would disavow the need for violence. In their estimation, the price of freedom would not be armed revolt but, in varying degrees, economic and political change. The possibility of violence was one reason why the King of 1966 was not in favor of the term *black power*. King supported the goals of black power as they were articulated in economic and political terms. "Dr. King, the head of the Southern Christian Leadership Conference, said that

23. Cruse, *Crisis of the Negro Intellectual*, 428.
24. Roberts, "Negro Nationalism," 51.

as long as there was hope that the movement would succeed, he expects no defections to the black power movement."[25]

I believe that Harold Cruse overstates the case in suggesting that there are no organizational expressions of Garveyism throughout the Caribbean. In many Caribbean nations, the overthrow of colonialism and the advent of political independence was and is an expression of Garvey's advocacy of democratic traditions that honor majority rule. Most Caribbean nations received their political independence in the 1960s, excepting, of course, Haiti, which became a republic in 1804. Additionally, the Rastafari faith traces its origins and its central beliefs to the teachings of Marcus Garvey. In an interview with *The Daily Gleaner* in Jamaica, only months prior to his death, Malcolm X was asked about the influence of his mother, who was from the Caribbean, on his thinking. Malcolm responded:

> [M]ost people in the Caribbean area, are still proud that they are black, proud of the African blood, and their heritage; and I think this type of pride was instilled in my mother, and she instilled it in us, too, to the best degree that she could. She had—despite the fact that her father was white—more African leanings, and African pride, and a desire to be identified with Africa. In fact she was an active member of the Marcus Garvey movement. My father, besides being an active worker in the Marcus Garvey movement, was a Christian clergyman—a Baptist minister. He was lynched in Lansing, Michigan, in 1954, by being thrown under a street car. . . . Every time you see another nation on the African continent become independent, you know that Marcus Garvey is alive. It was Marcus Garvey's philosophy of Pan-Africanism that initiated the entire freedom movement, which brought about the independence of African nations and had it not been for Marcus Garvey, and the foundations laid by him, you would find no independent nations in the Caribbean today. . . . All the freedom movements that are taking place right here in America today are initiated by the work and teachings of Marcus Garvey. The entire Black Muslim philosophy here in America is feeding upon the seeds that were planted by Marcus Garvey.[26]

Malcolm X could not escape the influence of Marcus Garvey since both his parents were active in Garvey's Universal Negro Improvement

---

25. Ibid.

26. A. Jacques Garvey, *Garvey and Garveyism*, 306–7.

Association (UNIA). James Cone reminds us that what Martin Luther King, Jr. was to the American South, Malcolm X was to the American North:

> The great migration of blacks from the rural South to the urban North, which began before the First World War and continued through the 1950s, marked a significant change in the context and texture of their lives. The contrast between what blacks expected to find in the "promised land" of the North and what they actually found was so great that frustration and despair ensued, destroying much of their self-esteem and dignity. Blacks expected to find the *freedom* which had eluded them for so many years in the South; that is, they expected to have—like other Americans—the right to live wherever they chose and to work and play with whomever they chose.[27]

Things turned out differently. In some ways, the North turned out to be worse than the South, as black people were crammed into urban centers, paying exorbitant prices for rent, food, and other necessities and being harassed by white police who showed no respect for black people. Black hopes were dashed as the promised land proved to be a mirage. "As de jure segregation defined black life in the South, de facto segregation was a way of life in the North," Cone writes. "Blacks were confined to the ghetto, with no future to look forward to except an endless repetition of mental and physical pain and suffering. . . . Some people claimed that for blacks the quality of life in the North was even worse than in the South, because of the devastating effects of the ghetto upon the personalities of its inhabitants."[28] Cone concludes that in this context, no one made a greater impact on the black masses than Marcus Garvey. Malcolm X embodied Garvey's teachings and was to black people in the North what Martin Luther King, Jr. was to black people in the South. Both of these leaders regarded the work and influence of Marcus Garvey as foundational.

In 1965, Martin Luther King, Jr. was invited to Marcus Garvey's home in Jamaica to address students at the University of the West Indies. At a reception held in his honor at the National Stadium, in which he received the keys to the capital city of Kingston, King said: "In the light of the many unpleasant and humiliating experiences with which I have to live, I am glad

---

27. James H. Cone, *Martin & Malcolm & America: A Dream or a Nightmare* (Maryknoll, NY: Orbis, 1992) 90.

28. Ibid.

to feel like somebody in Jamaica. I really feel like a human being."[29] I recall vividly hearing Dr. King express how he felt fully human in Jamaica. Perhaps it was in part because he experienced what it felt like being part of a black majority and not having to be preoccupied with issues of racial equality or the erasure of Jim Crow laws that circumscribed the lives of black people. During the visit to Jamaica, Martin Luther King, Jr. laid a wreath at Marcus Garvey's shrine with over two thousand persons in attendance. He spoke of the ways in which Garvey's life and mission informed his own work for civil and human rights:

> Marcus Garvey was the first man of color in the history of the United States to lead and develop a mass movement. He was the first man, on a mass scale and level, to give millions of Negroes a sense of dignity and destiny, and make the Negro feel that he was somebody. You gave Marcus Garvey to the United States of America, and he gave to the millions of Negroes in the United States a sense of personhood, a sense of manhood, and a sense of somebodiness. As we stand here let us pledge ourselves to continue the struggle in this same spirit of somebodiness . . . , in the conviction that all God's children are significant . . . that God's black children are just as significant as His white children. And we will not stop until we have freedom in all its dimensions.[30]

In most Caribbean communities there is a black majority, and in others, like Puerto Rico and Cuba, there is an African ethos that shapes the culture and history of the people. Because of the predominance of African culture in the Caribbean and the opportunity to live from the perspective of a black majority, it was extremely difficult to see as applicable to the Caribbean experience a movement in its early years, like Dr. King's, that was preoccupied with racial equality and the abolition of Jim Crow laws that circumscribed the life of black people in relation to whites.

In the Caribbean, there are many similarities between Afro-Caribbean and African American ways of life, and Dr. King's own life and heritage testified to this. Also, this explains why King could work so effectively with Harry Belafonte, Stokely Carmichael, Sidney Poitier, and other black artists and activists of Caribbean background, who donated their time, talents, energy, and resources to the civil rights movement in the United States in the

---

29. A. Jacques Garvey, *Garvey and Garveyism*, 308.

30. Ibid.

1950s and 1960s.[31] The central reality is that both Afro-Caribbean and African American people came out of the experience of slavery and endured the Middle Passage across the Atlantic to work and die on plantations in the New World. On both sides of the Atlantic we suffered from persistent poverty and complicated racial and ethnic identities. But in the Caribbean, we have had to live longer than our North American brothers and sisters with plantation slavery and plantation ethics. The slave trade was practiced for over a hundred years in the Caribbean prior to its introduction to Virginia in 1619, and even then the blacks were from the Caribbean.

Perhaps because of our longer history with slavery, we made peace with the status quo, and because we see the world from the perspective of a black majority, we have become more complacent in relation to social ills that frustrate the lives of our people. In the 1950s and 1960s, the majority of our financial institutions in the Caribbean were owned and managed by American and European companies. The University of the West Indies was an arm of the University of London. The Queen of England was head of commonwealth countries throughout the Caribbean, and the French, Spanish, and Dutch islands looked to their imperial masters for political and economic leadership. The Christian churches throughout the islands were an arm of churches in either the United States or in Europe, where hymns, liturgy, and sermons worshiped a white God. And yet the perception was that because we were a people who embraced an African ethos in music, art, and lifestyle, we did not need to expunge the white bias in our society. We were complacent because we were part of a black majority; we told ourselves that we lived life on our terms, and if change were to come, perhaps it would be from Africa, as Marcus Garvey and the Rastas taught us, and not from the United States and the movement led by Martin Luther King, Jr.

31. Lewis V. Baldwin, *To Make the Wounded Whole: The Cultural Legacy of Martin Luther King, Jr.* (Minneapolis: Fortress, 1992) 177.

10

The Relationship of Revolutions

Martin Luther King, Jr., the Civil Rights Movement, and Political Change in the Bahamas

Crystal A. DeGregory

America would see the dark-skinned minority, long oppressed and exploited, slowly rise, stand, flex muscles, and confront an overpowering white majority. . . . Many of the freedom-fighters found their way to the Bahamas and discovered kindred spirits among the black leaders [including] Martin Luther King [who] came and met the brothers of the third-world revolution.

DAME DORIS L. JOHNSON[1]

IN THE MORE THAN four decades since the assassination of the Reverend Dr. Martin Luther King, Jr., historians, social and cultural theorists, and even

---

1. Doris L. Johnson, *The Quiet Revolution in the Bahamas* (Nassau: Family Islands, 1972) 27.

theologians have struggled to both qualify and quantify the value of his life and legacy. This struggle was born out of a much larger conundrum—how to piece together this dynamic movement of loosely connected protests spread over the vast black South and beyond. Historians, for example, often became enthralled in the cult of personality that has since become part and parcel of the movement in the wake of King's demise. Dominated by the "Great Man Theory," their early social histories depicted the movement as a top-down entity, driven by charismatic personalities, not the least of which was King. Even when grassroots studies began emerging in the late 1970s and 1980s, King often remained at the center of movement historiography.[2]

It is a place that King earned by virtue of his sacrifice and service to the mid-twentieth century nonviolent struggle for freedom, justice, and equality. While tempting, to argue that the nature of his sacrifice and service was singular in nature is not only ahistorical; it is counterproductive because it is irrefutable that the modern civil rights movement was driven by thousands. While history now knows the names, faces, and stories of many of these men and women—most black and others white, fired up by the young, tempered by the wisdom of the old, Southerners together with Northerners—there are many more it will never know. King, however, was likely known to each and every one of them. If the distinctive quality of King's contributions is to be successfully argued, it is mostly for this reason. King's sacrifice and service is singular in its scope.

Consequently, this generation of scholars has inherited the mammoth task of interpreting the many dimensions of King. As arguably the most celebrated black leader of his generation and the most widely recognized figure in the modern civil rights movement, King offered easily documented contributions to every major campaign against Jim Crow in the American South between 1955 and his death in 1968. Even so, there are numerous indicators of the largely unexplored global dimensions of King's life and work. There are several signs that even King was aware of this connection. His speeches were punctuated with the terms "world house," "a world-wide neighborhood," "a single neighborhood," or a "human family," long before economic theorists became enraptured with the term *globalization* during the 1980s.[3]

2. See Steven F. Lawson, "Freedom Then, Freedom Now: The Historiography of the Civil Rights Movement," *The American Historical Review* 96.2 (1991) 456–71; Charles W. Eagles, "Toward New Histories of the Civil Rights Era," *Journal of Southern History* 66.4 (2000) 815–48.

3. See Martin Luther King, Jr., *Where Do We Go from Here: Chaos or Community?*

Efforts to situate King within the context of his "world house" vision are, for this reason, long overdue. Reticent about treading through the unchartered waters of King and the globalization of his ideas, values, and nonviolent ethos, historians have just now begun searching for King's role in struggles outside of the United States. Challenges, however, remain. Then-fledgling figures in the anticolonial movements of Africa, Asia, South America, and the Caribbean often left scant records of their rise to rule. In some instances, they may not have foreseen the need to keep meticulous records; in others, they may have been determined to wipe away the details of their historical record. Either way, their actions often make it difficult, if not impossible, to sew together the disparate threads in the fabric of global strivings for democracy.

Such is the case for the Commonwealth of The Bahamas, which began its transformation from a mere British colonial outpost, dominated by the hegemonic rule of a handful of whites, to a nation independent and governed by blacks, during the same period in which American blacks waged the earliest campaigns of the modern civil rights movement.[4] Using the histories of the King-led American civil rights movement and the political change secured by the Lynden O. Pindling-led Progressive Liberal Party of The Bahamas, this essay traces the relationships between the personalities, tactics, and aspirations of both efforts. Framing the discussion within the context of the formative years of its principal figures, it explains the shared motives of both King and Pindling and of their movements. Their histories are supported by the introduction of additional American and Bahamian leaders who give special attention to seminal moments in each of their lives. In doing so, it reveals the shared nature of two seemingly disparate revolutions through the cultivation of relationships that fueled the cross-pollination of ideas and ideals.

(Boston: Beacon, 1968) 167; James M. Washington, ed., *A Testament of Hope: The Essential Writings and Speeches of Martin Luther King, Jr.* (New York: HarperCollins, 1991) 209. See also Lewis V. Baldwin, "Living in the World House: Martin Luther King, Jr. and Globalization Theory and Praxis," unpublished paper, Vanderbilt University (Spring 2012) 1–3; Andrew Hurrell, "Globalization," in *The Concise Oxford Dictionary of Politics*, ed. Iain MacLean and Alister MacMillan, 2nd ed. (Oxford: Oxford University Press, 2003) 222–25.

4. The literature on The Bahamas and other former British colonies adheres to the standards of British English, and consequently, the spelling of some words will be different from their American usage. This author will allow direct quotes to remain unchanged, with British spellings of certain words (e.g., colour, coloured, labour, labourers) occurring.

SPHERES OF BAHAMIAN SOCIAL LIFE AND THE STRUGGLE FOR INDEPENDENCE

Centuries after Christopher Columbus stumbled onto the Bahama Islands in 1492, the archipelago of more than seven hundred low-lying islands and over two thousand cays remained for the most part obscure, remote, and uncultivated well into the twentieth century. It was not until the late eighteenth century, however, that the influx of the American Loyalists transformed the islands into a true settler colony. Just as the Loyalists' social, economic, and political systems predominated Bahamian society, the coming of the Loyalist slaves—and later their descendants—fortified The Bahamas' predominately black racial demographic into the mid-twentieth century.[5]

In general, the colony's race relations and economic legacies were born out of their preceding systems of European slavery and colonialism. Despite the mostly unsuccessful nature of Bahamian large-scale plantation agriculture and even the emancipation of Bahamian slaves in 1838, almost three decades before their American counterparts, the colony's social conditions during the 1950s were most akin to the American South. Perpetuated by the roguish capital-oriented business ethics of white foreigners, the resulting chasm of social stratification was widened, based largely on color, and to a lesser degree on class.[6]

The racial makeup, geographic isolation from its Caribbean counterparts, and dispersion of the Bahama Islands across six hundred miles caused the clearest social stratifications in the city of Nassau, on the island of New Providence. Rife with snobbery, its leading citizens formed a close-knit group that economically and politically controlled Bahamian life. As a result of their virtual monopoly on Nassau's more successful commercial ventures (usually import and export businesses) and the guile of their lawyer cartel, they dominated political offices via official appointments and elections. Normally aiding each other because of familial ties, they

---

5. For general information on and histories of The Bahamas, see Michael Craton, *The History of the Bahamas* (Waterloo, Ontario: San Salvador, 1997); Michael Craton and D. Gail Saunders, *Islanders in the Stream: A History of the Bahamian People*, vol. 2, *From the Ending of Slavery to the Twenty-First Century* (Athens: University of Georgia Press, 1999); Paul Albury, *The Story of The Bahamas* (London: Macmillan Caribbean, 1975).

6. Craton, *History of the Bahamas*, 311–12.

strong-armed the colony's economy and the political and administrative machinery.[7]

Seeking to preserve their racial purity, whites formed separate educational institutions and segregated themselves in churches as well as Sunday school attendance. Generating an apartheid-like situation of race-based discrimination, several other spheres of Bahamian social life also observed *de jure* segregation—among them were Nassau's banks, hotels, cinemas, barbershops, and virtually all social intercourses like clubs, lodges, dances, and even sporting events.[8] Below this white merchant/lawyer class were members of the colored and black middle class, whose color ranged from "near white" at the top to "off black" at the bottom. Coloreds, like everyone else in Nassau society, "knew their place . . . [and any] attempt to cross lines, up or down, was severely frowned on."[9] While well-educated darker coloreds were acceptable and sometimes interacted with lighter-skinned ones, the colored group was "self-stratified" according to skin color. Status within its communities was based on color and to a lesser extent economic success.[10]

The massive grouping of black laborers followed them; they mainly settled in the "Over-the-Hill" district as well as farther settlements including Adelaide, Fox Hill, and Gambier Villages.[11] Perceived in general as socially inferior, and culturally despised by the elite and middle classes (due in part to their limited education, use of creolized English, and African retentions in their religious observances), the black masses were barred from political and civic life and mostly performed undesirable and laborious services.[12] As historian Michael Craton pointedly observed, "The worst aspect of living for the majority of Bahamians, however, was not poverty, which was familiar and largely shared; it was the system of virtual *apartheid* by which the white minority in Nassau dominated the economy, monopolized

---

7. D. Gail Saunders, *Social Life in the Bahamas, 1880s–1920s* (Nassau: Rosebud, 1996) 65–67.

8. D. Gail Saunders, *Bahamian Society after Emancipation* (Kingston, Jamaica: Ian Ran, 1994) 10; Saunders, *Social Life in the Bahamas, 1880s–1920s*, 7–14.

9. D. Gail Saunders, "The Social History of the Bahamas, 1890–1953," PhD diss., University of Waterloo (1985) 78; Etienne Dupuch, *Tribune Story* (London: Benn, 1967) 64.

10. Saunders, *Social Life in the Bahamas, 1880s–1920s*, 89.

11. Ibid., 7 and 22.

12. E.g., laborers, domestics, seamen, sponge fisherman, farmers, small storekeepers, pedlars, and artisans.

political power, and did its utmost to keep non-whites in segregated areas and subordinate roles."[13]

The slow but sure transformation of the Bahamian middle class and black masses began with the return of Bahamian troops from service in the world wars, which, along with the steady emigration of Bahamians to the United States, intensified their racial awareness.[14] The 1950s postwar growth of the tourism industry exacerbated racist attitudes among whites in The Bahamas who argued that racial divisiveness was essential to Bahamian society if the colony was hosting American tourists who were accustomed to racial segregation.[15] In fact, political scientist Colin A. Hughes suggested that Bahamian society was deeply affected by its relatively high numerical ratio of whites to blacks, the close proximity of the southern United States and its "Jim Crowism," as well as cultural ties among Bahamians—black and white alike—and the United States.[16]

Published in 1972, just one year before the Bahama Islands were granted independence, Doris L. Johnson, who was the first Bahamian female election candidate, member of parliament, cabinet minister and president of the senate, unabashedly and unapologetically wrote *The Quiet Revolution in the Bahamas* as "but one attempt to vindicate the democratic process in the face of other tempting choices open to [then] emerging nations." In a clear declaration of what she hoped were the global implications of the study, Johnson was convinced that *The Quiet Revolution* "should inspire hope among all freedom-loving people of the world."[17] Still, it was her compatriot, Lynden Oscar Pindling, the islands' first black premier and prime minister, who best captured the *zeitgeist* of a British colony on the precipice of black-ruled independence. "In a world of bloody conflict, the phenomenon of a bloodless revolution effecting a change of government is indeed remarkable," wrote Pindling. "[F]or some four hundred and fifty years,

---

13. Michael Craton, *Pindling: The Life and Times of the First Prime Minister of the Bahamas* (Oxford: Macmillan Caribbean, 2002) 9.

14. See Saunders, "The Role of the Coloured Middle Class in Nassau, 1890–1942," *Ethnic and Racial Studies* 10 (1987) 484–65.

15. Sadly, their contention was at least true in part. Michael Craton noted: "Such *de facto* segregation was undoubtedly strengthened during the 1920s and 1930s in order to gratify the racist sensibilities of white visitors form the United States South—whose prejudices extended to include Jews and Chinese as well as blacks." Craton, *Pindling*, 10.

16. Colin A. Hughes, *Race and Politics in the Bahamas* (New York: St. Martin's, 1981) 21.

17. Johnson, foreword to *The Quiet Revolution in the Bahamas*.

the white man had dominated the life of the [Bahama] islands politically, economically, and socially. Black inhabitants, though early exceeding the white population in numbers, were subject to many forms of degradation, from the downright beastliness of slavery to the more economic and social indignities of inequality."[18]

Pindling's words were characteristic of a man hailed as the "Father of the Bahamian Nation." Because his achievements even now continue to tower over his country's political, social, and economic landscape, his personal history and that of the nation are so inextricably linked that it is impossible to consider one without the other. The same is true for several then-leaders of emerging Caribbean nation states, many of whom, like Pindling, led their countrymen to full political enfranchisement as well as independence. Former British colonies such as Jamaica, Trinidad and Tobago, and Barbados were the earliest sites of decolonization during the 1960s. Their leaders' names have since become synonymous with the countries they led. In Trinidad and Tobago, there was T. Uriah Butler, Albert Gomes, and Eric Williams; in Jamaica, Norman Manley and Alexander Bustamante; in Barbados, Grantley Adams and Errol Barrow; in Grenada, Eric Gairy; and Robert Bradshaw in St. Kitts.[19] Because his West Indian counterparts largely came of age in the decade prior to Pindling, whose short but sure stature resembled King's in appearance, they had the most in common with King. Perhaps this is, at least in part, why Pindling repeatedly hailed King as one of his most important ideological mentors.

MARTIN LUTHER KING, JR. AND THE CIVIL RIGHTS MOVEMENT: AN INSPIRATION FOR FREEDOM FIGHTERS IN THE BAHAMAS

In 1929, the same year that Black Tuesday signaled the onset of the Great Depression, Martin Luther King, Jr. was born into an Atlanta, Georgia, community he described as having an "unsophisticated simplicity." His family, however, could boast of a line of Baptist ministers that stretched back to his maternal great-grandfather. Initially named Michael King at birth, he was the namesake of his father. But while his college-educated mother, Alberta Williams King, was soft-spoken and easygoing, his father,

18. Lynden O. Pindling, preface to Johnson, *The Quiet Revolution in the Bahamas.*

19. See Franklin W. Knight, *The Caribbean: The Genesis of a Fragmented Nationalism* (New York: Oxford University Press, 1978) 179–80.

also a college graduate, was "as strong in his will as he [was] in his body." In what could have been a strategic move, the elder King later assumed the name Martin Luther, and began referring to his son as Martin Luther, Jr.[20]

Like his father and maternal grandfather, A. D. Williams, the younger King was a Morehouse man, but he seriously considered becoming a doctor or lawyer before yielding to his "inherited calling." His acceptance of the call to ministry was in no small measure, due to the time he spent at Morehouse, which nurtured his "growing awareness of social and political issues."[21] Having entered college at age fifteen, King was younger than most of his peers. Even his fun-loving and easygoing nature did not keep him from becoming the mentee of then-Morehouse President Benjamin Elijah Mays. Described by King as "one of the great influences in my life," Mays was learned and lettered, providing a strong counter model to the "shackles of fundamentalism" and anti-intellectualism he thought was common in the Ebenezer Baptist Church of his childhood. King was only one of the countless Morehouse Men who, inspired by Mays' "Morehouse Mystique," became leaders in the struggle for social justice.[22]

By the time he graduated Morehouse in 1948, King's course in the ministry was set; he entered Crozer Theological Seminary in the fall of the same year. At Crozer, King was first introduced to the life and teachings of Indian lawyer turned nonviolent theorist Mahatma Gandhi. King's interest in nonviolence as well as his intellectual development grew during his doctoral program at Boston University, where he worked with Edgar S. Brightman and L. Harold DeWolf.[23] Once he fulfilled the residential requirements for the PhD in 1954, King, who had married New England Conservatory of Music vocal student Coretta Scott the previous year, sought the pastorate of a church. In September 1954, the Kings moved into the parsonage of Montgomery, Alabama's Dexter Avenue Baptist Church, and the Reverend King began his first and only full-time pastorate.[24]

Lynden Pindling was born in Nassau's Mason's Addition community just a little more than a year later than King to Arnold Pindling, a

20. Martin Luther King, Jr., *The Autobiography of Martin Luther King, Jr.*, ed. Clayborne Carson (New York: Warner, 1998) 1–4.

21. Ibid., 5–16. See also Clayborne Carson, "Martin Luther King, Jr.: The Morehouse Years," *The Journal of Blacks in Higher Education* 15 (1997) 121.

22. Carson, "Morehouse Years," 121–25; King, *Autobiography of Martin Luther King, Jr.*, 13–16.

23. King, *Autobiography of Martin Luther King, Jr.*, 21–27.

24. Ibid., 30–47.

policeman, and Jamaican émigré Viola Bain Pindling, the only daughter of a Bahamian boat captain. Having left the police force to open his own store, Pindling's father was enterprising; and perhaps like Daddy King, Arnold Pindling could easily be associated with "rectitude and discipline." Conversely, Pindling's mother, like King's mother Alberta Williams King, was "naturally sympathetic" and "genuinely godly." His family also had high hopes for him and in the fall of 1943, he began his tenure at Government High School (GHS), which "had been designed to be a place for the children of the poorer classes to be educated to fill the lower ranks on the civil service."[25]

Pindling had won his place at GHS while childhood playmate Sidney Poitier attended Eastern Senior School, an important difference in the trajectory of their lives. Pindling left GHS in 1946 at age sixteen, but even while working in downtown Nassau he and his father "had their sights raised higher." With the knowledge that a career in law was "the only means by which intelligent black Bahamians could short-cut the route to the moderate heights of wealth and status to which they could aspire," Pindling boarded his first airplane in September 1948 to attend the University of London and Inns of Court in London, England.[26]

Having met and hobnobbed with many personages who later became postcolonial leaders, Pindling returned to Nassau in 1953 with his LLB degree; he was among the wave of Bahamian foreign-educated black intellectuals returning home with greater exposure to political activities through their shared colonial West Indian experiences. As a "training ground for those who would prove the leaders of the subsequent generation once independence was achieved," London provided Pindling with an "appreciation of how white minorities used political and economic power to perpetuate minority rule . . . and entrench[ed] their wealth at the expense of the black majority."[27] And it was very important that he did. The 1950s postwar growth of the Bahamian tourism industry had so entrenched the wealth and power holdings of the colony's white elite class that the economic gulf between whites and blacks was now compounded by the growing success

---

25. Craton, *Pindling,* 16–19, 27; King, *Autobiography of Martin Luther King, Jr.,* 3–4.

26. Craton, *Pindling,* 25, 30–31.

27. Interview with Sir Lynden O. Pindling, July 16, 1996. As quoted in D. Gail Saunders, "The Making of a Leader: The Ascendancy of Lynden Pindling as Leader of the Progressive Liberal Party, 1953–1963," unpublished paper, 1998, 8; Craton, *Pindling,* 33.

of tourism and its offshoots in construction, finance, real estate, and foreign investment.[28]

Established in October 1953 by a group of three light-skinned Bahamians with Out Island roots, the Progressive Liberal Party (PLP)—The Bahamas' first successful party—ushered in the age of formal party politics in The Bahamas. While the name "conveyed to the Bahamian people the direction the Party would follow," the PLP's platform outlined its objectives as "representative and reformist" but "not revolutionary or racialist."[29] Pindling was among the party's earliest recruits, as was the "heroic black populist orator" Milo B. Butler and the fiery lawyer Randol Fawkes, who had been self-exiled in the United States during his suspension from the bar from 1954 to 1955. Despite lasting only about a year, Fawkes' stay in the United States allowed him to participate in the excitement around the burgeoning modern civil rights movement. He was in Washington, DC, during the time of the now-historic *Brown vs. Board of Education* decision, and he sat in Harlem's Abyssinia Baptist Church when Ethiopian Emperor Haile Selassie I described "how Mussolini's armies in 1935 sprayed his homeland with mustard gas killing people and crops and poisoning rivers." Fawkes and his wife Jacqueline witnessed a recital of Paul Robeson whom he described as a "prophet preaching the fatherhood of God and the brotherhood of man." As Robeson sang, Fawkes' thoughts drifted to his homeland. "I thought of my people back home and their struggle against seemingly insuperable odds."[30]

Upon his return to Nassau in mid-1955, Fawkes became central leader in the revival of the Bahamian Labor Movement. As the founder and legal adviser of the Bahamas Federation of Labour (B.F. of L.), a federation of unions and skilled workers, the indomitable Fawkes' mass appeal was particularly attractive to the PLP. Fawkes' chances of transforming the party's liberal platform to a labor charge, however, grew slimmer with the passage of time.[31] At the time, Fawkes was singular in his rhetoric; his ideology was "a complete change in the status quo." "Colonialism is a sickness in our society," declared Fawkes to an impressive audience at the Southern

28. Saunders, "Role of the Coloured Middle Class in Nassau, 1890–1942."

29. Craton, *Pindling*, 51; Cyril Stevenson, "A Short History of the Progressive Liberal Party," *The Herald*, November 15, 1983. See the Web site of the Progressive Liberal Party: www.myplp.com.

30. Randol F. Fawkes, *The Faith that Moved the Mountain* (Nassau: Fawkes, 1979) 65–67.

31. Craton, *Pindling*, 55.

Recreations Ground. "It robs the rulers and ruled of human dignity. The only therapy capable of creating the conditions for a new social order is a new government."[32]

Even though the momentum from the Fawkes-organized first Labor Day celebration undoubtedly carried him and Pindling, who was his running mate, to a stunning victory in their district, Pindling was elected as party leader over him. Whereas the party's founders thought Fawkes was erratic and radical, to them, Pindling was pragmatic and, perhaps most importantly, did not enunciate—and was therefore not believed to have—an extensive racial agenda.[33] Although he was at odds with PLP party leaders, as a show of solidarity, the PLP members—whom the masses dubbed the "Magnificent Six"—sat together in the House of Assembly, despite the speaker's refusal to recognize them as a party. The Fawkes-led labor union "embraced not only the industrial objects of the working class but also many of its [the PLP's] political, educational and socio-economic ideals."[34] Fawkes' tireless efforts to revolutionize labor conditions generated the fervor, which set the stage for the colony's most successful act of civil disobedience—the 1958 General Strike.

The initial disagreement which led to the strike occurred on November 1, 1957, between the Taxi-Cab Union, a unit of independent taxi drivers and owners, and the hotel and tour bus operators. Taxi drivers had long complained about the loss of wages to tour companies who were more able competitors for tourist traffic. The opening of the new airport at Windsor Field—more than eleven miles west of Nassau city—should have meant larger fares for taxicab drivers, but tour companies arranged with the Hotel Association to provide transport. When the Airports Board's facilitation of an agreement proved short-lived, the Union—led by PLP member Clifford Darling—blockaded the street to the airport for twenty-four hours. In that short time, several planes returned to Miami with their passengers, an act that was sensational enough to garner the attention of the "Bay Street Boys"—so named because they controlled Bay Street, the commercial district of Nassau—and the international press. After a week, the union's efforts to mediate with the hotel-tour bus faction were still futile and the Taxi-Cab Unions leaders grew impatient.[35]

32. Fawkes, *Faith that Moved the Mountain*, 76.

33. Craton, *Pindling*, 58.

34. Fawkes, *Faith that Moved the Mountain*, 93.

35. D. Gail Saunders, "The 1958 General Strike in Nassau," *The Journal of Caribbean History* 27 (1993) 93–94; Craton, *Pindling*, 79–81.

Fawkes and the B.F. of L. answered the Taxi Union's request for support by calling for a general strike to "dramatise the fight of all Bahamians for freedom and social equality."[36] At the stroke of midnight on January 13, 1958, the organizing meeting for the strike began at Federation Hall. In his speech to the crowd, Fawkes chose "Once in the Life of every man and Nation comes the moment to decide" as the subject of his address:

> I hid nothing from the audience. They knew the purpose of the meeting. They knew that failure in what we were about to do could mean certain jail sentences and for the leaders even worse. I recited the experiences of the children of Israel and how despite the hardening of the heart of Pharaoh, they struck out for freedom. I made references to the recent Martin Luther King bus strike in Montgomery, Alabama, and told them if they listened carefully they could still hear the marching feet of their brothers and sisters in Africa as they declared the independence in Ghana.[37]

In haste and perhaps overreaction, the governor flew in British troops from Jamaica to pacify the fears of Nassau whites, more so than to keep the nonviolent protests in order. While the *Tribune* story reported that "injury and bloodshed seemed inevitable," the strikers confined their protests to peaceful picketing and a boycott of Bay Street–owned shops.[38] From the outset, the strike was nonviolent. "It was always our conviction," reflected Fawkes, "that a bloody revolution would defeat our purpose; besides, it would be exactly the signal government wanted to spray down innocent men, women and children." To this effect, the message of every speech and pamphlet was consistent: "Be calm, stay calm. Let us win this battle with a mighty meekness."[39] And like the movement afoot in the American South, under Dr. King's leadership, the strike was bolstered by music, including Negro spirituals like "Go Down, Moses," and lyrics were created and sung to the tune of "John Brown's Body."[40]

On November 25, 1958, the B.F. of L. played host to the Reverends King and Ralph Abernathy. In his speech to a full audience at the Federation Hall, King congratulated them on their historic stand during the

---

36. Fawkes, *Faith that Moved the Mountain,* 101.

37. Ibid., 100–101.

38. *Tribune,* January 15, 1958.

39. Fawkes, *Faith that Moved the Mountain,* 106 and 108.

40. Ibid., 126–28.

continuing strike. "The whole world is moving forward today and you must move with it. If you cannot fly, run; if you cannot run, walk; if you cannot walk, creep but in any case keep moving."[41] Once back in Birmingham, King responded to Fawkes. In a letter to Fawkes, dated December 15, King wrote:

> I too, was greatly helped by my visit to Nassau. I will long remember the expressions of genuine goodwill and moral support on the part of the people of your community. Please allow me to again express my personal appreciation to you for your determined courage and dedication to the cause of Freedom and Human Dignity. I am sure that your name will long live in the annals of your nation's history for your willingness to suffer and sacrifice for a cause that you know is right.[42]

Times had changed since Fawkes was a boy. As he pointedly observed: "To them [the people] the British monarchy and the white colonial administration were no longer sacred cows."[43] The seventeen-day strike ended abruptly after a picket line disbanded; its leaders, including Fawkes, were escorted away by police. Still, the move not only exacerbated tensions; when news of the strike hit the American, Canadian, British, and West Indian presses, it garnered international support.[44] Probably encouraged by the negative publicity—especially the American press' reaction to the unrest—the Colonial Office introduced recommendations for substantial, yet far from sweeping, constitutional and political changes. Its recommendations included reapportioning the colony's constituencies, introducing unconditional male suffrage at age twenty-one, abolition of company vote, and the limitation of the plural vote to two. As a result, the 1958 General Strike effected salient and salutary developments in Bahamian society.[45]

Widely hailed as "the champion of the working man," Fawkes' image and influence were also enhanced by the strike. As the "largest and most damaging strike in the history of the Bahamas," the walkout made the strikers "aware of the powerful weapon they possessed in the organisation of

41. King, as quoted in Fawkes, *Faith that Moved the Mountain*, 164.

42. Martin Luther King, Jr. to Randol F. Fawkes, December 15, 1958. Reprinted in Fawkes, *Faith that Moved the Mountain*, 165.

43. Fawkes, *Faith that Moved the Mountain*, 104.

44. Saunders, "1958 General Strike in Nassau," 95; Michael Craton, *Pindling*, 84.

45. Craton, *Pindling*, 85; Hughes, *Race and Politics in the Bahamas*, 66–67; Saunders, "1958 General Strike in Nassau," 97–98.

labour."[46] Like the strikers, PLP leaders must have realized the labor movement's power and most certainly recognized the influence they could seize from Fawkes and the B.F. of L. if they controlled their following. By the time of the 1960 by-election, Pindling and the black PLP leadership had already begun to "woo" the black Bahamian masses. Once the "crowd's hero," Fawkes had faced numerous attacks that climaxed with a sedition charge in late 1958. Despite the PLP's monetary contribution to his successful defense, Fawkes, who believed that PLP leaders conspired to divide his laborite following, founded the Bahamas Labour Party in June 1959. While the PLP vehemently denied the charge, the masses, which had considered Fawkes their "Moses," grew increasingly inclined to Pindling and the PLP.[47]

More moderate members of the PLP leadership, however, continued to articulate a non-racialist platform. Increasingly pushed to the margins of the party, PLP Chairman H. M. Taylor echoed these opinions in his editorial, "Is the PLP a Negro Party?," in which he contended that the party's ostensible racial exclusiveness was because whites opposed the "freedom" sought by blacks, refused to join the party, and benefited from the masses' defeat.[48] He reminded readers that that party had not added the plank that attacked "Jim Crowism" to the PLP platform until the party's second convention.[49] However, the PLP's win of all the by-election's four seats in May 1960 not only increased political, racial, and class tension, the win gave Pindling the support he needed to shake the early PLP's moderate, middle-class, and non-racialist foundations. The same year, he began recruiting members of the young black intelligentsia, including black middle-class lawyers Paul Adderley and Orville Turnquest as well as journalist Arthur Foulkes.[50]

Pindling's decision may have been inspired, at least in part, by developments afoot in the United States. On July 7, 1960, L. B. Thompson, a representative of the March on the Conventions Movement, read Martin

---

46. Henry Taylor, *My Political Memoirs* (Nassau: H. Taylor, 1987) 240.

47. Saunders, "Making of a Leader," 12; Craton, *Pindling*, 86.

48. Reprinted *Herald*, February 27, 1960. As cited in Hughes, *Race and Politics in the Bahamas*, 75.

49. The plank read: "The 'Jim Crow' practices now being carried out in the Bahamas are cause for serious concern and are strongly condemned by the Party as undemocratic, un-British, un-Christian and against the principles of the United Nations Universal Declaration of Human Rights. Having this in mind the Party pledges to eradicate this evil." Ibid.

50. Craton and Saunders, *Islanders in the Stream*, 312; Craton, *Pindling*, 89.

Luther King, Jr. and American black labor leader A. Philip Randolph's "Joint Platform Proposals" to the 1960 Democratic Party's platform committee. Among the proposals' many demands were calls for the acknowledgment of the wave of nonviolent demonstrations across the South, enforcement of the *Brown* decision, and protection of nonviolent activists from white terrorism as well as the protection of black voting rights.[51] As if its domestic agenda was not lofty enough, the proposal also made global demands: "We demand that this convention and its candidates take a clear moral stand against colonialism and racism of all kinds, everywhere, and especially in Africa where apartheid has led to the massacre of hundreds of people seeking only to live in freedom in their own land."[52]

Just one week later, Pindling was in Chicago, Illinois, attending the July 1960 Elks National Convention as the guest of Andros businessman and Elks leader Clarence Bain. The trip coincided with a sit-in led by Dr. King in Georgia, for which the convention's delegates held an all-night vigil to greet buses of protesters arriving from the South. Even though "Pindling found the emotive power of the occasion almost overwhelming," biographer Michael Craton noted:

> Lynden Pindling was even more impressed by the civil rights movement's chief leader. Martin Luther King's rhetoric was as emotionally inspiring as Abraham Lincoln's, and his method of making symbolic gestures, advocating non-violent mass demonstrations, and appealing to liberal sentiments in the wider world, were proving hugely effective.[53]

In the coming years, Pindling increasingly sought to employ the qualities King embodied. The steady growth of the young black PLP intelligentsia led to the formation of the National Committee for Positive Action (NCPA). By adding the role of "inspirational leader" of the PLP think-tank to his existing responsibilities as Parliamentary Leader and member of the PLP executive group, Pindling became the master of balancing "a light-footed minuet, assiduously attending all meetings, listening and agreeing, a

---

51. See "Joint Platform Proposals to the 1960 Democratic Party Platform Committee, Read by L. B. Thompson, 7 July 1960," in Clayborne Carson et al., eds., *The Papers of Martin Luther King, Jr.*, vol. 5, *Threshold of a New Decade, January 1959–December 1960* (Berkeley : University of California Press, 2005) 482–85.

52. Ibid., 485.

53. Craton, *Pindling*, 114.

learner and a friend to all, while waiting on events."[54] Bahamian suffragettes finally secured the right to vote as well as the right to run for the legislature with the passage of the Franchise Bill in July 1961.[55] Although the PLP officially supported the issue of women's suffrage, it seemed like they had some "misgivings on the subject"—misgivings that may have been warranted given the party's loss in the 1962 general election to the Bay Street Boys, who had formed the United Bahamian Party (UBP) in 1956.[56]

In the following year, Pindling again had the opportunity to witness King in action. Inspired by King's "Letter from Birmingham Jail," penned in April 1963, Pindling traveled to Washington, DC, four months later to participate in the August 28 March on Washington. He listened to the now-iconic "I Have a Dream" speech shoulder to shoulder with more than two hundred thousand other participants, including black film stars Sidney Poitier and Harry Belafonte. While Belafonte and Pindling shared being of part Jamaican parentage, Pindling and Poitier shared a friendship forged in their Bahamian childhoods. Born in Miami, Florida, in 1927 to Bahamian tomato farmers Reginald and Evelyn Outten Poitier, Poitier had moved with his family from their native Cat Island to Nassau when he was ten. It was there that he and Pindling worked alongside each other in Arnold Pindling's Over-the-Hill store.[57]

At age fifteen, Poitier's troublesome adolescent years led his frustrated and bewildered father to send him to live with his brother in Miami. Poitier, who was functionally illiterate, possessed a "stubborn independence" that was both a blessing and a curse to a teenage boy with a West Indian accent in the heart of Miami's Liberty City. Poitier had "followed a long pattern of Bahamian migration to Miami, but he could not abide in the Deep South"; he moved to New York City amid the Great Migration in 1943.[58] The sixteen-year-old lied about his age in order to join the army during World War II and served for a little more than a year. Alone once again in America's busiest city, Poitier fought to explore his boyhood love for the

54. Ibid., 91.

55. Ibid., 92–93; Hughes, *Race and Politics in the Bahamas*, 89.

56. Bahamas Monthly Intelligence Report, Secret and Confidential, February 1961, CO 1031/2140, 59.

57. Craton, *Pindling*, 114; "Premier Pindling Joins Old Pal Poitier at the Top," *Jet*, February 2, 1967, 49.

58. Adam Goudsouzian, *Sidney Poitier: Man, Actor, Icon* (Chapel Hill: University of North Carolina Press, 2004) 23–26 and 32.

cinema. Through consistent efforts at self-improvement, Poitier joined the American Negro Theater.[59]

Poitier came of age as an actor during the 1940s and in 1950 made his film debut in *No Way Out,* in which he played a black doctor trying to negotiate racial violence amid post-World War II riots. The Bay Street Censorship Board banned the film, along with *Lost Boundaries* and *Pinky,* which they deemed racially inflammatory.[60] A group formed for the purpose of acting "as watchdog on the abuses of government," the Citizens' Committee argued that people had a right to information "regardless of barriers." Composed of members of the black professional class, including Randol Fawkes, the committee successfully fought for the film's viewing.[61]

By the 1960s, Poitier was on his way to being hailed "the Martin Luther King of the movies." He chose roles that "portrayed a compelling humanity" in films such as *The Defiant Ones, A Raisin in the Sun,* and *Lilies of the Field,* which premiered in 1963. In April of the following year, Poitier won the Academy Award for best actor, becoming the first black American to do so.[62] The year 1964 was also momentous for The Bahamas, which achieved internal self-rule while still under white colonial domination. Despite having declared his support for the Pindling-led PLP, Poitier returned to Nassau amid much fanfare in early May. In a campaign dubbed "Sidney's Comin' Back Home," Poitier's car led a two-hour motorcade while scores of black Bahamians lined the streets. Others stood atop cars and roofs, and some even sat in trees as the island's colonial elite honored Poitier with an exclusive reception at the Government House.[63]

Coincidentally, the year was also seminal in the life of Martin Luther King, Jr. Exhausted from his nearly incessant participation in nonviolent campaigns across the South, King was actually in an Atlanta hospital when his wife Coretta telephoned on October 14 to report that he had been selected as the recipient of the Nobel Peace Prize.[64] Having been unsure whether or not his work had sufficient international appeal when he was

---

59. Ibid., 39–41.

60. Craton, *Pindling,* 48; Goudsouzian, *Sidney Poitier,* 75; Fawkes, *Faith that Moved the Mountain,* 45.

61. Fawkes, *Faith that Moved the Mountain,* 45.

62. Goudsouzian, *Sidney Poitier,* 3 and 219.

63. Ibid., 219.

64. King, *Autobiography of Martin Luther King, Jr.,* 255; David J. Garrow, *The FBI and Martin Luther King, Jr.* (New York: Norton, 1981) 121.

nominated, King had initially been reticent to believe that he had any real chance at winning the prize.

King's Nobel acceptance speech in Oslo, Norway, would be one of only a handful of opportunities enabling King to speak before a captive audience of international listeners. On December 11, 1964, King used the opportunity to rail against white domestic terrorism at home in the United States and white colonial oppression abroad, in places like South Africa, India, Mexico, and the Congo:

> I have the audacity to believe that peoples everywhere can have three meals a day for their bodies, education and culture for their minds, and dignity, equality, and freedom for their spirits. I believe that what self-centered men have torn down, other-centered men can build up. I still believe that one day mankind will bow before the altars of God and be crowned triumphant over war and bloodshed, and nonviolent redemptive good will proclaim the rule of the land. . . . I still believe that we shall overcome![65]

King, while shorter than most imagined, never failed to enchant his audiences with the rich baritone of his voice and the beauty of his words. When the voice of thirty-five-year-old King rang out, people around the world listened intently to the words of the Nobel's then youngest ever recipient. And as Ron Ramdin observed, "Around the world, people who had never heard of King now listened."[66] They were words that united the American nonviolent struggle for civil rights to the rising tide of anticolonial struggles in India, Africa, Latin America, and the Caribbean. They were words inspired by King's unyielding belief in the ability of nonviolence to secure democracy for humankind. They were words that may have been written, at least in part, aboard a Bahamian fishing boat floating in a clearing. Boatbuilder, fisherman, and Bimini native Ansil Saunders, who was King's fishing guide at the behest of Congressman Adam Clayton Powell, Jr., refers to the clearing, just beyond the narrow, mangrove-lined Bonefish Creek, as "Holy Grounds."[67] Given the beauty of the clearing, it is easy to imagine that some of King's words were inspired by his time in Saunders'

65. See Martin Luther King, Jr., "Nobel Prize Acceptance Speech (1964)," in Washington, *Testament of Hope*, 224–26.

66. Ron Ramdin, *Martin Luther King, Jr.* (London: Haus, 2004) 93.

67. David J. Garrow, *Bearing the Cross: Martin Luther King, Jr., and the Southern Christian Leadership Conference* (New York: Morrow, 1986) 136; Kennedy Warne, *Let Them Eat Shrimp: The Tragic Disappearance of the Rainforests of the Sea* (Washington, DC: Island, 2011) 67–68.

boat. "I refuse to accept the idea that man is mere flotsam and jetsam in the river of life, unable to influence the unfolding events which surround him," King declared. "I refuse to accept the view that mankind is so tragically bound to the starless midnight of racism and war that the bright daybreak of peace and brotherhood can never become a reality."[68]

Located just fifty miles off the coast of Florida, the Bahamas' western-most islands, the Biminis, had been the home of Ernest Hemingway in the mid-1930s, and by the time of King's 1964 visit, they were the favorite place of the embattled Adam Clayton Powell, Jr. Powell, like his father before him, served as pastor of Harlem's Abyssinian Baptist Church, which had become the nation's largest black Protestant church under his headship. Powell's rise to political preeminence had begun in the 1930s and gained momentum in the mid-1940s, when he began his congressional career based on a platform that opposed poll taxes and lynching while calling for fair employment practices for African Americans.[69]

Physically striking, charismatic, and flamboyant, Powell earned a reputation for "advancing civil rights," "progressive positions," and "an activist federal government." As one of only two African Americans in the U.S. Congress between 1945 and 1955, he was also unapologetically black. The bane of white Southerners, his famous "Powell Amendment" was a rider he tried to attach to dozens of appropriations bills that withheld federal funds from states that racially discriminated against blacks.[70] And as Andrée Reeves keenly observed, "Powell seemed to have a black mandate. . . . The more whites criticized him, the surer black America was that it had a true black representative in Adam Powell."[71]

Increasingly powerful, Powell became chairman of the House Education and Labor Committee in 1961. His once cooperative relationship with King, however, had been badly damaged the previous year when Powell pressured King to disassociate himself from his special assistant and New York SCLC office director Bayard Rustin. Forced to "save face" for the good

---

68. Washington, *Testament of Hope*, 225–26.

69. Taylor Branch, *Pillar of Fire: America in the King Years, 1963–1965* (New York: Simon & Schuster, 1998) 525. For more biographical information on Powell, see Charles V. Hamilton, *Adam Clayton Powell, Jr.: The Political Biography of an American Dilemma* (New York : Atheneum, 1991) and Wil Haygood, *King of the Cats: The Life and Times of Adam Clayton Powell, Jr.* (Boston: Houghton Mifflin, 1993).

70. Andrée E. Reeves, *Congressional Committee Chairmen: Three Who Made an Evolution* (Lexington: University Press of Kentucky, 1993) 112–13.

71. Ibid., 113.

of the cause, King folded under Powell's threat to lie about the nature of King and Rustin's relationship, and accepted Rustin's reluctant resignation.[72]

Powell's threat of libel, while seemingly successful, was characteristic of the growing recklessness of his political maneuvering. Allegations of misappropriation of funds grew in the wake of Powell's frequent trips to his island retreat of Bimini, as did the political misfortunes following the loss of a slander case levied against him by "bag lady" Esther James. Refusing to pay James court-ordered damages, Powell ignored court-ordered subpoenas and evaded subsequent contempt warrants for failure to appear. Once hailed "Mr. Civil Rights," Powell set up camp on Bimini, returning to his Harlem district only on Sundays, when it was illegal to serve the warrants.[73]

Powell's stints at his Bahamian island retreat had grown exponentially by the time of King's 1964 visit. An experienced angler, when Powell was not enjoying his favorite pastime, his fishing yacht, "Adam's Fancy," was tied at Brown's Dock. He enjoyed not only the fishing Bimini offered, he enjoyed its people. "Another aspect of Bimini that I liked was the people," recalled Powell. "They reminded me of my church congregation in that everybody knew at least a part of everyone else's family. By now I know most of the people on the island and it is still the place to go when I want to escape from the world. Escape," he noted, "can be a very difficult and very precious thing for the person in public life."[74]

Likewise, King probably sought an escape from the demands of his own life and work, but even his stay on the small, virtually desolate island of South Bimini had not escaped the hawkeyed vigilance of the Federal Bureau of Investigation (FBI). Director of the FBI J. Edgar Hoover had been outraged that King was to receive the Nobel honor; he was also angry about the conclusions of the Warren Commission concerning the assassination of John F. Kennedy, who was suspected in some circles of a growing support for civil rights legislation. Hoover publicly denounced King in one news story as "top alley cat" and dubbed him "the most notorious liar" in subsequent interviews.[75]

72. For more on the debacle, see Garrow, *Bearing the Cross*, 138–40; Martin Luther King, Jr. to Adam Clayton Powell, Jr., June 24, 1960.

73. Haygood, *King of the Cats* (Boston: Houghton Mifflin, 1993) 294.

74. Adam Clayton Powell, Jr., *Adam by Adam: The Autobiography of Adam Clayton Powell, Jr.* (New York: Dial, 1971) 220.

75. Garrow, *FBI and Martin Luther King, Jr.*, 121–22. See also Ben A. Franklin, "Hoover Assails Warren Findings," *New York Times*, November 19, 1964; "Off Hoover's Chest," *Newsweek*, November 30, 1964, 30; and "The FBI and Civil Rights—J. Edgar Hoover Speaks Out," *U.S. News & World Report*, November 30, 1964, 56–58.

When the story of Hoover's accusations broke, King was still in Bimini. His Atlanta office responded to Hoover directly in a telegram that bore King's name: "I was appalled and surprised at your reported statement maligning my integrity. . . . I have sincerely questioned the effectiveness of the FBI in racial incidents, particularly where bombing and brutalities against Negroes are at issue, but I have never attributed this merely to the presence of Southerners in the FBI."[76] The telegram was not enough to discourage a deluge of helicopters that had begun descending upon the little islands in the stream as soon as the story broke. Andrew Young, who traveled with King to Bimini, "knew something big had struck," as did Biminites. The accompanying onslaught of reporters led King to hold a press conference at the Big Game Fishermen's Lodge, during which he said,

> I cannot conceive of Mr. Hoover making a statement like this without being under extreme pressure. He has apparently faltered under the awesome burden, complexities and responsibilities of his office. Therefore I cannot engage in a public debate with him. I have nothing but sympathy for this man who has served his country so well.[77]

It was the final time that the world was certain of King's presence in The Bahamas, but the influence of the movement he led was again apparent the following year. On April 27, 1965, a day that has since been dubbed "Black Tuesday," PLP leader Lynden O. Pindling, frustrated with the UBP's continued gerrymandering practices, walked over to the Speaker of the House of Assembly's chair, shouting, "This is the symbol of authority, and authority in this island belongs to the people. Yes, the people are outside and the Mace belongs outside too!" At some point during his monologue, he had picked up the Speaker's Mace, the symbol of the House's authority. He moved with it to a window and threw it out, where a crowd of Bahamians watched it crash and break into pieces. Skillfully avoiding his impending arrest, Pindling, flanked by his fellow PLP members, made it out of the House and into the cheering crowd.[78]

---

76. Garrow, *FBI and Martin Luther King, Jr.,* 122–23. See also Martin Luther King, Jr. to J. Edgar Hoover, November 19, 1964; John Hubers, "Dr. King Rebuts Hoover Charges," *New York Times,* November 20, 1964.

77. Branch, *Pillar of Fire,* 527; Hubers, "Dr. King Rebuts Hoover Charges."

78. Johnson, *Quiet Revolution in the Bahamas,* 52; Craton and Saunders, *Islanders in the Stream,* 340; Hughes, *Race and Politics in the Bahamas,* 107; Craton, *Pindling,* 119–20.

With the knowledge that the UBP would send the riot police, Pindling mounted a post office van to tell the crowd what had occurred as well as why it had taken place. As he looked across the gathered crowd, he saw supporters displaying placards with messages like "Blood, Sweat and Tears" and "Boycott Bay Street." In her account in *The Quiet Revolution*, Doris Johnson recounted: "Echoing their American counterparts, the black demonstrators sang, 'We Shall Overcome,' the theme song of the civil rights movement in the United States. They added 'Showers of Blessing' when a light rain began to fall about 11 o'clock and the 'Amen' from *Lilies of the Field*."[79]

Following the momentous day's end, the PLP and black Bahamian masses fortified their commitment to ousting the UBP. Over the next two years, the Pindling-led PLP called on friends both at home and abroad for support. Still self-exiled in Bimini, Adam Clayton Powell, Jr. campaigned for the PLP, as did Oscar winner Sidney Poitier. Having been reunited in the cause of the American civil rights struggle, Pindling and Poitier remained in contact with each other following the March on Washington. During a critical point in the campaign, Poitier, who was in The Bahamas lending Pindling and the PLP his support, called Harry Belafonte in New York in the middle of a Saturday night to have him locate, purchase, and arrange next-day delivery of badly needed walkie-talkies.[80]

Unwittingly, the UBP had chosen January 10, 1967, as the next general election date. The biblical significance of "the tenth day of the first month" in the exodus story of the Israelites' victory over the Egyptian Pharaoh had not escaped them. The PLP seized the opportunity presented by their faux pas. They made the theme music from the film *Exodus* their campaign song and added to it the civil rights movement standard, "We Shall Overcome," and Poitier's "Amen." Meanwhile, recordings of Martin Luther King, Jr.'s "I Have a Dream" speech wafted from jukeboxes across Nassau.[81] The polls closed at 6:00 P.M., but it was nearly midnight when the election results were finally in. Claiming that "the island of New Providence awoke with one wild, almost incredulous, raucous cry of jubilation," Doris Johnson writes,

> Men, women and children, many in bedclothes, streamed out of their homes and began to dance in the streets. They clapped hands,

79. Johnson, *Quiet Revolution in the Bahamas*, 54.

80. Sidney Poitier, *This Life* (New York: Knopf, 1980) 317–18; Goudsouzian, *Sidney Poitier*, 255.

81. Goudsouzian, *Sidney Poitier*, 255; Craton, *Pindling*, 131–32; Johnson, *Quiet Revolution in the Bahamas*, 83.

threw hats and posters into the air. They seized banners and began triumphant parades in every direction, everyone laughing, shouting, singing, caught up in one irresistible wave of rejoicing. All over the island the frenzied beat of the goatskin drums and the chatter of cowbells sent up a happy din. The black man's day had come.[82]

Ironically, the PLP's day did not come until two independents, one of whom was Randol Fawkes, broke the party's stalemate with the UBP. Led by Pindling, the PLP boasted a black cabinet that marched into the House of Assembly as a crowd of spectators looked on. In 1973, Pindling, a strong admirer of Martin Luther King, Jr., became the first prime minister of an independent Bahamas, masterfully leading the PLP to dramatic victories in six successive elections until it was defeated by the Free National Movement (FNM) in 1992. It was an unprecedented success made possible by the link between the two men, born just one year apart, and their respective movements, worlds apart in different nations.

82. Johnson, *Quiet Revolution in the Bahamas*, 89.

11

Toward Prospects for Peace

*Martin Luther King, Jr., Latin America, and
an Example of Colombian Nonviolence*

Peter Cousins

In Latin America, for example, national reform movements have almost
despaired of nonviolent methods; one of the most powerful expressions of
nonviolence may come out of [an] international coalition of socially aware
forces, operating outside government frameworks.

MARTIN LUTHER KING, JR.[1]

THIS CHAPTER EXPLORES MARTIN Luther King, Jr.'s influence across Latin
America and examines in some detail a citizen-led, nonviolent initiative
in Colombia in the light of Kingian thinking. This South American nation continues to experience the turmoil of an internal armed conflict, and
although a new round of negotiations between the Colombian government

1. Martin Luther King, Jr., *The Trumpet of Conscience* (San Francisco: HarperSan-
Francisco, 1989; originally published in 1968) 63.

and Revolutionary Armed Forces of Colombia (FARC) are scheduled to begin in the final quarter of 2012, the focus here is not on the likelihood of a successful outcome; nor is it my purpose to survey previous high-level attempts at making peace. I look instead at how nonviolence has been adopted at the grassroots in a particular context of extreme violence, and relate this to Martin Luther King, Jr's approach to conflict transformation during the civil rights campaign in 1960s America.

The chapter draws on the literature where appropriate in considering the spread of his ideas across Latin America. On Colombia, however, many of the reflections are my own, based on two years of experience as an international accompanier with the American FOR in the Peace Communities of San José de Apartadó and Bogotá. The chapter starts by considering King's own understanding of nonviolence as it extended beyond relationships between individuals to take on regional, national, and ultimately international implications. Such a discussion is essential for relating King to the Latin American context.

REFLECTIONS ON THE NONVIOLENCE OF MARTIN LUTHER KING, JR.

The careful selection of three of King's texts for the A.J. Muste Memorial Institute's dedicated *Essay Series* charts the progression of King's thinking; a sermon preached in 1957, "Loving Your Enemies"; followed by the eloquent and moving "Letter from Birmingham Jail" (1963); leading up to his vehement critique of U.S. foreign policy in the "Declaration of Independence from the War in Vietnam" (1967). These essays reflect and develop the themes of the "pilgrimage to nonviolence" that King underwent and that he recounts elsewhere in a chapter of the same name.[2]

Here the reader can appreciate how King's reading of Mohandas K. Gandhi positioned him to write his 1957 sermon. His conviction that love could transform relationships only at the individual level was challenged and eventually fatally wounded by his growing understanding of *satyagraha*. This process would lead King to declare, as early as 1958, that "Gandhi was probably the first person in history to lift the love ethic of Jesus above mere interaction between individuals to a powerful and effective social force on a

---

2. I owe a debt of gratitude to Michael Randle for bibliographical advice on Martin Luther King's writings. See Martin Luther King, Jr., *Stride Toward Freedom: The Montgomery Story* (New York: Harper & Row, 1958) 90–107.

large scale." King continued: "It was in this Gandhian emphasis on love and non-violence that I discovered the method for social reform that I had been seeking for so many months."[3] At this juncture, King was primarily interested in how the Gandhian concept of love expressed through nonviolent action could be applied in the struggle against Jim Crow in the American South.

In any case, King integrated Gandhian ideas into his preaching, taking up the question of love in his 1957 sermon.[4] His homily was premised on the imperative that action for justice could not reduce itself to a zero-sum affair, but must necessarily leave open the way to the reconstruction of relationships, captured in the dichotomy "enemy-neighbour."[5] Convinced that love would eventually triumph over "our most bitter opponents" and issue forth in justice, King went on to declare: "One day we shall win freedom, but not only for ourselves. We shall so appeal to your heart and conscience that we shall win *you* in the process, and our victory will be a double victory."[6]

This sentiment was conveyed, for example, in the advice given by King to Afro-Americans following their victory in the Montgomery bus boycott: "Remember that this is not a victory for Negroes alone, but for all Montgomery and the South. Do not boast! Do not brag!"[7] Yet this transformative love, *agape*, also came to embed itself in King's overarching vision of nonviolent resistance, whose application he defended in "Letter from Birmingham Jail" in 1963. Here King articulates the four basic steps that the nonviolent resister ought to take before arriving at a decision to pursue a nonviolent campaign—namely, the gathering of facts to determine if injustices exist, attempts at negotiation, self-purification, and direct action.[8] By 1963, the year of his imprisonment at Birmingham, King had also identified the six features of nonviolent resistance that characterized his activities across the South. In all of these instances, one detects echoes of Gandhi. King referred to the six features collectively as the "philosophy of nonviolence," and the

3. Ibid., 97.

4. A. J. Muste Memorial Institute, *Essay Series* 1 (New York: A. J. Muste Memorial Institute, n.d.) 3–12.

5. Ibid., 5. See also Martin Luther King, Jr., "Loving Your Enemies," in Clayborne Carson et al., eds., *The Papers of Martin Luther King, Jr.*, vol. 6, *Advocate of the Social Gospel, September 1948–March 1963* (Berkeley: University of California Press, 2007) 429.

6. A. J. Muste Memorial Institute, *Essay Series* 1, 11; Carson et al., *Papers*, 6:428.

7. King, *Stride Toward Freedom*, 164.

8. See A. J. Muste Memorial Institute, *Essay Series* 1, 14–16; Martin Luther King, Jr., *Why We Can't Wait* (New York: New American Library, 1964) 78.

following merits further consideration when considering King's methods in broad context:

(1) Nonviolence is not cowardly: "it does resist." Here King clarifies the difference between *passive nonresistance* and *active nonviolent resistance*.

(2) Active nonviolent resistance does not set out to belittle the opponent, but to gain his friendship and understanding through persuasion.

(3) Nonviolent resistance distinguishes between "sin and sinner" and aims only to defeat the evil act.

(4) Nonviolent resistance encompasses the possibility of being subjected to violence, without permitting retaliation. "Unearned suffering is redemptive."

(5) Nonviolent resistance does not give in to hate.

(6) Nonviolent resistance is founded on the "conviction that the universe is on the side of justice."[9] Here the element of incurable optimism and hope enters the equation, both of which are grounded in a certain understanding of the Christian faith, and also in the willingness of committed human beings to become co-activists and co-sufferers with God.

These six features are inextricably tied to another principle that figured prominently in King's philosophy, namely, noncooperation. Like nonviolence, this principle extended beyond King's regional commitments in the American South and also his national commitments to take on universal meanings. The idea here is that from both a moral and rational standpoint, noncooperation rather than cooperation with an evil system is always preferred.

This chapter omits deeper discussion of the civil rights movement in the American South, as our focus lies elsewhere, and that matter has already been well established. I shall return to the above six features or principles in due course.

---

9. This expression of faith should be read alongside King's assertion that "human progress never rolls in on wheels of inevitability" and his call to action in the here and now. See A. J. Muste Memorial Institute, *Essay Series* 1, 23–24; King, *Stride Toward Freedom*, 102–7.

KING'S THINKING ON AMERICA'S ROLE IN LATIN AMERICA AND THE WORLD

With the passage of time, King's international standing increased. In 1964, he was awarded the Nobel Peace Prize. As the United States' participation in the Vietnam War scaled up towards it apogee, King delivered a lecture, a version of the "Declaration of Independence from the War in Vietnam," at Riverside Church in New York City, in which he condemned this bellicose activity. To those questioning and criticizing his involvement with the antiwar movement, King replied: "And when I hear them, though I often understand the source of their concern, I am nevertheless greatly saddened, for such questions mean that the inquirers have not really known me, my commitment or my calling. . . . I believe that the path from Dexter Avenue Baptist Church—the church in Montgomery, Alabama, where I began my pastorate—leads clearly to this sanctuary tonight."[10]

It is clear that by 1967, the year of this Riverside speech, King saw aligning himself with the peace movement as the outworking of his involvement in civil rights campaigns over the preceding decade. In other matters, too, one finds consistent threads throughout his work. Many of his interventions over the years bore witness not only to his persuasion that the universe leaned towards justice, but also to his faith in his country, invoking for his cause the universal values that gave rise to the birth of the United States. In his Nobel Prize lecture, in Oslo, Norway, in December 1964, King declared before the world that "nonviolence is the answer to the crucial political and moral question of our time—the need for man to overcome oppression and violence without resorting to violence and oppression."[11] These words embodied both a challenge and a warning, coming, as they did, at a time when America was deeply entrenched in Vietnam.

Stridently unsympathetic towards America's military action in Vietnam, King, convinced that "civilization and violence are antithetical concepts," connected the war with America's activity elsewhere in the world. Quoting an American official abroad who, as early as 1957, felt that the United States was in danger of ending up on the wrong side of history, King asserted:

10. A. J. Muste Memorial Institute, *Essay Series* 1, 36; James M. Washington, ed., *A Testament of Hope: The Essential Writings and Speeches of Martin Luther King, Jr.* (New York: HarperCollins, 1991) 232.

11. Quoted in Washington, *Testament of Hope*, 224.

During the past ten years we have seen emerge a pattern of sup-
pression which now has justified the presence of U.S. military
"advisors" in Venezuela. The need to maintain social stability for
our investments accounts for the counterrevolutionary action of
American forces in Guatemala. It tells why American helicopters
are being used against guerrillas in Colombia and why American
napalm and Green Beret forces have already been active against
rebels in Peru.[12]

At another point in 1967, King viewed the growing despair of nonviolent methods in Latin America as largely a product of America's policies in
that part of the world. He noted that "many young men, even many priests"
had "joined guerrilla movements in the hills." King lamented that "so many
of Latin America's problems have roots in the United States of America,"
and he called for "a solid, united movement, non-violently conceived and
followed through," to bring pressure to bear on "the capital and government power structures concerned, from both sides of the problem at once."
In King own thinking, this was possibly "the only hope for a nonviolent
solution in Latin America today." He believed that "one of the most powerful expressions of nonviolence" could conceivably "come out of that international coalition of socially aware forces, operating outside governmental
frameworks."[13]

Although one does not find a great concentration on Latin America
in King's *œuvre*, we clearly see that he was keenly aware of the problematic
nature of U.S. involvement in that part of the world and in the Western
Hemisphere as a whole. The Colombian insurgent movement to which
King referred in 1967 was the FARC, which had formally constituted itself
the year before (Colombia's other surviving guerrilla outfit, the smaller National Liberation Army or ELN, was by this time also active). King's own
mention of the FARC may sound anachronistic, but it speaks to the intractable nature of Colombia's conflict. The focus of this chapter now shifts to
the Americas in general, and then to Colombia in particular.

12. Quoted in ibid., 240. See also A. J. Muste Memorial Institute, *Essay Series* 1, 47.
13. King, *Trumpet of Conscience*, 63.

KING AND NONVIOLENCE ELSEWHERE IN THE AMERICAS

No government in Latin America or the Caribbean possesses nuclear weapons. Indeed, some countries south of the United States borders possess only very limited armed forces, and others do not maintain a military of any kind.[14] Meanwhile, Ron Pagnucco and John D. McCarthy point out that organized nonviolence has a short history in the region.[15] In view of this, the obvious question is, how is it that we should find ourselves talking about nonviolent resistance there at all?

Throughout the twentieth century, the shadow of the military loomed larger across Latin America. Many countries, particularly in the Southern Cone and in Central America, fell under the control of military dictatorships, often known as bureaucratic-authoritarian regimes.[16] King's rise to prominence in the United States did not go unnoticed here and elsewhere in the Western Hemisphere. For some people, his message and methods had a resonance far beyond the particular circumstances obtaining in the deep southern United States in the 1950s and 1960s. Two such figures included Hélder Câmara and Adolfo Pérez Esquivel. Hélder Câmara was the archbishop of Olinda and Recife in Brazil between 1964 and 1985. His occupancy of the see coincided with the period of military dictatorship in the country. Câmara was seized of concern at the great disparities of land distribution and wealth in Brazil at the time.[17] The resultant poverty—indeed poverty wherever it was to be found—was one element of what Câmara referred to as "injustice," "basic violence," or "violence No. 1."[18] As the title of

14. Ross Ryan, "Editorial—A Special Issue: Violence in Latin America and the Caribbean," *Peace and Conflict Monitor*, April 1, 2012. Online: http://www.monitor.upeace.org/innerpg.cfm?id_article=892.

15. R. Pagnucco and J. D. McCarthy, "Advocating Nonviolent Direct Action in Latin America: The Antecedents and Emergence of SERAJ," in *Religion and Politics in Comparative Perspective*, ed. B. Misztal and A. Shupe (Westport, CT: Praeger, 1992) 127.

16. R. Pagnucco, "The Transnational Strategies of the Service for Peace and Justice in Latin America," in *Transnational Social Movements and Global Politics*, ed. Jackie G. Smith et al. (Syracuse: Syracuse University Press, 1997) 125.

17. Bruce Kent, *The Non-Violence of Hélder Câmara* (London: Catholic Truth Society, 1977) 5.

18. However, Câmara felt strongly that the Church itself had nothing to fear from poverty and the loss of privilege: "Providence has already delivered us from the Papal States. When will the hour of God come which will bring the Church back to rejoin Lady Poverty?" Quoted in Kent, *The Non-Violence of Hélder Câmara*, 5. He once declared that

one of his books, *Spiral of Violence*, suggests, such conditions would almost inevitably beget revolt or "violence No. 2," followed in turn by repression of any uprising, or "violence No. 3."[19]

A 1966 letter to Martin Luther King from the missionary Earl M. Smith, who represented the U.S. wing of the Fellowship of Reconciliation (FOR), looks at the dissemination in Brazil of the former's ideas.[20] The possibility arises of translating King's *Strength to Love* into Portuguese. Smith then alludes to Câmara's interest in receiving a visit from King, stating that the archbishop "has been practicing some significant nonviolence."[21] Indeed, in his book, Câmara goes on to advocate for the use of peaceful intervention against each of the three kinds of violence that he identified.[22] To this end he encouraged the growth of a movement, Action for Peace and Justice. In an echo of King, he concluded that "if I joyfully spend the rest of my life, of my powers, of my energies in demanding justice, but without hatred, without armed violence, through liberating moral pressure, through truth and love, it is because I am convinced that only love is constructive and strong."[23]

Perhaps unsurprisingly, we find that *Spiral of Violence* is dedicated to Mohandas Gandhi and Martin Luther King, Jr. This alone says something about the global impact of nonviolence, and about how the minds and hearts of great leaders from around the world have come together around the use of that method as a moral imperative. In another sense, it seems to speak in some measure about the impact of Gandhi and King on parts of Latin America, and especially Brazil.

The military regime tried hard to silence Câmara,[24] but his preaching and practicing of nonviolence yet won him and his Gandhian-Kingian

---

"we, the *Excelentisimi* [i.e., the bishops], are in need of a most excellent reform" (author's translation). See Câmara, "Prefiero mil veces ser matado que matar." Online: http://www. eurosur.org/acc/html/revista/r37/37hprf.htm.

19. Hélder Câmara, *Spiral of Violence* (London: Sheed & Ward, 1971) 25–37.

20. I owe this point to Susana Pimiento Chamorro, who drew my attention to the existence of the letter. From Martin Luther King, Jr. to Earl M. Smith (1966), The Library and Archives of the Martin Luther King, Jr. Center for Nonviolent Social Change, Inc., Atlanta, Georgia.

21. Ibid.

22. Câmara, *Spiral of Violence*, 41–55.

23. Ibid., 82; Kent, *Non-Violence of Hélder Câmara*, 82.

24. Peter Winn, *Americas: The Changing Face of Latin America and the Caribbean*, 3rd ed. (Berkeley: University of California Press) 379.

ideas a national and even international audience, and he traveled widely. He also attracted fellow bishops to his cause.[25] Few in Latin America actually obtained this stature, though in neighboring Argentina, Adolfo Pérez Esquivel was to become the figurehead for an entire continental movement.

Pérez Esquivel served as the first Coordinator General of the *Servicio Paz y Justicia* (Peace and Justice Service), or SERPAJ, and would be awarded the Nobel Peace Prize in 1980 while at the helm of this organization. He was already renowned as a sculptor when, in 1971, he became a pacifist following a spiritual crisis. Thereafter he engaged in the defense of human rights in Argentina and elsewhere, founding or participating in a number of organizations. Between 1975 and 1978, he was subjected to periods of imprisonment in Brazil, Ecuador, and Argentina.[26]

SERPAJ itself came into being independently of Pérez Esquivel. Since the 1940s, the International Fellowship of Reconciliation and its American branch, with which Dr. King affiliated, had worked to create FOR chapters in Latin America, including in Uruguay, Argentina, and Brazil.[27] The FOR capitalized upon these initiatives in the 1960s by sending two prominent Catholic activists, Jean and Hildegaard Goss-Mayr, to the region.[28] Their task was to "convert the Roman Catholic Church in Latin America to nonviolence,"[29] in view of the absence of any such tradition there within that body. Hélder Câmara's contact with Earl M. Smith developed in this context, the latter working closely with the Goss-Mayr's. In the second half of the 1960s, FOR leaders from the United States and others involved heavily in the civil rights movement, such as Glenn Smiley, came to Latin America to bear their own witness to nonviolence. They were apparently effective in both Protestant and Catholic circles.

SERPAJ's establishment was preceded by two important meetings, one in 1966 and a second in 1971. At Montevideo in 1966, the first international assembly in Latin America on nonviolence, consisting of more than sixty delegates from around the region and beyond, gathered at the behest of Earl Smith. Martin Luther King, Jr. himself sent a representative. The meeting had a consultative character and some in attendance did not fully subscribe

25. Ibid.

26. See http://www.serpajamericalatina.org/home.htm, "Premio Nóbel."

27. Pagnucco, "Transnational Strategies," 125.

28. A fuller account of their journey can be found, in Spanish, on SERPAJ's Web site. See http://www.serpajamericalatina.org/home.htm, "Reseña Histórica."

29. Ibid. See also Pagnucco, "Transnational Strategies," 125.

to the philosophy or practice of nonviolence, though all concurred in the importance of addressing Latin America's social problems.[30] The 1971 summit took place at Arajuela, Costa Rica, and was billed as the *Primer encuentro sobre la noviolencia activa* (First meeting on active nonviolence). Archbishop Câmara gave the inaugural discourse.[31] On this occasion, a concrete way forward was discerned: SERPAJ's predecessor was founded, the *Servicio para la Acción Liberadora en América Latina—Orientación No-Violenta* (Service for Liberating Action in Latin America—Non-Violent Orientation), and a newsletter of the same name was to be set up, edited by Smith.[32]

Following SERPAJ's founding, three years later, Jean Goss reflected back on the situation faced by those first activists in terms of embedding a tradition of nonviolence in Latin America:

> Ya era evidente en 1971 que la tradición noviolenta-pacifista europea y de Estados Unidos, de predominancia intelectual, que no existía en América Latina, no se le podía imponer desde el exterior. También se hizo evidente que la lucha en Latinoamérica debía ser concebida dentro del proyecto global de liberación individual y colectivo, inserto en la situación histórica del continente. Las experiencias de otros pueblos (Gandhi, Dolci, King) deben ser conocidas, pero ellas servirán solamente para hacer brotar las propias iniciativas de América Latina.[33]

All the work undertaken to enable an indigenous nonviolent movement to emerge bore fruit at Medellín (Colombia) in 1974, when SERPAJ was formally constituted. Though organized again by Earl Smith and the Goss-Mayr's, the conference "had a distinctly Latin American character, and the newly established *Servicio* became a truly Latin American organization.

---

30. Pagnucco, "Transnational Strategies," 126.

31. Ibid.

32. Pagnucco and McCarthy, "Advocating Nonviolent Direct Action," 134.

33. See http://www.serpajamericalatina.org/home.htm, "Reseña Histórica." Author's translation: "In 1971 it was already obvious that the European and North American nonviolent-pacifist tradition, predominantly intellectual in character and which did not exist in Latin America, could not be imposed from the outside. It also became clear that the struggle in Latin America had to be considered in the context of individual and collective liberation across the globe, while part of the historical situation of the region. Other peoples' experiences (Gandhi, Dolci, King) need to be known, but they will serve only to bring forth Latin America's own initiatives."

Only Latin Americans could vote at the meeting. Conscientization[34] was the watchword of the conference."[35] Elsewhere, Pagnucco remarks that SERPAJ's vocation was to "strengthen communication and coordination of action among isolated non-violent Latin American groups and to educate and train people in the theory and practice of nonviolence."[36] Adolfo Pérez Esquivel, by then heavily involved in the defense of human rights, was designated SERPAJ's first Coordinator General at Medellín.

Events in the Latin American Catholic Church also favored a continental nonviolent movement. Six years prior to the founding of SERPAJ, Medellín had played host to an important meeting of the Latin American Catholic Bishops' Conference, at which the prelates of the region first articulated their "preferential option for the poor," thus "opening the windows" for other radical pronouncements at the Second Vatican Council. The nascent nonviolent movement, though not in essence religious—as evidenced by the involvement of the secular War Resisters' League alongside FOR in the exploratory period of the 1950s and 1960s—broadly, though not uniformly, "found important support in the Church in Latin America."[37]

Despite this progress, SERPAJ has never consisted of an unvarying regional organization. Like FOR, its basic units are the national chapters, which implement broad priorities ("lines of action"), determined at four yearly Continental Assemblies, in ways considered most appropriate for each nation's circumstances.[38] In the first eight countries to form national chapters between 1974 and 1982, military dictatorships provided the political backdrop. Pagnucco points out, however, that "there were no purely domestic human rights movements in Latin America during the 1960s, 1970s and 1980s, just as there were no purely autarkic regimes."[39] Indeed, he privileges transnational links between allies as an essential component in the ongoing construction of a nonviolent movement in Latin America, highlighting the significance of Jimmy Carter's election as president of the United States. Carter retained Andrew Young, a man close to Martin Lu-

---

34. This word is closely associated with Paolo Freire and his *Pedagogy of the Oppressed*. Freire, a Brazilian educator, advocated new models of learning, and his ideas received wide coverage in Latin America and beyond.

35. Pagnucco and McCarthy, "Advocating Nonviolent Direct Action," 135.

36. Pagnucco, "Transnational Strategies," 126–27.

37. Ibid., 125.

38. Pagnucco and McCarthy, "Advocating Nonviolent Direct Action," 136.

39. Pagnucco, "Transnational Strategies," 129 and 140.

ther King, Jr. in the Southern Christian Leadership Conference (SCLC), as ambassador to the U.N. Young then appointed a number of civil rights campaigners to his team, including the human rights activist Brady Tyson, who already worked closely with FOR and SERPAJ in particular. Tyson would go on to spearhead raising awareness at the U.N. of the Argentinian junta's repressive practices.[40]

The value of supranational ties for SERPAJ has also manifested itself in cooperation between national chapters in three major geopolitical nuclei of action: the Southern Cone, the Andean region, and Central America/Caribbean.[41] Indeed, its very origins lie in sustained efforts to cultivate a nonviolent movement across Latin America, country by country. The manner of its birth has led Pagnucco and McCarthy to speak of those who helped SERPAJ into being as "movement midwives"—purveyors of "skills and knowledge to facilitate creations that are ultimately out of their hands"—a role that SERPAJ itself would in turn exercise.[42]

Two examples from Argentina should suffice. The military dictatorship installed itself on March 24, 1976. Seeing the writing on the wall, Pérez Esquivel and SERPAJ Argentina spent the preceding months helping to establish two human rights organizations. A secular Permanent Assembly for Human Rights, consisting of trade unionists, politicians, and academics, was joined by the Ecumenical Human Rights Movement, composed of cross-denominational religious and lay people (but lacking the support of the Argentinian Catholic hierarchy, whose tendencies were conservative). Both organizations would collaborate with national chapters in defense of human rights as the political space available for dissent contracted.[43]

As the regime settled in, the picture in respect of human rights became more acute. Under General Jorge R. Videla, legislative and judicial institutions were dissolved, political and trade union activities proscribed, and civilians tried in military courts. The authorities resorted to secret detention, torture, and murder. Another practice was the "disappearing" of opponents, to which some thirty thousand people would eventually

40. See ibid., 130.

41. See http://www.serpajamericalatina.org/home.htm, "Reseña Histórica." The source continues: "Si bien hasta el presente esta esquema no ha logrado su efectivo funcionamiento . . . continúa planteándose como el más adecuado." Author's translation: "Even though this structure has not fully functioned to date . . . it remains the most appropriate one."

42. Pagnucco and McCarthy, "Advocating Nonviolent Direct Action," 138.

43. Ibid., 142. See also Pagnucco, "Transnational Strategies," 142.

be lost. Pérez Esquivel supported a group of mothers of the disappeared, who held the government responsible, as they organized themselves into a group known as the *Madres de la Plaza de Mayo*.[44] Initially numbering only fourteen, their number grew as the ranks of the disappeared swelled. SERPAJ accompanied the mothers in the square and prepared sessions on nonviolence for them. The mothers themselves were watched, and they twice had to cease their regular Thursday meetings, eventually returning to the square in both instances. On occasion, they gathered more covertly, applying certain techniques to identify themselves, including white headscarves indicative of their peaceful intentions. The *Madres* acquired a global profile and were thus instrumental in drawing the world's attention to a practice that the government sought to keep out of the public eye.[45]

These examples demonstrate SERPAJ's place in supporting the creation and development of independent nonviolent organizations. Furthermore, the *Madres* tapped into international concern, which was also mobilised to good effect when Pérez Esquivel himself was incarcerated by the junta. At that time, he was nominated for the Nobel Peace Prize by Irish activists. This was duly awarded to him in 1980, generating a virtuous circle of sorts, as it carved open a space for public discussion of human rights in Argentina and, according to Pérez Esquivel himself, rendered the *milieu* for SERPAJ-Argentina workers and human rights activists safer.[46] Pagnucco contends that "Pérez Esquivel's receipt of the Prize had a greater impact in Argentina than Martin Luther King, Jr.'s receipt of the Prize had in the United States."[47]

Be that as it may, the debt owed to King's ideal is established. The words that follow, closing the present section, show that underpinning Pérez Esquivel's tireless activism lay an unshakable belief in the same forces that so moved King and indeed Hélder Câmara: "We struggle by rendering operative the force of love in the battle of liberation. Active nonviolence is a response, a step forward (whether the world realizes it or not) that is based

---

44. Named after the square in central Buenos Aires where they would congregate.

45. Peter Ackerman and Jack Duvall, "Argentina and Chile: Resisting Repression," in *A Force More Powerful: A Century of Nonviolent Conflict* (New York: Palgrave, 2000) 267–78; Pagnucco and McCarthy, "Advocating Nonviolent Direct Action," 142; L. Bruschtein, "Por el camino de la no violencia," http://www.comisionporlamemoria.org/investigacionyenseñanza/materiales/dossiersddhh/dossier2serpaj.pdf.

46. Pagnucco and McCarthy, "Advocating Nonviolent Direct Action," 143–44.

47. Pagnucco, "Transnational Strategies," 138 n. 7.

on the gospel. Nonviolence is a way of answering evil and injustice with truth, and hate with love."[48]

A NONVIOLENT INITIATIVE FROM COLOMBIA

Valiant attempts to explore in English the full complexity of Colombian society, its conflict or its history, have been made by Pearce,[49] Bushnell,[50] and, very recently, LaRosa and Mejía.[51] As noted at the outset, high-level diplomacy in pursuit of a resolution to the conflict is not the focus here. Bouvier, in her own striking terms, has pointed out that the literature on Colombia privileges the study of the violence and its consequences[52] over peace initiatives; and insofar as the latter have been the object of attention, they are chiefly considered from the point of view of track I negotiations rather than grassroots and nonviolent peace building.[53] Her own volume is perhaps the most accessible and comprehensive attempt at remedying that to date, alongside García Durán's more technical study (2007) in Spanish.[54] This chapter does not cover all this ground and cannot hope to do so.

Colombia has long been a country haunted by violence. Economic and political tensions led to episodes of violent conflict between Conservative and Liberal Party factions in the nineteenth and early twentieth centuries. Liberal leader and reformer Jorge Eliécer Gaitán was brutally assassinated

---

48. Quoted in T. Messman, "A Dialogue on Nonviolent Resistance and Liberation Theology," in *Basta! No Mandate for War: A Pledge of Resistance Handbook*, ed. K. Butigan, M. Pastrick, and T. Messman (Philadelphia: New Society, 1985). The dialogue is now available online: http://paceebene.org/nvns/nonviolence-news-service-archive/dialogue-nonviolent-resistance-and-liberation-theology.

49. See Jenny V. Pearce, *Colombia: Inside the Labyrinth* (London: Latin American Bureau, 1990).

50. David Bushnell, *The Making of Modern Colombia: A Nation in Spite of Itself* (Berkeley: University of California Press, 1993).

51. Michael J. LaRosa and German R. Mejia, *Colombia: A Concise Contemporary History* (Lanham, MD: Rowman & Littlefield, 2012).

52. "Violontology" (the study of violence), undertaken by *violontólogos*, entered the scholarly realm with the publication of *La violencia en Colombia* (Guzmán Campos, Fals Borda, and Umaña Luna) in 1962.

53. Virginia M. Bouvier, ed., *Colombia—Building Peace in a Time of War* (Washington, DC: United States Institute of Peace, 2009) 6–7.

54. M. Garcia Duran, *Movimiento por la paz en Colombia, 1978–2003* (Bogota: CINEP, 2007).

in 1948.[55] While continuously plunged deeply into cycles of violence and instability, Colombia promotes itself as Latin America's longest-standing democracy, and indeed the formal electoral cycle has never been interrupted—although the presidency was taken in a *coup d'état* in 1953, later validated by Colombia's senate. A power-sharing arrangement between the two main parties, Conservative and Liberal, from 1958 to 1974 meant that elections merely ratified candidature decisions taken by the parties. This arrangement was itself a response to rocketing levels of lethal violence across Colombia in a period known simply as *La Violencia*, which resulted in an estimated two thousand deaths.[56] The violence gradually morphed into the armed conflict between state forces and illegal armed groups—guerrillas, paramilitaries, and their successors—that continues to this day.

Violent conflict in Colombia has not gone unchallenged. Strategic nonviolent action has occurred "at the level of municipalities within Colombia, particularly in Afro-Colombian, indigenous and peasant, and peace communities." Some of these communities, such as San José de Apartadó, "have mobilized as independent actors," dedicated to "resisting cooptation into the illegal armed forces," and also "proposing alternative visions of peace and development." Equally important is the fact that these communities "have articulated demands based upon nonviolence influenced heavily by Christian values, principles and discourse,"[57] a development that recalls Martin Luther King, Jr.'s ethical approach in the United States. From 1997 to 2009, another nonviolent force, called "No to the FARC," held marches against the Revolutionary Armed Forces of Colombia (FARC), a Marxist guerrilla organization, and also spearheaded demonstrations and other actions in the interest of "peace and negotiations."[58]

Another remarkable example of nonviolence in Colombia is the emergence of Luis Botero, one of its natives, who has devoted serious attention to the levels of violence in his country and throughout Latin America. Botero has actually led Lead4Tomorrow's efforts for peace in Colombia since the start of its mission there in 2012. Lead4Tomorrow specializes in the development and mobilization of leaders around violence prevention,

55. International Center on Nonviolent Conflict, "Colombia: Opposing Violent Insurgents, Social Violence and a Corrupt State (1990–Present)," February 2009, 2. See http://www.nonviolent-conflict.org/index.php/movements-and-campaigns/movements-and-campaigns-summaries.

56. Ibid.

57. Ibid., 5.

58. Ibid., 4.

and it works with many organizations and institutions in Latin America, Africa, Asia, the Pacific Islands, and the United States, promoting conflict resolution and nonviolent education and skill-building. Since 1999, Botero has also worked closely with Bernard Lafayette, Jr., one of Dr. King's former aides in the SCLC, and under Lafayette's guidance has become a "certified trainer in nonviolence" through the University of Rhode Island in the United States. In 2001, Botero became the first person in Colombia's history "to hold a public sector position in nonviolence when he was named Nonviolence Advisor to the Governor of the State of Antioquia, Colombia, Guillermo Gaviria." In this capacity, Botero coordinated the program in nonviolence in Antioquia, which is aimed at promoting "a change from a culture of violence to a culture of nonviolence in both Antioquia and the city of Medellín."[59] Since 2005, Botero has continued his nonviolent activities as "an international lecturer and trainer," proudly claiming the title of Education and Training Global Team Leader for the Center for Global Nonkilling, and more recently Latin America Programs Coordinator for Lead4Tomorrow. Botero's primary concern currently involves reducing domestic violence "as the central cause of violence" in Colombia and Latin America as a whole. Lead4Tomorrow also plans to provide training in nonviolence "for cross-sector leaders in Latin America" and to work with families "to reinforce the important role of parenting in creating a culture of nonviolence" for subsequent generations.[60]

But in contrast to Dr. King's movement in the United States, nonviolent action in Colombia has been characterized as "sporadic," "fragmented," and lacking "a unified strategy." Also, since 1994, nonviolent activists have, for the most part, targeted the guerrillas, while not giving the proper and necessary attention to "visible human rights violations" and the "anti-democratic practices" carried "out by the state or military." Those organizations that do seek to challenge the state or military, such as the Colombian Commission of Jurists, have continuously been subjected "to harassment and spying by State agencies, including the Department of Administrative Security."[61] Such effort to discourage and ultimately end nonviolent actions aimed at eliminating the "anti-democratic practices" of the state or military clearly evoke memories of King and his struggle with certain elements of the federal government in America.

59. "Lead4Tomorrow in Latin America." See http://www.lead4tomorrow.org/?p=116.

60. Ibid.

61. International Center on Nonviolent Conflict, "Colombia," 4–5.

CONCLUSION

The turmoil of violent conflict still threatens the well-being and survival of people in Colombia and other parts of Latin America, thus frustrating the prospects for formal peace processes. The ferocity of guerrilla groups and right-wing paramilitaries that in many cases work with drug producers and drug traffickers,[62] thereby heightening the spiral of violence, is likely to continue. But as long as there are creative nonviolent forces such as the peace communities, no matter how small, there is hope for the people of Colombia and of Latin America in general. Martin Luther King, Jr. often spoke of the potential vitality and effectiveness of "the creative minority" in bringing peace, stability, and wholeness to a violent, unstable, and suffering world.[63] There is still hope that Latin America will someday achieve, through peaceful means, the kind of economic security (antipoverty programs, land reforms, etc.) and social reform (stronger family ties, elimination of glaring cases of domestic violence, the true flowering of democracy) necessary for her people to live in harmony and community. This was Dr. King's hope for Latin America[64]—and for the entire world.

62. Ibid., 3.
63. See King, *Stride Toward Freedom*, 224; Washington, *Testament of Hope*, 318–19.
64. King, *Trumpet of Conscience*, 63.

12

An American, but Not an Imperialist
Martin Luther King, Jr. in Cuba

Francisco Rodés

These are revolutionary times; all over the globe men are revolting against old systems of exploitation and oppression. The shirtless and barefoot people of the land are rising up as never before.

MARTIN LUTHER KING, JR.[1]

ON APRIL 4, 1968, I was spending several weeks working as a volunteer during the sugar cane harvest when I first heard the shocking news of the death of Martin Luther King, Jr. As we sat on bundles of harvested cane eating our lunch and listening to a loudspeaker providing music and occasional news, we heard the announcement that King had been assassinated.

I lowered my head in consternation when I heard several comments being made around me. One of my fellow workers said, "Look at that.

1. Martin Luther King, Jr., *The Trumpet of Conscience* (San Francisco: Harper & Row, 1968) 33.

They have killed him even though he is one of them." In Cuban terms, the speaker was pointing out that King was just another American, someone who formed part of the Empire.

I took the opportunity to explain to those around me that King was a martyr, a fighter for racial justice and for the rights of the most humble of people. I said he was certainly an American but not an imperialist. He belonged to the poor and to those committed to nonviolence. Moreover, not all Americans are imperialists, I said.

Quickly a circle of workers gathered around me, interested to learn of a type of Christianity that was new to them—Christianity committed to a better world. It was only following his tragic death that the interest in King's life grew dramatically in Cuba.

During those years, Cuban attention to international affairs was intense but was directed to those Caribbean nations to our south. A year earlier, guerilla leader Ernesto "Che" Guevara had died in combat in Bolivia. The Cuban Revolution was exerting a strong influence on youth movements and leftist groups, and even Latin American Christians had begun a theological reflection that would give birth to liberation theology. It was a time of exaggerated political optimism, when a great many believed that building a society free of the ravages of capitalism was not only possible but was near at hand, maybe just around the corner.

At the time, the Cuban Revolution was struggling to survive. The United States erected an economic blockade. Mercenary groups infiltrated our borders and then unleashed their terror with the U.S.-coordinated Bay of Pigs invasion. Yet we survived. Meanwhile, churches in Cuba found themselves challenged to minister in the new Cuba, full of patriotic fervor and a new social vision appealing to idealistic youth with dreams of a Cuba free of poverty, illiteracy, and all of the wrongs that had been a part of our society.

Inevitably, Cuban churches, like the American churches in Dr. King's time, faced a crisis. The Cold War had deeply influenced many people, generating a fervent anticommunism in the majority of religious leaders. The conflict between the government and the Catholic Church was especially fierce. The Church lost its educational institutions and the majority of the Spanish clergy were expelled. Confrontations with some religious groups, like the Jehovah's Witnesses, created an atmosphere of general condemnation of religion, which was accused of being an ally of reactionary forces.

Of the various political currents that inspired our revolutionary leaders, a certain dogmatic, Soviet-style Marxism became the political norm, prompted in large measure by the need for alliances to withstand pressure from the United States. Popular education materials imported from the Soviet Union identified the confrontation between scientific materialism and idealism (which included religion per se) as the root of ideological contradictions. The patriotic song used at that time was "The Internationale," one verse of which states, "no more supreme saviors, no Caesar, no bourgeois, no God; we will make our own salvation." This form of Marxist fundamentalism was proclaimed with missionary zeal in special schools of "revolutionary instruction" and was taught as a part of the regular program of study from junior high school through graduate school.

Some popular forms of religion, which fused a mixture of African cults and Catholic saints, were open to these revolutionary ideas, since most practitioners were among the poorest of Cuban society. On the other hand, evangelical (Protestant) churches had a conservative tradition with a vision of the mission of the church focused on personal conversion and an eschatology of "the Great Tribulation" that, in many cases, identified Moscow as the beast of Revelation 13. These churches did not have the capacity to give an adequate answer to the new challenges. Many young people abandoned the churches because they were more attracted by the construction of a new society than by the prospect of sitting in a church pew.

Thus, it is not surprising that the church windows were closed to the outside world, which was seen as being dominated by hostile and dangerous forces. A large number of pastors abandoned the country, concluding that the hour of the church had passed and that God was no longer among our people.

However, at the same moment in Cuban history, a few pastors and laypersons were touched by the free wind of the Holy Spirit and developed a theological vision that drew us into the world. We wanted to demonstrate that the church was not necessarily reactionary, that Jesus was also a revolutionary in his day, as King had often said in his own country as he sought to rally the forces in the interest of civil rights.

Timidly, and with fear and trembling, we met to reread the Bible, seeking a word from God for the new situation. Fortunately, we found support, first in the global church. Because of our ecumenical connections, we had contact with Christians of great vision. They spoke to us of another way to be faithful disciples of Jesus as persons committed to the transformation of history and not just its repudiation. They helped us understand the parallels between the Marxist critique of religion and the protests of the prophets of Israel, who charged that religion had become a cult divorced from justice, with the Law and the Temple evolving into idols. This disturbing theme helped us become aware of the idolatry in the church itself.

Later, we pondered King's "Letter from Birmingham Jail" (1963), in which he confessed his disillusionment upon contemplating the beautiful architecture of the churches in the American South and asked, "What kind of God is worshipped by these people?"[2] Having exposed the truth that many Christian leaders in the American South were more interested in maintaining the status quo, and in a God who seemed oblivious to human suffering, Martin Luther King, Jr. helped us take a critical look at our own ecclesiastical institutions in Cuba.

We also were inspired by pivotal figures such as Dietrich Bonhoeffer, whose uncompromising stand against Nazi power resulted in his execution. Bonhoeffer inspired us to come to understand a God who works "on Mondays," in the midst of a secular and, in some senses, a post-Christian society.

At that time, we also learned about Camilo Torres, a priest who was very influential among university youth and who was killed while fighting as a guerrilla in Colombia. Torres, much like King, said that we could only call ourselves followers of Jesus when we practice effective love for the poor. With him, many other Christian youth took up the fight as guerrillas, creating a revolutionary mystique. The idea of nonviolent struggle was not very popular at the time.

All of these winds stirred the flame of a call to live faithfully within the large public policy issues of the day. However, evangelicals, nurtured in a tradition of commitment to the church and devotion to the Bible, felt emptiness and were not completely at ease. We needed to discover resources in our own tradition. It was here that Dr. King became a guiding light. King was a man of the church, a Baptist preacher with Bible in hand, defending the cause of the oppressed. Quickly, he became the hero of the new generations of Christians in Cuba. We were still unfamiliar with the breadth of his thought, but the little we did know inspired us to live a faith committed to the disinherited. King's witness—and through him an introduction

---

2. Martin Luther King, Jr., *Why We Can't Wait* (New York: New American Library, 1964) 91. King raised this question with greater intensity and clarity in Martin Luther King, Jr., "Who Is Their God?," *The Nation*, October 13, 1962, 209–10.

to Mohandas K. Gandhi—gave us concrete examples of active nonviolent resistance in the face of injustice. Most importantly, King's life provided a new way to read the story of Jesus.

We were beginning to chart a course between the polar options of a sectarian form of Marxism, on the one hand, and a rabidly reactive anticommunism on the other. We knew instinctively that our social vision needed to cohere with sound biblical insights. We felt the need to have the light of God's Word illuminate our way on this tumultuous journey.

In 1971, I was invited to speak at a meeting of Baptist youth in Havana, the theme of which was "The Validity of the Message of Christ for Our Action." This gathering of more than two hundred youth and young adults was exploring questions of Christian testimony in Cuban society. I prepared myself to present the biblical foundations for a responsible Christian presence in the world. I chose three key themes to shed light on this topic: the incarnation, as God's method for influencing the world; the kingdom of God, as the stimulus for announcing a better world; and the struggle against the principalities and powers, as the prophetic task in the face of evil. It was upon these three pillars that I sought to base the Christian commitment amidst the historic circumstances in which we were living. The influence of the thinking of Martin Luther King, Jr. was the main source for this reflection.

THE INCARNATION REVISITED AND REINTERPRETED

Understanding the basic meaning of the incarnation requires a major shift in our way of understanding the form in which God's mission in the world is realized. In Jesus' statement, "As the Father has sent me, so I send you" (John 20:21b), the word "as" indicates a specific model for accomplishing the mission of evangelization. This is none other than the incarnation, the presence in soul and body in the world, just as Jesus exemplified. We evangelical Christians have understood evangelization primarily as a kind of religious marketing, as if the gospel were just another product to offer, a piece of merchandise for sale. This is not to depreciate verbal proclamation, but only to affirm the content expressed in our actual lives.

To make this point, I said there are times when we need to vacate our pulpits, illustrating with a story of when King was invited to give a sermon in an ecumenical meeting of Christians in Geneva. Due to the exceptional demands of his work, he made the difficult decision to cancel his travel plans. Instead, he sent a recording of the speech, which was reverently received though the pulpit was empty. Since King was present in all of the important moments of the struggle, it was not possible for him to remain comfortably within the walls of the church.

Unfortunately, when all is said and done, there's usually a lot more said than done, which is what Jesus must have had in mind when he answered the disciples of John the Baptizer who were inquiring whether he was the awaited Messiah. Jesus did not respond with a great sermon or a philosophical argument. He simply answered, "Go back and report to John what you hear and see. The blind receive sight, the lame walk, the dead are raised, and good news is preached to the poor" (Matt 11:4–5).

To speak of the incarnation in the Cuba of the 1960s and 1970s meant the church needed actively to engage the pain of the world. Even if those committed to Communism did not clearly understand the motivation behind our actions, it was time to demonstrate the true nature of the church through deeds and not just with words.

One way we vividly demonstrated this conviction in our context was to volunteer in our nation's vital sugar cane harvest. Since the earliest days of colonial rule—first under the Spanish, then under the United States, and, in some respects, under the Soviets—Cuba's fertile soil has been exploited for the production of sugar. Though the situation has dramatically changed in the last generation, our economy was one big sugar factory. At the time, this was the principal resource we could offer in international trade. Given this reality, some of us in the church chose to show our solidarity by joining the throngs of people who left the cities to harvest cane.

It was arduous work. We lived in rustic shelters, rising with the dawn and working until dark. It was during one of these excursions that I heard the news of King's murder, and it prompted in me a strange mixture of both sadness and pride. Our presence as Christians in that setting caused suspicion among coworkers. They asked me if I had a "Nixon grant," the term used of those the government had sent to work in the country because they had put their names on a list of people who wished to leave Cuba.

Many churches, too, had a difficult time understanding this expression of Christian witness. I had to go before a congregational meeting to explain my reason for participating in the harvest. Happily, in the end they came to understand and support my action.

The path of the incarnation is marked by the love of God—"For God so loved the world" (John 3:16)—and also by the spirit of humility, which is the same attitude as that of Christ Jesus, "who, though he was in the form of God . . . , emptied himself, taking the form of a slave, being born in human likeness. And being found in human form, he humbled himself and became obedient to the point of death—even death on a cross" (Phil 2:6–7).

This path was not popular with those who thought that opening church doors and inviting people to come in was all that was necessary to fulfill the task that God has put in our hands. Dr. King's witness helped us understand that we are saved *for* the world, not *from* it.

Even more, some of us felt that spending a few days doing agricultural work was not enough. We believed it was too easy to stand in the pulpit and preach about sacrifice without having any other working obligations. This concern over the difference between pastors and laypersons led me to ask my congregation's permission to become a bi-vocational pastor. The church approved my unusual request.

Soon I found work with a farm produce distribution business, a job I held for fifteen years. This kept me closely involved with working-class people of humble means. I shared with them work that was exhausting but gratifying, since it dealt with distributing food. This bi-vocational experience of living in two different settings was not easy, and sometimes things became confused in my mind. There were days when at the beginning of a church service I found myself almost saying, "Dear fellow workers, let us pray to God," or in a labor union meeting saying, "Brothers and sisters in Christ."

Most Cuban pastors did not make this choice. In fact, there were more bi-vocational pastors prior to the revolution than after. There were times when I endured accusations from my peers of being a collaborator.

It is difficult to know the exact results of my bi-vocational choice. Only four of my work companions were baptized in the church. However, many coworkers began to see the church with new eyes. I never was an anonymous worker, but always something of a curiosity.

The importance of my dual career was less about my impact on the workplace as it was about the impact of the workplace on me. It kept me in touch with the reality of everyday life. It made me a better pastor. It resulted in important friendships I would otherwise have never had.

RETHINKING THE KINGDOM OF GOD AND UTOPIA

A second theme I presented to the Baptist youth gathering in 1971 was the importance of rediscovering that the central message of Jesus was not the salvation of the soul, but the announcement of the kingdom of God. The notion of "kingdom" points to a messianic hope, a new order that has burst upon the world and that Jesus made visible through miracles of healing and all of his redeeming work among those marginalized by economic and political institutions: the hungry, the orphaned, and abused women, among others. The coming of the kingdom means the unfolding of what Dr. King called "a revolution in values,"[3] resulting in a new social order based on the law of love. With great enthusiasm, we learned of the New York City pastor Walter Rauschenbusch, one of the founders of the Social Gospel movement, which placed the theme of the kingdom of God at the center of the Christian mission.

We linked this new perspective to the language of utopia, which does not yet exist but provides a horizon and calls us to the struggle for the age in which the prophets' dreams of justice and universal peace are fulfilled (see Isa 65:20–25). For us, *utopia* and *the kingdom of God* began to resonate; both expressed the hope of a better world, both provoked transformative actions.

We concluded that it was hypocritical to pray "thy kingdom come" while not being committed to the signs of the kingdom—life, justice, and peace. We were aware that neither socialism nor any other social system could be equated with the kingdom. However, we did see in laws that favor the poorest among us a sign, an indication that events were moving in the direction of the kingdom. The dream of a new world and the signs that this was coming in our midst motivated us to live with joy and hope, working so that the kingdom would also be visible among us.

There is no doubt that Martin Luther King, Jr. was this type of dreamer. He believed that another world of brotherhood, which he named the beloved community, could be a reality in our world. Although he at times noted that he himself might not live to see it, he could view it from afar, like Moses viewing the promised land without being able to walk its ground. Indeed, on the very eve of his assassination in 1968, speaking to a crowded church in Memphis, Tennessee, King, with great emotion, said,

---

3. Martin Luther King, Jr., *Where Do We Go from Here: Chaos or Community?* (Boston: Beacon, 1968) 186; James M. Washington, ed., *A Testament of Hope: The Essential Writings and Speeches of Martin Luther King, Jr.* (New York: HarperCollins, 1991) 631.

Like anybody, I would like to live a long life. Longevity has its place. But I'm not concerned about that now. I just want to do God's will. And He's allowed me to go up to the mountain. And I've looked over. And I've seen the promised land. I may not get there with you. But I want you to know tonight that we, as a people, will get to the promised land.[4]

This promised land was the dream about which King spoke so eloquently and forcefully in his well-known speech given during the 1963 March on Washington. This kind of dreaming is what we mean by utopia. He said, "I have a dream that one day . . ." This serves as an irrefutable proof of his perspective. It entails a deep dissatisfaction with the present and the confidence and hope of a better world. This is what sustains us in Cuba.

The following statement by King reveals this passionate utopian spirit in its fullness, with a particular focus on the global dimension:

Today as the world lies in darkness and in the hope
of the Good News, I boldly affirm my faith in the
future of humanity.
I reject the belief that in the current situation
human beings are not able to make a better world.
I firmly believe that, even in the midst of exploding bombs
and thundering cannons, there remains the hope of a shining tomorrow.
I dare to believe that one day all inhabitants of the world
will be able to have three meals a day for the life of their bodies,
education and culture for the health of their spirit,
equality and freedom for the life of their hearts.
I also believe that one day all of humanity
will acknowledge God as the source of their love. I believe that
saving and peaceful goodness will one day become law.
The wolf and the lamb will be able to lie down together, each
person will be able to sit under his fig tree, in his vineyard,
and no one will have reason to be fearful.
I firmly believe that we will triumph.[5]

In Cuba, we saw signs of that kingdom of God in everyday events. The 1960s and 1970s were a time of important changes in Latin America. Renewed by the Second Vatican Council, the Catholic Church awoke to

4. Quoted in Washington, *Testament of Hope*, 286.

5. King expressed this kind of indomitable hope in various ways and in many of his sermons, speeches, and writings. See King, *Where Do We Go from Here?*, 180–81; King, *Trumpet of Conscience*, 62 and 77–78; King, *Why We Can't Wait*, 22.

the problems of today's world. In 1968, Latin American bishops, meeting in Medellín, Colombia, proclaimed the necessity of the socioeconomic liberation of the continent. Thousands of organized local groups in Brazil and other countries searched the Scriptures for messages to address the oppression their people were experiencing. They found themselves rereading old texts with new eyes. Protestant and Catholic theologians created a new language, apart from academic abstractions and digressions. Theologian José Míguez Bonino of Argentina introduced the phrase "a faith in search of effectiveness."[6] Poor people became favored participants in theological dialogue as they searched for sense in a world without sense. European theological dialogue about secularism had little to contribute. On the political front, socialist candidate Salvador Allende won democratic elections in Chile with a program of sweeping changes.

We young Cuban pastors worked intensely to raise awareness in our churches because we believed that the Christian church has a place and a message to offer in times of change. We translated progressive position papers, distributed texts by Martin Luther King, Jr., and organized retreats focusing on Christian social responsibility. We sought to forge a new generation of Christians with social awareness. We were able to bring together a considerable number of workers, students, and young people in general.

But our optimism was premature, and we underestimated the power of the establishment. Firmly based social structures showed their ugly faces. The Ronald Reagan era began, and a meeting called by his advisors in Santa Fe produced a document that warned of the danger posed by liberation theology to the interests of the United States.[7] Repressive regimes focusing on "national security" began to appear. Military dictatorships savagely suppressed their people. Thirty thousand died or "disappeared" in Argentina alone. The sunset of hope had begun. The kingdom of God was not as close as we had thought. Other contradictions awaited us in the near future and pushed back even further the horizon of the utopia of which we dreamed. We still had much to learn.

In Cuba, the churches were moving at an agonizingly slow pace toward social awareness. Rumors circulated that our group of young pastors were Communist fellow travelers and that we were ecumenical heretics who opposed everyone who lacked a social commitment. Cuban Baptist

---

6. *"La fe en busca de eficacia"* (1968).

7. See Paul Farmer, *Pathologies of Power: Health, Human Rights, and the New War on the Poor* (Berkeley: University of California Press, 2003) 299 n. 6.

organizations excluded us from programs, and internecine fighting within these groups became more and more bitter. There was no dialogue, only the exclusion of anyone who thought differently.

At this point, it was becoming clear that the concept of the kingdom of God carried with it some elements that distinguished it from human utopias. The cross and the resurrection, as Dr. King so often said,[8] highlighted a path of suffering, self-denial, and momentary defeat that in truth is no more than the darkness before the splendor of the resurrection dawn.

The kingdom of God does not guarantee a steady, upward movement. There are failures, steps backward, and a cross of infinite pain that must be taken up. As Martin Luther King taught with his very life, opposing violence is a risky venture. King's followers walked this path with great difficulty, practicing a reflection and spiritual meditation that gave them the capacity to suffer violence without inflicting it. For Christians, the resurrection is the assurance that the kingdom is not totally annihilated. Life surges up with more power than death. As a Latin American poet has written, "All the flowers can be cut off, but no one can stop the coming spring."

A second distinguishing element in the good news of the kingdom of God is that Christian hope provides a unique perspective in a time of apparent stagnation. This hope does not offer a refuge for those who have failed. Rather, it is an ointment that opens the eyes to other realities, to small things that seem insignificant but that contain the promise of life.

Jesus spoke of a mustard seed, of the hidden treasure, of the children, and of the leaven hidden in the dough. The kingdom breaks out among us in small, simple things. It is not necessary that there be a seizure of political power; there is another power that rises up from below, from the simplest links of society, in the family and in the community. That is where ethical values are created—the values that fertilize the soil for the building of a better world. These are lessons that were missed by the revolutionaries who saw their dreams of a more just society frustrated and deferred.

ON THE PRINCIPALITIES AND POWERS

These struggles made us ask ourselves: against whom are we fighting? What is preventing the world from being transformed and our own churches from being renewed? Why are social structures so resistant to a change that would benefit the majority? It seemed as if we were swimming against

8. Washington, *Testament of Hope*, 42.

a current that was much stronger than we were and that was pulling us further and further from the kingdom.

Orthodox Marxism attempts to give an answer, teaching that society is conditioned by its economic struggles. Marxism argues that political power is built on these economic structures, which give rise to ideologies and produce a culture. So when control of the economy changes hands, the superstructure changes, almost automatically. A socialist society that takes ownership of the means of production creates the conditions for satisfying the material needs of its members. This results in a new culture and a new ideology.

However, things are not quite so simple. Human beings are more than the sum of their material needs. In addition, the so-called superstructure enjoys a certain amount of independence. Classical Marxism did not take into account what the Italian thinker Antonio Gramsci later called the existence of a hegemonic power that enjoys relative independence from political and economic power. This power expresses itself through the institutions of the civil society, such as the customs and traditions of the people. This perspective takes into account the influence of traditional culture, religion, and customs. This hegemonic power serves as a counterweight to political power and in the long run can totally debilitate it. This thinking allows us to understand that part of the success of the civil rights movement led by King is attributable not only to the justice of its demands, but also to the fact that it was rooted in the traditions of the black church.

Another factor contradicting classical Marxist theory is the undeniable fact that human desires sometimes count for more than needs. Thus, it is not surprising to see those living in barely habitable dwellings in a very poor country using the latest model of television and a cellular phone. For them, there seems to be no relationship between wants and needs. It would be interesting to research the degree of influence the power of consumerism had in the crumbling of the socialist camp.

All of this brings us to the biblical categories of "principalities and powers," which help us understand the powers that dominate society and even our own churches. These powers can be of great blessing, as was the case in the traditions of black churches. On the other hand, they may include negative influences—political and religious fanaticism and xenophobia, for example.

Those of us in Cuba were faced with the challenge of how to find a biblical basis for the existence of the oppressive realities that go beyond exclusively individual limitations and that are difficult to pinpoint. We saw how Martin Luther King, Jr. understood and faced the racism that was part of the laws and traditions of the South and that was reflected in the thinking of many sincere Christians—and even in the passivity exhibited by some of his own people.

Fortunately, the book *These Rebellious Powers* (1966), by Albert H. van den Heuvel, provided us with an answer. We discovered that the words, "principalities and powers," mentioned so often in the New Testament, form a conceptual foundation on which we can base our understanding of mental structures, traditions, prejudices, and unjust laws. In other words, principalities and powers can be used to refer to everything that conditions the lives of people and that acts as a net in which people become trapped. Thus, the term "principalities and powers" came to play a key role in our thinking. Van den Heuvel writes, "When powers isolate, bind, sow enmity, create loneliness, demand idolatry, and produce selfishness, conservatism and traditionalism, it is time to remember the invitation of the Messiah to join with Him in throwing these powers from their thrones."[9]

Van den Heuvel argues that in his Letter to the Colossians, Paul connects this idea of powers to the Jewish religious traditions that restrict freedom. Thus, it is appropriate to apply the categories of principalities and powers to all structures, ideologies, traditions, and other parts of society that become oppressive. Later, theologian Walter Wink explored this theme in depth in his well-known *Powers* trilogy.

Certainly, the vision of Ephesians 6:12 nurtured Dr. King's spirit as he clarified the structural dimensions of the sins of racism and segregation: "For we wrestle not against flesh and blood, but against principalities, against powers, against the rulers of the darkness of this world . . ."

While I am not certain if Martin Luther King, Jr. used these same biblical arguments in referring to his struggle, I am convinced that he handled the racial conflict from this perspective and with the belief that one must oppose injustice without dehumanizing the perpetrators.[10] From this perspective, a racist is the victim of powers that have blinded him, and therefore the racist deserves the compassion that could help him redeem himself from his sin. In the methods of Gandhi, King also found the way to

---

9. Albert H. van den Heuvel, *These Rebellious Powers* (London: SCM, 1966).

10. See Martin Luther King, Jr., *Stride Toward Freedom: The Montgomery Story* (New York: Harper & Row, 1958) 102–3.

educate the masses in the awareness that it is love, rather than hate, which motivates all of their sacrifices.[11]

We in Latin America are familiar with ethnic and racial prejudices, which attribute the crushing poverty of indigenous peoples and blacks to supposed flaws in their character and a lack of discipline. We are convinced, however, that this poverty was brought about by the oppression of the powerful, which has created institutional mechanisms that perpetuate injustice. Poverty is not a divine punishment; nor is it due to a lack of will on the part of the poor. Instead, it is due to those structures that are the modern principalities and powers. The most painful aspect of this reality is that a feeling of inferiority has been internalized by the poor. As a result, the poor are not able to free themselves from fatalism and dependency on their supposed protectors, who, while not giving them a decent life, at least guarantee them a certain amount of security.

TWO TOOLS FOR THE OPPRESSED IN LATIN AMERICA

In the face of these realities, two tools have come to the aid of the oppressed people of Latin America. We mention them because in some way they will have an impact on the Cuban situation. One is popular education, created by the Brazilian Paulo Freire. This consists of nothing more than empowering the poor to uncover the true reasons for their poverty. The poor then becomes the main players, active subjects who have something to say and who have developed a critical awareness of reality. Popular education creates spaces for horizontal dialogue, which is participative and inclusive. It raises self-esteem and produces a commitment to make necessary changes. It is a very valuable tool against fatalism, authoritarianism, and the principalities and powers. Dr. King understood this as well as anyone in his time, and this is why he included education—along with religion and nonviolent direct action—among the approaches essential for overcoming oppression.[12]

The second tool, liberation theology, introduces a new method for developing theology. It does not begin with what theologians or learned scholars said in the past; instead, it consists of a dialogue with the subjects

---

11. Washington, *Testament of Hope*, 12–20. Also see King's Palm Sunday sermon on Mohandas K. Gandhi, in Clayborne Carson et al., eds., *The Papers of Martin Luther King, Jr.*, vol. 5, *Threshold of a New Decade, January 1959–December 1960* (Berkeley: University of California Press, 2005) 145–57.

12. King, *Stride Toward Freedom*, 33–34.

of history, namely, people. Over time, theology has developed through conversations among those in the community of faith and the surrounding culture, and the dominant thought and philosophy in the academy. This has been an exchange of ideas, involving both give and take. Theological development has been marked by evolving concepts with a philosophical emphasis and has become primarily an academic exercise involving a small number of specialists. In the process, it has lost its evangelical and prophetic edge.

Latin American theology does not ignore the heritage achieved through years of reflection and theoretical development, but it has forged a new focus, based on real life and the oppressive circumstances being lived by a majority of poor people. Indeed, the central affirmation of this theology is the assertion that the God of Scripture is One who listens and responds to the cries of slaves. In Latin American theology, faith concepts are not questioned by illustrious thinkers, but by the poor, who pose the great questions of justice and the love of God. Latin American theology begins with the practice of liberation. Therefore, by its very nature it critiques all theological reflection that contributes to the perpetuation of a situation of suffering and oppression.

The first liberation theologians on our continent were the Dominican friars, headed by Pedro de Córdoba and Antonio de Montesinos, who used the pulpit of a parish on the island of Hispaniola to denounce the crimes and abuses that the Spanish *conquistadores* were committing in indigenous communities. From that point, there began a spring of prophetic voices, headed by Fray Bartolomé de las Casas, which gave life to a form of speaking of God that was different from the traditional because it represented the voice of the oppressed.

So in this sense other liberation theologies have arisen in the world. In one way or another, they all position themselves alongside those who have suffered discrimination or who have been marginalized. All have an element of the prophetic denunciation of all ideologies that justify and contribute to the persistence of oppression. Thus, it is possible to speak of a feminist theology, which unmasks the machismo hidden in language, customs, and religion. Nor can we fail to mention black theology, which has made a major contribution to the unraveling of the enormous load of racism in Western culture and has put forth a theology that dignifies and values the contributions of black culture and traditions.

Though well educated, holding a doctorate in theology, Martin Luther King, Jr. was not an academic theologian in the traditional sense. His life was not connected to a university classroom. However, to read his writings is to plunge into the depths of liberating thought. King's way of thinking moves awareness in the direction of transforming human beings focused on themselves into instruments of peace and into the builders of a new world. So here in Cuba, we see King as being in the best tradition of authentic liberation theology. And, like Antonio de Valdivieso, Monseñor Romero, and many other Latin Americans whose commitment was to read history "from below," King sealed his commitment to the poor with his own blood.

MARTIN LUTHER KING, JR. AND TRANSFORMATIONS IN CUBA TODAY

Now we address the most current aspects of the influence of Martin Luther King, Jr. in Cuba today. To do so, it is necessary to acknowledge that because of our long-term economic ties to Eastern Europe, the events that occurred there in 1989, with the fall of the Berlin Wall and all that followed, still have a profound impact on our society today. Although our country had the capacity to sustain itself and survive (against the experts' dire predictions), the magnitude of that economic disaster was so great that one can compare it to an earthquake that destroys 80 percent of the productive capacity of the country.

As an example, prior to 1989, sugar was produced by a well-developed agricultural system with advanced equipment used on state farms and cooperatives and was sold at guaranteed, protected prices. After 1989, production fell from 7.5 million tons to only 1.5 million tons. The decline in sugar production resulted from a range of factors, among which was the U.S. embargo and the fact that Eastern European nations were no longer buying sugar at guaranteed, protected prices.

The country was left bankrupt, with the United States embargo tightening to the point where the American administration even went after Cuban reserves in U.S. dollars held by foreign banks. In fact, Swiss banks were fined for holding Cuban funds in U.S. dollars. For Cubans, the horizon that had been utopian was reduced to a struggle for personal and family survival.

Up to that time, Cuban socialism had guaranteed a modest standard of living. In 1989, the rationing of basic items allowed some easing of the crisis, but in the 1990s the problem of food, transportation, and medicine became the top daily priority. The situation was captured in the popular saying *"No es facil!"* ("It isn't easy!"). This phrase was repeated thousands of times and became the trademark of the new situation.

Words of Saint Paul also became true in that difficult time: "But we have this treasure in clay jars, so that it may be made clear that this extraordinary power belongs to God and does not come from us. We are afflicted in every way, but not crushed; perplexed, but not driven to despair; persecuted, but not forsaken; struck down, but not destroyed" (2 Cor 4:7–9).

A new spirituality of resistance challenged pastors and theologians to persevere in standing with the suffering, desperate Cuban people. We were challenged to resist in the face of all that seemed hopeless, without knowing where we were headed; to resist the frustration of those who saw no way out, except to leave the island; and to resist those who feared an outbreak of social chaos and saw no solution aside from the strengthening of repressive measures.

There was very little international support for us. Lucius Walker, a prophet and follower of Martin Luther King, Jr., stepped up from the very country that was blockading Cuba.[13] Walker, the director of the Interreligious Foundation for Community Organization (IFCO) in New York, organized the first Pastors for Peace Caravan at the beginning of the 1990s. His goal was to challenge the U.S. blockade by taking to Cuba humanitarian supplies donated by the North American people. Donations were gathered in 120 cities, first in the United States and later in Canada. This help was directed to Cuban schools, hospitals, and churches. Pastors for Peace defied U.S. law, crossing the U.S.-Mexican border with buses loaded with supplies destined for Cuba.

Once, a bus carrying donations for the Martin Luther King, Jr. Center in Havana, inaugurated in April 1987, was detained. Members of the caravan went on a hunger strike for many days despite extremely high summer temperatures. They were supported by Havana pastors, who began another hunger strike in front of the U.S. Interests Section on the island. Finally, the bus was released and Havana residents joyfully welcomed the caravan members.

---

13. Walker died of a heart attack at age eighty as this article was being written. Besides his work with IFCO and Pastors for Peace, Walker was pastor of Salvation Baptist Church in Brooklyn, New York.

The example of Dr. King no doubt inspired the Pastors for Peace in their peaceful disobedience of unjust laws. These caravans have been repeated every year. By 2010, a total of twenty-one caravans have reached Cuba. They have made a difference in the image our people have of what it means to be a pastor. I have experienced this change in the way I am treated in Cuban institutions. All I need to say is that I am a pastor and I am received and listened to with a great deal of respect.

The men and women of the Pastors for Peace caravans risked jail and thousands of dollars in fines for violating the embargo laws. It distresses us that the great press establishment of the United States has not given coverage to these heroes, who have offered such a powerful testimony of loving solidarity and of bravery in confronting unjust laws. Martin Luther King, Jr. would feel proud in the company of the men and women who continue walking the path that he walked.

THE MARTIN LUTHER KING, JR. MEMORIAL CENTER IN HAVANA

Ebenezer Baptist Church, located in the Marianao municipality of Havana, founded the Martin Luther King, Jr. Memorial Center. Since its beginning as a modest institution in the shadow of the church, it has grown and expanded its influence beyond normal church boundaries. Because it rose up to meet the difficult times through which the country was passing, it presently enjoys national prestige and recognition. But we will let the Center speak for itself:

> The Martin Luther King Memorial Center is a macro-ecumenical organization of Christian inspiration. Based among the Cuban people and their churches, it contributes in a prophetic manner to the solidarity of the people and to their aware, organized, and critical participation, devoted to the defense of a fulfilled life for everyone and the respect for natural rights. This contribution is made from the perspective of popular education and a theology which is of the people, critical, liberating, and contextualized.[14]

A project of the Baptist church and the Cuban Ecumenical Council, the King Center opened with the help of a U.S. delegation that included Bernard Lafayette and other religious leaders who stood with King in the

14. Natalia Cruz, "A Bridge between U.S. and Cuban People," *People's Daily World*, May 6, 1987, 5A.

civil rights movement.[15] The Center has a clear focus on training, which is oriented not just toward churches, but also toward society generally. This training is designed to develop new attitudes toward conscious participation in public life, with the broad goal of the defense of life and of nature. The Center's macro-ecumenical character allows for an openness to the religious rainbow of Cuban society, which includes religions of African origins. These religions are active not only among the black population but also extend into many other sectors of Cuban society. This inclusive perspective is faithful to the inspiration of Dr. King, who welcomed those who joined the struggle, whether Jews or Muslims or simply people of conscience.

One of the basic contributions made by the Center is popular education. It is important to clarify that, although the King Center is not the only institution that promotes popular education, in our judgment it is training the largest number of people from all sectors of Cuban society, without excluding anyone. The courses that train popular educators have reached out to hundreds of activists throughout the country. This has created a network of persons who remain in contact and have organized themselves and hold national meetings in which feedback is provided by participants coming from a diversity of local experiences. It is also important to emphasize that popular education is central to the Center's mission, which keeps alive a spirit of self-criticism, of a horizontal relationship among its members, and of a model of democratic participation by all of its workers.

This contribution is very significant for us, since one of our social problems is the excessive state centralization of social organization. This is something we have inherited from the "real socialism" of Eastern Europe. This phenomenon confuses socialism with state control and gives rise to the bureaucratic and authoritarian methods that attempt to direct all social activities. It also has created a citizenry that is obedient and passive, lacks creativity, and faithfully follows the directions that come down from "above." This results in a participation in decision-making that is very mechanical and readily achieves artificial unanimity.

To this must be added the fear of the destabilization of our society, fostered by the United States. This provokes a defensive reaction from Cuban authorities when confronted with opinions different from the official position.

This contribution of popular education by the King Center certainly constitutes a movement from the ground up, attempting to create a culture

15. Ibid.

of authentically democratic participation by all sectors of the society. It does not receive any official governmental support or recognition. However, more and more leaders from various levels of government are becoming aware of the importance of popular education. In my opinion, this is one of the more interesting developments in Cuban society today. Within it lies a powerful germ of transformation.

The King Center's other hallmark is its commitment to a popular theology that is critical, liberating, and contextualized. This reflects the influence of Latin America's liberation theology. The provision of theological education is made together with the Latin American Biblical University of Costa Rica. Numerous theologians make periodic presentations at the King Center, featuring short-term courses followed by home study by each participant.

Since this second contribution of the King Center is linked directly to Cuban churches,[16] it is important to point out that in the last twenty years Cuban churches have experienced a staggering growth, with their memberships multiplying three or four times. Managing this rapid growth has been challenging, particularly in the adequate preparation of pastoral leaders. More than a few end up as pastors shortly after their coming to faith. This is especially true among the Pentecostal churches. In addition, the economic crisis has allowed young leaders to be easily influenced by dependency upon agencies and persons who donate money from abroad, primarily from the United States, and who import inappropriate Christian education traditions. In most cases, such foreign influences have produced sectarian divisions, an indifference to social participation, and disrespectful proselytizing.

The impact of the King Center's programs of popular theology on Christianity in Cuba is still modest. Clearly, though, it is one of the educational projects with the greatest promise in the training of pastors and laypersons in our country.

Another contribution of the King Center is in the area communications. With a broad program of publications, especially through its prestigious magazine, *Caminos*, the Center does justice to Cuban authors from the field of sociology as well as to theologians and biblical scholars. In addition, the publishing house *Caminos* has published a considerable number of works by Cuban authors.

16. For one of the best treatments of the origin and significance of the King Center in Havanna, see ibid.

A VISION FOR THE TWENTY-FIRST CENTURY

Thus far in our Cuban pilgrimage, the inspiration of Martin Luther King, Jr. has nurtured our vision and given us strength to confront difficult situations. Today, we want to move ahead with the same confidence as we seek to embrace the future. Hope is not the same thing as optimism. Hope allows us to face honestly the disquieting questions in our country's life. The revolutionary romanticism of the 1960s and 1970s, when we proudly proclaimed "Cuba: The First Free Territory of the Americas," no longer inspires confidence.

We urgently need to acknowledge the devastating impact on our life caused by the collapse of socialist governments elsewhere, especially the colonial legacy of our dependence on the Soviet Union. On the other hand, time has passed and a new generation has arisen. Earlier generations have given way, slowly but surely, to the coming of later generations, each with its own anxieties and new vision. Despite the fact that the power structures are the same and the heroic and defensive rhetoric is unchanged, the underlying pattern of beliefs that Gramsci called a "hegemony" is never more evident.

Today, nationalist fervor has cooled. Outbursts of patriotic pride are greeted with suspicion. Such enthusiasts are suspected of being opportunistic, or serving as government functionaries, or are persons of privilege insulated from the difficult times and shortages of the common people.

However, the majority of our citizens are not disenchanted. The love of Cuba throbs in our very beings. In the event that we would have to face aggression from abroad, thousands upon thousands of arms would be raised to defend our homeland. In addition, melancholy and sadness are not a part of the Cuban character. Our African roots give us precisely the energy and ability to find humor and entertainment in the midst of the worst of situations.

What is true is that the utopian horizon, the dream of a new society, has been reduced until it occupies only a small space in daily life. The struggle for survival has eroded the vision of the future. The horizon of need is more immediate and rudimentary. Adequate housing, the care and well-being of our children, meaningful work—these are what occupy us more than before. Outright hunger does not afflict a significant portion of our citizens, as in many industrialized nations, but we live on a very thin margin. Scarcity takes its toll, diminishing our expectations, discouraging participation in the larger life of our communities.

In this situation, inequalities in standards of living have arisen, something we were not accustomed to in earlier decades. The necessary opening to international tourism, the arrival of foreign corporations, and the receipt of money from family members living abroad have produced a shocking differentiation in levels of consumption. There are beautiful stores where goods can only be purchased with a type of currency that is not the same in which salaries are paid. We know heroes and veterans of wars of liberation who live in precarious conditions, while their neighbors make a show of their wealth. So in this contradictory life today, one might ask, has utopia disappeared completely from the hearts of the Cubans? No, it has not. Let me illustrate with a story.

In 2006, I traveled from Caracas to Havana on a flight I will never forget. The passengers around me were people who had never flown before. The majority were elderly, of humble origins, with skin tanned by the sun. Some had indigenous features. They were bound for Cuba as part of a program called Operation Miracle, which would enable doctors to operate on the eyes of thousands of people from the most humble levels of society. In Cuba, operating rooms were prepared and hotels were waiting. Medical personnel would work around the clock so that in a matter of months hundreds of thousands of poor people would regain their sight. As I sat on the plane, I pondered on how much matters were different. Today, change is not coming through guerillas seizing power. Today, the provision of health is the great task—the sending abroad of life for the poor.

This is something that does not capture the attention of the world media: the contributions of an army of thirty thousand Cuban doctors and nurses giving service in places where others do not go—in jungle and mountain hamlets. It is not surprising that when the recent earthquake devastated Haiti, 150 Cuban doctors were already there serving that impoverished country. As I write, a search for persons with physical and mental challenges is being conducted throughout the countryside and towns of various countries in Latin America. Once located, these people will be offered medical and technical assistance to improve their quality of life. These brigades of Cuban personnel work in the most remote places. It truly is impressive.

I have known these doctors, who work in ways similar to medical missionaries in the most inhospitable places, risking their lives to bring health. They do receive a modest economic benefit, but the sacrifices they are making cannot be compensated with money. In our own country of Cuba, there is much human wealth in the thousands of professionals who serve with true selflessness, without receiving sufficient compensation for their efforts. They are true signs of the kingdom, the light of utopia that does not go out.

Of course, this brief account does not cover the full spectrum of the Cuban reality, with all its lights and shadows. So it is understandable how we who live on the island find ourselves frequently caught in the tension between uncertainly and faith, seeking a new language that will help us not to lose our direction but rather to follow in the footsteps of Martin Luther King, Jr.

TOWARD A THEOLOGICAL INQUIRY

I have spoken of how, in the early days of the revolution, theology derived from biblical teachings regarding the kingdom of God, the incarnation, and the principalities and powers served to orient our mission as the church in a new context. In the same way, the inspiration of the example of Martin Luther King gave us the strength for our social commitment. Despite the pressure of urgent pastoral and social duties that did not leave much time for theoretical reflection, those first two decades were fertile ones for theological creativity. Profound articles and essays appeared in modest ecumenical publications, often mimeographed. Even with all the limitations, it was the first time that authentic Cuban theological reflections had come to light. One of the best writers is theologian and pastor Sergio Arce Martínez. We remember gratefully his essay, "The Mission of the Church in a Socialist Society," which shed great light on our social practice.[17]

However, the same cannot be said of the present day. I feel as if we are walking through an arid desert, without fresh thinking relevant to our situation. In more progressive ecumenical circles there is too much stale repetition of old promises and triumphalist claims that have grown hollow. In ignoring the stress of our condition, we have little that is meaningful to say to our people. We have ceased being prophets because we are not grounded in our own reality.

If we consider theology to be a faith dialogue with people in the historical context in which we have been called to live, it behooves us as theologians to seek a more intimate encounter with lived experience, free from all propaganda and apologetics. We must listen to the simple people,

17. Also his *The Church and Socialism: Reflections from a Cuban Context* (New York: CIRCUS, 1985).

to the humble people. We must be disposed to dialogue with our hearts and minds fully open.

The most creative truth-tellers in our culture are artists, poets, dramatists, and cinematographers. Vital theology must be done in conversation with such people. They survey reality, put their ears to the ground, and listen to silent shouts. Their work becomes a reflection of an era. Any visitor coming from another country who gets close to our current literature will find that it is a far cry from that of earlier times. No longer does it parrot past ideologies. Such artists are listening to both the confusion and the affirmations being made, the fears and the hopes. We need to listen with them.

Our filmmakers, in particular, are reaching a larger audience and addressing important public questions of purpose and meaning. The new films reflect the contradictions, frustrations, and lack of hope, as well as the quiet heroism, joys, and dreams of a people who have been called upon to live through a singular historic experience. In some cases, these films have become a true catharsis by which the public sees itself portrayed. In other cases, these films have served as a probe, making people uncomfortable and causing them to think.

For instance, the film *Suite Havana* (2008), directed by Fernando Pérez, moves people deeply as it details the daily lives of various average individuals as they go about their daily business with one thing in common: the protagonists were motivated by their own specific, but different, dreams. These dreams were no longer those of a great utopian society, but were nonetheless beautiful and legitimate.

The primary job of Cuban theology today is to spend less time speaking, and more time listening to everything that this complex time in our history has to say. It does not help to repeat old slogans and tired analysis from the good old days, whatever days they may have been. As the Peruvian theologian Gustavo Gutiérrez says so well, we must learn again to "drink from our own wells."[18] The ancient, urgent questions of our Scripture and tradition must be raised anew among the living, not simply asserted from the past. Doing so will require large doses of evangelical humility and reverent silence.

---

18. Gustavo Gutiérrez, *We Drink from Our Own Wells: The Spiritual Journey of a People*, trans Matthew J. O'Connell (Maryknoll, NY: Orbis, 1983).

SOME GUIDEPOSTS TO FOLLOW

A popular reading of the Bible, an offspring of popular education, is an essential methodology for our journey, in the way that encourages the free expression of people's insights. In this process, there is no specific interpretation of the Bible enforced by the pastor or teacher. Instead, the reading is done from the perspectives of the real lives of the participants. Even when aided by the most serious of exegetical tools, the text is read from personal experience, from the moving of God in our present experience. In this way, the Scripture again becomes "living water," refreshed daily from the lived experience of longing for God's righteousness. The result is not necessarily predictable. The Spirit liberates the illuminating and relevant message.

The Martin Luther King, Jr., Memorial Center is developing a program of the popular reading of the Bible, and this is being put into practice in numerous communities, with very encouraging results. I should clarify that this method of Bible study is not done at the mercy of capricious interpretations of Scripture. The model used is faithful to the best tradition in hermeneutics. Popular Bible reading is a communal activity in which the reading interprets reality and reality reinterprets the meaning of the Scripture.

The limitation of this method is that it is difficult to systematize the results to produce consensus conclusions. However, there is no doubt that the ideas produced by such a reading of the primary material of Scripture produces valuable ingredients for later theoretical formulation. Perhaps the most important theological contribution is the connection it establishes between the utopia of the kingdom and the individual life experience within communities of faith. Think of the image of a great net that is knotted at thousands of tiny points where its threads cross. These knots represent the realizations of many individual dreams. There is no need to divorce personal and familial aspirations of happiness from the kingdom. In Jesus we find that there is a link between the small and the great, between the insignificant seed and the powerful tree.

A second guidepost for us is the example of Martin Luther King, Jr., whose civil disobedience movement began in a meeting in a church in Montgomery, Alabama. The U.S. civil rights movement, surely among the greatest social movements of the twentieth century, was rooted in the church. Recognizing the distance that separates Cubans from the experiences of the black church in the American South, and without any messianic pretensions, I nevertheless affirm that the churches of Cuba have an important contribution to make to society. Local Christian communities and small prayer and Bible study groups are privileged spaces where the basic humanity of each participant can be affirmed. Ecumenical theologian J. H. Oldham wrote that

> The first indispensable task is to restore substance to the human person. . . . There is no way to restore substance and depth to [human life] except by living. . . . Human living is living in relations with other persons and can acquire meaning and depth only in those relations. Since the number of persons with whom an individual can have direct and close relations is limited, the art of social living has to be learned and practiced in small groups, of which the family is the chief. . . . There is nothing greater that the church can do for society than to be a center in which small groups of people are together entering into the experience of renewal and giving each other mutual support in Christian living in secular spheres.[19]

Our country's entrance into the worst of the economic crisis coincided with the arrival at our churches of waves of people seeking help and a message of hope. Churches became centers of help, offering not only a word of encouragement but also, to the extent of their means, medicine and food. Many people were victims of depression and became disoriented and perplexed in the face of a situation that was totally beyond their power to control. For the generations without any exposure to religion, it was a great discovery to find in the communities of faith an atmosphere of warm fellowship and genuine community. Those families divided as a result of some members emigrating from Cuba found a new family and were given love and care.

One of the traditional moments in the Christian liturgy is passing the peace. In Cuban churches, this is a meaningful expression of affection. Everyone exchanges warm embraces, resulting in a bit of chaos in the middle of the service. But this moment is much appreciated because the love of family is being expressed spontaneously. Another significant and unscripted ritual is the sharing of thanksgiving and prayer requests, allowing anyone present to mention joys or sorrows, triumphs or failures. This is how we live into the Apostle Paul's instruction to "rejoice with those who rejoice, weep with those who weep" (Rom 12:15).

19. J. H. Oldham, "A Responsible Society," in *The Church and the Disorder of Society* (New York: Harper 1948) 126.

Another contribution of the churches comes in the realm of ethics. The Cuban economic crisis resulted in a crisis in values. When unable to secure what was needed, some resorted to illicit strategies, including pilfering items from places of employment, prostitution, and the black market. Alcohol consumption rose significantly, as did the frequency of divorce and other social problems. Here the churches assumed greater relevance as agents affirming positive values. Indeed, the Cuban government itself acknowledges this contribution. There is of course a dark side to the church's growth, particularly the spread of "prosperity theology," which identifies material wealth as divine blessing and poverty as judgment. This is a curse everywhere market values infect the church's faith.

Overall, the positives outweigh the negatives. Churches in Cuba are increasingly important sources of community and sustenance, meaning and mediation.

FROM MYSTICISM TO SPIRITUALITY

Martin Luther King, Jr. certainly would not be completely satisfied with churches that limit themselves to offering support to those who come to them and that, in the end, are focused on themselves in competition with other churches.[20] There is no doubt that in these times the spirit of cooperation between the various communions has suffered. The ecumenical movement suffers from anemia. Despite the presence of Protestant churches in considerable numbers, this lack of unity has resulted in their having no prophetic voice in the larger society. As such, we Protestants mirror the world's disunity and lack the capacity for dialogue and the maturity to accept diversity.

The clarity of our witness has suffered, making it difficult for us to resist the principalities and powers. In a society like ours, which is attempting a more democratic and human socialism, the church should be able to offer a significant contribution. Sadly, however, there is little desire for a prophetic role. Our evangelical vocation has been reduced to religious marketing for institutional growth, a problem that King said so often haunts the church.[21]

20. See King's sermon "Cooperative Competition, Noble Competition," in Clayborne Carson et al., eds., *The Papers of Martin Luther King, Jr.,* vol. 6, *Advocate of the Social Gospel, September 1948–March 1963* (Berkeley: University of California Press, 2007) 583.

21. Martin Luther King, Jr., "Transformed Nonconformist," unpublished version of

What then is the illness that is paralyzing Protestant Cuban churches? Where are we falling short? It may be surprising for one like myself—a lifelong activist and promoter of social conscience—to assert that the problem arises from a poverty of authentic spirituality. Each day I am more convinced that the lack of spirituality is what cripples our mission and our calling not just to the church but to the larger culture. Let me explain by making an artificial distinction between mysticism and spirituality.

In 1980, my wife and I were collaborating with the Baptist Seminary in Nicaragua, living in the euphoric times following the Sandinista Revolution that had defeated the cruel Somoza dictatorship. The great majority of Nicaraguans adored their new national leaders, who were for the most part young and who enjoyed great prestige. They were brave men and women who risked their lives fighting in the mountains against a powerful army. Some had been tortured, while others had given up comfortable lives for the sake of a new society. They were an example of the purest revolutionary mysticism. They sacrificed their all on the altar of a better world. This mysticism placed the heroes above the common people, as if they were higher beings.

But ten years in power were enough to corrupt, with a few honorable exceptions. The Sandinistas lost the 1990 election and an unheard of thing happened—what Nicaraguans called the "piñata phenomenon." Many of these revered leaders, like children grabbing the candy falling out of a birthday piñata, appropriated for themselves everything they could before giving up power. Sometime later while visiting Nicaragua, I was told that some of those former guerilla commanders were now millionaires. What had happened to their values? The Somoza regime had been overthrown, but its spirit had been resurrected.

Of course, heroes are not really superior to the rest of humanity. They are also vulnerable to temptations, and nothing seduces more than power and wealth, as Dr. King so often noted. This is, I believe, how the account of the temptations of Jesus at the beginning of His ministry should be read. It was not enough for Him to receive the anointing for the messianic task. It was necessary to go through a process of self-emptying and purification, rejecting idols and despising the power and grandeur of this world.

---

sermon, Ebenezer Baptist Church, Atlanta, Georgia (January 16, 1966) 4–5 (housed at the library and Archives of the Martin Luther King, Jr. Center for Nonviolent Social Change, Inc.); Martin Luther King, Jr., *Strength to Love* (Philadelphia: Fortress, 1981) 59.

This, too, was part of Martin Luther King, Jr.'s preparation. The disciplines of humility and sacrifice are essential to good leadership and are the doorway to authentic spirituality. Near the end of his life, in a sermon at his own church, Ebenezer Baptist, King reflected on how he wanted to be remembered; his words underscore my point:

> If any of you are around when I have to meet my day, I don't want a long funeral. And if you get somebody to deliver the eulogy, tell them not to talk too long. . . . [Just have them say] that I was a drum major for justice; say that I was a drum major for peace. And all of the other [accomplishments] will not matter. . . . I won't have any money to leave behind. I just want to leave a committed life behind.[22]

The courage to go unrecognized, save in the memory of God, also marked José Martí, Cuba's national hero. Near his death at the age of forty-two, Martí wrote, "I am ready to disappear." He knew he wasn't irreplaceable. He had no desire for reverence. This is, in fact, why he is so dearly remembered for a life of exceptional spirituality, reflected in his personal relations and his capacity for loving even his own enemies.

Nelson Mandela is another person who displays the spirituality of humility and sacrifice. He emerged from twenty-seven years in prison to lead his country through the depths of the hatred that had grown during the decades of apartheid. Then, after one term as president, he refused to run for reelection, entering private life without other ambitions. He, too, found in Dr. King a model and source of inspiration.

In *Contemplation in a World of Action,* Thomas Merton maintained that nonviolence must not simply be a practice in the world but also a discipline of the soul. "He who intends to act and do things for others or for the world without deeply studying who he is, and what is liberty, integrity, and the ability to love," Merton contended, "will not have anything to communicate to others, except the contagion of his own obsessions, his aggressiveness, his egocentric ambitions, and his doctrinaire prejudices."[23]

To paraphrase Paul's well-known hymn to love to the church at Corinth (1 Cor 13:1–13), we could say that "mysticism has us to share goods, to provide food for the poor and give our bodies to be burned, but spirituality says that without love, everything is worthless."

22. "The Drum Major Instinct," in Washington, *Testament of Hope,* 267.

23. Thomas Merton, *Contemplation in a World of Action* (Notre Dame: University of Notre Dame Press, 1998) 160–61.

Spirituality is deep water, subterranean. It feeds the springs and rivers that run on the surface. Many torrents are produced when it floods, but they dry up and only leave an empty and dry riverbed. But deep waters do not dry up. So is it with authentic spirituality.

We are living in a time when it is necessary to dig many new wells in Cuba in order to feed a spirituality to renew our society and our churches. And I would say more: not only in Cuba, but in all of Western Christianity we are subject to new principalities and powers. Who doesn't feel numbed by the power of technological consumerism, which penetrates to the bones of even the poorest, instilling a deep craving for material wealth? Who is not distressed at the era of violence that invades even family space, exacting a terrible cost in the most intimate of relations?

Jesus invited people to Him as Living Water (John 7:38) and offered spiritual traits that should mark the Protestant churches of Cuba as we offer a timely word to the longings of our age. Dr. King is also meaningful in this regard. Even with the limitations that have already been pointed out, the churches are a reserve of hope, with great potential for healing and life. With proper formation, this well of living water can be refreshed and deepened and purified.

Ironically, the historical forces that produced the Protestant Reformation's attempted renewal of spiritual life added to its distortion. Medieval piety, among various spiritual traditions, was harshly criticized for promoting superstitious practices. Protestantism was closely tied to Enlightenment thinking, with its confidence in the power of human reason. Such reliance on human discourse, preaching in particular, became the defining characteristic of the reforming movement. And with it came a certain "flattening" of the word, an overly optimistic, even arrogant, confidence in the power of rational thought. *Credo*, Latin for "I give my heart to," was transformed into creed, the assertion of orthodox ideas and propositions.

In this postmodern age, there is renewed appreciation of mystical experiences, a search for spirituality. As a result, many in the West have turned to Eastern religious traditions. Others have found a new orientation for their faith in the charismatic movement. Especially in Latin America, the neo-Pentecostal movement, in a variety of manifestations, represents the largest non-Roman Catholic religious force.

The lesson to be learned is one that theologian Hans Küng frequently emphasizes: if spirituality does not characterize Christianity in the twenty-first century, Christianity will not survive.

The spirituality we need, however, is not the kind that separates heaven from earth. Again, listen to Dr. King's insistence that any religion or spirituality that professes to be concerned with the souls of persons and "is not concerned with the slums that damn them, the economic conditions that strangle them, and the social conditions that cripple them is a dry-as-dust religion."[24]

Authentic spirituality springs from an unconditional love for the world for which Jesus died. Of course, not all forms of spirituality are the same. In effect, there are distortions of spirituality that become ways to escape reality. However, it is not so easy to draw a line between what we could call good and bad spirituality. It is necessary to take into account which people are practicing one type of spirituality or the other and in what context each type of spirituality is being practiced.

I wish to affirm that spirituality with Jesus as its source involves an ascent of the Mount of Transfiguration, where ecstasy breaks out and where the veil between heaven and earth, sacred and secular, is very thin and porous. Here, eyes are opened to a new way of seeing the world, consciousness is awakened, and love is stirred. These produce the desire to embrace all that has been excluded. Simultaneously, this spirituality has the power to resist seduction and sustain hope, even in the midst of despair.

For Cubans, Martin Luther King, Jr. was not just a social reformer. His reforming impulse was anchored in a profound spirituality, which gave him the energy to struggle and enabled him to see the possibilities for transformation latent in all human beings. His sermons reveal a depth of thinking that penetrates to the deepest levels of consciousness. His concepts of redemptive love, forgiveness, and reconciliation spring from a very rich interior, reflecting Jesus' assurance that those who follow His lead will unleash "streams of living water."

Despite their frailties, churches can serve as a reservoir of hope, with a potential for healing and life, for cleansing and refreshment. But the journey is not easy, as Dr. King's own life shows. Deepening our spirituality involves a new conversion—a breaking with old religious habits, ways of thinking, and deep-rooted customs. Only the spirit of God can cause this type of growth in believers.

---

24. King, *Stride Toward Freedom*, 36.

13

Martin Luther King, Jr. in the Holy Land

The Tragedy of His Absence[1]

Rabbi Everett Gendler

Today, we particularly need Hebrew prophets because they taught that to love God was to love justice; that each human being has an inescapable obligation to denounce evil where he sees it and to defy a ruler who commands him to break the covenant. . . . The Hebrew prophets are needed today because decent people must be imbued with the courage to speak the

---

1. The choice of this title for this chapter is not meant to suggest that King never visited the Holy Land. He and his wife did indeed make a trip to that part of the world, and King's plan for another trip before his death was never fulfilled. However, King and his nonviolence, for whatever reasons, were never an active presence in resolving the conflicts in the Holy Land in his time, and this is indeed "tragic." See King's Easter Sunday sermon, "A Walk through the Holy Land," delivered at the Dexter Avenue Baptist Church, Montgomery, Alabama, on March 29, 1959, in Clayborne Carson et al., eds., *The Papers of Martin Luther King, Jr.,* vol. 5, *Threshold of a New Decade, January 1959–December 1960* (Berkeley: University of California Press, 2005) 164–75; Martin Luther King, Jr., *Strength to Love* (Philadelphia: Fortress, 1981) 30.

truth, to realize that silence may temporarily preserve status or security but that to live with a lie is a gross affront to God.

MARTIN LUTHER KING, JR.[2]

Like Moses, his spiritual predecessor in the struggle on behalf of Divinely guided human liberation, Martin Luther King, Jr. was "a traveling man": many arduous routings, many challenging detours, many bruising encounters on the freedom trail. As with Moses, so with King: the Holy Land was an important point of reference in his religious life. In contrast to Moses, however, who could only climb the mountain to see the promised land from afar, King was able to visit part of the land in March 1959. The occasion was returning home from his visit to India, where, with Coretta, he had visited significant sites in the life of Gandhi and deepened his understanding of nonviolence.

In the Holy Land he was deeply moved as he followed the paths that Jesus had walked on the Mount of Olives and in the Garden of Gethsemane, as well as the burial places of Abraham, Isaac, Jacob, Sarah, and others. But as he pointedly remarked, he was at that time unable to experience the fullness of the land because of the separation barrier between Jordan and Israel. In the biblical narrative, God the Creator was first experienced as God the Liberating Redeemer in the exodus from Egypt, following which He directs His people toward the promised land. As I understand this narrative, the failure of Moses to set foot in the land did not compromise its status as the final destination in this Liberation narrative, with all the later inspiring revolutionary effects throughout the history of the struggle for justice and human dignity. By contrast, the absence of King may have affected the destiny of this land in our age, diminishing its capacity to serve as a place where the liberating and healing power of the Divine was again made manifest. Regrettably, neither King nor Gandhi before him managed to bring to the promised land his charismatic embodiment of the efficacy and the power of nonviolence, thus depriving it of their desperately needed

2. Martin Luther King, Jr., "My Jewish Brother," *New York Amsterdam News*, February 26, 1966, 1 and 12; Martin Luther King, Jr., "An Address," delivered before the Synagogue Council of America (December 5, 1965) 8–10 (housed at the library and archives of The Martin Luther King, Jr. Center for Nonviolent Social Change, Inc., Atlanta, Georgia); Israel Goldstein, "Martin Luther King's Jewish Associations," *The Jerusalem Post*, October 22, 1964, 3.

contributions to the reconciliation of contending claims and conflicting claimants.

NONVIOLENCE IN THE HOLY LAND? THE ISRAELI-PALESTINIAN CONFLICT IN HISTORICAL CONTEXT

Nonviolence in the Holy Land? On first hearing, the phrase does, indeed, sound like an oxymoron. Yet nonviolence has a lengthy, although largely fitful and frustrated, history in that strife-afflicted region sacred to the three Abrahamic traditions, Judaism, Christianity, and Islam. A brief review of a few incidents from the modern history of Israel/Palestine may be helpful in setting the context for what Martin Luther King, Jr.—had he indeed set foot in the land—might have contributed to the resolution of this seemingly intractable conflict. Since it was his regular practice to apply nonviolent principles to the particular conditions of a situation, we need at least some sense of the background of the present impasse in Israel-Palestine.

A word of explanation about the selection of these few background incidents may be helpful. For reasons of space, they must be few in number and abbreviated in their presentation. They are not intended as a full portrait of the issue in all its shadings; rather, they are strokes, integral to the texture of the situation, yet sometimes not noticed, whose appearance King surely would have discerned, filled out, and brought vividly to our attention. All are extracted from the overall canvas representing two deeply felt forces tragically colliding, both of which are too often oblivious to the similarities between them.

We are most accustomed to reading of conflicts and clashes between Israeli Jews and Palestinian Arabs, often violent. Indeed, the violent expressions of the profound differences between Jewish and Arab positions with respect to Israel/Palestine have gained most attention from observers as well as participants in the conflict. Yet significant nonviolent elements and initiatives have been present from the beginning of the modern period of this ancient struggle. Some of the early Zionists, for example, were aware of the Palestinian presence in the land, and they hoped to overcome the possible resistance of the residents through an expansion of opportunities. Moses Hess in 1861, a generation before Herzl, "had imagined that a highly Westernized element such as the Jews would be welcomed by the Arabs because of the leadership that Jews would provide in creating in the entire region an advanced economy and an advancing society."[3] While this attempt to convert a zero-sum game to one of an expanding sum that could be shared was not universal among the early Zionist thinkers, others as well sought to forge common purpose with the Arab residents.

Chaim Weizmann, central to the diplomacy that yielded the Balfour Declaration, corresponded directly with Emir Feisal Husseini, a prominent leader who was the Arab representative to the Paris Peace Conference of 1919, and the two signed an agreement. In a letter to Lord Herbert Samuel in 1919 that accorded recognition to the common interests of both peoples, Husseini said, "I . . . very much regret to know of the opposition of the Damascus Press to Zionism. I personally deprecate any differences between the Arabs and the Jews who ought to unite their efforts in word and deed for promoting the development and happiness of our country."[4] In addition, he signed an agreement accepting the immigration of Jews into the country and their development of it, subject to the protection of the rights of the Arab peasant and tenant farmers.[5] Although an eminent representative, Husseini was himself a resident of the Hejaz (Saudi Arabia) and was not able to represent accurately the far more negative feelings of the local residents of the region.

Despite little positive response from those in the Arab communities, there continued to be Jewish Zionists and others associated with the B'rith Shalom (Covenant of Peace) movement who sought a more conciliatory path, among them Judah Magnes, Martin Buber, and Ernst Simon. More ambiguously, Chaim Arlozoroff, a prominent early leader of the labor Zionist movement, also attempted to find ways for Arab-Jewish cooperation. His never-solved murder in June 1933 deprived the Zionists of a figure more central to the politics of the movement, yet keenly aware of the importance of achieving Arab-Jewish understanding.[6]

Regrettably, this attempt to cultivate a commonality with the Arabs of the region was itself compromised by other goals of early Zionism: the reassertion of the dignity of manual labor; the determined effort to expand Jewish occupations beyond the middleman-commercial role imposed by

3. *Encyclopedia Judaica (EJ)*, 1971 ed., s.v. "Zionism," 16:1056.

4. Ibid., 1050.

5. Doreen Ingrams, *The Palestine Papers, 1917–1922: Seeds of Conflict* (New York: George Braziller, 1973) 55.

6. Susan Lee Hattis, *The Bi-National Idea in Palestine during Mandatory Times* (Haifa, Israel: Shikmona, 1970) 84–86.

the Russian rulers; and a quest for self-reliance that sought independence from outside forces, in this case the Arab inhabitants of the land. Each of these goals was understandable, even commendable, yet their combined effect was to marginalize and so exclude the Arabs from full participation in the expanding opportunities brought by the new settlers.

Adding to the difficulties of avoiding injuries to peasants, while in the process of legally acquiring land, was the opaque complexity of title procedures in the Ottoman Empire. For reasons clearly presented by William R. Polk, a long history of subterfuge and misrepresentation had come to characterize the peasant registration of land in the Ottoman Empire, thus making it especially difficult to determine the true owner of the land. To avoid the government's conscription of their sons as well as to protect their land rights more effectively, peasants often registered their land in the name of an important and influential man who could, through his influence, defend their traditional land rights. This resulted in a severe discrepancy between the legal title to land and the actual possession and cultivation by peasants over many generations. Hence, for example, when a Zionist purchasing group in 1921 openly and legally purchased an extensive plot of land in the Emeq from the Beirut Christian family of Sursuk, some eight thousand peasants who were actually living on the land, many with only a dim grasp of the technicalities of title deeds, were evicted to make way for the intended settlers.[7] This tragic dispossession was entirely legal, yet it grievously violated the traditional peasant attachment to the land and the simple peasant sense that to live on the land and to cultivate it over generations constituted title to the land.

Polk movingly describes both the feeling of attachment to the land as well as the traditional sense of entitlement among those living on the soil. He contrasts peasant feelings with the Bedouin mentality, for whom there is no fixity in relation to the land: "For the settled peasant . . . land is one's *own* land, where ancestors were born, where they built, tilled, are buried, and where sons will be born. Land is a visible extension of man—as it were, the summary of life. In its terraces, holy places, and graveyards, the individual achieves a sort of immortality. . . . It is perhaps the strongest emotional attachment known to peasants the world over."[8]

---

7. William R. Polk, "The Arabs and Palestine," in *Backdrop to Tragedy: The Struggle for Palestine*, by William R. Polk, David M. Stamler, and Edmund Asfour (Boston: Beacon, 1957) 229–37.

8. Ibid., 231.

Consequently, "land was the ultimate value to be saved at all sacrifice; in the peasant's mind it *was* saved so long as he worked it, buried his dead in it, and raised sons upon it. To him it was incomprehensible that through the edicts of a distant government, whose authority he had hardly ever felt, the land had ceased to be his."[9] This legal situation compounded the difficulties of finding ways to minimize the destructive effects of Jewish settlement on the lives of those who had long lived on the land.

Harsh external circumstances also contributed to the lack of continuing attention to this vital element that was destined to have so profound an effect on the continuing effort to increase Jewish settlement in the Holy Land. Twenty years after Hess's hope to create a common cause between the Jews and the Arabs came the assassination of Czar Alexander II, followed by widespread pogroms against Jews throughout the Russian Empire and adjacent lands. Profoundly disheartening to Jews was the passivity of the government, which failed to defend them against the mob violence, and still more so the apparent acquiescence of even progressive elements in Russia in this brutal wave of bloodshed. Populist movements (the Narodniks) tended to view the uprisings as a "first necessary revolutionary convulsion,"[10] thus showing little concern for the Jews. The Kishinev pogroms in 1903 further fueled the mass exodus of Jews from Russia and surrounding lands; between 1881 and 1914, the number of Jews who fled totaled approximately 2,400,000. Most went to the United States, but there were some among them who, despite difficulties, did immigrate to Palestine. Later, during the disturbances following World War I, over one hundred thousand Jews were slaughtered in Russia and Poland by Ukrainian and counter-revolutionary troops. Long before the unprecedented horrors inflicted by Adolph Hitler, such events contributed to a sense of urgency that focused attention elsewhere than on conciliatory ways of resettling persecuted Jews in their ancestral homeland.

In resisting the perceived threat from Jewish immigration, Arabs in the beginning took largely nonviolent measures to protest the development. In her valuable comprehensive study of Palestinian nonviolence during the first Intifada, Mary Elizabeth King identifies antecedents in the widespread use of nonviolent methods, especially protest and persuasion, by Palestinians during the 1920s: "formal statements, declarations,

9. Ibid., 235–38.
10. *EJ*, 1043.

petitions, manifestos, assemblies, delegations, processions, marches, and motorcades."[11] Because these methods failed to achieve their proclaimed end, the halting of Jewish immigration to Palestine, many Arabs were discouraged from further using such tactics as they turned increasingly to violent protests. What followed was a long, complex, painful, and all too familiar history of continuing Jewish determination to create again, this time in their historic land of origin, a refuge for their perpetually persecuted, in collision with an equally determined Arab resistance to what was perceived as a threat to the longtime residents of the land. The Balfour Declaration explicitly affirmed that it favored and would facilitate "the establishment in Palestine of a National Home for the Jewish people." In the very same complex sentence, it explicitly affirmed, "in the achievement of this object . . . nothing shall be done which may prejudice the civil and religious rights of existing non-Jewish communities in Palestine." Details of how this was to be accomplished were lacking, and consequently it failed to gain the cooperation of the Arabs in this admittedly difficult endeavor.

Throughout the period of the British Mandate, a few voices were audible from both parties that sought to achieve this end. The members of B'rith Shalom, mentioned earlier, worked tirelessly for a binational state that would recognize and take account of the deep longings of both peoples for this land. In his moving testimony at the hearings of the United Nations Special Committee on Palestine (UNSCOP), Professor Ernst Simon introduced his remarks by reminding the Committee that "the members of the League [for Jewish Arab Rapprochement and Cooperation] still believe in man, in the brotherhood of nations, in the progress of mankind, and in the eventual triumph of the progressive forces within it."[12] There followed the more concrete statement of Aharon Cohen: "In our view, there is no conflict between the real interests and just aspirations of the two peoples. The Jews want freedom to develop unhindered their national home through immigration, settlement, and political independence. The Arabs seek progress, political independence, a rise in their standards of life, freedom from want and ignorance, freedom from economic backwardness and feudal domination."[13] Although few Arab voices were heard in agreement with this position, at least one positively responding group, Falastin al-Jedida

11. Mary Elizabeth King, *A Quiet Revolution: The First Palestinian Intifada and Non-violent Resistance* (New York, Nation Books, 2007) 32.

12. Hattis, *Bi-National Idea in Palestine*, 311.

13. Ibid., 312.

(The New Palestine), was formed in 1936 by Fauzi Darwish el-Husseini, a cousin of the Grand Mufti. The group had little growth during the following decade, but it did sign a document of understanding with the League on November 11, 1946, pledging to work together "to preserve the unity of the country and work for a solution of its political problems through an Arab-Jewish agreement on the basis of the [following] principles: full cooperation between the two nations in all fields; political equality between the two nations in Palestine as a means of obtaining the independence of the country; Jewish immigration according to the absorptive capacity of the country and the joining of the shared and independent Palestine in an alliance with the neighbouring countries in the future."[14]

On November 23, 1946, Fauzi Darwish el-Husseini was murdered by unknown Arab nationalists. While speculating about whether Arab masses could ever be converted to this viewpoint, Susan Lee Hattis remarks: "The Arab masses had been told for 30 years that there was nothing to compromise about with the Zionists. . . . To reverse this trend a man of extraordinary qualities and with an ability to command great authority was required."[15] She leaves unanswered whether or not Darwish el-Husseini was such a figure.

Whatever hindsight one may direct at the situation through the first decades of the twentieth century, a full violent collision between the two nationalist movements was not averted. The United Nations Special Committee on Palestine in 1947 proposed a partition of the land; the proposal was accepted by the Zionists, rejected by the Arabs, with the Arab-Israeli War of 1948 following immediately the end of the British Mandate in May 1948. The de facto partition of the land finally came about, followed by the subsequent armistice agreements of 1949 between the warring parties. Additional national armed clashes occurred in 1956, 1967, and 1973, with a major change in the territorial arrangement as a result of the 1967 Six-Day War, when Israel occupied the West Bank and Gaza, formerly held by Jordan.

Throughout the years following the 1949 truce, smaller-scale armed clashes and guerilla actions continued, along with consistent Arab efforts to isolate, boycott, and refuse recognition to the State of Israel. Following the Six-Day War, the Arab League adopted its widely known policy of three no's: no peace with Israel, no recognition of Israel, no negotiations with Israel. Within Israel itself, the Palestinian resistance was marked by the

14. Ibid., 305.
15. Ibid.

increasing use of suicide bombers, whose attacks on civilians caused not only human casualties and material destruction but also a heightened sense of anxiety and insecurity among the Israelis. This regrettably reenforced the memories of the recent mass extermination of six million Jews at the hands of the Nazis during World War II. The result was heavy military retaliation by the Israelis along with hardened attitudes on both sides.

During this period, however, some resident Palestinian civic leaders and activist intellectuals began to explore nonviolent alternatives to the mutually injurious violent tactics then widespread among both Israelis and Palestinians. Mary Elizabeth King provides a lucid, detailed, thorough report of this important development in chapters 7 and 8 of *A Quiet Revolution*.[16] The Arab Thought Forum convened a three-day international conference in Amman in November 1986, with Dr. Gene Sharp, a pragmatic Western analyst and the author of *The Politics of Nonviolent Action*,[17] and Narayan Desai, the principled Gandhian director of the Institute for Total Revolution, among the major presenters. Some developments in Israel during those years are vividly and engagingly presented in Sari Nusseibeh's *Once Upon a Country*,[18] offering numerous instances of these ideas in application. Illustrative is Military Order 854 and the Palestinian response.

In 1980 the military government of the West Bank and Gaza ordered that "all foreign professors, whether Palestinian expatriates or internationals, apply again for work permits, and that they sign a loyalty pledge, specifically stating that they would not engage in opposition to the military government or have any dealings with a 'hostile' organization as defined by the Israelis, namely the PLO." The order was, on Nusseibeh's analysis, calculated "to undermine our academic freedom and prevent a full-fledged civil society from taking root by threatening hundreds of professors . . . with deportation if they engaged actively in politics."[19] Although the administration at Birzeit University, fearing the consequences of refusal, agreed to go along, the professors ignored the order. They publicized the issue in the Palestinian and Israeli communities and the Israeli and foreign press, gaining widespread support. The President of the Israeli Academy of Sciences

16. King, *Quiet Revolution*, 127–201.

17. Gene Sharp, *The Politics of Nonviolent Action*, 3 vols. (Boston: Porter Sargent, 1973).

18. Sari Nusseibeh, *Once Upon a Country: A Palestinian Life* (New York: Picador, 2007).

19. Ibid., 189.

set up a committee of Israeli academics "to investigate the legality and morality" of the order; their findings supported resisting the order. A minor scuffle, during which an Israeli officer was pushed by a student and fell to the ground, resulted in the military government ordering a three-month shutdown of the university and deporting seven professors. Still refusing to sign after the university was reopened, the professors received orders from the PLO's headquarters in Amman that they submit to the Israeli order. After consulting with representatives from all the West Bank and Gaza universities, the professors decided to resist the PLO as well, finding that it was "against the PLO's best interests" to submit to its order. With the support and urging of Abu Jihad, the PLO was ultimately persuaded to defer to the judgment of the local leadership. Later the U.N. called for Israel to rescind Military Order 854, as did the International Commission of Jurists; the support of Israeli academics continued as well. In response, while refusing to rescind the order, the military government did suspend it for one year; at the end of the year "they just chose not to enforce it."[20]

From this episode Nusseibeh gained the following crucial insight into Israeli psychology: "only after the first hint of violence" did they take action. Expanding on the importance of this moment of insight, he continues: "For thirty-five years every shot we took at the occupiers had ricocheted back at us tenfold: more land was seized, more people expelled, more of our future trampled upon. It was a losing battle, because they had a strategy, whereas we had only emotions. Now, for the first time, we were discovering our strength. The Israelis had nothing in their repertoire to defeat a dedicated nonviolent campaign of civil disobedience."[21]

What an invaluable discovery! The further exploration, both in theory and in practice, of nonviolent strategies by the East Jerusalem Activist Intellectuals, as Mary Elizabeth King calls them, did indeed prepare the way for the unprecedented two-year Intifada that began in 1987. A valuable fuller account of what turned out to be preparations for that uprising is found in Nusseibeh's memoir, including such unforgettable episodes as the swimming pool nonviolent "bombshell," a classic case of "moral jiujitsu," in which the nonviolence and goodwill of the victim appeals to the conscience of the victimizer and forces the victimizer to waste his energy and to surrender moral balance.[22] Along with various nonviolent actions

20. Ibid., 197.
21. Ibid., 191–92.
22. Ibid., 239–40.

that challenged the consciences of the occupying authorities, Nusseibeh recounts also the transformative experience of his encounters with "two American Jewish visionaries," Professor Herbert Kelman and his wife, Rose. On reflection, Nusseibeh found himself conceding the deep wisdom of the Kelmans' insistence that "Palestinians and Israelis would eventually have to sit down and negotiate a deal."[23] After much soul-searching, to his own surprise he reluctantly found himself ready to enter into negotiations with the Israelis on the basis of the pre-1967 borders. In effect, of course, that meant recognition of the permanent presence of the State of Israel; by the same token, it also meant the implicit recognition by the Israelis of a Palestinian state. Such antecedents and others constitute fascinating vignettes in Nusseibeh's record of further discoveries about nonviolence along with first attempts to apply those discoveries.

Perhaps it comes as a surprise to many readers that the first Palestinian Intifada ("uprising," literally "shaking off"), from 1987 to 1989, was predominantly, though not entirely, nonviolent. Yet Mary Elizabeth King assembles massive, convincing evidence that this was the case. How do we explain the discrepancy between the actuality and the impression? How did it happen that the quantitatively minor amount of stone-throwing, mostly by Palestinian youths, so outweighed the vastly greater employment of pure nonviolence? The simplest, most compelling explanation is, I think, offered by Dr. Gene Sharp and Colonel (retired) Robert Helvey in their trenchant treatments of strategic nonviolent struggle.

Sharp, whose powerful theoretical work contributed directly to the 1995 success of Otpor! (Resistance!) students in Serbia and to the disciplined nonviolent movements in Tunisia and Egypt of the Arab Spring of 2011, has insisted throughout his writings that mixing even a little violence compromises and weakens any nonviolent movement by reducing outside sympathy and support, lessening the almost inevitable disaffection among opposing troops when facing resolute nonviolent resisters, and reducing the numbers of those attracted to the nonviolent movement.[24]

Helvey, his natural strategic gifts impressively honed by thirty years in the military, addresses the issue with characteristic illuminating directness. In *On Strategic Nonviolent Conflict,* he titles one chapter "Contaminants" and points out that contaminated fuel "can cause an engine to misfire and sputter ... [or]stop the engine from running at all." On the basis of extensive

23. Ibid., 221.

24. Gene Sharp, *Waging Nonviolent Struggle* (Boston: Porter Sargent, 2005) 390.

personal experience and research, he says bluntly, "A single act of violence may provide the government with a convenient rationale for brutal retaliation. . . ."[25] Especially pertinent to our issue is a further assertion:

> Extreme examples of violence provoking violent retaliation were the Palestinian terrorist groups Hamas and Islamic Jihad and the suicide bombings against Israeli citizens during the second Intifada. Because the Palestinian Authority failed to aggressively disassociate itself from these terrorist acts, Israeli public support for a negotiated homeland for Palestinians evaporated, and the international community began backing away from influencing restraint on Israeli settlement policies and Israel's violent occupation of the West Bank.[26]

Although the above does not constitute a full analysis of the complex situation, its basic truth should not be overlooked: positions again hardened on both sides.

Sadly, even the largely nonviolent first Intifada was not recognized as such. Part of this may indeed have been the result of the contamination from the widespread stone-throwing. However understandable as the spillover of almost unbearable frustration, and admittedly less lethal than bombs and bullets, it nevertheless is not a nonviolent tactic. In the words of the old (half correct) nursery rhyme, "sticks and stones can break my bones, but words will never hurt me." Being the target of a hail of stones is both fear-inducing and anger-provoking; witnessing such events does not incline the viewers to trust the purely peaceable intentions of the stone-throwers. These physical threats to the soldiers almost totally nullified the usual disconcerting effects of courageous, restrained, determined nonviolent human confrontations on consciences, reducing seriously the effectiveness of the Intifada.

Another likely factor was the long-term conditioning of the Israelis to associate any Palestinian opposition with violence, blinding them to the differences of this first Intifada. Reuven Gal, a former chief psychologist for the Israeli Defense Forces, remarked that Israeli officials regarded the Intifada in purely military terms: "The best proof is in the fact that Israel never handled the intifada by police forces or semi-military forces, but

25. Robert L. Helvey, *On Strategic Nonviolent Conflict: Thinking about the Fundamentals* (Boston: Albert Einstein Institution, 2004) 117.

26. Ibid.

handled the intifada by brigades and divisions of the army—mobilizing full brigades, full divisions. . . . Not police, not riot control."[27]

In all likelihood, contributing further to this failure of recognition was the simple unfamiliarity of nonviolent protest to most people in the region. More than forty years had passed since Gandhi was alive, and more than twenty since Martin Luther King, Jr. had been alive and active in the United States. Even though people power had toppled Marcos in the Philippines the previous year, this was a period before the Velvet Revolution, the fall of the Berlin Wall, the liberation of Latvia, Lithuania, and Estonia, and the overthrow of Milosevic in Serbia, all largely by nonviolent methods. This unfamiliarity may also have contributed to the failure of the Israeli authorities to explore the potential contribution that a nonviolent movement offers for a mutually respectful resolution of the issues.

THE ISRAEL-PALESTINE IMPASSE: WHAT WOULD BE MARTIN LUTHER KING, JR.'S APPROACH?

With the foregoing as an admittedly abbreviated background sketch, let us now try to imagine how Martin Luther King, Jr., had he lived to enter the Holy Land, might have contributed to the resolution of this conflict. One suggestive hint comes from a preliminary plan, first sketched in the autumn of 1966, for a visit that was still being actively planned at the time of his murder. The Reverend Andrew Young, at the time King's primary coordinator, relates that he and King—along with the Reverend Sandy Ray, the prominent pastor of a major black church in Harlem, and then-Governor of New York Nelson Rockefeller—formulated a tentative proposal for five thousand pilgrims to visit sacred sites in Israel and Jordan sometime in September 1967. At the time of preliminary planning, the sacred sites in East Jerusalem were under the rule of the Jordanians, those in West Jerusalem under the Israelis. Consequently, not coincidentally, this massive tourist influx, with its promise of a large infusion of highly desired foreign currencies to both economies, would require active coordination and cooperation from Jordan and Israel. When Jordanian officials raised questions about the feasibility of accommodations and facilities for such a large number of visitors, Dr. King insisted that five thousand be the number; he wanted the nonviolent intervention to be of significant scale. Hotel reservations were made and deposits confirmed in December 1966. The trip never

27. King, *Quiet Revolution*, 9–10.

materialized because of the Six-Day War of June 1967, and urgent events in the United States fully occupied Dr. King during the ensuing months.[28] In the spring of 1968, before there was time to formulate fresh plans for a comparable trip under the changed circumstances, Dr. King was murdered in Memphis. Informed imagination, then, must provide the speculative sketch of what King might have contributed to the solution of the Israel-Palestine impasse. And rather than try to reconstruct that earlier period of time, it is more relevant to think in terms of the situation that Dr. King, were he alive, would confront today.

Dr. King would surely have sensed a situation that on first sight defied satisfactory solution, for he was endowed with penetrating vision as well as elevating dreams. At the same time, he lived with the conviction, founded in faith, that God would not ultimately abandon God's beloved human creations to final frustration and futility. How, then, might we imagine him working toward a solution?

Key to King's approach was his commitment to "a tough mind and a tender heart," which is, not by accident, I think, the title of the opening sermon in his *Strength to Love* (1963). By a tough mind, he meant "incisive thinking, realistic appraisal, and decisive judgment. This tough mind is sharp and penetrating, breaking through the crust of legends and myths and sifting the true from the false." The tough-minded individual, as a consequence, "has a strong, austere quality that makes for firmness of purpose and solidity of commitment."[29] However, without an accompanying tender heart that provides "the capacity for genuine compassion," one will never be able to bridge the gap between oneself and the other. This deficiency leaves human beings isolated, passionless, denied the warmth and beauty of friendship and the capacity genuinely to relate to their fellow humans.

Also essential to King's approach was his commitment to finding a solution to the conflict that represented a recognition and response to the humanity of both parties. Unforgettable is this passage from "Loving Your Enemies": "To our most bitter opponents we say: 'We shall match your capacity to inflict suffering by our capacity to endure suffering. We shall meet your physical force with soul force. Do to us what you will, and we shall continue to love you. . . . One day we shall win freedom, but not only for

---

28. Telephone interviews with Ambassador Andrew Young (November 2011).

29. Martin Luther King, Jr., *Strength to Love* (New York: Harper & Row, 1963) 2.

ourselves. We shall so appeal to your heart and conscience that we shall win *you* in the process, and our victory will be a double victory."[30]

Briefly summarized, King's commitment was to a method of non-violent action that (*a*) resisted evil; (*b*) sought not to defeat or humiliate the opponent, but to win the opponent's friendship and understanding; (*c*) directed its attack against structures of evil rather than against those persons doing the evil; (*d*) maintained a willingness to accept suffering without retaliation; (*e*) attempted to avoid not only external physical violence but also internal violence of spirit; and (*f*) was "based on the conviction that the universe is on the side of justice . . . [that] there is a creative force in this universe that works to bring the disconnected aspects of reality into a harmonious whole."[31]

Thus, King did not view conflicts as zero-sum games. He practiced a Gandhian *satyagraha*, the aim of which "is neither to harm the opponent nor to impose on them a solution against their will. The aim is to help both parties to achieve a more secure, creative, and truthful relationship. . . . *Satyagraha*, then, involves consistent effort in the search for truth while converting the opponent into a friend as part of the process. It is not used *against* someone; it is done *with* someone."[32]

Since King took great care to begin the consideration of any intervention with a tough-minded "realistic appraisal" of the situation, what might the first outcome of such an appraisal have been? We had earlier characterized the impasse as the collision between two deeply felt, passionately asserted claims to a particular territory. The elemental nature of any conflict over a parcel of land, if not mediated by an accepted code of law, is succinctly and vividly captured in the following excerpt of a poem by Carl Sandburg:

> "Get off this estate."
> "What for?"
> "Because it's mine."
> "Where did you get it?"
> "From my father."
> "Where did he get it?"
> "From his father."

30. Ibid., 40.

31. Martin Luther King, Jr., *Stride Toward Freedom: The Montgomery Story* (New York: Harper & Row, 1958) 102–3, 106–7.

32. Robert J. Burrowes, *The Strategy of Nonviolent Defense: A Gandhian Approach* (Albany: State University of New York Press, 1996) 109.

"And where did he get it?"
"He fought for it."
"Well, I'll fight you for it."[33]

Faced with this stark reality, I can imagine King immediately look-ing for alternatives to such a belligerent confrontation. Had there been any examples of land disputes in this area settled by means other than "we'll fight you for it"? Indeed, there were examples, among them the lengthy, impressively disciplined nonviolent resistance of the Druze inhabitants of the Golan Heights to the 1967 Israeli occupation, the later declaration of annexation, and the subsequent attempts to redefine the status of the Druze and to impose identity cards and citizenship. The specifics of the conflict are succinctly and clearly presented by R. Scott Kennedy.[34] The Golani Druze, organized around "realistic objectives," were able to forge commu-nal unity "through a consensus process" and compromise, and related it to the Israeli soldiers in quite striking ways. "Villagers defied a strict curfew confining them to their homes to place tea and cookies outside their doors for the Israeli soldiers. They engaged soldiers in conversation and chose not to curse them. . . ."[35]

What were some of the results? When soldiers were ordered to take repressive actions against the villagers, they "were really being torn apart, because they couldn't handle that type of nonviolence. . . . [T]he morale and discipline of Israeli soldiers began to break down."[36] A humanizing process was taking place that radically changed the terms of the confrontation. The villagers were somehow able to recognize that the perpetrators of the unjust policies were themselves human beings. Acting on this recognition, they reached toward the soldiers with one of the most basic of human gestures: food (tea and cookies, no less!). Could the toughest of combatants fail to be moved by this elemental act of human recognition? The soldiers, in turn, not threatened physically yet deeply challenged emotionally, could not continue to regard simply as "enemies" the human beings who had fed them as if they were their own children. Principled nonviolent action, as

33. Carl Sandburg, from *The People, Yes* (New York: Harcourt, Brace, 1936) end of section 37.

34. R. Scott Kennedy, "Noncooperation in the Golan Heights: A Case of Nonviolent Resistance," in *Civilian Jihad: Nonviolent Struggle, Democratization, and Governance in the Middle East*, ed. Maria J. Stephan (New York: Palgrave Macmillan, 2009) 119–29.

35. Ibid., 125, 126.

36. Ibid., 126.

practiced by Gandhi and King, applies political pressure while simultaneously releasing the transformative power of humanization of the enemy. In
combination, these serve to establish a new basis upon which the opposing
forces can reach an agreement. A striking illustration of this is Budrus, a
Palestinian village whose residents discovered that the planned Separation
Barrier would pass directly through their village. This projected path would
destroy thousands of olive trees upon whose produce the livelihoods of
some villagers entirely depended, skirt the village school, cut through the
cemetery, and isolate Budrus from nearby Palestinian villages. A stirring
documentary recorded some highlights of the ten-month nonviolent resistance campaign organized in the village under the leadership of Ayed Morrar.[37] Morrar explicitly recognizes the right of Israel to protect its citizens
against terrorist attacks from the Occupied Territories, but insists that the
barrier be erected along the Green Line, not on Palestinian land. His comprehension of what the Israelis have at stake, together with the disciplined
nonviolent approach accepted by all factions in the village, attracted both
international support as well as active participation from a number of Israeli Jews who see and object to the manifest injustice of the proposed path.
Their presence is "like a dream" to the Palestinian organizers, and there
are moving testimonies to the humanizing effects of this Israeli presence:
"Now I know that not all Israelis are bad and hate us," Morrar thought. The
demonstrations continue despite increasing injuries from the escalating
severity of the Israeli soldiers' reactions and a number of arrests. Finally,
after more than fifty demonstrations, an alternative path is proposed by the
Israeli authorities that saves 95 percent of the land and olive trees, avoids
the cemetery, and is out of sight of the school. While space precludes a full
analysis of the dynamics at work, even this brief sketch directs attention to
the potential of nonviolence for resolving some of the issues in this seemingly intractable conflict.

Another issue that King would immediately see as a serious impedi-
ment to a satisfactory solution of the dispute is the rapid, continuing growth
of Israeli settlements within the Occupied Territories. Now numbering
more than three hundred thousand, the occupants of these settlements
come for two major reasons. For the estimated vast majority, the cheaper
housing subsidized by the state, along with convenient transportation networks established by the state to make commuting to work easy and safe,

37. *Budrus*, written and directed by Julia Bacha, DVD (2009). For more information,
see www.justvision.org/budrus.

are attractions not to be resisted. For others, the sense of historic rights and responsibilities to settle in particular sacred places is the primary motivation. To each of these, I can imagine King applying judiciously his cauterizing method that initiates the ultimate healing process.

Dr. King, like Gandhi, was realistic. He knew that appeals to conscience often need the heft of economic consequences in order to have full effect. Both in Montgomery and in Birmingham, the economic effects of boycotts and selective buying campaigns forced those in power to face the full human meaning of their segregation policies. By analogy, a carefully focused policy of economic penalties, imposed upon the State of Israel for its subsidized enabling of settlement activities, would almost certainly have immediate salutary consequences. The exemplary action of President George H. W. Bush is instructive in this respect. Confronted by Prime Minister Menachem Begin's policy of encouraging Israeli settlements in the West Bank, which was in direct contradiction to clearly enunciated U.S. and U.N. principles, President Bush simply stated that U.S. guarantees of Israeli loans would cease if these policies continued. Faced with the certain consequence of much higher interest rates that Israel would have to pay if the U.S. no longer guaranteed the loans, Begin immediately suspended the settlement activities.

Where are the economic leverage points today that could be used to end and reverse the current settlement policies? Widely acknowledged to be major obstacles to a peaceful resolution of the Israeli-Palestine conflict as well as a serious threat to a genuinely democratic Jewish state, these policies would, I imagine, receive immediate, careful scrutiny from King. Where do the funds come from that maintain settlement amenities and underwrite new activities? Are some charitable donations from abroad? These would invite immediate investigation by their respective governments for possible violation of philanthropic guidelines. Are there discernible Israeli governmental subsidies for transportation systems, including road building and maintenance as well as vehicles? Foreign governments that genuinely oppose these settlement policies might respond by reducing their own foreign aid or trade concessions by commensurate amounts. In each case, the proposed actions would be narrowly focused on the grievance, avoiding any overall implication of rejection of the legitimacy of Israel's existence. King might in fact suggest—as he did in 1967[38]—that such an intervention,

---

38. In 1967 King put out at least two statements affirming Israel's "right to exist in a state of security," and asserting the obligation of "the great powers" to "recognize that the

besides supporting valid demands of the Palestinians, will further affirm the legitimacy of Israel by securing for the Palestinians their rights to self-determination, thereby validating the full United Nations Special Committee on Palestine proposal that became the accepted resolution of the United Nations General Assembly in 1948.

The challenge of those settlers religiously motivated to reside in certain areas requires a different approach, again one for which King was ideally equipped. Here a direct confrontation with the meaning of the biblical promise is required. I can well imagine Dr. King's dear friend, fellow marcher, and spiritual brother, Rabbi Dr. Abraham Joshua Heschel, directing King to sources that would speak to the convictions of the religious settlers. One such source—dense, difficult, yet of great value for this task—is an astonishing article by Rabbi Dr. Andre Neher, "Rabbinic Adumbrations of Non-violence: Israel and Canaan," which introduces us to a significant strand in classical Jewish tradition that is highly critical of Joshua for his methods in settling the land. Beyond the personal condemnation of Joshua implied in the sobriquets "*lista'a,*" *robber baron,* and *pirate,* the text insists that Joshua's true mission was to achieve "a peaceful co-existence of Hebrew and Canaanite in the Land of Canaan."[39] The full implications of this critique for the dangerous dogmatism found among many settlers cry out for expanded interpretation and application.

Following up this approach, I also imagine Heschel further coaching King in how to broaden the perspectives of dedicated religious settlers. Among these resources would surely be the stirring cry from Amos: "'Are you not like the Ethiopians to me, O people of Israel?' says the LORD. Did I

Arab world is in a state of imposed poverty and backwardness that must threaten peace and harmony." King felt that peace "for Israel means security" and "territorial integrity," and that peace for the Middle East means "Arab development." He called for a Marshall Plan to deal with poverty and illiteracy in the Middle East, noting that "we must work passionately and unrelentingly through the United Nations to grapple with this years-old problem" in that part of the world. One finds here possible suggestions concerning how King might approach these issues today. See transcript of an interview with Martin Luther King, Jr. on *Issues and Answers* (June 18, 1967), by Tom Jerriel, ABC Atlanta bureau chief, and John Casserly, ABC Washington correspondent (housed at the library and archives of the King Center, Atlanta, Georgia); "Draft Statement Regarding SCLC's Participation at The National Conference on New Politics: Resolution on the Middle East," Chicago, Illinois (September, 1967) 1–2 (housed at the library and archives of the King Center, Atlanta, Georgia).

39. Andre Neher, "Rabbinic Adumbrations of Non-violence: Israel and Canaan," in *Studies in Rationalism, Judaism and Universalism: In Memory of Leon Roth,* ed. Raphael Loewe (London: Routledge & Kegan Paul, 1966) 169–96, esp. 178.

not bring up Israel from the land of Egypt, and the Philistines from Caph-tor and the Syrians from Kir?" (9:7).

In *The Prophets*, Heschel also cites the startling passage from Isaiah proclaiming the day when "Israel shall be the third with Egypt and Assyria" and that designates Egypt as "my people" and Assyria as "the work of my hands"!

> On that day Israel shall be the third with Egypt and Assyria, a
> blessing in the midst of the earth, whom the LORD of hosts has
> blessed, saying, "Blessed be Egypt my people, and Assyria the
> work of my hands, and Israel my heritage." (Isa 19:24–25, NRSV)[40]

What's that? God redeeming Philistines (might we read Palestinians)? Egypt as God's people, and Assyria the work of God's hands? The radical potential of such citations to loosen the shackles of the current terms of discussion, to provide a fresh view of the problem by this cleansing of the eyes of perception, hardly needs explanation.

Along with this economic-religious-spiritual approach of King to the perplexing problem of settlements, I imagine one additional element that must be mentioned even if space precludes any discussion. What shall happen to those displaced, perhaps, in this process? How are they to be re-settled? With what resources? Or are they to remain where they are, with a mutually acceptable status defined in the details of an anticipated two-state solution? Or should there be a single, overarching state with safeguards for the rights of all to dignity, security, and self-determination? What is certain is that King's tender heart would not ignore this dimension in any settle-ment assisted by the measured, effective intervention of his tough, realistic, strategic mind.

Space precludes further imagining of how King might have contrib-uted to the solution of these perplexing issues. One overall element that affects every aspect of the confrontation, however, must be mentioned in closing: the prevailing sense of trauma and victimhood that distorts each side's perception of present realities. The late Anthony Shadid, until his un-timely death a seasoned and sensitive Middle East correspondent for the *New York Times*, wrote in a dispatch from Ramallah in the spring of 2002:

> The Israeli-Palestinian war is often seen through the lens of one
> side or the other. Israelis, in more numbers than ever before, see

---

40. Abraham J. Heschel, *The Prophets* (Philadelphia: Jewish Publication Society, 1955) 33 and 185.

the conflict through the lens of terrorism. They feel a nation be-
sieged by the lurking threat of suicide bombings that has disrupted
lives. . . . Palestinians see that same conflict through the lens of
occupation. While Israelis may fear walking their streets, Palestinians point out that they cannot even enter theirs. The curfews, the
checkpoints, the overwhelming superiority of arms Israel wields,
have produced the humiliation of occupation that is stretching
into a second generation. . . . [N]either side comprehends the
other's pain.[41]

How else can one account for the disregard or belated recognition of important changes in the situation? Other than persisting holocaust trauma
reinforced by the counterproductive Palestinian strategy of terrorism, what
can explain the failure to explore eagerly the startling Arab Peace Initiative
of 2002? In contrast to the infamous "three no's" of 1967, this proposal—
publicly offered by King Abdullah of Saudi Arabia, ratified by all members
of the Arab League, and reendorsed in 2007—proposed normalizing relations between the entire Arab region and Israel, in exchange for a complete
withdrawal from the Occupied Territories (including East Jerusalem) and a
"just settlement" of the Palestinian refugee crisis based on U.N. Resolution
194 (which calls for a diplomatic resolution to the conflict and resolves
that any refugees "wishing to return to their homes and live at peace with
their neighbors" should be able to do so, or if they otherwise wish, to be
provided with compensation). Notwithstanding the need for further clari-
fication, this offer testifies that, contrary to popular rhetoric, there is indeed
someone with whom to negotiate. To begin to understand this continuing
self-fulfilling and self-defeating denial of evident reality, explorations such
as Avraham Burg's soul-searching *The Holocaust Is Over: We Must Rise
from Its Ashes*[42] seem essential.

For Palestinians, it would seem that the persistent pain of defeat and
occupation—encapsulated in the term *nakba*, "the catastrophe"—has impeded their recognizing such important resources for a just resolution of
the conflict as the human conscience, especially when coupled with traditional Jewish self-understanding. We have already glimpsed, in the cases of
Military Order 854, along with the Druze and Budrus, how effective this

---

41. Anthony Shadid, "Unholy War into the Heart of Darkness: Four Days in the Israeli-
Palestinian Combat Zone," *Boston Globe*, May 12, 2002. Online: http://www.boston.com/
news/world/middleeast/articles/2002/05/12/unholy_war_into_the_heart_of_darkness/.

42. Avraham Burg, *The Holocaust Is Over: We Must Rise from Its Ashes* (New York:
Palgrave Macmillan, 2008), esp. chapter 6, "Lessons from the Holocaust," 69–90.

element can be. The frequent Israeli invocation of *tohar haneshek*, "purity of arms," even if it has come to sound increasingly hollow in recent years, is but one testimony to the continuing power of this human reality. King never lost sight of its vital importance as a resource that contributed to the resolution of conflicts in a manner affirming the basic human needs and dignity of all the contenders.[43]

Martin Luther King, Jr. was an activist, a cauterizer, but above all a healer. When he would intone, "There is a balm in Gilead," his warm, resonant voice, coupled with the intensity of his conviction, seemed to bring to many of us a measure of healing at the mere hearing of those unforgettable words. This was never hollow rhetoric; it truly characterized the insistent yet loving quality of his interventions. If at times they hurt, the pain was always in the service of ultimate health, ever and again striving to "bring the disconnected aspects of reality into a harmonious whole."[44] How desperately the Holy Land needs King's Divinely inspired spirit of informed, incisive, loving intervention!

43. For example, the late distinguished scholar Nahum N. Glatzer cites this Talmudic characterization of the Jews from Yebamot 79a: "SIGNS This people is known by three signs: Being compassionate, shamefaced, and charitable. Everyone who has these three signs is worthy of cleaving to this people." *Hammer on the Rock: A Short Midrash Reader* (New York: Schocken, 1948) 36. For a powerful recent example of this continuing activity of the Jewish conscience in relation to the Israeli-Palestinian situation, cf. David N. Myers, *Between Jew and Arab: The Lost Voice of Simon Rawidowicz* (Waltham, MA: Brandeis University Press, 2008), with the full translation of Rawidowicz's startling essay.

44. Martin Luther King, Jr., "Some Things We Must Do," unpublished version of an address, Montgomery, Alabama (December 5, 1957) 3 (housed at the library and archives of the King Center, Atlanta, Georgia).

14

From the Mountaintop to the Roof of the World

Martin Luther King, Jr. and the Tibetan Plateau

Mary Gendler

I've been to the mountaintop. Longevity has its place. But I'm not concerned about that now. I just want to do God's will. And He's allowed me to go up to the mountain. And I've looked over. And I've seen the promised land. I may not get there with you. But I want you to know tonight that we as a people will get to the promised land.

MARTIN LUTHER KING, JR.[1]

---

1. Excerpted from King's last speech, "I See the Promised Land," in James M. Washington, ed., *A Testament of Hope: The Essential Writings and Speeches of Martin Luther King, Jr.* (New York: HarperCollins, 1991) 286.

ON FIRST VIEWING, MARTIN Luther King, Jr. and the Tibetan Plateau may seem an unlikely pairing. Even though Dr. King and the Dalai Lama are both Nobel Peace Laureates, their awards were decades apart. At the time of King's assassination in the spring of 1968, most of us in the West had not heard of the Dalai Lama and were quite unaware of the issues of human rights, personal dignity, and self-determination for Tibetans under Chinese occupation. Nonetheless, the pairing of King and the Tibetan struggle is not inappropriate, as the following incident will attest.

My husband, Rabbi Everett Gendler, and I happened to be in Dharamsala at the time that the director of the Teachers Training Institute for the Tibetan exile school system was suddenly summoned to Delhi for a week of important meetings. Besides his administrative and supervisory tasks, he was also teaching two courses in English-language-medium skills to full classes of teachers in training. While the administrative and supervisory tasks could wait a week, the classes were meeting daily and needed substitute teachers immediately. Pema Dorjee, director of the program, had met us earlier and asked if we could come two hours daily to teach his classes while he was in Delhi. We agreed to do so.

Since these were teachers in training for the first two years of English-language studies, we thought that it might be instructive and useful to take a simple children's book, read it together in class, and illustrate, by suggested questions, how to enliven and personalize the readings for the students. For texts we decided to use two that we had along—one a brief biography of Dr. Martin Luther King, Jr., the other a biography of Rosa Parks—one for each class. This was the beginning of our efforts to establish King's relevance for the Tibetan cause.

The results of this approach were startling. As the future teachers adapted the issues that Dr. King and Rosa Parks had faced to the personal situations of Tibetans under Chinese occupation, it was clear that there were numerous parallels. Among the questions raised by the Tibetans were: How can our children develop feelings of self-respect when the surrounding society treats us as inferior? How can adults retain feelings of self-worth when limited to menial, ill-paying work? Discussing such questions generated intense feelings, and by the end of the week we felt so much a community that we decided to have a ceremonial farewell dinner together. Since it was a Friday night, our joint planning included elements of our traditional Sabbath observances along with elements of traditional Tibetan worship. The shared ceremonies were quite moving, we socialized during the meal, and as we approached the end of the evening, it occurred to Rabbi Gendler and me: "Let's teach them 'We Shall Overcome' to summarize both the evening and the week." "Do you know 'We Shall Overcome'?," we asked hesitantly, preparing internally to teach them the various verses. "Of course!" came the reply. "Do you want it in English or in Tibetan?" What a surprise for us, yet on reflection, how obvious. Long ago, members of this Tibetan community had recognized their kinship with Dr. King and the U.S. nonviolent freedom movement. They had adopted "We Shall Overcome" as one of their own hymns of affirmation, and so total was the adoption that they had long before devised an entire set of lyrics in Tibetan. After such an experience, can anyone doubt King's significant presence in the Tibetan Plateau? How did this come to be? Here's the amazing tale.

THE TRIP TO TIBET: A JOURNEY FOR PEACE

Following our retirements in 1995—Everett as rabbi of a congregation in Lowell, Massachusetts, and Jewish chaplain and instructor at Phillips Academy Andover, and me as a clinical psychologist—we packed our bags and set out for several months of traveling in Asia. Our only commitment was an audience we had set up with the Dalai Lama in Dharamsala, India, for November. Although not explicitly verbalized, we were both wondering what the assignment for the next phase of our lives would be. The answer was not long in coming.

In October 1995, following a glorious trek in the Annapurna Mountains, we decided to go Tibet. We had met some Tibetans in Nepal on previous trips, and a few years earlier we had gone to Dharamsala, the seat of the Tibetan exile government, and had met the Dalai Lama. We found that they were a sympathetic people, and we believed their cause was as just as any taken on by King and black Americans thirty years earlier. We did not know a lot about the situation, but we did know that the Chinese had invaded and overrun Tibet in 1949, and that despite Chinese promises to allow the Tibetans autonomy, they gradually tightened the knot. On March 10, 1959, now called "National Uprising Day," the Tibetans rose up against the Chinese, who were, they thought, threatening the Dalai Lama. Fearing for his life, the young Dalai Lama was spirited out of Tibet, while brave warriors demonstrated their opposition to the Chinese occupation. Possessing superior arms and power, the Chinese suppressed the uprising, and

Tibet came under the rule of the Communist regime in Beijing. Over one hundred thousand Tibetans followed the Dalai Lama into exile in India.

Tibet, having been closed to the world until quite recently, had enormous allure. Who could resist? So, despite our misgivings about giving the Chinese our foreign currency, we rationalized that we should go to Tibet even though Tibetans in India and Nepal could not. Perhaps we might learn something that could be of use to them. How prescient this was would be apparent soon.

We booked through a Tibetan travel agency in Kathmandu, Nepal, and made sure that we would also be working through a Tibetan travel agency in Tibet. We wanted to have a Tibetan guide so that we would not be bombarded with propaganda from a Chinese guide. We were puzzled, however, when the agent in Nepal cautioned us, as we were leaving the agency, "Try to get along with your guide." What could he mean? "Never mind," we said to ourselves. "We are actually going to fabled Tibet!"

Upon arrival, we found that the countryside was stunning, the mountains and lakes still pristine. As we drove past the gorgeous, turquoise-colored Yamdrok Tso Lake, we gaped in sheer joy and amazement. But then we saw a partially completed nuclear power plant, a monstrosity that will pollute the water forever. Across the road, in the distance, we observed people wearing white suits and face masks emerge from an opening in the mountain. Were they workers from uranium mines? Perhaps so.

After having destroyed 95 percent of Tibet's monasteries during the Cultural Revolution, the Chinese government has recently restored a few of them. These few were impressive and beautiful, from what we could see, although mostly devoid of active religious use. Barkhor Square, the heart of Lhasa, which houses the Jokhang, the holiest temple, still had a Tibetan feel. There were many stalls selling Tibetan holy goods, such as statues, prayer wheels, and prayer shawls. Pilgrims from all over Tibet, dressed in their finest clothes, were prostrating themselves before the temple, then walking around it, chanting prayers and turning prayer wheels. The scene there was quite lively and felt genuinely Tibetan. But there was a shadow side. We were warned that there were video cameras on the roof of the temple so that the authorities could keep an eye on everything that happened there. The Tibetan ambience there was in contrast to much of the rest of Lhasa, which even as early as 1995 was being made into a replica of a Chinese development city, with wide streets, ugly cement buildings, bars, and stores. The Potala, the palace of the Dalai Lama, had been turned into a tourist site, with hundreds and hundreds of people, mostly Chinese, walking around the massive building. Most distasteful, however, was a stall set up on one of the terraces where one could dress up in Tibetan clothes and have one's picture taken!

We knew that Tibet was being changed by the occupiers, and we steeled ourselves in anticipation. The ugly Chinese concrete buildings, the bulldozed monasteries, the brothels, the strong military presence were expected, though not welcomed. We had also expected to receive some ill treatment from the Chinese occupiers. Well, we did have several bad experiences—not with the Chinese, but with Tibetans! This was a shock to us, for we had heard and read glowing reports from a few tourists who had gone to Tibet, and only bad things about its occupiers. Nevertheless, we could not overlook the very real, rough, rude encounters we had with a group of nomadic pilgrims on our first day in Tibet, and the lying and cheating to which we were subjected by both of our Tibetan guides (the first dumped us after two days because we were too old!) and by shopkeepers in Lhasa were quite disturbing. This was such a startling contrast to the Tibetans we had met in Nepal and in India, all of whom had been unfailingly polite and friendly. Why such a difference here? Might it have to do with the conditions they live in under the Chinese occupation?

It is not much of a stretch to assume that the ominous, relentless, controlling, and sometimes deadly Chinese presence in Tibet might well be a major source of these behaviors. Abuse begets abuse. There is no question that few Tibetans in Tibet have escaped abuse from the Chinese occupiers over the last fifty years, either personally or through members of their family, friends, and neighbors. Having one's country invaded and taken over by another country; having one's cherished monasteries demolished and stripped of art and religious treasures; having thousands of monks and nuns dispelled, beaten, and often imprisoned for daring to keep a portrait of the Dalai Lama in their rooms; having any expression of dissent punished with imprisonment, torture, and death; having one's revered leader sent fleeing for his life; having a mass immigration of Chinese, who now threaten to become the majority; seeing the physical resources of one's country exploited and stolen; having one's schools use Chinese as the basic language; seeing the best jobs and opportunities go to Chinese; being forced to have an operation to control the number of children one can have (a frightening reality for women, who sometimes refuse to seek medical care for this reason); being forcibly resettled if one is a nomad . . . This list could go on and on. What happens to people when they are put in this position, forced to endure such treatment? It is not too hard to imagine that they will feel anger, frustration, and a lack of control over their lives and all they hold dear. These feelings can, and often do, lead to depression, anger, a sense of hopelessness and helplessness. Under such circumstances, it is not surprising that some begin to exhibit antisocial behaviors. Where are they to direct these pent-up feelings? How are they to survive, emotionally and physically, under such conditions? Can the methods of Martin Luther King, Jr. be effective in this situation?

The situation for the Tibetans is only getting worse. To this day, the Chinese exercise ironfisted control over Tibet, and swift action ensues against those who try to resist, whether violently or nonviolently. Many Tibetans feel they have no alternatives. They are in a classic double bind. Indeed, their sense of hopelessness has recently driven twenty-nine Tibetans, mostly monks and nuns, to self-immolate, in a desperate attempt to get the world to notice their suffering under the Chinese occupiers. The Tibetan people are strong, and they take refuge in their religion and the Dalai Lama. This strong faith helps them cope, but it does not give them back their country or their freedom. Is there anything to be done about this situation? Memories of Dr. King and the struggle in the United States occasionally surfaced as we pondered this question.

TOWARD DIRECT ACTION: THE BIRTH OF A PROGRAM

Feelings can be understood as a form of energy, and energy can be directed in many ways. If the negative energy engendered by these insults and maltreatment can be channeled into positive actions that hold the promise of ameliorating their situation, there is a good chance that people will begin to feel less frustrated and more empowered. Without this redirection, the potential for eruptions is high, as was seen in the uprising and riots in Lhasa in 2008. We had witnessed similar eruptions—riots—in the urban ghettos of America in the late 1960s, as the struggle for black freedom reached fever pitch. As King put it in those times: "The Negro has many pent-up resentments and latent frustrations. . . . If his emotions are not released in nonviolent ways, they will seek expression through violence; this is not a threat but a fact of history. . . . This normal and healthy discontent can be channeled into creative direct action."[2] Perhaps if the Tibetans inside and

2. Martin Luther King, Jr., *Why We Can't Wait* (New York: New American Library, 1964) 88.

outside of occupied Tibet learned new ways to resist nonviolently, as was the case with King and his followers in the United States, they could direct their energy into planning and executing actions with the potential to make their lives more tolerable. The strength of the current regime in China makes overt political resistance quite dangerous at this time, but there are other things the Tibetans could do to improve their lives while waiting for unrest in China to shake the regime. The Tibetans could still better their lives by improving their economic and educational situations, and by finding ways to hang on to their culture, their language, their religion, and their heritage. No dictatorship has ever lasted forever.

When Rabbi Gendler was still teaching at Andover, one of the courses he offered was called "Nonviolence in Theory and Practice." Along with the campaigns and teaching of Martin Luther King, Jr. and Mohandas K. Gandhi, he used the work of a Western sociologist, Dr. Gene Sharp, who offers an active strategic approach to practicing nonviolence. We thought that perhaps the Tibetans living in Tibet, as well as those in exile, might feel less frustrated if they had some new nonviolent tools to employ in their struggle against the Chinese. We were convinced that the ideas and tactics of King and Gandhi could be appropriated and applied here.

Over the course of many years, Dr. Sharp has studied nonviolent actions and movements around the world, first among them the campaigns of Gandhi and King. He has systematized his findings in an approach that he calls "strategic nonviolence." He has written many books on this subject, including a widely distributed booklet called From Dictatorship to Democracy.[3] Rather than the spontaneous and often disastrous demonstrations calling for the return of the Dalai Lama, which are inevitably met by a violent response from the Chinese, Sharp's method suggests a more reasoned approach, based upon a careful and detailed analysis of the whole situation. Before taking any action, the strengths and weakness of both sides should be noted and analyzed. Hard questions must be asked and answered. Where does the power lie? Which institutions are most powerful and which are most vulnerable? What are your goals? What are the changes sought? What problems should be addressed first? Should protests and actions be directed toward the political sector, the economic structure, or social areas?

3. See Gene Sharp, From Dictatorship to Democracy: A Conceptual Framework for Liberation, 4th ed. (Boston: Albert Einstein Institution, 2010). Sharp's three-volume work on the politics and the theoretical dimensions of nonviolence, The Politics of Nonviolent Action: Power and Struggle (Boston: Porter Sargent, 1973), is among the best available in print.

Ultimately, all of this information should be used to create a grand strategic plan. Once this plan is in place, smaller campaigns, targeted at specific goals, need to be carefully devised and revised as necessary. Martin Luther King, Jr. had identified this as an important step in any action campaign, irrespective of the geographical context in which it might occur.

Our idea was to bring Dr. Gene Sharp to India to conduct some training seminars for the Tibetans in exile. We thought that if some of the Tibetans could learn this broader and more inclusive approach to nonviolent struggle, their campaigns could be more successful. It would be up to them to figure out how to get this information into Tibet. Before broaching this with the Dalai Lama, we telephoned Dr. Sharp to see if he was willing to come to India to teach this seminar. We called and he agreed, in principle, to come.

Our audience with the Dalai Lama fortuitously fell on the first day of Chanukah, the dark-of-winter Jewish celebration of light and liberation. Was it serendipity, auspicious coincidence, or divine guidance? The biblical passage selected by the rabbis for this holiday declares, "Not by might, nor by power, but by my spirit, says the LORD of hosts" (Zech 4:6). For our own observance of the eight days of the holiday, we improvised a Chanukah menorah (candleholder) out of a brass bowl used by Tibetans for ritual purposes, and affixed nine Tibetan beads with crazy glue to hold the candles. We shared the biblical passage with His Holiness, chanted the traditional blessings, and lit the candles. The Dalai Lama stood with us as we recited the prayers. The sharing of rituals between faiths creates a special bond. To meet in the realm of the spirit is to connect at a very deep level. This Martin Luther King, Jr. knew very well. Certainly, sharing the evocation of the Spirit while participating in the gospel singing, as the black churches did during the civil rights movement, was powerful indeed.

After the ceremony, we told the Dalai Lama about our trip to Tibet and what we had experienced there. We also shared our thinking about why some of the Tibetans behaved this way, and our ideas about how to remedy this. We explained Dr. Sharp's approach to nonviolent action, and His Holiness became quite excited and jumped from his chair and cried, "Yes, yes, we must learn more about it! We must set aside two weeks for it!" Thus was born our project, which has extended far past the initial two weeks and now stretches over the past fifteen years.

Dr. Sharp went to India three times to give high-level seminars to Tibetan educators, monks, administrators, and lay leaders. We felt strongly that the common people should also have an opportunity to learn about this material. With the backing of the Tibetan exile government, we began to give popular seminars and workshops throughout the Tibetan diaspora in India. Between 1995 and 2012, we traveled to almost all of the Tibetan settlements in India, introducing Tibetans to these new ideas about how to struggle nonviolently against Chinese occupation in Tibet. We spoke in elementary and secondary schools, universities, monasteries, community gatherings, merchant groups, women's associations, student associations, and also to teachers, administrative staff, veterans, old people, young people, the educated and the uneducated. In the schools we communicated in English; in the settlements we needed a translator.

Our presentations ranged from a one-hour talk, to half and full days, to two days, a week, and, in a few instances, two full weeks. In all of the seminars lasting more than an hour, after having presented some methods of strategy, we always broke the listeners into groups to discuss ways of applying these ideas in Tibet. How they had been applied decades earlier in King-led civil rights campaigns, which drew on the physical presence and spiritual power of ordinary people, was always uppermost in our thinking.

"Nonviolence is a people's movement," we told the participants in our seminars. "It is not just 'important' people who cause the changes. Every single one of you is important. Every one of you can make a difference. Your ideas matter. Look at Rosa Parks, a simple seamstress whose single act of resistance, her refusal to give up her seat in a bus, changed history." By involving each and every person and encouraging them to participate actively in the process of trying to regain their homeland and maintain their unique culture, we were actually training them to take an active role in determining their future. In other words, some level of self-determination, as King so often said, is essential if people are to live out the full measure of their personhood.

One question we frequently had them address was this: what can be done to help improve the economic conditions of people in Tibet? We would assign a different segment of society—monks, city dwellers, farmers, nomads, students—to each group, whose members were tasked with coming up with concrete suggestions and actions designed specifically for their segment of society. These were then shared with the larger group. We certainly did not expect them to solve the problems in one seminar, but we were trying to teach them how to approach these kinds of problems in a strategic way. In response to the above questions, they shared ideas ranging from setting up small-scale co-ops and improving farming methods to frequenting only Tibetan merchants. Their call to boycott Chinese goods brought to mind Gandhi's khādī movement in India, the worldwide boycott of gold from South Africa, and the bus boycott organized by King and others in Montgomery, Alabama. Wherever we spoke, interest was always high, and the participants often reported that they felt the seminar was too short and that they wanted more.

Preservation of their language, culture, traditions, and religion is crucial for the Tibetans' survival as a people, with or without independence from China. We asked the students to think deeply about the question, what can you do to help Tibetans maintain their language, religion, and culture? Develop strategies for different groups, as before, depending on their situation. Here, again, the participants came up with many good ideas. We especially liked the strategic thinking shown by a group of ninth grade girls. They said, "Open a disco in Lhasa. Fill it with bright lights and loud music. The Chinese will be happy to see this, because they want to corrupt the Tibetan youth. Some kids would come in and dance, but in the basement would be a classroom where young people could go for classes in Tibetan language, history, and religion." Some years later we were pleased to hear about a particular action initiated in Tibet. Called "White Wednesday," the Tibetans in an area of what used to be called Amdo made a pledge to wear Tibetan clothes and to speak only Tibetan to each other every Wednesday. Reminding themselves and proclaiming to other Tibetans that they are still Tibetan, and proud to be so, reveals their determination to hold tight to their culture and traditions, and solidifies their identity as "Tibetan." These kinds of actions bring to mind the multitude of ways in which King and the civil rights movement brought a sense of self-worth and pride to blacks in America. Asserting that they would be downtrodden and mistreated no more, they, led by King, took matters into their own hands and nonviolently marched, protested, "sat in," showed pride in their culture, and proclaimed to the world that they were equal to all and deserved to be so treated! As Dr. King so often said, "Oppressed people cannot remain oppressed forever. The yearning for freedom eventually manifests itself."[4]

In addition to teaching how to analyze a situation and devise strategies, we also included a discussion of feelings, especially anger and fear. Remembering the strong feelings we had experienced with Dr. King in Albany Georgia; Birmingham, Alabama; and Selma, Alabama, we felt it

4. King, *Why We Can't Wait*, 82 and 87.

important to warn about the effects these very human emotions can have on demonstrators. It is important both to acknowledge these feelings and to explore ways to overcome them. Controlling one's anger enables one to think more clearly and not give in to blind rage and destructive action when involved in demonstrations or other nonviolent actions. Controlling and moving past fear is necessary to achieve success, especially in situations where there is a threat of violence on the part of police, soldiers, or others.

We have only to remember how frightening it was to walk arm in arm past armed police and their snarling dogs in Selma, as we marched toward the Edmund Pettus Bridge, to understand the importance of such training. One often hears about the courage of soldiers engaged in violent warfare, but nonviolent warriors deserve at least as much praise for their courage, as they knowingly take action against a more powerful foe with nothing more than their courage to protect them. As King said, "Courage is an inner resolution to go forward in spite of obstacles and frightening situations. . . . Courage breeds creative self-affirmation."[5] The nightly gatherings in churches in Selma provided a much-needed infusion of comfort and solidarity, which fortified participants to face the potential dangers of the following day. King also used these evening meetings to teach how to participate in nonviolent actions. For example, in Montgomery, as the time came for blacks to ride the buses again, the leadership issued a list of "integrated bus suggestions" about how to behave, to maintain calm and courtesy, and to resist reacting to provocative behavior from white people.[6] We felt that Tibetans had much to learn from this if they were to find in nonviolent action a workable method for achieving justice.

RELATIONS WITH THE CHINESE: BUILDING COALITIONS

Relations with the Chinese are another area that we addressed in our teaching. It is all too easy to demonize the "other"—the Chinese people, in this case. Indeed, one teacher at a Tibetan boarding school wondered, "Are we teaching our children to hate?" This is a grave danger, and it is an issue that we try to address in the seminars. "Are *all* the Chinese people responsible for what is happening to the Tibetans? Are *any* of them on your side? Could

5. Martin Luther King, Jr., *Strength to Love* (Philadelphia: Fortress, 1981) 118–19.

6. Martin Luther King, Jr., *Stride Toward Freedom: The Montgomery Story* (New York: Harper & Row, 1958) 164 and 169.

Tibetans make friends with them? What might be the result if you did?" This is a new idea for many of the young people, especially, and they are surprised and intrigued. Drawing on our knowledge of King and experiences with race relations in America, we often used role-play to encourage them to think about ways of making these connections.

We also talked about the tremendous amount of unrest and dissatisfaction there is in China among the Chinese people. Again, the Tibetans are always surprised and heartened to hear this. Perhaps there are ways of forging an alliance with these elements of the Chinese population? The Tibetans have done brilliantly in engaging outside help, especially Westerners, in their struggle to regain their land. Now, perhaps, they need to reach out to Chinese dissidents and other sympathetic Chinese.

Here the example of King and the civil rights movement stands out boldly. King reached out to the white community for support. Although there were a few courageous Southern whites who supported him, there were many whites who came from the North to support the cause. Blacks and whites together marched side by side under sometimes very trying circumstances. Some whites even lost their lives. While we were in Selma, a white Unitarian minister, the Reverend James Reeb, was clubbed to death by a white racist, right around the corner from where we were staying. Two young students, Michael Schwerner and Andrew Goodman, who had come from the North to aid in voter registration, were murdered, along with James Chaney, by members of the Klu Klux Klan before they could even begin their work in Philadelphia, Mississippi. But Northern whites continued to answer King's call, despite the personal dangers involved. Both morally and practically, the participation of white people in the civil rights struggle was very important. We felt that the Tibetans should know all about this as they think in terms of building coalitions with well-meaning and progressive-minded Chinese for much-needed change.

THE ROLE OF SPIRIT IN NONVIOLENT RESISTANCE

The role of spirit—whether it is referred to as *ahimsa* (Gandhi), *agape* (King), or *compassion* (Dalai Lama)—has been the underpinning of many approaches to nonviolent social change. This was most certainly the case with Gandhian *satyagraha* campaigns, which stressed the spiritual significance of love in peaceful protest. In *Stride Toward Freedom*, King writes, "Gandhi was probably the first person in history to lift the love ethic of

Jesus above mere interactions between individuals to a powerful and effective social force on a large scale. Love for Gandhi was a potent instrument for social and collective transformation. It was in this Gandhian emphasis on love and nonviolence that I discovered the method for social reform that I had been seeking for so many months."[7] It is important to note that King understood not only the social significance and the political implications of nonviolence on a global scale, but also its spiritual dimensions.

King, a Baptist minister, knew and lived in the spirit, and he reached out to leaders of all religions while highlighting the role of prayer and spiritual discipline as central ingredients in nonviolent struggle. Rabbis, including Abraham Joshua Heschel and Everett Gendler, supported King, recruited for him, and marched, prayed, and sang alongside him. Catholic priests and Protestant ministers of all denominations likewise answered King's call. Convinced that change in its most authentic and positive expression must first occur within, in the hearts of people, before it can be translated into the social, political, and economic order, persons of different faith traditions stood at the forefront of the nonviolent protest campaigns that transformed America. Similarly, Tibetan monks and nuns have often spearheaded the resistance in Tibet.

NONVIOLENT REVOLUTIONS AS CASE STUDIES

We also included in our teachings in Tibet case studies of many successful nonviolent revolutions, large and small, around the world. First among them, of course, stand Gandhi's *satyagraha* campaigns in India and King's civil rights campaigns in the United States. These two struggles stand out as formative and as models for all the others that have followed. Successful nonviolent campaigns in the Philippines removed the dictator Marcos; in Serbia the student group Otpor! (Resistance!) ousted "the Butcher of the Balkans," Slobodan Milosevic; and in Norway during the Second World War teachers successfully resisted the Nazification of the schools. The list could go on and on. The recent exciting nonviolent revolutions in Tunisia and Egypt drew on the work of Dr. Sharp, which rests on the foundation laid by King and Gandhi. Knowing of other countries and peoples who have actually ousted deadly dictators and regimes through peaceful means, gives Tibetans hope that they, too, may someday succeed.

7. Ibid., 97.

As King declared so many times, the yearning for freedom and self-determination is universal, and brave people all over the world put themselves at risk to obtain it. In the case of oppressed people, the recurring issues are how to gain the necessary courage, how to overcome fear, how to deal with grief and loss, and what to do with one's anger, rage, frustration, helplessness, and despair. The answers never come easy, but they lie in part in the power that comes through the human encounter with the spiritual or supernatural realm.

During the height of the civil rights movement in the United States, the black community, in collaboration with white Northerners who went South to participate in the demonstrations, gathered in churches at night after every action. There they heard Dr. King speak, prayed, listened to sermons, received instructions for further actions, and sang their hearts out while standing shoulder to shoulder and holding each other's hands. We were fortunate enough to experience one of these gatherings in Selma, Alabama, and can still feel the warmth, the glow, the sense of oneness with hundreds of people we didn't even know. The genius of the way that King addressed frustration, anger, and rage is confirmed by the spontaneous reactions of the Tibetans in India to the deeply disturbing events of 2008.

In 2008, partly due to the upcoming Olympics, which the Chinese were using to showcase their accomplishments, there were demonstrations in Tibet. These began peacefully, but as the Chinese responded with more and more force, the Tibetans rioted, burning some Chinese stores and killing some Chinese. The Chinese government responded with even greater force, killing, injuring, and imprisoning an untold number of Tibetans. How did the Tibetan exile community deal with this? Of course they were frightened, angry, upset, worried, and feeling helpless. But, as did King, who also experienced the effects of alternating cycles of rioting and government crackdowns, they devised a psychologically sound way of channeling these feelings.

For over a month in Dharamsala, India, there was a nightly candlelight procession, which wound its way through the town to the courtyard of the Dalai Lama's temple. Led at times by monks and at other times by laypersons, more than a thousand people—old and young, businesspeople, students, families—participated in this nightly coming together, comforting and gaining hope and courage from each other, reasserting their devotion to a free Tibet, and strengthening their commitment to working toward this end. They sang Tibetan songs, prayed, and received instructions for further actions. An open-air replica of the churches of King's days!

THE ROLE OF YOUNG PEOPLE: A NEW SPIRIT OF ACTIVISM

King recognized the importance of having young people involved in freedom movements worldwide, for he observed firsthand their contributions to the civil rights cause. Students played a vital role in the soda fountain sit-ins in Nashville, Tennessee. Well trained by King's friend and associate, the Reverend James Lawson, students—well dressed, polite, and presentable—offered a respectable image to the watching world.[8] In Birmingham, Alabama, young people responded by the thousands to King's call to participate in the campaign. They volunteered to march, to go to jail, and to put their lives on the line for freedom. King, who knew well the sympathy young people could elicit in the hearts of the general public, described, with some delight, the efforts of one principal to keep the students in by locking the gates, only to have them climb over it and run "toward freedom." As King said, "The movement was blessed by the fire and excitement brought to it by young people such as these."[9]

The Tibetan youth are likewise quite involved in the cause of Tibetan freedom. Indeed, the three most politically active organizations are composed primarily of students and young people. Most of the students we spoke to were passionately interested in learning new ways to resist. One of the most moving examples involving young people that we witnessed occurred in the aftermath of the 2008 uprising. Along with adults, more than twenty of them took their turn sitting in a small, cage-like structure where they remained for twenty-four hours without eating or drinking. Seeing these young Tibetans voluntarily committing themselves to such an uncomfortable ordeal, I was reminded of the brave children in Birmingham,

8. See Part 1 of the PBS documentary *A Force More Powerful* (2000), written, produced, and directed by Steve York. Also see the many accounts of student activism in Clayborne Carson, *In Struggle: SNCC and the Black Awakening of the 1960s* (Cambridge: Harvard University Press, 1981) 9–190; David Halberstam, *The Children* (New York: Random House, 1998); John Lewis with Michael D'Orso, *Walking with the Wind: A Memoir of the Movement* (New York: Simon & Schuster, 1998); Raymond Arsenault, *Freedom Riders: 1961 and the Struggle for Racial Justice* (New York: Oxford University Press, 2006).

9. King, *Why We Can't Wait*, 98–99.

who, without flinching—and armed with the Kingian nonviolent ethic—bravely faced vicious police dogs and high-powered water hoses as they marched for freedom and dignity. There seemed to be a spiritual bond that literally transcended time and space.

THE QUESTION OF LEADERSHIP IN NONVIOLENT MOVEMENTS

Successful nonviolent campaigns have come in many different guises. In both India and the United States, there was a charismatic leader who mobilized oppressed people and guided them to victories in their peaceful protests and campaigns. Gandhi and King supremely symbolized the significance of having this kind of leader. On the other hand, in the Philippines, Latvia and Estonia, Egypt, Tunisia, Serbia, and many more countries, there was no charismatic leader, but rather concerned citizens who took the helm, inspired the populace, and guided them to the successful overthrow of brutal dictators. Interestingly enough, Tibetans have embraced aspects of both approaches in their enduring quest for freedom.

The Tibetans, of course, have the Dalai Lama, whose spiritual teachings and commitment to nonviolence have inspired not only Tibetans but also millions of others around the world. Like King, he has a broad vision that he has articulated in his proposal to make Tibet a "zone of peace." Unlike Gandhi and King, however, he is not a "field general." He has set the context and parameters of the nonviolent struggle to regain control of Tibet but has left it to the people to find the precise ways of doing so. This, we believe, is why he welcomed our suggestion to bring in this "new" approach to nonviolent struggle, an approach that owes much to our reading of Dr. Sharp and our own experiences in the United States during the King years.

As a leader, King realized the importance of creating an organization that could sustain the effort between the civil rights campaigns. Along with other black preachers, he created the Southern Christian Leadership Conference (SCLC). Understanding the wisdom of this approach, in 2007 we founded in Tibet an NGO (nongovernmental organization), or an Active Nonviolence Education Center (ANEC). Staffed entirely by Tibetans, it provides workshops and ongoing classes for Tibetans in India, produces publications, does outreach, and offers internship possibilities to Western tourists and college groups who come to Dharamsala with the intention of learning more about nonviolence.

363

THE PRACTICAL SIDE OF NONVIOLENT STRUGGLE: PLANNING AND TRAINING

In reviewing and sharing details of Dr. King's campaigns with people in Tibet, we have been repeatedly impressed by the importance placed on proper planning of the actions, and on the need for intense preparation and training for those participating in freedom movements. In *Why We Can't Wait*, King describes the kind of detailed planning that figured into preparations for demonstrations, sit-ins, marches, and other forms of non-violent direct action in Birmingham. At one point, King and his aides had to count "the number of stools, tables and chairs to determine how many demonstrators should go to each store."[10] King also describes the sixty-five nightly meetings held in Birmingham in order to prepare the community for action there; the careful screening of interviews with individuals; the training with socio-drama; and the pledges required of participants that they could endure violence without responding.[11] Students for a Free Tibet (SFFT), an international youth movement, provides such training in preparation for various "actions" they are planning. As our program is education, rather than action-based, the "training" Rabbi Gendler and I do is focused on understanding the process and strategic thinking that goes into a nonviolent campaign, and contemplating how to implement these ideas in practical, concrete, and successful ways.

UNIVERSAL TRAINING IN NONVIOLENT METHODS

The Dalai Lama has spoken movingly about the creation of a zone of peace.[12] How might Tibetans prepare themselves more directly for the realization and defense of the Dalai Lama's vision of a zone of peace? To this end, several years ago we wrote a proposal that we titled, "Universal Nonviolence Training: The Moral Equivalent to Military Basic Training." In the essay, we proposed that the Tibetans set up a program to train all of their students—and perhaps twelfth graders in particular—in all different aspects of nonviolence, not only nonviolent defense, but also nonviolent

10. Ibid., 56.

11. Ibid., 60–61.

12. Dalai Lama, "Five-Point Peace Plan: Address to the U.S. Congressional Human Rights Caucus" (September 21, 1987). Online: http://www.dalailama.com/messages/tibet/five-point-peace-plan.

living. What does this mean? This means not only a thorough grounding in the type of nonviolent strategic defense mentioned above, but also the development of a just and honorable society. In a zone of peace, none of the citizens should be without access to basic needs. These include food and water, housing, clothing, education, health and hygiene, and the possibility of life-sustaining work.

As stated previously, the population should also be aware of their customs and traditions—art and music, dance, folklore, religion, language. This, too, as King and the movement in America demonstrated, is important in any genuine crusade for human freedom. A common base of knowledge concerning what makes Tibetans uniquely Tibetan will instill a sense of pride and cohesion among the populace. Grounded in compassion, about which the Dalai Lama speaks so movingly and persuasively, the goal is to create a nation dedicated to living moral, fruitful, satisfying lives. Politically, Tibet would be neutral, but also capable of defending itself nonviolently if necessary. The buffer this would create between China and India would be invaluable. How much safer the world would be if the Dalai Lama's vision could be fulfilled! How beneficial this would be not only for Tibet but also for the world! It should be noted that although we focus on Tibetans in this particular essay, this in no way rules out the hope that this kind of training might become available in other countries.

In December 2011, we had the opportunity to launch a pilot program of Universal Nonviolence Training. At six thousand feet in the Himalayas at that time, the hardy Tibetans were less chilled than we pampered Westerners! But the spirit generated from our work together warmed our hearts, even if our fingers and toes were freezing. We spent eleven intensive days together—Rabbi Gendler and me, two of ANEC's staff, and twenty-one ninth through eleventh graders, all but four of whom had come from Tibet as young children. These youngsters had walked across the Himalayas at night in the dead of winter. Scantily clothed, they left their families and risked their lives to get an education and to live in freedom. Although some of the students were in contact with their families, most were not. Despite their suffering, they were normal, cheerful, friendly, and outgoing youngsters, quick to laugh and sensitive to injustice and wrong. Their resilience is amazing, their commitment to the Tibetan cause unwavering. Their courage, sacrifice, and character are inspiring and moving. A world filled with people like them would be fine indeed! They loved the workshop, which they attended faithfully, despite the cold. My favorite student, a young man with a ready smile and quick tongue, told me that before the workshop he had planned to join the army after completing school so that he could fight the Chinese. Now, after the workshop, he had decided not to do so, because he could see that he could work for Tibetan freedom nonviolently. King was apparently right about the powerful impact that lessons in nonviolence can have on the human psyche and spirit. In Judaism we have a saying: "If you save one life, it is as if you have saved an entire world."[13] Well, it may take more than one in this case, but how many more young people are there like my favorite student, not just among Tibetans, but around the world? What kind of opportunity are we missing?

Martin Luther King, Jr.'s vision of a just and peaceful world is being sustained by the Dalai Lama and the Tibetan people, whose search for dignity and freedom through nonviolence is a testimony to this universal and enduring message: "We shall overcome."[14] Indeed! Whether in English, Tibetan, Hindi (and who knows how many other languages), the words "we shall overcome someday" and the melody that goes with them warm the heart and send courage to all humans who suffer oppression, even those living amid the highest mountains of the world. King's "dream" echoes the dreams of all people, and his method of attaining that dream through nonviolence still inspires all people.

13. Talmud, Sanhedrin 37.
14. King, *Why We Can't Wait*, 61.

Index